Virtualizing Desktops & Apps with Windows Server 2012 R2 Inside Out

Byron Wright
Brian Svidergol

PUBLISHED BY
Microsoft Press
A division of Microsoft Corporation
One Microsoft Way
Redmond, Washington 98052-6399
Copyright © 2015 by Microsoft Corporation

Library of Congress Control Number: 2014952206
ISBN: 978-0-7356-9721-8

Printed and bound in the United States of America.

First Printing

Microsoft Press books are available through booksellers and distributors worldwide. If you need support
related to this book, email Microsoft Press Support at mspinput@microsoft.com. Please tell us what you
think of this book at http://aka.ms/tellpress.

This book is provided "as-is" and expresses the author's views and opinions. The views, opinions and
information expressed in this book, including URL and other Internet website references, may change
without notice.

Some examples depicted herein are provided for illustration only and are fictitious. No real association
or connection is intended or should be inferred.

Microsoft and the trademarks listed at http://www.microsoft.com on the "Trademarks" webpage
are trademarks of the Microsoft group of companies. All other marks are property of their respective
owners.

Acquisitions Editor: Alison Hirsch
Project Editor: Rosemary Caperton
Editorial Production: nSight, Inc.
Technical Reviewer: Todd Meister; Technical Review services provided by Content Master, a member of
CM Group, Ltd.
Copyeditor: Ann Weaver
Indexer: Lucie Haskins
Cover: Twist Creative • Seattle

Contents at a glance

Table of contents

What do you think of this book? We want to hear from you!

Microsoft is interested in hearing your feedback so we can improve our books and learning resources
for you. To participate in a brief survey, please visit:

http://aka.ms/tellpress

What do you think of this book? We want to hear from you!

Microsoft is interested in hearing your feedback so we can improve our books and learning resources
for you. To participate in a brief survey, please visit:

http://aka.ms/tellpress

Introduction

If you want to learn about using Microsoft technologies to implement application and desktop virtualization, then this book is for you. If you need to support users who roam among multiple computers and platforms, then this book will help you identify, select, and implement options for user state virtualizations. If you are implementing application virtualization by using Microsoft Application Virtualization (App-V), then this book will help you learn how to design and configure an App-V deployment. It also will teach you how to sequence applications for deployment. If you want to implement virtual desktops to simplify hardware upgrades and support mobile users, then this book will teach you about both session-based virtual desktops and virtual machine–based (VM-based) virtual desktops. It also will teach you how to secure remote access to virtual desktops by using Remote Desktop Gateway (RD Gateway). Finally, to ensure that your application and desktop virtualization meets the performance requirements of your users, you will learn about monitoring application and desktop virtualization.

This book assumes that you have a working knowledge of Windows client and server administration or have access to that information. So, we assume that you understand basic facts like how to connect a computer to a domain, how to create and apply Group Policy, and how to work with management tools. This book focuses on implementing the application and desktop virtualization technologies that layer on top of Microsoft Windows Server 2012 R2. Each of the technologies covered in the book is examined from a real-life perspective. This book provides examples and recommendations for implementation.

System requirements

The following are the recommended system requirements necessary to implement the technologies described in this book in a development environment:

- A processor with Second Level Address Translation (SLAT) support

- Windows 8.1 (Enterprise edition recommended, Professional edition minimum)

- Windows Server 2012 R2

- Microsoft Desktop Optimization Pack (MDOP)

- At least 8 GB of random access memory (RAM)

- A hard drive with at least 128 GB of free space

- A CD-ROM or DVD-ROM drive

- A mouse or other pointing device

- A 1024 x 768 or greater monitor display

Acknowledgments

We'd like to thank Alison Hirsch at Microsoft Press for helping us get started on this book and ensuring that we were on the right track. We'd also like to thank Rosemary Caperton at Microsoft Press for getting us to the finish line. Finally, we'd like to thank Michael McMann, Brad Joseph, Phil Helsel, and Tony Jamieson from Microsoft Learning Experiences for working with us on a new development process.

Byron would personally like to thank Tracey, Samantha, and Michelle for tolerating the occasional late night required to get a large project like this done.

Brian would personally like to thank his wife Lindsay, his son Jack, and his daughter Leah for supporting him in another project. He would also like to thank Elias Mereb, Charles Pluta, and Bob Clements for their continued support and expertise.

Free ebooks from Microsoft Press

From technical overviews to in-depth information on special topics, the free ebooks from Microsoft Press cover a wide range of topics. These ebooks are available in PDF, EPUB, and Mobi for Kindle formats, ready for you to download at:

http://aka.ms/mspressfree

Check back often to see what is new!

Errata, updates, & book support

We've made every effort to ensure the accuracy of this book and its companion content. You can access updates to this book—in the form of a list of submitted errata and their related corrections—at:

http://aka.ms/VirtApps/errata

If you discover an error that is not already listed, please submit it to us at the same page.

If you need additional support, email Microsoft Press Book Support at *mspinput@microsoft.com.*

Please note that product support for Microsoft software and hardware is not offered through the previous addresses. For help with Microsoft software or hardware, go to *http://support.microsoft.com.*

We want to hear from you

At Microsoft Press, your satisfaction is our top priority, and your feedback our most valuable asset. Please tell us what you think of this book at:

http://aka.ms/tellpress

The survey is short, and we read every one of your comments and ideas. Thanks in advance for your input!

Stay in touch

Let's keep the conversation going! We're on Twitter: *http://twitter.com/MicrosoftPress.*

CHAPTER 1

Desktop and application virtualization

Virtualization technologies separate access to resources from the actual physical resources. One of the more commonly used virtualization technologies that you may be aware of is virtual machines (VMs). When you use VMs, the hardware resources of a single computer are divided and allocated to multiple VMs. Each VM behaves as if it's an independent computer even though all the VMs share a set of resources. VMs are only one example of virtualization. In addition to VMs, this book explores other virtualization technologies that you can use to create virtualized desktops and applications, such as a Remote Desktop Services (RDS) and Microsoft Application Virtualization (App-V).

You can gain a number of benefits by implementing virtualization:

- Flexibility in resource allocation

- Isolation of conflicting applications

- Better remote access to applications and data

- Improved roaming experience for users

Overview of virtualization technologies

Before you begin implementing virtualization technologies, you need to understand your options. After you understand benefits of each virtualization technology, you can select those that meet your business needs and are appropriate for your environment.

Microsoft virtualization technologies can be roughly categorized as follows:

- **User state virtualization**   Simplifies the use of multiple devices by synchronizing user state information across multiple devices

- **Application virtualization**   Simplifies application deployment by giving users access to applications without the typical application installation process

1

- **Desktop virtualization**   Simplifies desktop deployment by centralizing control and configuration of desktops

- **Storage virtualization**   Makes allocation and management of storage more flexible than volumes created by using traditional tools such as Disk Managementis

Many virtualization technologies, such as Storage Spaces and RDS, are included in Windows Server 2012 R2. Other virtualization technologies, like App-V and User Experience Virtualization (UE-V), are part of the Microsoft Desktop Optimization Pack (MDOP).

Inside OUT

MDOP technologies

MDOP is a collection of technologies that can be used to simplify the management of desktops. However, you can't purchase MDOP as a stand-alone product. You are eligible to obtain MDOP only if you are a Microsoft Software Assurance customer.

> ➤ For more information about how to evaluate and obtain MDOP, see MDOP Information Experience on the TechNet web site at *http://technet.microsoft.com/en-us/library/hh563900.aspx.*

The technologies in MDOP are as follows:

- Microsoft Application Virtualization (App-V)   Virtualizes applications and simplifies software deployment

- Microsoft User Experience Virtualization (UE-V)   Synchronizes application configuration across multiple devices used by a single person

- Microsoft Advanced Group Policy Management (AGPM)   Simplifies the management and maintenance of Group Policies that are used to manage desktops

- Microsoft BitLocker Administration and Monitoring (MBAM)   Simplifies the deployment and management of BitLocker for desktops

- Microsoft Diagnostics and Recovery Toolset (DaRT)   Diagnoses and repairs desktops

- Microsoft Enterprise Desktop Virtualization (MED-V)   Provides a solution for deploying Windows Virtual PC–based VMs to Windows 7 desktop computers

CHAPTER 1

User state virtualization

User state is the combination of files and settings that create a user environment. This includes user data such as the Documents folder and user-specific settings such as mail profiles and desktop configurations.

By default, each user on a computer has separate user state information that is stored locally on that computer. If a user logs on to a second computer, the user state information does not move automatically with the user and must be configured on the second computer. In an environment where users move between multiple computers, this can be inefficient.

To simplify the user experience when roaming among computers, you can implement user state virtualization, as shown in Figure 1-1. User state virtualization makes user state information independent of a single computer. Depending on the user state virtualization technology used, user state information synchronizes among multiple computers or it is stored in a central location that is accessible to all computers.

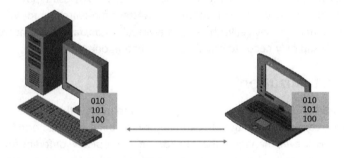

Figure 1-1 User state virtualization

User state virtualization technologies include:

- **Roaming user profiles**   Stores user profiles on a central server and copies the user profile to each computer when the user logs on

- **Folder Redirection**   Stores user profile data such as Documents on a central server that multiple computers can access

- **Credential Roaming**   Allows user certificates to roam with users independently of their user profile

- **Microsoft User Experience Virtualization (UE-V)**   Synchronizes application settings among multiple computers and across different operating system versions

How can user state virtualization make a user more productive? Here is an example. Susan has three devices: a desktop computer, a Windows phone, and a tablet. Susan uses each of these devices at different times of the day. The desktop computer is in her office, and she uses it for most of the work day. She takes the tablet with her to client sites because it's easier to carry. She also uses the tablet while commuting to work on public transit. The Windows phone is with her all the time, and she uses it when she doesn't have any other devices with her. She browses the web on all three devices.

Without user state virtualization, none of the configuration information is synchronized among Susan's three devices. If she is researching a project and creates a set of favorites in Internet Explorer, each device maintains a separate set of favorites. As Susan moves from device to device, she doesn't have all the favorites and wastes time searching for information that she has stored on another device. With user state virtualization, favorites synchronize among devices and Susan only needs to search for information one time.

Application virtualization

You can use virtualized applications to provide applications to users without installing the apps on the user's desktop computer. To a user, the app appears to behave like a normal, locally installed application. However, managing that application is completely different from managing a locally installed application. You manage and update virtualized applications centrally.

In general, virtualizing applications provides the following benefits:

- Faster and easier application deployment

- Easier application updates deployment and management

- Elimination of conflicts between applications

- May allow possibility of running of applications not compatible with the locally installed operating system

App-V from MDOP is the technology most people think of for application virtualization. When you deploy applications by using App-V, the applications run in a local virtualized environment. The virtualized environment prevents applications that you deliver by using App-V from conflicting with locally installed applications or other applications that App-V delivers.

App-V does doesn't allow you to run applications that are incompatible with the locally installed operating system. For example, a Windows XP application that is isn't compatible with Windows 8.1 can't be distributed to Windows 8.1 computers by using App-V.

NOTE

The terminology used when discussing application virtualization can be confusing because the same term can be used multiple ways. You will see *application virtualization* used as a generic descriptor for multiple technologies. You also will see *application virtualization* used to describe the specific Microsoft technology App-V. Remember that App-V is only one technology that can be used to virtualize applications. *App-V* is used only to refer to Microsoft Application Virtualization, the specific technology that is part of MDOP.

App-V copies files for the application to a computer just before running the application in the virtualized environment. This makes deployment much faster than standard application deployment, which requires an installation process. When you update an application deployed by using App-V, the updates automatically deploy to the clients. Figure 1-2 shows how App-V isolates applications and runs them locally.

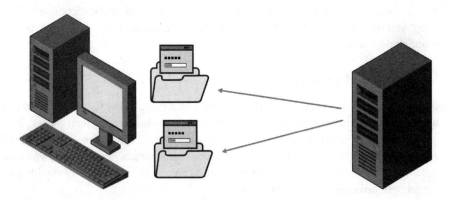

Figure 1-2 Applications delivered by using App-V

RemoteApp is a second Microsoft technology that you can use to virtualize applications. It is part of RDS, which is included with Windows Server 2012 R2.

When you use RemoteApp to deliver applications, the applications are installed and executed on a remote server instead of on the desktop. The user interface for the application displays on the user's desktop by using RDP. Because the application is never installed on the desktop, an application delivered by RemoteApp won't conflict with locally installed applications. Figure 1-3 shows applications delivered by using RemoteApp.

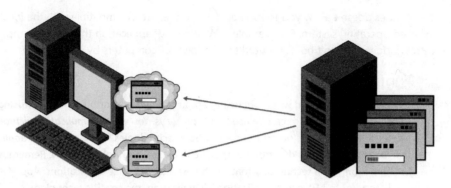

Figure 1-3 Applications delivered by using RemoteApp

You can use RemoteApp to distribute applications to client operating systems that can't run the applications locally. For example, if an application that is isn't compatible with Windows 7 is installed and runs properly on Windows Server 2012 R2, you can use RemoteApp to access the application from computers running Windows 7.

To deploy an application by using RemoteApp, you provide the users with a method to connect to the application. This is much faster than the traditional application installation process. When you update the application on the central server hosting the application, the application is updated for all users.

Desktop Virtualization

Desktop virtualization provides users with access to a complete virtual desktop that operates similarly to a desktop computer. There are several server-based and client-based virtualization technologies that can be used to provide virtual desktops. Client Hyper-V is available in Windows 8 and Windows 8.1 to run VMs. Session-based virtual desktops and VM-based virtual desktops share the physical resources of a central computer to provide users with access to virtual desktops over the network.

Client Hyper-V

Client Hyper-V is a technology that enables you to use VMs when Windows 8.1 is installed on physical hardware. This enables you to use the resources on a single computer to run multiple operating system instances at the same time. Each VM runs an independent operating system and behaves similarly to a physical computer. However, the VMs and the host operating system share the resources on the physical computer. Figure 1-4 shows a Windows 8.1 client computer using Client Hyper-V to run multiple VMs.

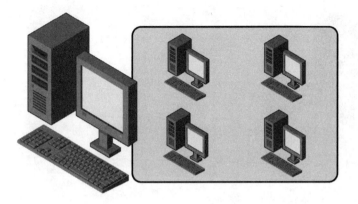

Figure 1-4 Client Hyper-V

Corporate datacenters commonly use Hyper-V in Windows Server 2012 R2 to host multiple VMs on a single physical server. Client Hyper-V in Windows 8.1 is the same technology included in Windows Server 2012 R2, with a few of the features removed.

Some uses for Client Hyper-V include the following:

- **Test environment**   You can test application and operating system updates by installing them on a VM rather than testing them on your computer's operating system. If you experience any problems with the update, you can revert to a previous point in time.

- **Application compatibility**   If your current operating system isn't compatible with an application, you can use a VM with a compatible operating system to run the application.

- **Demonstrations**   You can install and configure an application in VMs to perform demonstrations. This capability is particularly useful when you can't install the application on a single client computer.

Session-based virtual desktops

You can use session-based virtual desktops to provide multiple users with a virtual desktop from a central server. All applications are installed and executed on the central server, which is shared by multiple users at the same time. The central server is called a Remote Desktop Session Host (RD Session Host) server. Figure 1-5 shows session-based virtual desktops being accessed by multiple device types.

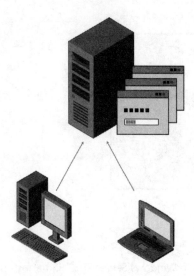

Figure 1-5 Session-based virtual desktops

Each user has an independent desktop when she connects to the RD Session Host server, and one user can't see what other users are doing. However, each RD Session Host server has limited resources, such as memory and disk throughput. The limited resources in each RD Session Host server limit the number of users who can connect and run applications at the same time.

When users connect to the RD Session Host server, screen display information, mouse movements, and keystrokes are sent across the network between the RD Session Host server and the client computer. RDP (the protocol that is used between client computers and the RD Session Host server) is efficient and consumes very little network bandwidth. This makes it possible to use a session-based desktop from remote locations over the Internet and other slow networks. In some cases, session-based virtual desktops are a replacement for accessing files directly over a virtual private network (VPN) for mobile users.

Remote desktop client software that uses RDP is available for many operating systems. Microsoft provides an RDP client for Windows clients, Windows Phone 8.1, Mac OS X, iOS, and Android. This means that you can access a session-based desktop regardless of the device type you choose to use. It also means that you can access a session-based desktop from almost anywhere you have Internet access.

NOTE

In Windows Server 2012 R2, the RDS server role provides session-based desktops. In Windows Server 2008 and older versions of Windows Server, this was called Terminal Services.

Some software isn't compatible with session-based virtual desktops because it isn't designed for multiple-session use. In such cases, you might be able to mitigate compatibility issues by using App-V to deliver the application to user sessions.

Benefits of session-based virtual desktops include

- **Better application performance for remote users**   When applications require fast access to centralized data, users in remote locations can use a session-based desktop to access the application. The session-based desktop is located close to the application data, which increases application performance over a remote user running the application locally.

- **Simplified application updates**   Updating an application on the RD Session Host server updates the application for all users. This can be easier than updating an application on multiple desktop computers.

Inside OUT

Application compatibility for session-based desktops

Most software can be installed and used for session-based desktops. However, some software is written in such a way that it's not compatible for multiple-session use. For example, an application may use a single central registry location instead of user-specific registry keys to track configuration. This would result in session-based users overwriting one another's changes while running the application.

One potential method to make applications compatible with session-based desktops is using App-V. Because App-V virtualizes the application, the application instance executed by each session-based user is isolated and conflicts are prevented.

VM-based virtual desktops

You can provide users with independent VMs that run Windows 8.1 as virtual desktops. A server that runs Windows Server 2012 R2 with the Hyper-V server role installed hosts the VMs. When you use VM-based virtual desktops, the creation of VMs is automated by installing RDS with the Remote Desktop Virtualization Host (RD Virtualization Host) role service. Users connect to the VMs by using RDP, which is the same as connecting to a session-based desktop.

Figure 1-6 shows multiple client types accessing VM-based virtual desktops on an RD Virtualization Host server.

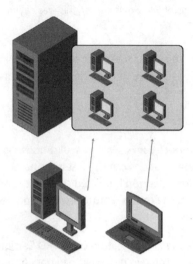

Figure 1-6 VM-based virtual desktops

When you implement VM-based virtual desktops, each user has an independent VM.
Resources that are allocated to each VM are exclusive to the user who is connected to that
VM. This guarantees that sufficient resources are available to applications that the user runs,
but it makes
VM-based desktops less efficient than session-based desktops because the same server hard-
ware can support fewer users.

Application compatibility is less of a concern when using VM-based virtual desktops. Generally,
if the application is compatible with the operating system on the VM, then it will work properly with VM-based virtual desktops. You can use VM-based virtual desktops for some applications that can't install on an RD Session Host server.

There are two variations of VM-based Virtual Desktop Infrastructure (VDI):

- **Pooled virtual desktops**   When you use this type of VDI, the VM for each user has the
  identical configuration. When the user logs off from the remote session, user state information is removed, and another user can access the VM. This is efficient because users
  don't consume resources when they are logged off. You might have 100 users for pooled
  virtual desktops, but because not all the users are logged on at the same time, only
  90 pooled virtual desktops are required.

- **Personal virtual desktops**   In this type of VDI, users have individual private VMs
  with varying configurations. When the user logs off from the remote session, user state

information is maintained, and users don't share the VMs. Users can be given the option to install software in their personal desktop.

Because resources for personal virtual desktops are dedicated to a single user, implementing personal virtual desktops is significantly more resource intensive than implementing pooled virtual desktops. Personal virtual desktops consume much more storage space than pooled virtual desktops. You also require more personal virtual desktops than pooled virtual desktops because personal virtual desktops are not shared.

Inside OUT

Selecting virtual desktop technology

Many virtual desktop deployment projects start with the assumption that personal virtual desktops are superior to other types of virtual desktops because personal virtual desktops are closest to having a personal physical computer. However, you need to identify the technology that is appropriate based on your users' needs and the cost to implement that technology.

In general, it's preferable to use session-based virtual desktops over other types of virtual desktops because they are the most efficient. If a scenario isn't suitable for session-based virtual desktops, then you should consider pooled virtual desktops. Consider personal desktops only if pooled virtual desktops and session-based virtual desktops are not appropriate

Storage virtualization

Storage Spaces is a storage virtualization technology in Windows Server 2012 R2 and Windows 8.1. You can use Storage Spaces to combine multiple local disks into a storage pool and then allocate spaces from the storage pool. When you create spaces in the storage pool, Storage Spaces allocates the disk space from the pool. You don't have control over which disks are selected for use in the storage space. After the space is allocated, it appears within the operating system as a normal volume.

When you use Storage Spaces and thin provisioning, you can increase the efficiency and flexibility of disk utilization. When you create a thin-provisioned space, the disk space isn't allocated for that volume until data is stored in the volume. So, you can over-provision disk space. For example, you can create several 1-terabyte (TB) spaces when there is only 2 TB of disk capacity in the storage pool. No matter how you allocate thin-provisioned spaces, the capacity of the storage pool limits the amount of data you can store.

Inside OUT

Virtual desktop terminology

Much of the Microsoft documentation about RDS and virtual desktops uses slightly different terminology from that of many other vendors. In most cases, when a vendor refers to virtual desktops, the vendor is referring to VM-based virtual desktops. Microsoft also refers to a session on an RD Session Host server as a session-based virtual desktop.

Similarly, other vendors typically use the term Virtual Desktop Infrastructure (VDI) to refer to the servers and software required to support VM-based virtual desktops. Microsoft expands the term VDI to include the servers and software required to support VM-based virtual desktops and session-based virtual desktops. In some cases, Microsoft documentation explicitly mentions session-based VDI and VM-based VDI.

To increase fault tolerance for data, you can create mirrored and parity spaces. Mirrored spaces create multiple copies of data and can be either two-way or three-way. Parity spaces are a more efficient way to protect against disk failure. With a minimum of three drives, a parity space protects you from a single-disk failure. With seven drives or more, a parity space protects you from two-disk failures.

Implementing mirrored and parity spaces is an alternative to using hardware-based RAID (Redundant Array of Independent Disks). Despite the fact that software-based RAID traditionally has poorer performance than hardware-based RAID, in most scenarios Storage Spaces offers approximately the same performance as hardware-based RAID. In a critical production environment, you should plan and test your implementation carefully to be sure that performance is acceptable.

NOTE

A computer that runs Hyper-V or RDS can use Storage Spaces to help manage local storage. However, you don't need to use Storage Spaces when implementing virtual desktops or application virtualization.

Usage scenarios for desktop virtualization

Like other technologies, you should implement desktop and application virtualization to meet the specific business needs of your organization. Not all desktop and application virtualization technologies are relevant to every organization. You need to understand the business benefits that desktop and application virtualization provides to determine whether they are relevant for your organization.

You might combine multiple Microsoft virtualization technologies to meet your needs. For example, you might implement pooled virtual desktops for users and then use either RemoteApp or App-V to deploy applications to those users.

Meeting legal and security requirements

You can use session-based virtual desktops or VM-based virtual desktops to provide users with virtual desktops that they can access remotely. Regardless of the method you use to implement desktop virtualization, you can use desktop virtualization to meet legal requirements for control of data and to increase data security. The main way that desktop virtualization increases security is by keeping all data in a central location. Data never downloads to the client computers that access virtual desktops. Losing control of the device that accesses the virtual desktop is less of a concern because credentials are required to use the device to access the virtual desktop.

When users connect to a virtual desktop by using a Remote Desktop client, they typically are able to copy data, save data, or print from the virtual desktop to the local client. However, you can disable this functionality to increase data security. Disabling this functionality can be part of a solution to prevent data from being taken outside the organization.

Some companies have remote offices in politically unstable areas where there is a risk that computer equipment could be stolen or seized. Because the security of the computer equipment is questionable, you want to make sure that no company data is stored on computers in those locations. Instead, you can provide users in those locations with access to virtual desktops that are stored in the main datacenter. This approach helps secure applications and their data.

You also might have computers in publicly accessible spaces. For example, a kiosk might run an application to provide guest access to catalog information. However, you don't want that information taken outside the office. In this example, if the kiosk accesses only a virtual desktop, then you have better control over the data.

Caution

By using desktop virtualization, you can prevent users from downloading data to a remote location. However, you can't prevent users from using other methods to capture data that they have permission to view. For example, users could take screenshots of reports even if they are unable to print or save the reports locally. You can make it more difficult to remove information, but you can't prevent it entirely.

Supporting desktop management tasks

When you implement desktop virtualization as a replacement for standard desktops, you simplify management of user computers and devices. However, desktop virtualization comes with its own set of management requirements.

In a standard computing environment, you need to keep client computers up to date by applying updates for the operating system and applications. You also need to monitor the deployment of updates to ensure that they were successful. You can simplify this process by using tools such as Windows Server Update Services (WSUS) and System Center 2012 R2 Configuration Manager, but it's still significant work to deploy and monitor updates. The updates for personal virtual desktops are managed similarly to those for standard client computers because they are all unique and maintain state.

Updates for session-based virtual desktops and pooled virtual desktops are done centrally. In both scenarios, you update and monitor a smaller number of computers than you would for standard desktops or personal virtual desktops.

Updates for session-based virtual desktops are performed on the RD Session Host server. When an application or operating system update is applied to the RD Session Host server, the update is performed for all users of that RD Session Host server.

For pooled virtual desktops, you update the starting image for the pooled desktops and redeploy the virtual desktops. Redeploying the pooled virtual desktops re-creates them from the starting image. After the virtual desktops have been redeployed, the operating system and application updates are included in all pooled virtual desktops.

In most organizations, replacing a user's computer is a relatively complex process. As part of the process, you need to ensure that the new computer has the correct applications for the user. You also need to migrate operating system and application settings from the old computer to the new computer. Finally, in some cases you need to migrate local data from the old computer to the new computer.

After implementing virtual desktops, no applications or data are stored on the client computer. Therefore, replacing the client computer does not require any migration of settings or data. You only need to configure the client to access the virtual desktop. This is true whether the replacement is done to retire hardware or to replace failed hardware.

Replacing a standard computer that has failed can take at least a few hours, if not a day or two. You typically design a virtual desktop deployment to be highly available. A user can connect from any computer with a remote desktop client, and the server infrastructure is redundant. At the very least, you should have redundant servers host the virtual desktops. In larger environments with multiple datacenters, you can configure recovery in a secondary datacenter. Clients then can connect to the virtual desktops in the secondary datacenter if an entire site fails.

Improving application compatibility

In most cases, applications can coexist without conflict when installed on a desktop computer or a virtual desktop. However, some applications have conflicting requirements for dynamic-link libraries (DLLs). In other cases, you can't run multiple versions of an application on the same computer. Both App-V and RemoteApp can help increase application compatibility.

App-V runs applications in a virtualized environment that isolates applications from one another and prevents file conflicts among applications. In some cases, two applications may need different versions of the same DLL. When you install applications locally, the last application installed may overwrite the DLL and cause the first application to break. When you use App-V, each application has its own copy of the DLL in its virtualized environment.

In some cases, applications just don't work well when installed on the same computer. For example, if you have two versions of Microsoft Office locally installed on the same computer, you can experience extended configuration sequences when switching between versions. If you deliver Microsoft Office by using App-V, the configuration sequence is avoided and you can switch quickly between the two versions of Microsoft Office.

RemoteApp also can be used to avoid application conflicts. When you use RemoteApp, the application is installed on an RD Session Host server and executes on that server. Therefore, an application delivered by using RemoteApp can never conflict with locally installed applications. However, you might need to install conflicting applications on different RD Session Host servers if you want to use RemoteApp for all of them.

Some applications can't be virtualized with App-V. For example, Internet Explorer can't be virtualized because it's integrated into the operating system. By using different versions of Internet Explorer on multiple RD Session Host servers, you can use RemoteApp to provide users with access to multiple versions of Internet Explorer if they are required for accessing application-specific websites.

Another concern for application compatibility is the operating system version. App-V does not resolve situations in which an application requires an older operating system. RemoteApp can help with operating system compatibility if the application is compatible with the operating system that is installed on the RD Session Host.

> ### NOTE
> Although you can't use App-V to allow applications to run on an incompatible operating system, there are specific instances in which App-V can help. For example, if the application installation sequence fails due to an operating system version check, but

the application will run after it's installed. App-V avoids the application installation process on the App-V clients and allows the application to distribute to computers without error.

Implementing desktop as a service

The idea of desktop as a service is to provide a Windows desktop like other cloud services. Software as a service is commonly available; Microsoft provides access to multiple instances of software as a service in Microsoft Office 365. Desktop as a service extends the concept of provisioning Windows desktops.

In a standard computing environment, provisioning a new desktop computer can take several days, depending on the processes that are in place. Among other issues, this can result in new staff and expensive consultants being unproductive while waiting for a new desktop computer.

When you use virtual desktops with Microsoft technologies to implement desktop as a service, you can provision desktops more quickly than traditional desktop computers. In some cases when users bring their own device, provisioning a new desktop can occur within minutes. In an organization that provides a client for accessing a virtual desktop, provisioning a virtual desktop is faster than provisioning a traditional desktop because fewer configurations need to be done on the client computer.

If you use a cloud-based provider of desktop as a service, you also might get the benefit of flexible payment and scalability. Basing cloud-based desktop as a service on a monthly fee per virtual desktop used is common. This enables you to provide desktop as a service to a few users without investing in expensive infrastructure. Cloud-based desktops also enable you to scale up quickly as required by increasing the number of seats you purchase from your provider.

Supporting the mobile user experience

Desktop and application virtualization provides benefits for all users, but there are additional benefits for mobile users. Mobile users can use desktop and application virtualization to take their desktop and applications on the road.

Many applications require fast access to a data source, such as a database hosted by Microsoft SQL Server. Most of these applications communicate frequently with the data sources and are not optimized to limit the amount of data that is read over the network. This makes it impossible for mobile users to use the application on a mobile computer with a VPN connection back to the office, because the VPN connection is too slow and its latency is too high. By using RemoteApp or a virtual desktop, mobile users can run the application while they are outside the office. For example, a sales person can run a line-of-business-application from a customer site to process sales orders. The line-of-business application is located on an RD Session Host server in the same datacenter as the data source for fast communication.

Access to data such as documents and spreadsheets also is slow over a VPN. Using a virtual desktop enables mobile users to run applications for editing documents and spreadsheets close to where the data is located. Using RDP is more efficient and provides better performance than accessing data files over a VPN.

Mobile users can use a variety of devices to access virtual desktops and applications. This is important because many mobile users use different types of devices when on the road. For example, many users prefer a tablet to a laptop when on the road because it's easier to carry. In some cases, users prefer to access information from their phones.

The requirement to support multiple types of mobile devices such as tablets and phones is expanding as companies begin to support Bring Your Own Device (BYOD). BYOD refers to users accessing organizational data and applications on their personal devices.

A key requirement for BYOD is supporting the wide variety of devices that are available. Remote Desktop client software is available for multiple operating systems. In addition to Windows operating systems, Microsoft provides a Remote Desktop client for Windows Phone 8.1, Mac OS X, iOS, and Android. The Microsoft Remote Desktop client supports accessing virtual desktops and applications that RemoteApp delivers. This allows users to select the device they want and retain access to their virtual desktop or RemoteApp applications.

Considerations for implementing virtualization

Desktop and application virtualization isn't a solution that solves all problems in all computing environments. Everyone in the computer industry is aware of poorly conceived and implemented projects that didn't deliver the promised benefits. Desktop and application virtualization is highly visible to users. When it isn't implemented properly, it reflects poorly on the information technology (IT) department that implemented it.

Many of the considerations for implementing desktop and application virtualization have a direct impact on user experience and, consequently, on the success of the project. The infrastructure you implement to support virtualization is important because it needs to have sufficient capacity and availability to support your users. It's also important to understand licensing considerations to ensure that all users are able to connect to and use the virtual environment.

User experience

User experience is an important consideration for the implementation of any technology project. When you implement virtualization for desktops and applications, user experience is critical. If the user experience for accessing a virtualized application or virtual desktop is worse than the experience of a standard client computer with locally installed applications, users will reject the solution.

A general rule of thumb is that virtual desktops must allow users to start using applications within 30 seconds. This is similar to the amount of time that users expect to wait for a computer to start. It shouldn't take several minutes to log on to a virtual desktop and begin using applications.

As you plan the implementation of virtual desktops, you need to consider what users will be doing with the desktops. It's relatively easy to implement virtual desktops to support standard applications such as Microsoft Office. Consider other applications with more complex requirements:

- Will users use applications that require audio?

- Will users use applications that require video?

- Will users use applications that require three-dimensional rendering?

- Do users require specialized hardware such as webcams?

- Do users need to perform Voice over Internet Protocol (VoIP) on the computer?

- Do users need to print to a local printer?

Before starting a virtualization project, you need to understand what users need to do. Then you need to ensure that your solution is capable of meeting those needs. If you don't properly identify and address user requirements, the project won't be successful.

Network connectivity

To provide an acceptable user experience, you need to have appropriate network connectivity between the clients and the RD Session Host server or the RD Virtualization Host server. Appropriate network connectivity isn't simply a matter of speed (also referred to as bandwidth). Network speed is a raw measure of how much data can flow over the network connection. An RDP connection requires at least 64 kilobits per second (Kbps) of bandwidth to function properly. A faster connection can better support network-intensive features such as video in a virtual desktop. However, raw speed isn't enough.

In addition to network speed, you need to consider network latency. Latency is the amount of time it takes to send a packet of data across the network to a remote device and receive a response. Higher latency results in lower throughput, regardless of the raw speed of the network connection. Throughput is the amount of data that you can transmit in a realistic scenario.

Latency is important because of the way that network communication is performed. If network communication were one-way, like the flow of water down a river, then the raw speed would be an accurate indicator of throughput. However, network communication usually is a two-way conversation, in which some data is sent and then a response is expected. The communication process has data going back and forth many times. Each time the communication changes direction, latency is introduced.

The type of network connection and the physical distance between the two computers influence the amount of latency in network communication. A dial-up or satellite network connection has relatively high latency. A local network connection has very low latency. You don't need to consider the distance between buildings in a campus environment when identifying latency. Latency is created over wide area network (WAN) connections that are thousands of miles. For example, latency over 2,000 kilometers (1,250 miles) is approximately 20 milliseconds (ms).

Figure 1-7 shows latency as measured by the Ping command. Notice that the latency varies from one ping request to the next. The lowest latency is 25 ms, and the highest is 85 ms.

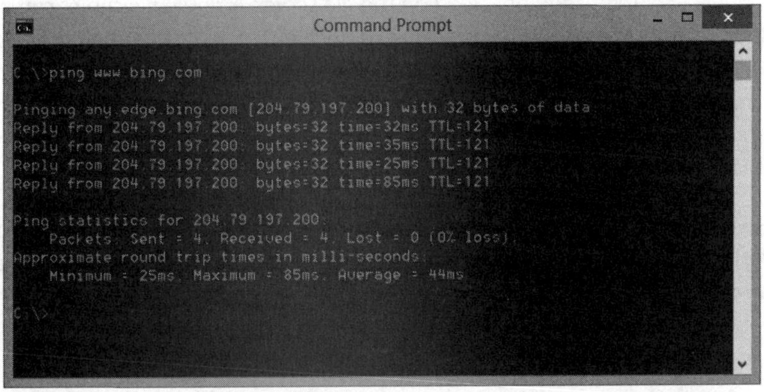

Figure 1-7 Latency measured by the Ping command

On shared wide area networks, such as Internet-based connections, the latency might fluctuate, which is a condition referred to as jitter. High amounts of jitter also can affect the user experience for some applications, such as VoIP and graphic design programs.

As part of implementing virtual desktops, you should include performance testing for network connectivity and scalability. This ensures that your virtual desktop implementation performs as required to support your users. You also should perform pilot testing to ensure that users are satisfied with the new system before deploying it to all users.

The aggregate network utilization that virtual desktops and applications on your network generate can be significant. The network traffic for virtual desktops and applications needs to coexist with other communication on your network. To ensure that enough network capacity is reserved for virtual desktops and applications, you can use Quality of Service (QoS) on your network.

QoS tags network packets with a priority number that network equipment uses to ensure that higher-priority communication isn't delayed. By marking virtual desktop and application communication with a higher priority, you ensure that the user experience is maintained. This is particularly important if your network is close to capacity or has other applications that can create large bursts of network traffic.

Infrastructure

A standard computing environment has applications installed on many client computers. If you use virtualization in your environment, many users utilize centralized servers. This has important implications for scalability and high availability.

In a standard computing environment, most of the scalability is achieved by adding client computers. For example, if the client computers are using a file server, each additional client computer puts very little additional load on the file server. A single file server can potentially service thousands of clients. For other scenarios, such as an application that uses a SQL server database, you need to be more diligent in monitoring the server utilization. However, it's not uncommon for a single SQL server to support at least hundreds of clients, depending on the application. Adding a few additional clients that use the SQL database adds a relatively small load to the SQL server.

The process for adding client computers is well understood and routine in most organizations. A typical deployment includes purchasing the new client computers and installing all of the necessary applications. Adding a few new clients generally adds little stress to the central servers. Scalability in a virtualized environment is more complex because each client adds much more load to the central servers.

In a virtualized environment, a server that performs a specific role, such as RD Session Host, can support a certain number of users depending on the workload those users generate. When one server has reached its maximum capacity, you need to expand capacity by adding servers and providing a method for automatically load balancing among the servers.

NOTE

The load-balancing method used to provide scalability depends on the role of the servers. For example, RD Session Host servers don't use traditional load balancing. The Remote Desktop Connection Broker (RD Connection Broker) service is responsible for providing load balancing for RD Session Host servers.

In a standard computing environment, if one client computer fails or an application on a client computer fails, there is a significant impact on one user but minimal impact on the overall organization. However, if you use virtualization in your environment, the impact of server failure is high because many users will be unable to work. Consider the following points about the impact of infrastructure failure for virtualization technologies:

- Session-based virtualization hosts sessions for many users on a single RD Session Host.

- VM-based virtualization hosts multiple VMs on a single RD Virtualization Host.

- Depending on the deployment model, App-V applications rely on an App-V publishing server.

- Applications delivered to computers by using RemoteApp rely on an RD Session Host.

To mitigate the risk of downtime associated with important centralized servers, you must make your infrastructure highly available. For each type of virtualization, different methods are used to enable high availability. High-availability methods include failover clustering and load balancing. You must ensure that you implement the appropriate methods for the type of virtualization that you implement.

Inside OUT

High availability and capacity planning

When you plan highly available infrastructure, you need to consider the performance after a component has been taken out of service. For example, if you have three RD Session Host servers and one is taken out of service, is there sufficient capacity in the two remaining RD Session Host servers to support all users? If you require three RD Session Host servers to support your users, you should have at least four RD Session Host servers in your environment to support high availability.

Having the fourth server in the example above is important in case of a server failure, but it more commonly is required for performing server maintenance. When you need to apply updates to one of the RD Session Host servers, you can take it out of service, apply the updates, and reboot the server without affecting users.

High availability for virtualized desktops and applications isn't just about making individual servers highly available. The entire infrastructure that supports those servers needs to be highly available. Other things that must be highly available include:

- Network equipment, such as switches and routers

- Network services, such as Domain Name System (DNS) and Active Directory Domain Services (AD DS)

- Datacenter infrastructure, such as cooling and power

Implementing high availability is expensive, but it's important for critical services. Otherwise, you risk having a large number of users unable to work when a relatively small part of your infrastructure becomes unavailable. The cost associated with the failure and the unproductive workers is very high.

NOTE

Due in part to the cost of implementing high availability for infrastructure, you often won't see direct cost savings associated with implementing desktop virtualization. Instead, you gain management benefits by implementing virtualization. If you are approaching desktop virtualization as a cost-saving measure, you should evaluate your assumptions carefully to ensure that they are accurate.

Licensing requirements

When you implement virtualization, you need to understand the licensing requirements for the solution you implement. Some types of virtualization require per-user client access licenses (CALs), and other types need one license for an entire organization.

NOTE

The following is general information about licensing for virtualization. Licensing can be a complex topic, depending on your scenario. Licensing options also change over time. Carefully identify the licensing requirements for your organization.

Session-based virtualization is based on the RDS server role in Windows Server 2012 R2. Server-side licensing is included as part of the license for Windows Server 2012 R2. Clients must have a separate CAL. RemoteApp also is session-based virtualization and requires an RDS CAL.

You can purchase user-based or device-based CALs for RDS. The CALs are shared among the RD Session Host servers. User-based CALs allow one user to connect to as many RD Session Host servers as required from multiple devices. Device-based CALs allow a single device to connect to as many RD Session Host servers as required and allows multiple users to use that device.

Inside OUT
Select user-based or device-based CALs

You should select user-based or device-based CALs based on your users' usage patterns. This will result in the most cost-effective deployment of RDS for your organization.

If users access their virtual desktop from multiple devices, user-based CALs typically are more cost-effective. For example, users who access their virtual desktop from a standard computer, a tablet, and their home computer require one user CAL. In the same usage scenario, three device-based CALs would be are required for each user.

If multiple users access desktops from an individual device, device-based CALs typically are more cost-effective. For example, in a call center with three shifts of 100 users all using the same 100 computers to access virtual desktops, you require one device-based CAL for each computer for a total of 100 device-based CALs. In the same usage scenario, you would require 300 user-based CALs for the 300 users who work the three shifts.

When you implement VM-based virtual desktops, you need to consider how to license both user connectivity to the RDS infrastructure that supports the VMs and the operating system that runs on the VMs.

NOTE
The restrictions on standard volume licensing and OEM licenses for operating systems make them unsuitable for use with a VM-based virtual desktop deployment.

To license the desktop operating system that runs on the VMs, you have two options:

- **Microsoft Software Assurance (SA) for Windows clients**   Windows client SA includes virtual access rights for VDI. This means that you can implement VMs at no charge if your desktop computers are licensed with Windows Client SA and you are accessing the VM from that licensed desktop computer.

- **Windows Virtual Desktop Access (VDA)**   VDA licenses allow a device to access a running VM and a Windows client operating system. You require this type of license for any scenario that Windows Client SA does not cover. Scenarios that require this license include contractors and access from employee-provided devices. This license is an annual subscription per device.

    ➤ For more information about Microsoft VDI and Windows VDA, see *http://go.microsoft.com/fwlink/?LinkID=510000&clcid=0x409.*

To license the RDS role services that provide VM-based virtual desktops, you can use either of the following:

- **Full RDS CAL**   A user or device RDS CAL that you purchase to access session-based virtualization also can be used to access RDS for VM-based sessions. This license also includes App-V for RDS licensing.

- **VDI Suites license**   For cases in which users don't need access to session-based desktops, you can use a VDI Suites license to provide access to the RDS for VM-based desktops. In addition, this license provides System Center 2012 R2 VM Manager licensing for the VMs. VDI Suites licensing is per device.

Licensing for App-V and UE-V is part of the licensing for MDOP. You can obtain MDOP licensing in two ways:

- As part of an enterprise agreement

- As an option when purchasing VDI Suites licenses

NOTE

MDOP licensing covers desktop operating systems. App-V for VM-based virtual desktops can be obtained through MDOP. Licensing for the use of App-V on a RD Session Host is included with the user's RDS CAL.

Application licensing in a virtualized environment varies depending on the licenses each vendor uses. You can't assume that an application that is licensed for use on a desktop computer also can be used for session-based virtual desktops or VM-based virtual desktops.

In the case of App-V distributed applications, you need to understand how you will track the deployment and usage of those applications. Then you need to find out how the application vendor handles licensing for App-V. For example, a vendor may require a license for each desktop to which the application is deployed. Or, the vendor may require a license for each desktop on which the application is available.

Challenges for implementing desktop and application virtualization

When you implement virtualization, you face challenges that you don't face in a traditional computing environment. You can mitigate each of these challenges, but you need to be aware that they exist to address them.

Providing consistent user state

Users require a consistent user state, regardless of whether they log on to a desktop computer or a virtual desktop. This allows the users to have a consistent configuration of applications and profile information such as favorites.

When users log on to session-based virtual desktops, they may be connected to different RD Session Host servers each time. By default, each RD Session Host server has a local profile for each user who logs on. The local user profiles are not synchronized among the RD Session Host servers. You need to implement some type of user state virtualization to keep the experience consistent for users.

Pooled virtual desktops are reset to their starting state at each logoff. Any user state information is lost at each logoff. Again, to allow users to retain information such their favorites, you need to implement user state virtualization.

Delivering unique apps to specific users

Session-based virtual desktops and pooled virtual desktops present the same applications to all users. Some users in your organization may require unique applications, but it might not be cost-effective to provide those applications to all users. In such cases, you can use App-V or RemoteApp to provide access to unique applications that specific users require. Both App-V and RemoteApp provide fast access to applications that are not installed on the local computer. This avoids the need to install the nonstandard applications on RD Session Host servers or pooled virtual desktops.

Monitoring performance of central servers

To ensure adequate performance on the central servers that provide virtual desktops and applications, you need to monitor the performance on the servers. You can perform monitoring in many ways, but one of the most effective is by using System Center 2012 R2 Operations Manager. Operations Manager can monitor performance and generate alerts when problems occur. Because Operations Manager provides a centralized monitoring console, it's easier to track server performance than by using native Windows tools such as Performance Monitor.

Identify virtualization technologies for business needs

Each organization has unique business needs. To help you further understand when it's appropriate to use different virtualization technologies, let's consider the business needs of a fictional company, A. Datum Corporation.

Improve roaming experience for users

A. Datum has a call center with 100 users. The users in the call center use an application that provides a script to follow during the calls and records user responses. This application needs to be configured on the first startup for each user. The configuration is stored in the local user profile. To avoid configuring this application each day, users try to use the same computer, but this isn't always possible.

To improve the user experience for the call center users, you should implement user state virtualization. User state virtualization synchronizes the application configuration among multiple computers and avoids the need to configure the application if users move among computers.

In this scenario, both roaming user profiles and UE-V will accomplish the user state virtualization that is required. The following are some things to consider:

- Roaming user profiles is the simplest method to implement Windows user state virtualization. There are no additional licensing costs for roaming user profiles because the functionality is part of the core Windows operating system.

- UE-V is part of MDOP. To implement UE-V, you must have a license for MDOP. If A. Datum does not have an enterprise agreement, it may not be able to obtain MDOP.

- UE-V is more complex to implement than roaming user profiles. You must implement client and server software. You need to configure UE-V to support the application.

Improve performance of apps for mobile users

A. Datum has 50 sales users who constantly visit client sites. The sales users currently use full laptop computers to run an application that allows them to enter sales orders from the client sites. To run the application, they connect to the A. Datum office by VPN.

Unfortunately, running the application over the VPN is very slow for the sales users. Over a VPN, there typically is high latency. High latency delays requests between the client software and the data source at the main office. This has been causing performance problems for the application.

In addition to the slowness concerns, the sales users have been requesting the ability for tablets to run the application. However, the vendor does not make an application for tablet operating systems. The sales users already have company email on their tablets.

To resolve the performance issues for running the application, you can use session-based virtual desktops, pooled virtual desktops, or RemoteApp. All of these solutions use RDP to connect to the main office and connect to a server or VM that is running the application. Sales users with tablets can use Remote Desktop to access all of these solutions.

When given a choice between using session-based virtual desktops or pooled virtual desktops, you should select session-based virtual desktops because pooled virtual desktops are more resource-intensive and consequently more expensive to implement. However, RemoteApp is the best solution for this scenario because the users only need remote access to the application, not an entire virtual desktop. RemoteApp reduces complexity for the users by providing only the application they need.

Provide remote access to apps and data

Many users want to work from home occasionally. However, most of the users don't have the necessary applications on their home computers and devices.

Some users have laptop computers with the necessary applications. The laptop users copy files locally onto their laptops, work on the files from home, and then copy the files back to a file share. Unfortunately, some users forget to copy the updated files to the file share. Occasionally, data is lost when users belatedly remember to copy the files after other users also have made changes.

A VPN like the one used by the sales users isn't a good solution for the users working from home. A VPN can provide access to the data at the main office, but it doesn't provide access to the applications. The users still would still need to have the applications installed on their home computers and devices, which may not be possible due to performance or licensing issues.

To provide users with access to applications from home, you can use virtual desktops or RemoteApp. Session-based virtual desktops are the best solution for users who work from home. They allow you to replicate the users' work environment with mapped drives and the same applications. They also are more cost-effective than pooled and personal virtual desktops. RemoteApp would be more difficult for users to understand when replicating a complete work environment.

Implementing session-based virtual desktops will resolve the problems caused by users copying files locally. There will no longer be a need for users to copy files to their laptops because they can access the files on their session-based virtual desktops.

NOTE
If users have desktop computers in the organization, then it is possible to use Remote Desktop and allow those users to connect directly to their desktop computers. If you implement this, you need to carefully consider the security requirements for remote connectivity and the licensing implications for the applications on the desktop computer. Most large organizations prefer to provide a centralized infrastructure for remote desktops.

Update apps efficiently

A. Datum's accounting application requires quarterly updates. The application is installed locally on computers, and a vendor performs all updates. The vendor manually runs updates on each computer. Because the vendor is charging for time to do the updates, you would like to simplify the update process. Also, the application doesn't run properly on server operating systems.

In many cases, you would use RemoteApp from an RD Session Host server to provide access to an application that you want to update centrally. However, because the accounting application can't be installed on server operating systems, you can't use session-based virtual desktops or RemoteApp based on session-based virtual desktops.

You can use pooled virtual desktops to provide access to the application. Pooled virtual desktops run a desktop operating system and therefore are supported for the accounting application. It's also possible to configure RemoteApp for pooled virtual desktops. With RemoteApp for pooled virtual desktops, each user is connected only to the application on each pooled virtual desktop.

If you use pooled virtual desktops, the application update process is simpler than updating multiple standard desktop computers. You update the image for the pooled virtual desktops and regenerate them.

You also could use App-V to deploy the application. Using App-V simplifies the application update process and requires less server infrastructure. After the App-V application is updated, it's automatically deployed to all clients using the application.

In this scenario, you must consider the application vendor's ability or willingness to support the deployment method. If the application vendor currently is doing manual updates of desktop computers, the vendor is unlikely to have much experience with more advanced technologies such as App-V. So, for support purposes, you may want to select pooled virtual desktops because the vendor is more likely to support this deployment method.

Provide unique apps and improve security

Research and development (R&D) users work in an open lab environment with shared computers. These users perform unique work and often need to install specialized applications. The current configuration is frustrating for users because sometimes the computer on which they have installed a specialized app is busy doing computations for another user. In some cases, users are removing apps that other users have installed. The labs have a limited amount of physical space, and it isn't possible to install a personal computer for each user.

The R & D department's apps aren't graphically intensive, but they are computationally and memory intensive. You need to guarantee that they have enough resources to analyze datasets.

Occasionally, A. Datum participates in joint ventures with other companies for research and development. Currently, R & D users take reference data on laptops to the joint venture location. You want to minimize the risk of A. Datum data being stolen.

The only virtualization technology that is suitable for the R & D users is personal virtual desktops. Only personal virtual desktops allow users to be given administrative permissions to install applications. Personal virtual desktops also retain state between user sessions so that the applications and their configuration will remain between sessions.

To ensure that all users have the necessary resources in their personal virtual desktops, you configure the resources allocated to the VM. You can configure the amount of memory and the number of virtual processor cores that are allocated.

Using personal virtual desktops is a security improvement for the joint ventures. The current system requires data to be taken offsite on a laptop that could be stolen or lost. If users are using a personal virtual desktop to access the data, the data is never stored on the laptop. If the laptop is lost or stolen, it does not include the data.

Planning and implementing user state virtualization

Technology users are becoming more mobile. However, when they are away from their main office, they expect the same technology experience with any device that they use—whether it's a phone, tablet, laptop, or desktop. Users don't want varying configurations among their devices because it can be confusing and it wastes their time.

Information Technology (IT) departments also want well-managed systems to offer users the experience level they have come to expect, without a labor-intensive process to make that happen. Windows operating systems include several technologies that make this possible. For example, you can use the Folder Redirection and Offline Files technologies together to redirect the path of local folders, such as the Documents folder, to a network location, while caching the contents locally for increased speed and availability. You can use roaming user profiles to redirect a user profile to a network location so that another device can provide the same user experience and data that a user has configured elsewhere. You also can configure the Primary Computer setting for a user to control which domain computers use roaming user profiles and which use redirected folders.

At the enterprise level, you can implement Microsoft User Experience Virtualization (UE-V) for user state virtualization. It synchronizes user applications and Windows settings to deliver a user's personal experience across many domain devices. UE-V integrates with existing management tools and provides detailed control and synchronized settings.

Understanding user state and user profiles

User state is a general term that describes settings and data that define the work environments for users on their devices. For each user, the user state is a collection of files and folders rather than a single file. In Windows 8.1, user state information is stored separately from files and settings that are specific to the operating system and applications.

Each user of a computer running a Windows client operating system has separate user state information. This means that every user has a user state that is independent of other users on the same computer. Windows client operating systems refer to user state as a user profile, which is stored in C:\Users. For example, a user with the logon name Aidan would have a user profile stored in C:\Users\Aidan. Figure 2-1 shows the contents of a user profile in Windows 8.1.

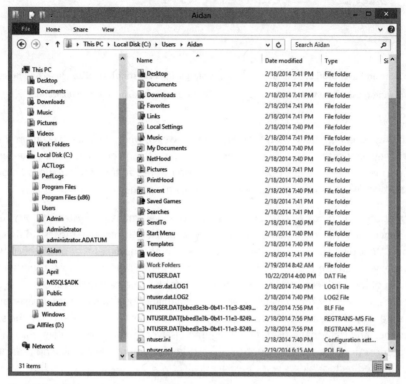

Figure 2-1 Contents of a user profile

User profile creation

When a user logs on to a computer for the first time, the operating system automatically cre-ates a local *user profile*. That local user profile is used for all subsequent logons to the same computer. If the user logs on to a second computer, a new local user profile is created on the second computer. By default, there is no synchronization of profile information among local user profiles. This means that modifications and documents that the user creates on one computer won't be used or available on other computers. Therefore, local profiles should be avoided if a user logs on to multiple devices.

Local user profiles are created from the default user profile stored in C:\Users\Default. When a user logs on to a computer for the first time, the default user profile is copied to the folder containing the local user profile for that user. The default user profile acts as a starting point that users can customize.

Inside OUT

Modifying the default profile

It's possible to modify the default user profile to establish a baseline for new profiles created on a desktop computer. In the early days of networking with Windows 95/98 and Windows NT, this was a common way to create a standardized user environment. In a modern computing environment, there are better ways to create a standardized user environment than modifying the default user profile. For example, you can use Group Policy to set and enforce almost any aspect of Windows 8.1.

If, after careful thought, you determine that modifying the default user profile is appropriate for your environment, then you can use the following methods:

- Copy files and shortcuts into the default user profile.
- Use registry editing tools to modify NTUSER.DAT in the default user profile.
- Create a new default user profile when you run Sysprep.

The supported method for modifying the default user profile is by using Sysprep. You create an XML file with CopyProfile enabled.

➤ For more information about using CopyProfile to modify the default user profile, see *http://technet.microsoft.com/en-us/library/hh825135.aspx.*

Data in the public user profile stored in C:\Users\Public is shared by all users on the local computer. Windows merges the public user profile folder contents with the user's own user profile when logging on. For example, if a shortcut is placed in the Desktop folder of the public user profile, then that shortcut appears on the desktop of each user. The shortcut file isn't copied to each user profile, but it's displayed as though it was.

If an error prevents a user's profile from loading properly, a temporary user profile is created. The user is informed that a temporary user profile is being used. This is important because when the user logs off, the contents of the temporary user profile are deleted. Any files or settings created and saved in the temporary user profile are lost.

TROUBLESHOOTING

Deleting a profile

In older operating systems such as Windows XP, administrators deleted a local user profile folder to force the creation of a new user profile. If you attempt this with Windows 7 or later client operating systems, it will force the user account to start using a temporary user profile. If you need to remove a local user profile and want it to be re-created properly, you need to remove it by taking the following steps:

1. On the Start screen, type advanced system and click View advanced system settings.

2. In the System Properties window, on the Advanced tab, in the User Profiles area, click Settings.

3. In the User Profiles window, click the profile you want to remove and click Delete.

If you do not remove a user profile properly, you need to edit the registry to remove references to it before it can be re-created.

The list of local profiles for a computer is located in HKEY_LOCAL_MACHINE \SOFTWARE\Microsoft\Windows NT\CurrentVersion\ProfileList. Each profile has its own key based on the SID of the user. To identify the key for the failing profile you need to delete, look at the ProfileImagePath value. This value is the file path to the profile and contains the name of the user.

User profile content

Most of the user-specific settings in Windows 8.1 are stored in the registry. These include user-specific operating system settings, such as desktop configuration, and application settings, such as profile configuration for Microsoft Outlook. The user portion of the registry is NTUSER.DAT.

A unique copy of NTUSER.DAT is stored in the user profile folder of each user. When a user signs in, the HKEY_CURRENT_USER registry key is linked to the HKEY_USERS registry key for that user. The HKEY_USERS key for a specific user links to the NTUSER.DAT file for that user.

Each user profile also has an AppData folder that is used to store application-specific data. Although individual settings such as options within an application can be stored in the registry, other application-specific information such as template files can't. When applications need to store user-specific data files, the files are stored in AppData.

Within AppData, there are three folders:

- **Local**   This folder contains application settings and data that are computer specific. In this folder, applications store data that should not roam between computers. Typically this data does not roam between computers because it's too large or isn't important. For example, cached files or temporary files do not need to roam.

- **LocalLow**   Like the local folder, this folder is used to store application data that is either too large or not important enough for roaming. However, this folder is for low-integrity applications to use to isolate data from those applications. For example, applications that run within Internet Explorer Enhanced Protected Mode use this location for their data and settings.

- **Roaming**   This folder contains application data and settings that can roam between computers. Data inside this folder isn't computer dependent and is limited in size, so it can roam with a user from computer to computer.

In addition to user settings, each user profile contains folders for user data. Some of the folders that store user-specific data are:

- **Desktop**   This folder contains any files and shortcuts that appear on the user's desktop. The data stored here is important because users often start applications from desktop shortcuts and may store frequently used files on the desktop.

- **Downloads**   Files downloaded from the Internet are stored in this folder. The size of this folder will vary significantly among users. For example, a typical office worker may occasionally download documents from the Internet, which will be a few megabytes. An administrator may regularly download large files for software updates or application installation.

- **Favorites**   This folder contains favorites that are created in Internet Explorer. Favorites are a critical part of user profiles because users want to retain a quick way to access frequently used websites.

- **Documents**   This folder is designed to hold personal user documents. However, in most corporate environments, users are discouraged from storing data files in their user profile because information on their desktop computer isn't backed up.

- **Music**   This folder is meant to hold music files. This folder is seldom used in corporate environments.

- **Pictures**   This folder is meant to hold picture files. Most users in a corporate environment will have a small number of pictures stored in this folder. However, users with job roles that specifically deal with pictures may store a very large number of pictures.

- **Videos**   This folder is meant to hold video files. Unless users have a job role that specifically deals with videos, this folder will typically have few, if any, files. However, because video files can be very large, even a few video files can be a large amount of data.

Understanding and planning user state virtualization

Centralized management and storage of user state is desirable because it provides users with mobility and flexibility and it helps IT departments manage costs and compliance. User state virtualization provides users with the ability to use multiple devices and have the same user state on each device. For example, if you modify the configuration of Microsoft Word on one computer, that updated configuration will be available on other computers on which you use Word. User state virtualization provides a consistent, familiar experience that enables users to increase their productivity. Users always will have access to their personal experience on any managed computer or device, and when user state virtualization is combined with Folder Redirection and Offline Files, their data will move with them.

You can implement user state virtualization to address the following challenges:

- **Backing up user data and settings**   Most organizations do not back up user data and settings from individual devices because it's too difficult to manage or too costly. If data is stored on a device such as a laptop or tablet and that device is lost, the data is lost with it.

- **Migrating the user state to new devices**   When users get a new device, it's time-consuming to manually migrate data and settings to a new device. If users keep a lot of local data, the migration process can take an hour or more.

- **Migrating the user state to new operating systems**   Companies typically do not perform an in-place upgrade when implementing a new operating system. Instead, they perform a clean installation of the operating system and then migrate user settings and data from the old computers. If the deployment process requires you to back up the user state before the operating system update and restore the user state afterward, it significantly slows down the operating system deployment process. With user state virtualization in place, some organizations even have enabled end users to redeploy the operating system on their computers without intervention from IT staff.

- **Making data and consistent settings available, regardless of the device**   Users can use many different devices types for work. For example, they can have a desktop computer in the office, an RDS server for remote work from home, and a tablet for use when out of the office. Users need to have consistent data and settings on all devices to support their productivity.

- **Consumerization of IT**   Many organizations are starting to allow users to bring in their own devices to access corporate systems. Even though some devices run operating systems other than Windows, they usually can browse the Internet and send and receive email, instant messages, and text messages. The challenge is to provide similar and familiar user environments and data to these devices.

User state virtualization provides a solution to these challenges. By using user state virtualization, organizations store users' data and settings in a central location and optionally cache them locally for offline usage when users are mobile. Typically, this location is a network share on a file server or network attached storage (NAS) device. The result is that when users roam, their data and settings follow them from computer to computer, including to their mobile devices. This effectively separates data that is user-specific and can roam from data that is computer-specific and must be stored locally.

User state virtualization also can mitigate productivity loss because of computer replacement. The central copy of the data is on a network, so it's restored easily in the event of a lost or stolen computer, and the user's settings can be reapplied automatically. When the IT department sets up the policy to allow offline access to a redirected folder, BitLocker Drive Encryption can be applied to the computer to help ensure data safety. A typical example of this type of user state virtualization is the use of Folder Redirection with Offline Files and a roaming user profile.

User state virtualization centralizes the storage of the user state that typically resides on users' computers, thus simplifying the backup and management of business-critical data. It also decouples user state from the operating system, which enables the same user state to be used on different operating systems. For example, the operating system can be reverted while the user state is preserved, such as with pooled virtual desktops when user profile disks are used. When you back up the central storage, the user state that was synchronized from users' computers also is backed up.

Centralized management of user state also provides the following benefits:

- **Ability to work from different computers**   Centralized data and settings can synchronize across different computers, thereby providing users with flexibility and mobility options that can improve productivity. Each computer at which a user signs in has the same settings and data.

- **Ability to work when disconnected from an enterprise's network**   User state virtualization technologies can automatically cache local updates to user data and settings so they can synchronize with the central store when network connectivity is reestablished.

- **Faster and easier user migration**   User state virtualization technologies enable the dynamic creation of the user state on new computers over the network, thereby simplifying migration. The user state information is copied from the central storage location and placed in the local profile.

- **Recovery from disaster scenarios, such as when hard disks fail or computers are lost or stolen**   Centralized data and settings that are backed up regularly can be restored automatically to new hard disks when the user logs on, thereby reducing the time required for organizations and users to regain productivity.

- **Using familiar user state data on devices**   When a user is working from a device that isn't a domain member (for example, a Windows RT tablet) or runs a non-Microsoft operating system, the user still can benefit from user state virtualization. Different devices can use other technologies, such as Virtual Desktop Infrastructure (VDI). In this scenario, a device receives a copy of a remote client desktop session, and user state virtualization adds the user state data to that session.

Microsoft has developed a planning strategy for enterprise user state virtualization. This strategy presents a systematic method of identifying an organization's user and IT needs to design and plan a suitable user state virtualization strategy. The key to planning the correct user state virtualization strategy for your organization is to assess the organization's business requirements.

The following steps guide you through the prevalent requirements for IT and the common user in most organizations. Each step contains job aids in the form of checklists that you can use to track relevant business requirements so that you can provide these requirements to IT infrastructure designers to assist in the user state virtualization planning process.

The user state virtualization planning strategy contains five steps that guide the planner through user and IT requirements, and it contains real-world scenarios that influence user state virtualization solution planning:

- Assess user data requirements

- Assess user settings requirements

- Evaluate compatibility considerations

- Evaluate infrastructure and manageability requirements

- Evaluate usage scenario considerations

These steps are not sequential, meaning that you can perform them in any order. However, to understand the suitability and importance of the various technologies, you should complete them all.

➤ **For more information about this planning strategy, download the Windows User State Virtualization Guide from** *http://go.microsoft.com/fwlink/?LinkId=286564.*

Assess user data requirements

The first step of the user state virtualization planning strategy is to assess user data requirements. This step involves identifying which portions of user data are important to the organization, discovering technology limitations, and identifying real-world considerations that apply to the organization.

In this assessment, you're concerned with user data that resides in user profiles. Data stored in shared folders isn't part of the evaluation for planning user state virtualization.

The main technologies available for managing user state data are Folder Redirection, roaming user profiles, and Offline Files. In general, it's beneficial to minimize the amount of data stored in user profiles. When user data is stored in a central file share, it's easier to back up and restore. Reducing the data in a user profile also speeds up the login process for users who have roaming user profiles.

One common way to reduce the amount of data in local profiles is by using Folder Redirection. The Documents folder is a logical place for users to store their data, but it's part of the local user profile. You can redirect Documents to a file share for shared data or a user home folder. If that data needs to be taken on the road with a mobile computer, then Offline Files can be used.

Folder Redirection can be used only for known common folders supported by Folder Redirection. If there are custom folders in the profile, then the only user state virtualization method that you can use is roaming user profiles.

Assess user settings requirements

Assessing user settings requirements addresses virtualization of the user settings. In this step, you identify which components of user settings are relevant to the business, discover technology limitations, and identify real-world considerations that apply to your organization.

The term *user settings* refers to user-specific customizations of applications and the operating system. Examples of user settings include: network drive mappings, printer connections, the Start screen layout, keyboard and mouse layouts, desktop wallpaper, and dictionary and spelling checker options in Microsoft Word. Such settings typically are stored either within the HKEY_CURRENT_USER portion of the registry hive or in configuration files in the AppData \Roaming folder in the user profile.

Roaming user profiles and UE-V can be used to virtualize user settings that are stored in the HKEY_CURRENT_USER registry hive. To virtualize user settings in the AppData\Roaming folder you can use Roaming User Profiles, UE-V, or Folder Redirection.

Roaming user profiles technology does not allow virtualization of specific keys or subkeys within HKEY_CURRENT_USER. However, UE-V does allow specific keys and subkeys to be virtualized.

In Windows 8.1, roaming user profiles allow background synchronization of HKEY_CURRENT_USER so that updates to the hive can synchronize to the profile server while the user is logged on, as opposed to synchronization only during logon or logoff. UE-V also synchronizes periodically.

Evaluate compatibility considerations

Evaluating compatibility for user state virtualization requires you to consider the compatibility of different operating systems, device types, and applications. When you design user state virtualization, you need to determine which settings can be virtualized and which can't. Some of the things you need to consider are:

- **Operating system compatibility**   The settings that a user configures in one operating system may not be valid in another operating system. In such a case, it isn't possible for the settings to be virtualized. For example, a user may have a roaming user profile that is configured for Windows 8.1. When logging on to an older computer running Windows 7, Start screen customization won't be relevant. Even for Windows 8.1, the RT edition of Windows 8.1 has different capabilities from Windows 8.1 Professional.

- **Device type compatibility**   The settings that are available for one type of device are not necessarily available for all devices. Bring Your Own Device (BYOD) introduces a wide number of device types, such as Apple iPads and Android-based devices. These devices typically have very different user states, and there may be very few settings that you can synchronize among the device types. The typical user state virtualization technologies such as roaming user profiles and Folder Redirection are not cross-platform.

- **Application compatibility**   The settings for applications typically are specific to that application. So, settings for Word 2013 can't be applied to another document editor on an Android device. You also need to be concerned about the version of a specific application. Word 2010 and Word 2013 have many settings in common that can be used across devices with the two different versions, but you can expect that Word 2013 will have settings that can't be applied to Word 2010.

Evaluate infrastructure and manageability requirements

Like any other technology that you implement, you need to ensure that the necessary infrastructure is available to support user state virtualization. For example, to support roaming user profiles, you need to have fast and low-latency connectivity between the clients and the roaming profile storage location. It's not a reasonable scenario to have roaming user profiles between physical locations with slow WAN links.

Another major consideration for infrastructure is availability and redundancy. Most of the user virtualization technologies centralize data storage in a location such as a file share. You need to be aware of what happens when that centralized location isn't available. For example, if you redirected folders to a central file share and that share isn't available, then the setting and data stored in that share are not available to users. You can mitigate this by making the central file share highly available or by using Offline Files.

From a management perspective, you need to identify how you will manage each of the user state virtualization technologies that you choose to implement. In many cases, you can implement user state virtualization by using Group Policy. Using Group Policy whenever possible simplifies configuration because you can create a single Group Policy object that is applied to many users. For example, you can implement Folder Redirection by using Group Policy.

Evaluate usage scenario considerations

To select the appropriate user state virtualization technologies, consider how your users work. The three commonly considered usage scenarios are

- **Assigned computer** Each user is assigned a dedicated computer, and the user works only with that assigned computer.

- **Occasionally roaming user** Users are assigned dedicated computers, but they occasionally might use public computers.

- **Always roaming user** Users are not assigned a dedicated computer; instead, they always log on to a computer within a shared pool of computers.

Assigned computer user scenario

Users with assigned computers might not need to use different computers in the organization. However, implementing a user state virtualization strategy can be useful because it provides the ability to centralize a user's business-critical data so that it can be backed up easily. User state virtualization also provides the ability to cache data files locally so that users can continue to work when remote network servers and mail servers are offline. If these users are assigned laptop computers, user state virtualization also provides the ability to work while traveling. Taking additional steps such as configuring Outlook connectivity to the Microsoft Exchange Server can improve the user experience in this scenario.

The following considerations are relevant to Folder Redirection, Offline Files, and roaming user profiles in an assigned computer user scenario:

- Use Folder Redirection to redirect users' data folders.

- Use Offline Files so that business users can continue working when they are disconnected from the network.

- Use the Slow-link mode of Offline Files so that users automatically work on locally cached copies of data when the network connection is slow.

- Enforce periodic synchronization of the Offline Files stored to the redirected folder on the corporate server so that the centrally managed business data remains current.

CHAPTER 2

- Avoid redirection of the AppData\Roaming folder unless it contains business-critical data.

- Avoid redirection of known folders such as Music and Videos unless they contain business-critical data.

- Avoid the use of roaming user profiles unless business-critical settings or data exist in the HKEY_CURRENT_USER hive of the registry.

The following considerations are relevant to Outlook and Exchange Server or Office 365 with an assigned computer user scenario:

- Configure Outlook in cached/offline mode to enable indexing and to allow users to continue working while offline.

- Avoid the use of .pst files for email storage. Office 365 supports large mailboxes, which negate the need for .pst files. For an on-premises implementation of Exchange Server, you should design the implementation to support large mailboxes or online archive mailboxes.

These configuration settings provide an optimal user experience for an assigned computer scenario. Users have access to all of their data immediately after they log on via Folder Redirection, and email is available after an initial download. The ability to search email messages and data files is immediate after initial indexing.

Occasionally roaming user scenario

The occasionally roaming user scenario applies to users who are assigned a primary computer but occasionally need to work from shared public computers or kiosks. User state virtualization provides the ability to cache user state on local computers and to synchronize user state across different computers in the organization. This benefits users when they work offline and when they log on to different computers, such as public kiosk computers. Taking additional steps such as configuring Outlook connectivity to Exchange Server can improve the user experience in this scenario.

The following considerations are relevant to Folder Redirection, Offline Files, and roaming user profiles with an occasionally roaming user scenario:

- Do not use Folder Redirection to redirect application settings stored in the AppData \Roaming folder, because users on a kiosk computer typically do not need to access application-specific files such as custom dictionaries or templates.

- Disable Offline Files so that redirected data files that the user accesses are not cached locally.

- Consider using mandatory profiles for kiosk computers, in which saving user settings isn't required.

The following consideration is relevant to Outlook and Exchange Server or Office 365 with an occasionally roaming user scenario:

- Configure Outlook to run in Online mode so that email isn't stored on the public computer. This will help ensure that the hard drives of public kiosk computers do not accumulate user profile data.

Always roaming user scenario

The always roaming user scenario applies to users who are not assigned personal computers, but instead always log on to an available computer from a pool of shared computers. Examples of such users are call center employees or employees in a help desk environment and users who log on to pooled virtual desktops in a VDI scenario. Taking additional steps such as configuring Outlook connectivity to Exchange Server can improve the user experience in this scenario.

The following considerations are relevant to Folder Redirection, Offline Files, and roaming user profiles with an always roaming user scenario:

- Use Folder Redirection to redirect users' data folders.

- Avoid using Offline Files so that hard drives of shared computers do not accumulate data from multiple users.

- Turn on indexing on the remote server to enable search for redirected data.

- Avoid redirection of the AppData\Roaming folder unless it contains business-critical data.

- Avoid redirection of known folders such as Music and Videos unless they contain business-critical data.

- Avoid the use of roaming user profiles unless business-critical settings or data exist in the HKEY_CURRENT_USER hive of the registry.

- Consider using UE-V to allow application settings to be synchronized across computers if required.

The following considerations are relevant to Outlook and Exchange Server or Office 365 with an always roaming user scenario:

- Configure Outlook in Online mode so that email does not cache on the local computer.

CHAPTER 2

- Configure Outlook to use Exchange Server for searches, which is the default functionality when Outlook is configured in Online mode.

- Consider using Outlook Web App instead of Outlook. Outlook Web App provides most of the functionality available in Outlook and can be used without any configuration of individual client computers.

This configuration emphasizes storing data on the central server, and data does not cache locally on the shared computers. Users will have access to all of their data immediately after logging on via Folder Redirection. Email also is available immediately after Outlook starts, and there is no need to wait for email to download. The ability to search email messages and data files is immediate because there is no need to build a local index. Instead, the indexes on Exchange Server are used for email searches and indexes on the file server are used for file system searches. This configuration minimizes network transmission of user state information every time a user logs on, but it will place an additional load on the supporting infrastructure, such as Exchange Server and the file system, because copies of email and data are stored on the network.

Configuring user state virtualization technologies

The most commonly used technologies for implementing user state virtualization are those included as part of Windows Server 2012 R2 and Windows 8.1. Any organization can implement these technologies with no additional licensing costs. User state virtualization technologies that are part of Windows operating systems include the following:

- Roaming user profiles

- Folder Redirection

- Offline Files

- Credential Roaming

- User profile disks

Configuring roaming user profiles

Roaming user profiles allow enterprises to store users' profiles on a central network location instead of storing them locally on the users' client computers. The roaming user profile structure is the same as that of local profiles, but the location of the roaming folder is different.

Roaming user profiles are stored on a network share so that they are accessible from any computer. When a user with a roaming user profile logs on to a new computer for the first time, the roaming user profile is copied to the new computer as a local user profile and used locally while the user is logged on. When the user logs off, the local user profile and all of the changes that have been made to it are uploaded to the network location to update the roaming user profile. Figure 2-2 shows this process.

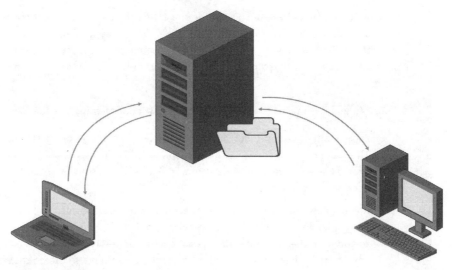

Figure 2-2 How roaming user profiles work

If a user modifies files or settings that are stored outside the user profile, they are not included in the roaming user profile. The modified files outside the profile are available only on the computer on which they were made—they do not roam with the user.

CHAPTER 2

Inside OUT

Performance issues with roaming user profiles

Roaming user profiles have been available since the early days of corporate computing with Windows NT and Windows 95/98. At the time, they were the only commonly available method to simplify roaming between computers. However, there can be some performance issues with roaming user profiles, and most organizations no longer use them.

Some of the performance concerns with roaming user profiles include the following:

- Large roaming user profiles can cause slow sign in and sign out performance. This is directly influenced by the data contained in the user profile. If the user profile has any large files, signing in and signing out is slow because the files need to be copied over the network

- Roaming user profiles occasionally become corrupted and need to be re-created. When roaming user profiles become corrupted, the changes aren't synchronized to and from the network storage location. Corruption typically is caused by network communication issues during sign out. Corruption also can be caused by applications that don't release registry keys quickly enough during the sign-out process. This problem is much less prevalent in Windows 7 and Windows 8.1 than it was with Windows XP, but it still occurs occasionally.

- If a user signs in to multiple computers at the same time, the changes at the last sign out overwrite changes from the previous sign out. Basically, the changes the user makes to the profile on the first computer are lost because the profile is copied from the second computer when the user signs out.

- If a user doesn't sign out from the computer, the user profile isn't copied back to the roaming user profile. This is a problem because many users leave their computers logged on for an extended period of time without signing out. Instead, their computer locks the screen or goes to sleep. Windows 7 and Windows 8.1 mitigate this problem somewhat by synchronizing NTUSER.DAT content in the background while the user is logged on. However, other files are not synchronized in the background.

Preparing a share for roaming user profiles

To prepare to use roaming user profiles, you need to create and configure a network share that holds the roaming user profiles. It's important to secure the network share properly because sensitive data could be contained in the roaming user profiles. For example, a roaming user profile contains the files in the Documents folder for a user. Users assume that this data is private and protected. Additionally, a roaming user profile contains any certificates that have been assigned to the user.

When you create a shared folder for roaming user profiles, you need to consider both share and NTFS permissions. The minimum share permission that you can provide for the shared folder is Modify. The Modify share permission is necessary to allow users to create, delete, and modify files in their own roaming user profile folder.

NTFS permissions for roaming user profiles need to be set at the root folder and at the folder for each roaming user profile. At the root folder, the minimum permissions you can assign are listed in Table 2-1.

Table 2-1 NTFS permissions for root folder in roaming user profile share

Account	Minimum Permissions	Applies To
System	Full Control	This folder, sub-folders, and files
Creator Owner	Full Control	Subfolders and files only
Administrator	Full Control	This folder only
Group containing users with profiles	List Folder/Read Data Create Folders/Append Data	This folder only

You typically do not create individual folders in the share for each roaming user profile. Instead, the Windows client operating system creates the folders for each roaming profile as part of the logon process. When you allow users to create the folders for the roaming user profiles, inheritance for NTFS permissions is disabled and the user is assigned as owner of the folder. The NTFS permissions assigned to each roaming user profile folder are listed in Table 2-2.

CHAPTER 2

Table 2-2 NTFS permissions for roaming user profile folder

Account	Permissions Assigned	Applied To
System	Full Control	This folder, subfolders, and files
User of the profile	Full Control	This folder, subfolders, and files

Configuring the user object for roaming user profiles

You can configure the user object with the path for a roaming user profile by using Active Directory Users and Computers or Active Directory Administrative Center. The path you configure is a universal naming convention (UNC) path for the share containing the user profiles and includes the name of the user. To simplify the creation process, you can use the environment variable %username%. The variable is substituted with the name of the user. For example, the actual UNC path with the username resolved might be \\LON-DC1\Profiles*April*.

Inside OUT

Roaming profile folder names

When the user folder is created for a roaming user profile, the extension V2 is added to the folder name. For example, the folder for April would be April.V2. This occurs for roaming user profiles with Windows Vista and newer Windows operating systems to distinguish them from roaming user profiles used by Windows XP. This extension name convention was created because Windows XP profiles were not compatible with Windows Vista and newer. You won't see the V2 listed in the user account, but you can verify it in the profile share. For Remote Desktop Session Host (RD Session Host) servers running Windows Server 2008 or later, the V2 extension also is used.

Perform the following steps to configure a user for a roaming user profile:

1. Open Active Directory User and Computers or Active Directory Administrative Center and locate the user account you want to modify.

2. Right-click the user account and click Properties.

3. In the user account properties window, on the Profile tab, set the Profile path as \\Server\ProfileShare\%username%, as shown in Figure 2-3, and then click OK.

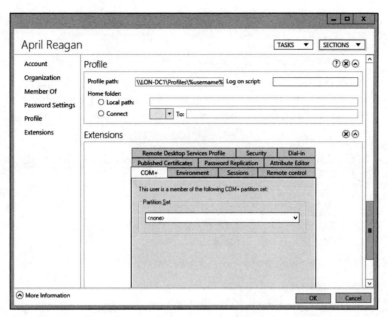

Figure 2-3 Setting the roaming user profile path in Active Directory Administrative Center

Inside OUT

Setting roaming profiles for specific computers

In most cases, you want a roaming profile to be used on all computers a user utilizes. However, in special use cases like a computer lab, you may want a different profile to be used based on the computer at which the user signs in. You can configure computer-specific roaming user profiles by using Group Policy.

To configure roaming user profiles for specific computers, perform the following steps:

1. Open the Group Policy Management Console and browse to the organizational unit containing the computer accounts.

2. Right-click the container that contains computer accounts and click Create A GPO In This Domain And Link It Here.

3. In the New GPO window, in the Name box, type a name for the GPO and click OK.

4. Right-click the new GPO, click Edit, and navigate to Computer Configuration \Policies\Administrative Templates\System\User Profiles.

5. In User Profiles, right-click Set Roaming Profile Path For All Users Logging Onto This Computer and then click Edit.

6. In the Properties dialog box, click Enabled.

7. In the Users Logging Onto This Computer Should Use This Roaming Profile Path box, enter the path to the file share where you want to store the user's roaming user profile, followed by %username%.

You also can use this Group Policy setting to configure roaming user profiles for an entire domain. However, it would be unusual to do so because you can specify only one path. In a large organization, it's likely that you would need at least separate profile shares for different physical locations. However, you may be able to use environment variables to make a single GPO possible for an entire domain.

Managing user profiles by using Group Policy

You can use Group Policy to manage user environments centrally, including many of the user profile settings. Group Policy includes many user profile–related settings that you can config-ure for users and computers.

In a GPO, user-specific settings for user profiles are configured in User Configuration\Policies\Administrative Templates\System\User Profiles. Some of the user-specific GPO settings that you can configure for user profiles include:

- **Exclude Directories In Roaming Profile**   AppData\Local and AppData\LocalLow folders, which are part of the local user profile, are excluded from roaming by default. By configuring this setting, you can exclude additional directories from roaming. For example, if a folder contains settings and data that can be used only on a single computer because an application is installed on only that computer or because only that computer is equipped with a specific hardware device.

- **Limit Profile Size**   You can limit the user profile size, and this limit applies to local profiles and roaming user profiles. By default, user profile size isn't limited. If you limit profile size and a user exceeds it, the user's profile won't synchronize with the network location if the roaming user profile is used.

In a GPO, computer-specific settings for user profiles are configured in Computer Configuration\Policies\Administrative Templates\System\User Profiles. Some of the computer-specific GPO settings that you can configure for user profiles include:

- **Add The Administrators Security Group To Roaming User Profiles**   By default, only the users have Full Control permissions to their roaming profile. If you configure this setting, administrators also will have full access and will be able to view user profile content. You should be aware that administrators always can take ownership of the files and folders and then modify permissions.

- **Delete Cached Copies Of Roaming Profiles**   By default, a local copy of the roaming user profile is kept on the computer when the user logs off. If you configure this setting, the local copy of the roaming user profile will be deleted when the user logs off.

- **Only Allow Local User Profiles**   By configuring this setting, only local user profiles will be used on the computer where this setting is effective. If a user who logs on is configured with a roaming user profile, a new local user profile will be created on the computer, and that profile will be used when the user logs on to that computer in the future.

- **Set Roaming Profile Paths For All Users Logging Onto This Computer**   If you want all users who log on to a computer to use roaming user profiles, you should configure this Group Policy setting. As part of the configuration, you can specify the network location where roaming user profiles will be stored. You should use the %username% variable in the path to specify a different profile directory for each user.

- **Prevent Roaming Profile Changes From Propagating To The Server**   When a user is configured with a roaming user profile, the user's roaming profile is copied from the network location to the computer the user logs on to. The user's changes write to the local copy of the profile, and by default, all changes from the local copy of the profile synchronize with the network copy when the user logs off. By configuring this setting, you modify this behavior and prevent synchronization of the local copy of the profile with the network copy when the user logs off. The result is similar to how the user would be configured with a mandatory profile.

- **Set The Schedule For Background Upload Of A Roaming User Profile's Registry File While User Is Logged On**   By default, a local copy of the roaming user profile, including the user registry file (NTUSER.DAT), synchronizes only when a user logs on and off. If you configure this setting, the roaming user profile still synchronizes only when the user logs on and off. However, you can specify the interval or time of day at which the local copy of the user registry file will synchronize with the network copy, regardless of whether the user logs off.

Mandatory user profiles

A mandatory user profile is a type of roaming user profile that prevents users from saving changes to their user profile. Like a typical roaming user profile, the profile is downloaded at logon. However, a mandatory profile does not synchronize to the network location when the user signs out. When the user signs in again, the original, unmodified profile is downloaded from the network location, and all previous profile changes are lost.

You convert a normal roaming user profile to a mandatory user profile by renaming the file NTUSER.DAT to NTUSER.MAN. The Windows client operating system recognizes this change and uses the profile as a mandatory user profile. The file NTUSER.MAN instead of the file NTUSER.DAT is loaded for the user portion of the registry while signed in.

You're more likely to use Group Policy than mandatory user profiles to restrict the user environment. However, in a kiosk scenario, mandatory profiles might be useful as a simple way to ensure that the profile is never modified permanently.

CAUTION

If you use mandatory user profiles for normal users and those users save files to either the desktop or My Documents folder, those files are lost when the user signs out. This is very risky in a typical work environment. You can mitigate the risk somewhat by using Folder Redirection to point common locations like Documents and the desktop to a network location that will be preserved between logons.

If a user signs in and the network location storing a mandatory user profile isn't available, the cached copy of the mandatory user profile is used. In this situation, profile changes from the last user, such as files on the desktop, will still be present when the user signs in because the user profile from the network isn't copied down to overwrite the local profile.

To ensure that users never get cached changes to a profile, you can create a *super-mandatory* user profile. When a roaming profile is super mandatory and the network location storing the profile isn't available, the user is unable to sign in.

To change a mandatory user profile to a super-mandatory user profile, you rename the folder containing the profile to include the .man extension. For example, if a roaming user profile is stored in the \\Server\Profiles\User1.V2 folder, you can rename the folder to User1.man.V2 and configure the user with the \\Server\Profiles\User1.man profile path.

Configuring Folder Redirection

One limitation of using roaming profiles is that if you configure users with roaming profiles, each time they log on, the entire profile synchronizes with the local copy on the computer. If a user logs on to a computer for the first time or if the local copy of the profile is deleted, this can cause the entire profile to download. Because the profile contains data folders, such as My Documents, Music, Videos, and Downloads, and these folders can contain large amounts of data, the process of downloading the entire profile can cause considerable network traffic and can take considerable time. This can result in very slow logons.

Similarly, when the user logs off, the entire profile must synchronize back to the network location, which can cause a slow logoff if a user added a considerable amount of data to her profile. To ensure that the logon and logoff process are performed quickly, it's recommended that you separate user data from the user profile but keep the user data on a network location. This way, the data can follow users, but it does not slow down the logon and logoff process.

Folder Redirection is a client-side technology that provides the ability to change the target location of user-specific folders within the user profile, such as Documents or Desktop. For example, an administrator can redirect the Documents folder from a local or roaming user profile to a separate network location. The content of a redirected folder is available from any computer on the network and isn't copied to the computer to which the user logs on, as with roaming user profiles.

Redirected folders are stored only on a network share, and users access them transparently in the same way as when they are stored in a local user profile. The Offline Files feature, which is enabled by default when redirected folders are used, provides users with access to content in redirected folders even if there is no network connectivity.

The Windows operating system supports the redirection of the following 13 folders that are found within user profiles. These folders are often referred to as *known folders*:

- AppData\Roaming
- Desktop
- Start Menu
- Documents

CHAPTER 2

- Pictures

- Music

- Videos

- Favorites

- Contacts

- Downloads

- Links

- Searches

- Saved Games

You can configure redirection of some folders manually from the user profile. For example, you can redirect the Documents folder to a network location, as shown in Figure 2-4. When you change the location, you have the option to move the existing data from the local profile.

Figure 2-4 Redirecting Documents to a network location

In most cases, you want to configure Folder Redirection for a large number of users. Getting this done is more efficient if you use Group Policy. You can configure Folder Redirection by modifying User Configuration\Policies\Windows Settings\Folder Redirection settings in a GPO.

When you use Group Policy to enable Folder Redirection, you can use basic or advanced settings. Basic Folder Redirection redirects the folder for all users to a single network share. Advanced Folder Redirection redirects the folder for users to different shares based on group membership, as shown in Figure 2-5.

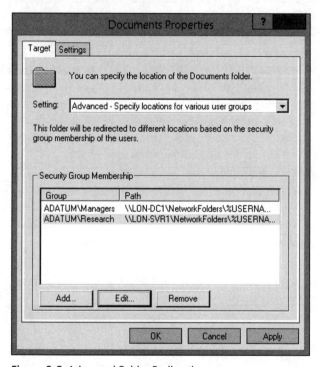

Figure 2-5 Advanced Folder Redirection

In a large organization, you won't be able to redirect all folders to a single network share. It isn't practical because the data storage requirements might be too large and it might overload that network share. In addition, users might be in various locations.

You can accommodate multiple shares for redirected folders with Basic or Advanced Folder Redirection. With Advanced Folder Redirection, you divide users based on group membership and direct their content to different file shares. You can accomplish this with Basic Folder Redirection by applying different GPO settings to different OUs. You can choose the option that suits your organization best.

Inside OUT

Setting Target Folder Location

Whether you select Basic or Advanced Folder Redirection, you must set the Target Folder Location. When you add a Target Folder Location in a GPO for Folder Redirection, there are four options:

- **Redirect To The User's Home Directory**   This option redirects the folder to the user's home folder. This is useful for redirecting the Documents folder because both locations are used for storage of personal data. Users consider it convenient that saving items to Documents automatically puts them in their home directory.

- **Create A Folder For Each User Under The Root Path**   This option redirects the folder to a specific network share and subfolders. This is useful when you want to store multiple redirected folders in the same location. For example, if you use this option for the Documents and Pictures folders with a root path of \\LON-DC1\NetworkFolders, then each item would be stored in \\LON-DC1\NetworkFolders\%username%\Documents and \\LON-DC1\NetworkFolders\%username%\Pictures, respectively.

- **Redirect To The Following Location**   This option redirects the folder to a specific folder that can be either private for the user or shared. You can redirect to a private folder with the path \\LON-DC1\NetworkFolders\%username%. You can redirect to a shared folder with the path \\LON-DC1\Data.

- **Redirect To The Local Userprofile Location**   This option redirects the folder to the local user profile. This isn't so much redirecting the folder as it is setting it back to the default location.

Each folder that you redirect has additional settings, shown in Figure 2-6, that are important to know. These setting are:

- **Grant The User Exclusive Rights To *Folder***   This option sets NTFS permissions to ensure that only the user has access to the redirected folder. This is enabled by default but should be disabled when multiple users are being redirected to a shared location.

- **Move The Contents Of *Folder* To The New Location**   When this option is selected, the contents of the redirected folder in the local user profile are copied to the redirected location. This is useful when implementing redirected folders to ensure that users retain access to all of their data. If you don't enable this option, the data remains on the local computer but to users it appears as if the data has been deleted.

- **Also Apply Redirection Policy To Windows 2000, Windows 2000 Server, Windows XP, And Windows Server 2003 Operating Systems**   This option applies the redirection policy to older operating systems. In most organizations, this option is now irrelevant.

- **Leave The Folder In The New Location When Policy Is Removed**   This option leaves the folder redirected when the user falls outside the scope of the policy. Effectively, this means the folder redirection change is permanent unless a new policy is created that forces the folder to be local again.

- **Redirect The Folder Back To The Local Userprofile When Policy Is Removed**   This option forces the folder to be part of the local user profile again if the user falls outside the scope of the policy. This can be useful as part of decommissioning Folder Redirection.

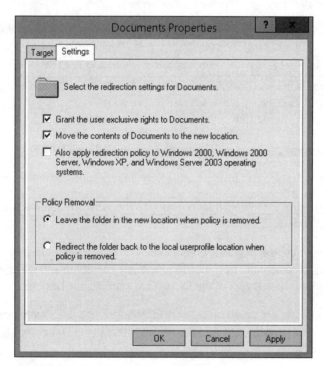

Figure 2-6 Folder Redirection settings

CHAPTER 2

Inside OUT

Redirecting Documents to home folders

It often is useful to redirect the Documents folder to a network location. To avoid having two network locations for personal files, the Documents folder commonly is redirected to user home folders. To redirect Documents to user home folders, perform the following steps:

1. In Group Policy Management, create a new GPO and link it to the OU containing the appropriate users.

2. Edit the new GPO and browse to User Configuration\Policies\Windows Settings \Folder Redirection.

3. Right-click Documents and click Properties.

4. In the Document Properties window, on the Target tab, in the Setting box, select Basic-Redirect Everyone's Folder To The Same Location.

5. In the Target Folder Location box, select Redirect To The User's Home Directory.

6. On the Settings tab, verify that the Move The Contents Of Documents To The New Location check box is selected and click OK.

Folder Redirection provides several advantages, which include the following:

- Content of redirected folders is available from any computer in the domain.

- Content of redirected folders does not copy to the local computer, which minimizes network traffic when a user logs on.

- Administrators can set quotas and permissions on redirected folders. By doing so, administrators can control how much space a user can utilize and whether the user can modify contents of that part of the folder—for example, the Desktop.

- Redirected folders are stored on network locations or network shares, not on local computers. If a local hard drive fails, users still can access data in redirected folders from a different computer.

- Contents of redirected folders can be backed up centrally because they are not stored locally on user computers. If Shadow Copies for Shared Folders is configured on a network location, users can access previous versions of their redirected files.

Configuring Offline Files

One of the common difficulties administrators experience is the management of user data on mobile computers. Even with improvements in mobile communication, mobile users need to keep files locally on their mobile computer for situations in which network connectivity is either unreliable or unavailable. The problem with users storing files on a mobile device is twofold:

- **Mobile computers are seldom backed up**   Most organizations have a policy in place that mobile computers are not backed up. This leaves the data stored on mobile computers vulnerable to hardware failure. Typically, a policy states that all files from mobile computers should be copied to a network share, but if the process isn't automated it's easy for users to forget.

- **Multiple copies of files**   When users take a copy of a file from the network and modify it, they may forget to copy the updated file back to the network quickly. In the meantime, other users might take copies of that file and make their own changes or modify the network version of the file. When there are multiple modified versions of a file, it can be difficult to merge the changes.

You can use Offline Files to help resolve data problems for mobile users. When you implement Offline Files, the files are cached locally on the mobile computer and automatically synchronized to the network share when there is connectivity. Automatic synchronization to the network share ensures that updated files are copied to a location that is easily backed up and reduces the likelihood of multiple file copies.

From the user's perspective, Offline Files are transparent. Users access the cached files on their computer by using the same network path from which they were cached. For example, Offline Files cached from a mapped drive M are accessible through the M drive even when the user is disconnected from the network.

When there is a slow or unreliable connection to a server, Offline Files can improve file access performance. For example, if a user is connected over a relatively slow VPN connection, Offline Files allows the user to work with a local cached copy of the file that is fast to open and save. After the file is saved, it's synchronized back to the server by Offline Files.

When you implement user state virtualization by using Folder Redirection, Offline Files can be an important part of ensuring that users have reliable access to their redirected folders. The most obvious benefit is for mobile computers for which Offline Files are used when the mobile computer is out of the office. Offline Files also provide reliable access to redirected folders if the server holding redirected folders experiences an outage.

Operating modes of Offline Files

The default mode for Offline Files is online mode. If the network file share is available, users access and modify files directly on the file share. As the files are updated on the network share, the cached copy of the file also is updated.

If the computer can't connect to the network share, it automatically switches to auto offline mode for that share. In auto offline mode, all file access and changes are performed by using the local cached copy of the files. The Offline Files client tries to access the file share every two minutes to reestablish online mode. While the folder is in auto offline mode, users can't access previous versions of the file.

The combination of online mode and auto offline mode works well for users with reliable connectivity to the network when they are in the office. However, if the network connection is slow or unreliable, you may want to force the cached files to be used. Forcing the use of cached files has the following benefits:

- Users experience faster access to files in redirected folders, especially potentially large folders such as the Documents folder.

- Network bandwidth is reduced, decreasing costs on expensive wide area network connections or metered connections, such as a 4G mobile network connection.

You can use the following methods to force the cached files to be used:

- **Configure Slow-Link Mode**   You can use Group Policy to configure the network latency at which cached files are used. By default, Windows 7 uses a threshold of 80 milliseconds (ms) and Windows 8.1 uses a threshold of 35 ms. You can use the Configure Slow-Link Mode setting to override the default values and set different latency thresholds for different UNC paths. Slow-link mode is useful to identify when the network connectivity is poor and use cached files automatically. This is useful for mobile users who connect by using a VPN or from a remote office with high network latency.

- **Enable always offline mode**   To ensure that a remote user does not have varying experiences, you can force Offline Files to always work with cached files regardless of the network latency. This can be useful if the network quality varies significantly over time. To enable always offline mode, you configure the Configure Slow-Link Mode setting with a value of 1 ms. This mode is available only in Windows 8 and newer. When this mode is enabled, background synchronization occurs every 60 minutes by default. You can change the background synchronization interval by configuring the Configure Background Sync setting in a GPO.

- **Manually switch to offline mode**   If you provide users with guidance on when to use Offline Files, you can instruct them how to manually enable offline mode by using File Explorer. In Windows 8, this option can be difficult to find. Figure 2-7 shows where the Work Offline option is located in File Explorer.

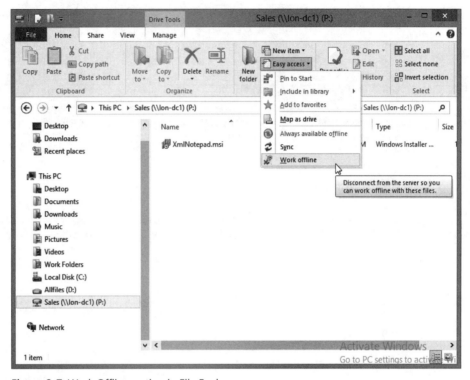

Figure 2-7 Work Offline option in File Explorer

Inside OUT

Offline Files synchronization problems

Offline Files has a bad reputation among some administrators because of how it was implemented in Windows XP. In Windows XP, the offline files only synchronized when the user logged on and logged off. For users who simply shut the lid on their laptop computer, the files would never synchronize. Starting with Windows 7, the synchronization process is done incrementally in the background. This means you're much less likely to experience this issue with current versions of Windows.

However, you should be aware that there still can be replication conflicts with Offline Files in current versions of Windows. A replication conflict occurs when a user modifies an offline copy of a file and another user modifies the original copy stored on the server before the offline copy is synchronized. When Offline Files encounters a situation in which both the offline copy and the original file have been modified, it can't integrate the changes in the two documents. When a replication conflict occurs, the user with the offline file is notified. At that point, it's the responsibility of the user to view both documents and rationalize the changes in both versions.

To prevent synchronization conflicts, it's a best practice to limit the files that are taken offline. One common strategy is to allow Offline Files for home folders where users have exclusive access but not for shared folders where multiple users can make changes.

Configuring shares for offline folders

When you share a folder on a computer running Windows Server 2012 R2, you can configure how files on that share are made available offline. To configure offline settings, perform the following steps:

1. On the file server, in File Explorer, right-click the shared folder and click Properties.

2. In the *Shared Folder* Properties window, on the Sharing tab, click Advanced Sharing.

3. In the Advanced Sharing window, click Caching.

4. In the Offline Settings window, shown in Figure 2-8, select the appropriate option for offline files and click OK.

Figure 2-8 Offline Settings for a shared folder

The default setting for a shared folder is Only The Files And Programs That Users Specify Are Available Offline. This is a reasonable setting to use because it provides users with the option to make files available offline but does not do it automatically. This minimizes the number of offline copies of a file and reduces the likelihood of a synchronization conflict.

The Enable BranchCache option is available if you have installed the BranchCache feature on the server. BranchCache is a file-caching solution for branch offices or remote users. However, unlike Offline Files, the cached copy of the file can be used only when the original copy of the file is online and it can be verified that the cached copy is up to date.

> ➤ **For more information about BranchCache, see the BranchCache webpage on TechNet at** *http://technet.microsoft.com/en-ca/network/dd425028.aspx.*

For shared folders for which you don't want any files to be taken offline, you can select No Files Or Programs From The Shared Folder Are Available Offline. You may want to select this option for shared folders that many users access to ensure that there is no possibility of synchronization conflicts.

For folders that are used exclusively by a single person, you should consider using the All Files And Programs That Users Open From The Shared Folder Are Automatically Available Offline option. Selecting this option provides the simplest way for users to make files available offline because it happens automatically as they use each file. For redirected folders, this is a good option because the users never need to identify which files are cached. The Optimize For Performance option is obsolete for Windows Vista and newer versions of Windows.

Configuring Offline Files in Windows 8

Users can make files or folders available offline by using File Explorer to browse to the file or folder, right-click the file or folder, and then select Always Available Offline. At that point, the file is cached locally and monitored for updates.

You also can configure several options for Offline Files from the Manage Offline Files option on the Start screen. This opens the Offline Files dialog box, shown in Figure 2-9. You can use this dialog box to do the following:

- Disable offline files

- Open Sync Center

- View your offline files

- Configure disk space limits for offline files

- Enable encryption for offline files

- Configure the interval for slow-link detection

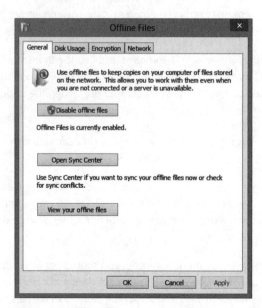

Figure 2-9 Offline Files settings in Windows 8.1

Encrypting Offline Files helps secure the cached files and prevent an unauthorized user from gaining access to them. If you don't encrypt the cached files, an unauthorized user with physical access to the computer can gain access to the cached files in minutes. With encryption enabled, it's extremely difficult for an unauthorized user to gain access to the cached files.

The use of metered networks, such as wireless networks from a mobile communications provider, is becoming more common for network devices. For example, some tablets use a subscriber identity module (SIM) card to connect with mobile data networks. Laptop computers also may have this functionality built-in or use a USB dongle to provide connectivity to mobile data networks. Mobile data networks typically charge based on the volume of data transmitted over the network, and subscriber plans have limited amounts of data included in a given service plan. All mobile broadband connections are configured as metered by default. Wi-Fi networks are not configured as metered connections by default, but you can configure them as metered connections.

NOTE

If you tether your mobile computer to a mobile phone that has data access, Windows 8.1 connects to the mobile phone by using Wi-Fi. Because this is a Wi-Fi connection, it won't be metered by default.

Windows 8 and Windows 8.1 can identify the use of metered networks for synchronization. Using cost-aware synchronization, Windows 8 and newer can deactivate background synchronization in the following scenarios:

- When the user is using a metered network connection, such as a 4G mobile network connection
- When the subscriber is near or over his bandwidth limit
- When the user is roaming on another provider's network

Cost-aware synchronization on metered networks helps users avoid unexpectedly high data usage costs when they use metered connections that have usage limits or while roaming on another provider's network.

Windows 8, Windows Server 2012, and newer Windows operating systems automatically track roaming and bandwidth usage limits for users when they are on metered connections. When users are roaming, near their bandwidth limit, or over their limit, the Windows operating system switches to offline mode and prevents all synchronization. Users still can initiate synchronization manually, and administrators can override cost-aware synchronization for specific users, such as executives. When the user no longer has the conditions that inhibit connectivity, normal synchronization occurs.

CHAPTER 2

Metered network connections usually have round-trip network latencies that are slower than the default 35 ms latency value for transitioning to offline mode based on slow-link detection. Therefore, these connections usually transition to offline mode automatically.

Using the Primary Computer setting

When administrators configure users with roaming user profiles and Folder Redirection, these settings apply to users regardless of the domain computer to which they log on. However, sometimes you might want to restrict roaming user profiles and Folder Redirection to be available only when a user logs on to specific computers. This could be because you do not want a user to leave any personal or company data when she logs off, or because you do not want to roam the user's settings and data between 32-bit and 64-bit client computers. For example, if your organization has a computer lab for training, you would not want roaming user profiles to be used in the computer lab.

Starting with Windows 8 and Windows Server 2012 in domain environments, you can apply this restriction by using the Primary Computer feature. By using the Primary Computer feature, an administrator can specify a list of computers, known as Primary Computers, for each domain user. Then, Folder Redirection, roaming user profiles, or both features are used only when a user logs on to a computer on her Primary Computer list, which can be controlled by using Group Policy.

To use the Primary Computer feature, the Active Directory Domain Services (AD DS) schema must be extended to at least the Windows Server 2012 level. A Windows Server 2012 or newer domain controller isn't required, but the AD DS schema must be extended. The Primary Computer feature works only when a user logs on to a Windows 8, Windows Server 2012, or a newer Windows operating system because older Windows versions ignore the Primary Computer setting. To configure Primary Computers for a user, include the list of computer names in the msDS-PrimaryComputer attribute in the user account. This attribute isn't included as a field in any of the graphical management tools. However, both Active Directory Users and Computers and Active Directory Administrative Center allow you to edit arbitrary attributes in user accounts.

To add a Primary Computer list by using Active Directory Administrative Center, perform the following steps:

1. In Active Directory Administrative Center, locate the user account you want to modify and open the Properties of the user account.

2. In the user account window, click Extensions and then click the Attribute Editor tab, as shown in Figure 2-10.

3. In the list of attributes, scroll down and double-click msDS-PrimaryComputer.

4. In the Multi-valued String Editor window, in the Value To Add box, type the name of a primary computer and click Add.

5. Repeat step 4 for any additional primary computers and then click OK.

6. Click OK to close the user account window.

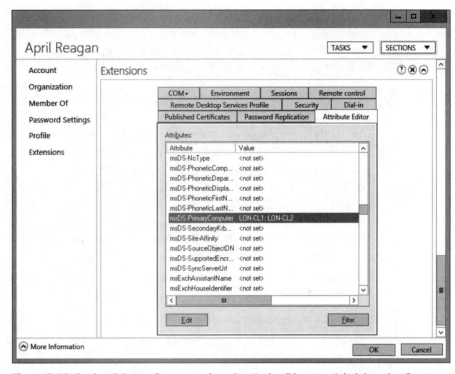

Figure 2-10 Setting Primary Computers by using Active Directory Administrative Center

After configuring the list of Primary Computers for a user, you also should enable the Redirect Folders On Primary Computers Only and Download Roaming Profiles On Primary Computers Only Group Policy settings.

Inside OUT

Bulk configuration of Primary Computers

Configuring Primary Computers by using Active Directory Users and Computers or Active Directory Administrative Center isn't scalable for large numbers of users. It would take days or weeks to configure the Primary Computers for users in a large organization. Instead, you need a scripted solution that can perform the task quickly.

Two older tools included in Windows Server 2012 R2 that you can use to do bulk configuration of Primary Computers are as follows:

- **Dsmod.exe**   This command-line utility can be used to modify user attributes. This utility is used as part of a batch file for bulk changes.

- **LDIFDE.exe**   This command-line utility uses an LDIF file to make bulk changes. The key to using this tool is correctly creating the LDIF file.

The simplest way to make bulk changes is by using Windows PowerShell. You can use the Set-ADUser cmdlet to make changes to user objects by using the msDS -PrimaryComputer attribute with the Add parameter. To script the process, you most likely will configure a list of users and their Primary Computers in a .csv file that can be read by Windows PowerShell. You can use the following syntax to add a Primary Computer for a user account:

```
Set-ADUser April -Add @{'msDS-PrimaryComputer' = 'CN=LON-CL1,OU=London
Clients,DC=Adatum,DC=com'}
```

You can use the following syntax to remove a Primary Computer for a user:

```
Set-ADUser April -Remove @{'msDS-PrimaryComputer' = ''CN=LON-CL2,OU=London
Clients,DC=Adatum,DC=com''}
```

Configuring Credential Roaming

Some organizations have deployed certificates to end users. Certificates can be used for encryption or authentication. If you have implemented certificates for end users, it's important to understand that the certificate is stored in the local user profile. If a user is issued a certificate while logged on at one computer and then logs on at another computer, the certificate isn't automatically available. One solution to this problem is to implement roaming user profiles. However, if you want to specifically allow certificates to roam with users, you can implement Credential Roaming.

Credential Roaming was introduced in Windows Server 2008 R2 and Windows 7 and is enabled by using Group Policy. When you enable Credential Roaming, existing user certificates are copied from the local profile into Active Directory as part of the user object. In the future, each time the user signs in to a new computer the certificates for the user are copied from Active Directory to the new local profile.

You configure Credential Roaming by using Group Policy, as shown in Figure 2-11. The Certificates Services Client - Credential Roaming setting is located in User Configuration \Policies\Windows Settings\Security Settings\Public Key Policies. In addition to enabling Credential Roaming, you can configure the following settings:

- **Maximum Tombstone Credentials Lifetime In Days**   Defines how long a credential is retained in Active Directory after it has been deleted locally.

- **Maximum Number Of Roaming Credentials Per User**   Defines the maximum number of certificates and keys that can be used by Credential Roaming. The default value of 2,000 should be sufficient for most organizations.

- **Maximum Size (In Bytes) Of A Roaming Credential**   Defines the maximum size of any one roaming credential. This limit ensures that the Active Directory database does not grow too large in organizations with many users.

- **Roam Stored User Names And Passwords**   Controls whether stored user names and passwords accessible in Credential Manager are included for roaming.

Figure 2-11 Enabling Credential Roaming

Enabling user profile disks

If you have implemented desktop virtualization with session-based virtual desktops or virtual machine (VM)–based virtual desktops, you can implement user profile disks to user profiles in a central location. User profile disks are similar to roaming user profiles because they store profiles in a central location. However, user profile disks are used exclusively for session-based virtual desktops or VM-based virtual desktops. For example, if you have multiple RD Session Host servers, user profile disks allow users to have a consistent profile regardless of the RD Session Host server to which they are connected.

When you enable user profile disks, a virtual hard disk is created for each user who signs in. When the user signs in, the virtual hard disk for that user is mounted as the storage location for the user profile. User profile information isn't copied or cached.

> ➤ See more information about user profile disks in Chapter 8, Planning and deploying session-based desktops.

Configuring User Experience Virtualization

UE-V is an enterprise solution that enables you to synchronize operating system settings, desktop app settings, and Windows Store app settings among computers in the same AD DS domain environment. Unlike roaming user profiles, which roam all settings in the profile among computers, UE-V allows you to be selective about which settings roam among computers.

With UE-V, nothing roams unless specifically enabled. UE-V provides several default settings location templates that define where each app stores its settings. You can create additional settings location templates, and UE-V will synchronize only those settings that are defined and enabled in the settings location templates.

NOTE

An administrator can control only if UE-V will synchronize the settings for Windows Store apps. An administrator can't control which Windows Store app settings will be synchronized.

UE-V stores settings on a network location as soon as a user closes an app, and those settings can synchronize on other computers without the user having to log off. Computers periodically synchronize their settings with a network location, and if computers have permanent connectivity to a network location, you can configure them to use those settings immediately.

UE-V synchronizes settings between applications on different operating system versions as long as the applications are stored in the same location. Regardless of how an application is deployed, UE-V can synchronize settings among locally installed applications on one computer, Microsoft Application Virtualization (App-V) applications on another computer, and RemoteApp programs on the RD Session Host. UE-V also can synchronize settings between Windows Store apps that run on physical and virtual computers, such as the virtual desktops that are used in VDI implementations.

NOTE

UE-V does not synchronize user data; it only synchronizes settings. If you need to synchronize user data, you can combine UE-V with Folder Redirection or roaming user profiles.

Windows 8 and Windows 8.1 allow users to link a Microsoft account with a domain account for authentication. When the two accounts are linked, UE-V only synchronizes settings for desktop apps. Users can synchronize other settings, such as operating system settings and Windows Store app settings, by using OneDrive. In UE-V 2.1, administrators can control if Windows Store apps will synchronize by using UE-V or OneDrive.

To use UE-V, you must have a supported operating system, as shown in Table 2-3. Notice that Windows Server is supported so that UE-V can be used on RD Session Hosts. For client operating systems, both 32-bit and 64-bit operating systems are supported.

Table 2-3 UE-V operating system requirements

Operating system	Edition	Architecture	Microsoft .NET Framework
Windows 7 SP1	Ultimate, Enterprise, or Professional	32-bit or 64-bit	.NET Framework 4 or newer
Windows Server 2008 R2 SP1	Standard, Enterprise, Datacenter, or Web Server	64-bit	.NET Framework 4 or newer
Windows 8 and Windows 8.1	Pro or Enterprise	32-bit or 64-bit	.NET Framework 4.5
Windows Server 2012 and Windows Server 2012 R2	Standard or Datacenter	64-bit	.NET Framework 4.5

Besides the requirements for supported operating systems, there are no additional random access memory (RAM) requirements for UE-V. Administrator user rights are required to install the UE-V agent, and you must restart the computer to make the UE-V agent operational.

You must install .NET Framework 4 or newer and Windows PowerShell 3.0 or newer before you can install the UE-V agent. A default installation of Windows 8 or Windows 8.1 meets those requirements. However, on Windows 7 SP1, you need to install Windows PowerShell 3.0 before you can install the UE-V agent.

UE-V compares local time on a client computer with the time stamp of the stored settings on a network location to decide if settings synchronization is required. Because of that, computer clocks on UE-V client computers should be synchronized, which is the default behavior in an AD DS environment. If computer clocks are not synchronized, older settings can overwrite newer settings, or newer settings might not be stored to the network location. This should not be a concern in most environments because client computers synchronize time by using domain controllers.

UE-V architecture

To understand how to implement and manage UE-V, you should be familiar with its high-level architecture and the items here that enable synchronization of settings between computers, as shown in Figure 2-12. Understanding these items here ensures that you can identify which items here need to be configured to obtain the configuration that you desire.

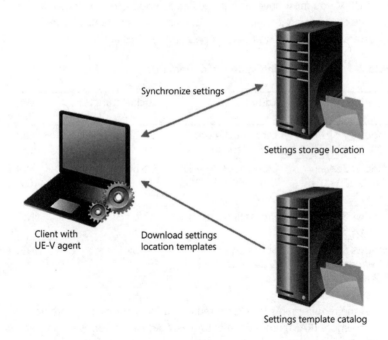

Figure 2-12 UE-V architecture

You must install the UE-V agent on every computer that will synchronize settings. The UE-V agent monitors changes to settings and synchronizes them between computers. It stores settings on a network location called the *settings storage location*, and it periodically synchronizes the local cache with the settings storage location. When you start an application, the UE-V agent applies settings from the local cache, and when you close an application, the UE-V agent stores the application settings to the settings storage location. Application settings are available for synchronization as soon as you close an application. However, remember that when you start an application, settings from the local cache, not settings from the settings storage location on the network, are used by default. In an environment in which a computer has permanent network connectivity, you can modify this behavior and always use the settings from the settings storage location on the network. Operating system settings apply when a user logs on, when a computer is unlocked, or when a user connects remotely to a computer. The UE-V agent saves settings when a user logs off, when a computer locks, or when a remote session disconnects.

A settings storage location is the network location where the UE-V agent stores the settings that are synchronized. Administrators can specify this location during UE-V agent installation, in AD DS as a user's home folder, or by using Group Policy. The settings storage location can be on any file share where users have read and write access. The UE-V agent verifies the location and creates a hidden system folder named SettingsPackages, where settings are stored.

A *settings location template* is an XML file that specifies the settings locations where values are stored on a computer, not the settings values. Only settings defined in the settings location templates are captured and applied on UE-V client computers. Several settings location templates, such as Microsoft Office 2010, Office 2007, Windows Internet Explorer 8, Internet Explorer 9, Internet Explorer 10, and desktop settings, are included with UE-V. You can create additional settings location templates by using the UE-V Generator. The UE-V Generator is included as part of UE-V.

A *settings template catalog* is a folder that stores settings location templates. This usually is a shared folder, although a settings template catalog also can be a local folder. By default, a UE-V agent reads new or updated settings location templates from this folder once per day. This is done by a scheduled task named Template Auto Update that runs daily at 3:30 A.M., and it applies the changes (modified, added, or removed templates) to the UE-V agent. If only the default settings location templates are used, the settings template catalog isn't used.

Desktop app settings, Windows settings, and Windows Store app settings are stored in settings packages, which the UE-V agent creates in the settings storage location. A *settings package* is a collection of settings that is defined in the settings location templates. A UE-V agent that runs on one computer reads and writes to a settings storage location independently of UE-V agents that run on other computers. The most recent settings and values are applied when the next UE-V agent synchronizes with the settings storage location.

UE-V includes several operating system and application settings location templates. When you need to synchronize the settings of additional applications, you can use the UE-V Generator to create additional custom settings location templates. The UE-V Generator monitors the registry, the HKEY_CURRENT_USER registry subtree, and file systems, including the AppData\Roaming and AppData\Local folders in user profiles, to discover where application settings are stored. You can modify a generated template and include it in the settings template catalog. You also can use the UE-V Generator for editing existing templates or for validating templates that were created in another XML editor.

Inside OUT

How UE-V applies synchronization settings

When you log on to a Windows operating system, UE-V synchronizes settings from a network settings storage location with the local cache. Then, the local cache synchronizes with the settings storage location every 30 minutes by default. Synchronization is triggered by a scheduled task named Sync Controller Application, which is created when you install a UE-V agent. You also can trigger synchronization manually by using Company Settings Center, which installs automatically during a UE-V agent installation.

When you start an application, UE-V applies settings to the application from the local cache. Application settings save to a network settings storage location when an application closes. A user doesn't have to log off and then log on to another computer to synchronize application settings, like when roaming user profiles are used. When using UE-V to synchronize settings, a user can be logged on to multiple computers at the same time. When you configure application settings and close an application, the application settings write to the settings storage location in a settings package. When the user starts the application on another computer, the UE-V agent reads and applies the application settings from the local cache on that computer. If the local cache has not yet synchronized with the settings storage location, you can wait for synchronization to occur, trigger synchronization manually, or modify the UE-V configuration to always use the settings from the settings storage location on the network. The user experience with UE-V is similar to having application settings roam with a user.

If computers have permanent connections to a settings storage location, you can configure the UE-V agent to always apply the settings from the network settings storage location and to bypass the local cache completely. You can do so by setting the synchronization method, SyncMethod, to None. For example, when installing a UE-V agent or by running the Set-UevConfiguration cmdlet.

Desktop background and Ease of Access settings are applied when a user logs on, when a computer locks, or when a remote connection establishes. To optimize the logon experience, these settings don't synchronize by default. You can enable the desktop background and the Ease of Access settings by using Company Settings Center, Group Policy, the Windows PowerShell cmdlet Enable-UevTemplate, or Windows Management Instrumentation (WMI). Like synchronizing application settings, a user doesn't have to log off to store Windows settings to the settings storage location. The UE-V agent saves settings when a user logs off, when a computer locks, or when a remote connection disconnects.

Users sometimes accidentally modify settings. By using UE-V, you can restore application or operating system settings to the initial values that were on a computer before the first UE-V synchronization of settings. UE-V can restore settings on a per-application or per–operating system setting basis. The settings are restored the next time a user starts the application or when a user logs on to an operating system. You can restore settings only by using Windows PowerShell or WMI—there is no GUI for that. UE-V provides the Restore-UevUserSetting Windows PowerShell cmdlet, which you can use to restore user settings for an application or a group of Windows settings.

CHAPTER 2

Comparing user state virtualization options

When you want to synchronize settings among the different devices to which a user logs on, you can use different solutions such as roaming user profiles, a Microsoft account, or UE-V. Table 2-4 summarizes the capabilities of each of these technologies.

Table 2-4 Comparison of user state virtualization options

Feature	Windows 7 roaming profile	Windows 8 roaming profile	Microsoft account	UE-V
Roam settings among multiple devices	Yes	Yes	Yes	Yes
Roam settings between physical and virtual applications	No	No	No	Yes
Apply settings periodically	No	No	No	Yes
Supported on devices that are not domain members	No	No	Yes	No
Supports Primary Computer attribute	No	Yes	No	No

Control which application to roam	No	No	No	Yes
Roam Windows Store app settings	No	No	Yes	Yes
Roam user data	Yes	Yes	Yes	No

A Microsoft account is the only solution that can synchronize settings even if devices are not domain members. However, it requires Internet connectivity because it stores settings in the cloud. You can synchronize Windows Store app configurations only when logging on with a Microsoft account or by using UE-V. When a user has a Microsoft account linked to his domain account, UE-V will synchronize desktop app settings only. You can use a Microsoft account and OneDrive synchronization to synchronize other settings. With UE-V 2.1, administrators can configure whether Windows Store apps will synchronize by using UE-V or a Microsoft account.

Inside OUT

Microsoft accounts for authentication

A Microsoft account provides you with a unified identity, which you can use for accessing Microsoft and non-Microsoft cloud services. You can link your domain or workgroup account with your Microsoft account, and you can use it for transparent access to the Microsoft Store and OneDrive and for logging on to Windows 8.1.

Roaming user profiles can synchronize only the entire profile, including the settings and data that are stored in the profile. You can't control which settings you want to synchronize. In contrast, in Windows 8 and Windows 8.1 you can control the devices on which you want to synchronize settings by configuring the Primary Computer user Active Directory attribute. Roaming user profiles copy to a file server only when users log off, and they do not synchronize periodically. When you configure Folder Redirection, redirected folders are exempt from this copying.

If you use UE-V to synchronize settings, you must install a UE-V agent on the device. UE-V can synchronize only those settings that are defined in the settings location templates, and it's the only solution that can synchronize settings between physical and virtual applications. In addition, UE-V is the only solution that applies settings periodically, not only when the user logs on. UE-V isn't included in the operating system, and you must obtain and license it separately. In contrast, roaming user profiles is a feature of domain-member devices that run any version of the Windows operating system.

Preparing to deploy UE-V

Before you deploy the UE-V agent to client computers, you need to prepare the necessary infrastructure. This includes:

- Configuring the settings storage location.

- Configuring the settings template catalog.

- Adding UE-V Group Policy administrative templates.

The settings storage location for UE-V is the file system location where the settings for a user are stored. You can configure either user home directories or a network share as the settings storage location. You can configure the UE-V agent with the settings storage location by using an installation parameter, a Windows PowerShell cmdlet, or Group Policy settings.

If you choose user home directories as the settings storage location, the home directory for each user must be defined in the AD DS user object for each user. The NTFS and share permissions that allow users to create and modify files in their home folder also are sufficient for UE-V.

If you choose a network share at the settings storage location, you need to ensure that the share has the correct permissions. Both Administrators and a security group containing the UE-V users should have Full Control share permissions on the network folder. The NTFS permissions for the root folder are described in Table 2-5.

Table 2-5 NTFS permissions for storage settings location shared folder

Account	NTFS permissions	Apply to
Administrators	Full Control	This folder, subfolders, and files
Creator/Owner	Full Control	Subfolders and files only
Security group of UE-V users	List Folder/Read Data Create Folders/Append Data	This folder only

A settings template catalog is required if you want to use UE-V to synchronize other application settings in addition to the settings that are provided by default. The settings template catalog is a network share where custom settings location templates are stored. If your UE-V deployment will use the settings template catalog, you should create and share a folder with the appropriate permissions, as shown in Table 2-6 and Table 2-7. You can configure the UE-V agent with the settings template catalog location by using an installation parameter, a Windows PowerShell cmdlet, or Group Policy settings.

CHAPTER 2

Table 2-6 Share permissions for a settings template catalog

Account	Share permissions
Everyone	No permissions
Domain computers	Read permission
Administrators	Read/Write permission

Table 2-7 NTFS permissions for a settings template catalog

Account	File permissions	Apply to
Creator/Owner	Full Control	This folder, subfolders, and files
Domain computers	List Folder Contents and Read	This folder, subfolders, and files
Everyone	No permissions	This folder, subfolders, and files
Administrators	Full Control	This folder, subfolders, and files

Most configuration of the UE-V agent is performed by configuring Group Policy objects with the appropriate settings. Windows Server does not include the UE-V configuration options in the Group Policy editor by default. You need to add the Group Policy administrative template for UE-V to enable the UE-V configuration options in the Group Policy editor.

Typically, larger Windows-based networks have configured a central store for Group Policy administrative templates. The central store lets you place the administrative templates in a single location, and they are available throughout the domain. If you have configured a central store, the administrative templates are copied to %SystemRoot%\SYSVOL\<AD DS name> \Policies\PolicyDefinitions on a domain controller. The template files will be replicated to all domain controllers. If you have not configured a central store for administrative templates, then copy the administrative templates to %SystemRoot%\PolicyDefinitions on the computer you're using to edit the Group Policy object.

Administrative templates are .ADMX and .ADML files. You can download the administrative templates for UE-V from the Microsoft Download Center at *http://go.microsoft.com/fwlink/?LinkID=510001.*

Deploying the UE-V agent

You can deploy the UE-V agent by using almost any software or operating system deployment tool, such as manual installation or Group Policy, or by including it in a standard desktop image. Table 2-8 describes the installation methods and when you would use each.

Table 2-8 UE-V agent installation methods

Method	Use this method when
Group Policy	You deploy software already by using Group Policy. You want to deploy the UE-V agent to existing computers. You want to deploy the UE-V agent after operating system images are deployed. You're configuring the UE-V agent by using Group Policy and not the command-line options. Computers have high-speed, persistent connections to the shared folder that contains the installation files.
Microsoft Deployment Toolkit 2013	You use the Microsoft Deployment Toolkit (MDT) for operating system deployment. You want to deploy the UE-V agent as part of an operating system deployment.
Microsoft Intune	You already use Microsoft Intune for client management. You want to deploy the UE-V agent without requiring an additional infrastructure. You have computers in multiple locations with limited connectivity between locations.
System Center 2012 R2 Configuration Manager	You already use System Center 2012 R2 Configuration Manager for application and operating system deployment. You want to use one deployment tool to deploy the UE-V agent to existing computers and during operating system deployment. Computers have high-speed, persistent connections to the distribution points where the UE-V agent installation files are located. You want to manage and maintain your application deployments centrally.
Scripted installation	You want to script the installation as part of an operating system installation, and you're not using MDT or Configuration Manager. You want to deploy the UE-V agent by using an electronic software distribution system. Computers might not have high-speed, persistent connections to the enterprise network, and installation from local media is required.

CHAPTER 2

You can install the UE-V agent by running AgentSetup.exe, AgentSetup32.msi, or AgentSetup64.msi. AgentSetup.exe detects the appropriate processor architecture and runs the correct .MSI file. If you run the .MSI file directly, you need to ensure that you have selected the correct .MSI for the processor architecture.

You can include command-line parameters during installation to configure the UE-V agent. For example, you can use the /norestart parameter to prevent the installation from restarting the computer after installation. The command-line parameters can be used for AgentSetup.exe or the MSI files.

The following example shows how to use AgentSetup.exe to perform an installation that installs silently, does not restart the computer after installation, and creates a logfile:

```
AgentSetup.exe /quiet /norestart /log "%temp%\UE-VInstall.log"
```

The following example shows how to use AgentSetup64.msi to perform an installation that installs silently, does not restart the computer after installation, and creates a logfile:

```
msiexec.exe /i "<path to msi>\AgentSetup64.msi" /quiet /norestart /l*v "%temp%
\UE-VInstall.log"
```

➤ For more information about the command-line parameters you can use for installing the UE-V agent, see Deploy Required Features for UE-V 2.x on TechNet at *http://technet.microsoft.com/en-us/library/dn458891.aspx.*

Inside OUT

Defining the settings storage location with %username%

Defining the settings storage location is a critical part of deploying the UE-V agent. If you define the settings storage location as a parameter, it's common to use the %username% variable to define the unique subfolder for each user to store settings. However, how you refer to the variable depends on the type of scripting you're per-forming. Table 2-9 shows deployment methods and an example of how you should refer to the %username% variable in each situation.

Table 2-9 Examples of using %username% for UE-V agent deployment

Deployment type	Example
Command prompt	StorageSettingsPath=\\server\share\%^username%
Batch script	StorageSettingsPath="\\server\share\%%username%%"
Windows PowerShell	StorageSettingsPath="\\server\share\%username%"
Configuration Manager	StorageSettingsPath="\\server\share\^%username^%"

Notice that you can't use quotes around the path at a command prompt. If the path includes spaces and you need to use quotes, you should use a batch file.

After the UE-V agent installs, you must restart the computer to make the UE-V agent operational. After the installation, a new service named User Experience Virtualization is installed. Also, the following six scheduled tasks are added:

- Collect CEIP Data

- Monitor Application Settings

- Sync Controller Application

- Synchronize Settings at Logoff

- Template Auto Update

- Upload CEIP Data

These tasks periodically synchronize the local cache with the settings storage location, check for updates in the UE-V settings location templates, and upload data if you joined the Customer Experience Improvement Program (CEIP). The UE-V agent installation also installs the Company Settings Center, which you can use to control which settings UE-V should synchronize, to trigger the synchronization manually, and to view the synchronization status of UE-V.

Managing the UE-V agent

After installing the UE-V agent, you can manage it by using Group Policy or Windows PowerShell. Windows PowerShell is useful when you're working with a single client computer, but to configure large numbers of computers, Group Policy is preferred. After you install the

UE-V Group Policy .admx and .adml files, the Microsoft User Experience Virtualization node appears under Policies\Administrative Templates\Windows Components in the Group Policy Management Editor window for both Computer Configuration and User Configuration. You can configure certain UE-V Group Policy settings only for computers, some only for users, and some for both. Table 2-10 lists the Group Policy settings you can configure.

Table 2-10 **Group Policy settings for managing the UE-V agent**

Policy setting name	Target	Policy setting description
Use User Experience Virtualization (UE-V)	Computers and Users	Allows you to enable or disable UE-V.
Settings Storage Path	Computers and Users	Configures where the user settings will be stored.
Settings Template Catalog Path	Computers Only	Configures where custom settings location templates are stored. This policy setting also configures whether the catalog will replace the default Microsoft templates that are installed with the UE-V agent.
Do Not Use The Sync Provider	Computers and Users	Allows you to configure whether UE-V will use the Sync Provider feature. This policy setting also allows you to enable notification to occur when the import of user settings is delayed.
Synchronization Timeout	Computers and Users	Configures the number of milliseconds (ms) that the computer waits when retrieving user settings from the remote settings location. If the remote storage location is unavailable, the application launch is delayed by that many ms.
Package Size Warning Threshold	Computers and Users	Allows you to configure the UE-V agent to report when a settings package file size reaches a defined threshold.
First Use Notification	Computers Only	Enables a notification in the notification area that appears when the UE-V agent runs for the first time.
Tray Icon	Computers Only	Enables the UE-V tray icon.

Do Not Synchronize Windows 8 Apps	Computers and Users	Defines if the UE-V agent synchronizes settings for Windows Store apps.
Roam Applications Settings	Users Only	A multiple policy setting that configures the roaming of user settings of each application.

When you install the UE-V agent, it includes the UE-V module for Windows PowerShell. This module includes 20 cmdlets for managing the UE-V agent. Some of the cmdlets are listed in Table 2-11. To get a list of all available UE-V cmdlets, run the following command:

```
Get-Command -Module uev
```

Table 2-11 Some of the Windows PowerShell cmdlets for managing the UE-V agent

Windows PowerShell cmdlet	Description
Get-UevConfiguration	View the effective UE-V agent settings. User-specific settings have precedence over the computer settings.
Set-UevConfiguration	This cmdlet has many parameters, and it's used to configure the UE-V agent.
Get-UevTemplate	Lists all the settings location templates that are registered on the computer.
Register-UevTemplate	Registers a settings location template with UE-V. After a template is registered, UE-V synchronizes the settings that are defined in the template between computers that have the template registered.
Restore-UevUserSetting	Revert application settings to their initial value, which were effective before UE-V synchronized its settings for the first time.

UE-V settings that can be configured in different places have the following order of precedence:

1. User-targeted settings that are managed by Group Policy

2. Computer-targeted settings that are managed by Group Policy

3. Configuration settings that are defined by the current user who uses Windows PowerShell or WMI

4. Configuration settings that are defined for the computer that uses Windows PowerShell or WMI

CHAPTER 2

This means that if the same UE-V settings are configured in multiple places, configuration in the user part of Group Policy has precedence over configuration in the computer part of Group Policy. Group Policy has precedence over locally configured settings.

Managing default settings location templates

UE-V only synchronizes settings that are defined in the locations specified by the settings location templates. Settings location templates are XML files that specify, for each application, where in the registry and on the file system the application stores its settings. UE-V includes several predefined settings location templates, and administrators can create additional templates for custom applications. Not all application settings can safely roam between computers. Settings that synchronize by using UE-V must meet the following criteria:

- **Settings must be stored in an accessible location**   UE-V can synchronize settings only in the HKEY_CURRENT_USER registry subtree and the AppData\Roaming or AppData\Local folders in a user profile. If an application stores its settings in other locations, you can't synchronize its settings by using UE-V.

- **Settings should not be specific to a particular computer**   Some settings, such as network configuration, are relevant only for a certain computer and should not synchronize with other computers.

- **Settings must synchronize without the risk of corrupting data**   For example, if settings are stored in a database file, these settings should not synchronize by using UE-V. You should consider another solution, such as storing the database file with configuration settings on a network location.

When you install a UE-V agent, it includes settings location templates for operating system settings and common Microsoft applications. You can view the list of registered settings location templates by running the Get-UevTemplate cmdlet, as shown in Figure 2-13. The settings location templates included with the UE-V agent are stored in the Microsoft User Experience Virtualization\Templates folder.

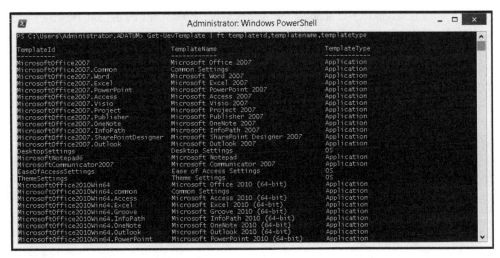

Figure 2-13 Results of Get-UevTemplate

The default settings location templates in UE-V 2.0 enable synchronization of the following settings:

- Office 2007 configuration

- Office 2010 configuration

- Internet Explorer options (Internet Explorer 8, 9, 10, 11)

- Windows accessories (Calculator, Notepad, Wordpad)

- Desktop settings (desktop background, folder options, region and language settings)

- Ease of access feature configuration

Inside OUT
Office 2013 settings location templates

The Office 2013 settings location templates can be downloaded for UE-V 2.0 from the template gallery. UE-V 2.1 is in beta at the time of writing. UE-V 2.1 includes the settings location templates for Office 2013 and Office 2010.

CHAPTER 2

Synchronization is enabled for the following applications by default. However, you can use Group Policy to disable synchronization for the default applications:

- Calculator

- Internet Explorer 8, 9, 10, 11

- Internet Explorer Common Settings

- Microsoft Office 2007 Applications (Word, Excel, and so on)

- Microsoft Office 2007 Common Settings

- Microsoft Office 2010 Applications (Word, Excel, and so on)

- Microsoft Office 2010 Common Settings

- Notepad

- Wordpad

Also, users can control which settings are synchronized by using the Company Settings Center. The Company Settings Center is added as part of the UE-V agent installation. It can be accessed from the Start screen or from the UE-V notification icon. Users can enable and disable the synchronization of Windows settings and application settings, as shown in Figure 2-14.

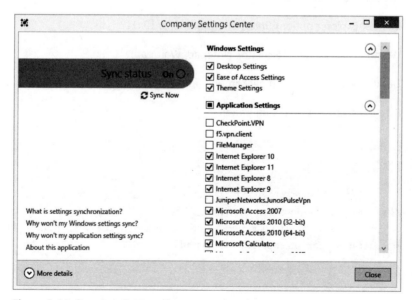

Figure 2-14 Company Settings Center

UE-V also synchronizes Windows Store app settings. Settings location templates aren't used for Windows Store apps because they synchronize only the settings that were configured to synchronize by the application developer. You can run the Windows PowerShell cmdlet Get-UevAppxPackage to view the list of Windows Store apps and their synchronization status.

You can use Group Policy to disable synchronization for some Windows 8 apps. Figure 2-15 shows the Windows 8 apps that are synchronized by default.

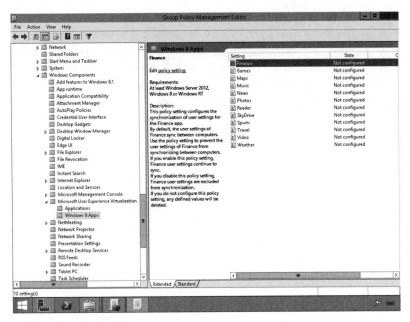

Figure 2-15 Windows 8 apps in UE-V

Creating and managing custom settings location templates

If you want to synchronize application settings that default settings location templates do not cover, then you must obtain or create additional settings location templates. You can obtain custom settings location templates online from the UE-V 2.0 template gallery. If a custom settings location template isn't available, you must create your own template by using the UE-V Generator.

Inside OUT

UE-V 2.0 template gallery

The UE-V 2.0 template gallery is a repository of downloadable settings location templates. The gallery is a community-driven project that includes templates created by Microsoft and templates uploaded by the community. You can find templates here for common applications such as Google Chrome, Adobe Reader, and Notepad++.

Although it's always important to test new software before deploying it into production, because the template gallery is community driven, it's even more important that you verify the functionality of any templates that you download before deploying them to users. You can access the template gallery at *http://go.microsoft.com/fwlink/p/?LinkId=246589.*

When you need to create custom settings location templates for an application, you can use the UE-V Generator to monitor where the application stores its settings and generate a settings location template. You can use the UE-V Generator only for locally installed applications. You can't use the UE-V Generator for applications delivered by App-V or RemoteApp. You also can't use the UE-V Generator for Java applications or Windows 8 apps.

The UE-V Generator isn't installed by default. You need to install it from the MDOP installation DVD. To install the UE-V Generator, run ToolsSetup.exe from the MDOP installation DVD or select it from the installation menu on the DVD, as shown in Figure 2-16.

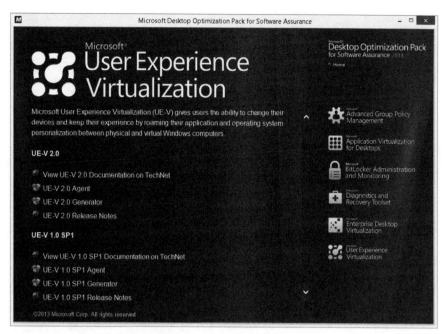

Figure 2-16 UE-V installation screen

To create a custom settings location template by using the UE-V Generator, perform the following steps:

1. Click the Start button, type User, and click
    Microsoft User Experience Virtualization Generator.

2. In the Microsoft User Experience Virtualization (UE-V) Generator window, click Create A
    Settings Location Template.

3. In the Create A Settings Location Template Wizard, on the Specify Application page,
    shown in Figure 2-17, enter the following items and click Next:

    - **File Path**   This is the path to the application executable that will be monitored.

    - **Command-Line Arguments**   This is any additional command-line arguments
       that need to be passed to the executable for it to function properly. In most cases,
       this box will be blank.

    - **Working Folder**   Some applications require you to provide a folder in which the
       application starts to locate additional files that the application uses. In most cases,
       when required, this will be the folder in which the executable is located.

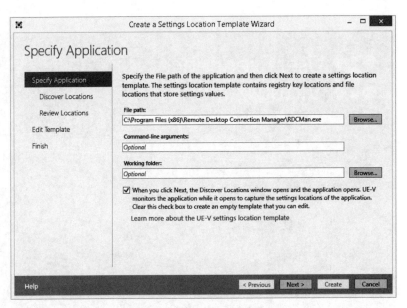

Figure 2-17 Creating a settings location template

4. Wait while UE-V Generator starts the application and monitors the settings locations.

5. After the application has completely started, close the application.

6. When location discovery is complete, click Next.

7. On the Review Locations page, you can review the registry and file locations that were identified by monitoring, as shown in Figure 2-18.

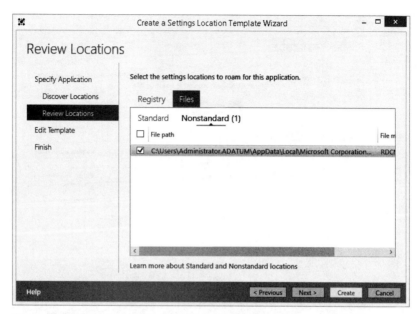

Figure 2-18 Reviewing discovered locations

8. Select the check boxes for the files and registry locations that you want to roam as part of the application and click Next. Standard locations are selected by default. Nonstandard locations must be selected.

9. On the Edit Template page, as shown in Figure 2-19, you can edit the template information before it's created.

    ■ On the Properties tab, you can modify Application properties such as the application name. Most of this information is gathered from properties of the executable file and does not need to be modified.

    ■ On the Registry tab, you can modify the registry settings that are being synchronized. You can add or remove keys. You also can adjust the scope to identify whether subkeys should be included.

    ■ On the Files tab, you can modify the list of file locations. To add a specific file, add the folder that contains the file and enter the file name as the file mask. To include all files in a folder, leave the file mask empty.

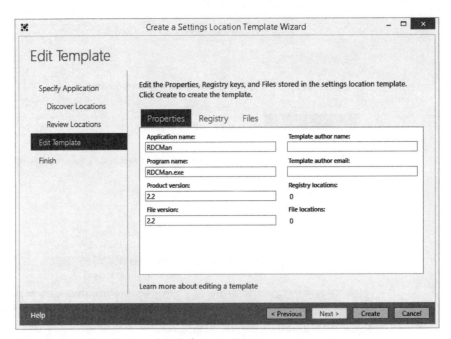

Figure 2-19 Editing the template before creation

10. When eyou're done editing the template, click Create.

11. In the Save As window, browse to the location where you want to save the file, enter an appropriate file name, and click Save.

12. On the Finish page, click Close.

Inside OUT
Standard, nonstandard, and excluded settings

When UE-V Generator monitors the files and registry keys an application uses, it divides the locations into standard and nonstandard. Generally, standard locations roam well between computers. The standard location for registry keys is HKEY_CURRENT_USER. The standard location for files is C:\Users\%username% \AppData\Roaming. Any registry keys or files outside these two locations are considered nonstandard.

Some registry key and file locations are excluded and not listed as standard or nonstandard locations. If you need to include an excluded location, you need to edit the template and add it manually. The excluded locations are as follows:

- HKEY_LOCAL_MACHINE

- HKEY_CURRENT_USER keys to which the user does not have Write access

- HKEY_CURRENT_USER keys for core Windows operating system functionality

- Files in C:\Program Files or C:\Windows

- Files in C:\Users\%username%\AppData\LocalLow

The UE-V Generator creates an XML file that the UE-V agent uses to roam settings for the application. You always should test a custom settings location template before you make it available to users. When that testing is complete, you deploy the custom settings location template to the settings template catalog file share.

Because the settings template catalog is a network share, you can just copy the XML file that the UE-V Generator created to that network share. Each UE-V client computer has a Template Auto Update scheduled task that runs once daily and updates settings location templates on a client. You can force the UE-V agent to apply custom settings location templates from a catalog immediately by running ApplySettingsTemplateCatalog.exe or by using the Windows PowerShell cmdlet Register-UevTemplate.

You also can use the UE-V generator to edit and validate existing templates. The interface for editing an existing template is the same as that for creating a new template. You're able to modify the file and registry locations for the application. Validating a template is done when you have manually edited the XML in a template. When you validate a template, you're verifying that it's still in the proper format.

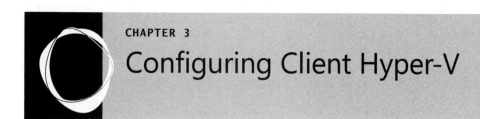

CHAPTER 3

Configuring Client Hyper-V

Microsoft Hyper-V is the current Microsoft solution for implementing virtual machines (VMs). Hyper-V was first introduced in Microsoft Windows Server 2008, and each release has been improved significantly with additional features. On the server side in Windows Server 2012 R2, Hyper-V is capable of supporting enterprise-level virtualization in datacenters that support hundreds or thousands of VMs. Implementing pooled and personal virtual desktops uses the Hyper-V feature in Microsoft Windows Server 2012 R2.

Client Hyper-V in the Windows 8.1 operating system and Hyper-V in the Windows Server 2012 R2 operating system are built on the same code base and provide the same basic virtualization functionality. Client Hyper-V also has the same administrative interface. Hyper-V in Windows Server 2012 R2 extends that functionality with enterprise features, such as network virtualization, Hyper-V Replica, and VM live migration, which are not part of Client Hyper-V.

Hyper-V enables multiple operating systems to run on individual VMs that share a physical computer. VMs can be isolated for testing or connected to a network. This chapter will introduce you to Client Hyper-V in Windows 8.1 and explain the fundamentals of working with VMs in a Client Hyper-V environment. You should be aware that all the features that this chapter covers also are available in Hyper-V in Windows Server 2012 R2.

Understanding Hyper-V

At its most basic level, Client Hyper-V enables you to subdivide the physical hardware in a computer running Windows 8.1 and allocate that hardware to VMs. This enables you to run multiple VMs on a single physical computer. Each VM is completely independent and can have its own operating system and applications.

Client Hyper-V represents virtualized resources as usable components to a VM's operating system. For example, one physical computer with one network adapter might have five different VMs that run in Client Hyper-V. In each of these VMs, a virtualized network adapter is associated with the single physical network adapter. This enables all five VMs to gain access to the network through the physical network adapter. Each virtual network adapter has its own

CHAPTER 3

IP address for communication on the physical network. Similar virtualization happens with other hardware components such as processors, memory, and hard disks.

VMs are commonly used for testing application and operating system updates. Without VMs, a technician could maintain a separate physical computer for this purpose. The use of VMs obviates the need for a separate physical computer and makes it easier to perform testing.

When you use a physical computer for testing, you normally need to image the computer between each test scenario to ensure that one test isn't impacting another. Imaging the computer takes it back to a known good state that matches the configuration of client computers in your organization.

You also can use VMs to run older applications that are not compatible with your current operating system. For example, if you have an application that works properly in Windows XP but not in newer operating systems, then you can install it in a VM running Windows XP. This enables you to use Windows 8.1 as your main operating system but still have access to the older application.

Finally, Client Hyper-V can be useful when you are outside the office and need to demonstrate software functionality. For example, if you are a salesperson for a specific piece of software that requires a complex environment, such as server operating system and SQL database, you could create that environment with VMs to perform demonstrations. Then that environment can travel with you when you visit clients.

Inside OUT

Dual booting

Many support professionals used to configure their computers to support booting to multiple operating systems. This typically was done so that they could do testing in various operating systems and could have the same graphical interface as users when providing support over the phone.

Dual booting is awkward to use because it requires support professionals to have multiple hard disk partitions. Each operating system instance is installed on its own partition. When the computer isn't initially configured to support this, it takes significant effort to modify the disk partitioning to allow for dual booting. In many cases, a second hard drive must be added to support dual booting.

Widespread use of virtualization has almost eliminated the need for dual booting. In most common scenarios, it's faster and easier to maintain a VM for testing than it is to have a second operating system installed for dual booting. However, dual booting still is required when testing anything that relates to physical hardware. For example, to do performance testing of physical hardware or to test driver updates, you can't use a VM.

Client Hyper-V is a feature that enables virtualization within Windows 8.1 Pro and Windows 8.1 Enterprise environments. Client Hyper-V uses the same virtualization engine as Hyper-V in Windows Server 2012 R2, and it contains the same core feature set. Client Hyper-V replaces the Windows XP Mode that is available for Windows 7. Some significant differences between Client Hyper-V and Windows XP Mode functionalities include:

- **Compatibility with Hyper-V in Windows Server**   Client Hyper-V supports the same standard functionality as Hyper-V in Windows Server. You can import and export VMs and virtual hard disks between Hyper-V and Client Hyper-V without conversion or modification.

- **Support for 64-bit VMs**   Client Hyper-V can provide both a 32-bit and a 64-bit virtualized hardware environment for VMs.

- **No application-level virtualization**   In Windows 7, Windows XP Mode enables a user to run an application in a virtualized environment while displaying it within a Windows 7 environment. That is, an application running in Windows XP Mode could appear to be part of the Windows 7 operating system. This was used to support applications written for earlier operating systems that were not compatible with Windows 7. In Windows 8.1, Client Hyper-V exposes the complete virtualized operating system in its own window.

Client Hyper-V architecture

When you install Windows 8.1, the operating system accesses the computer hardware directly with device drivers. Device drivers run in the kernel mode and have full system access. Programs such as Microsoft Office execute in user mode and have limited access to the system.

Inside OUT

User mode and kernel mode

Software can run in user mode or kernel mode for x86 and x64 processors. You also may see some documentation refer to running software in ring 3 and ring 0, which correspond to user mode and kernel mode. Software running in kernel mode has complete access to the hardware, including all memory areas. Therefore, it is important to restrict which software runs in kernel mode because this can impact the reliability of the overall operating system. Applications that run in user mode are restricted to their own memory space and have a limited ability to impact the overall operating system.

After you enable the Client Hyper-V feature, a thin hypervisor layer is added between the operating system and the physical computer hardware, which is one of the reasons a system restart is required. The currently installed Windows 8.1 operating system moves into a VM called the parent partition. The operating system in the parent partition is called the management operating system, from which you can create and manage additional VMs. Additional VMs that you create are called child partitions. Figure 3-1 shows the Client Hyper-V architecture.

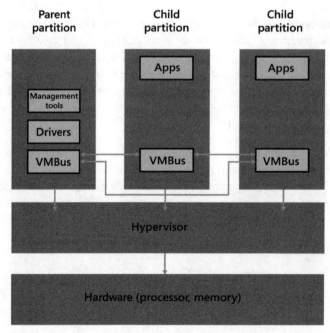

Figure 3-1 Client Hyper-V architecture

The virtualization stack runs within the parent partition, and by using device drivers in the parent partition, it has direct access to computer hardware. VMs can't access computer hardware directly. Instead, they are presented with virtual devices that communicate with virtual service providers in the parent partition through the virtual machine bus (VMBus).

Device access requests from child partitions redirect through the VMBus or through the hypervisor to the device drivers in the parent partition. The VMBus manages the requests, and it is the fastest communication channel between parent and child partitions. The parent partition hosts virtual service providers, and child partitions host virtual service clients, which redirect device requests to virtual service providers in the parent partition through the VMBus.

The VMBus is part of integration services that can be installed in the operating system of VMs. Newer operating systems such as Windows Server 2012 R2 and Windows 8.1 include integration services and automatically begin using the VMBus because the drivers are installed and available. For older operating systems, such as Windows Server 2003, Windows XP, or Windows Vista, you need to install integration services. Windows 7 includes an older version of integration services, but you should upgrade to the latest version of integration services after installation.

If integration services isn't available for a specific operating system, such as an unsupported Linux distribution, you can use device emulation instead. Device emulation is a less efficient method to provide VMs with access to hardware resources. Device emulation requires Client Hyper-V to present an emulated version of hardware that is well known and widely compatible. When the operating system in the VM identifies the emulated hardware, it loads the appropriate device driver for it.

Client Hyper-V in Windows 8.1 supports almost all of the features found in Hyper-V in Windows Server 2012 R2. The few features that are not included in Client Hyper-V are primarily high availability features that are not relevant for the scenarios in which Client Hyper-V would be used. Table 3-1 compares the features of Client Hyper-V and Hyper-V.

Table 3-1 Comparison of Client Hyper-V and Hyper-V

Feature	Description	Client Hyper-V in Windows 8.1	Hyper-V in Windows Server 2012 R2
Sleep and hibernate for physical computer and VMs	Putting a computer into sleep or hibernate mode keeps its current state while reducing power utilization. To support client computers for which this is likely to occur, Client Hyper-V saves all VMs as part of the sleep and hibernation processes.	Yes	No

CHAPTER 3

Virtual wireless network adapters	Allows Hyper-V hosts to connect directly to wireless networks by using a wireless network adapter in the physical computer.	Yes	Yes
Up to 64 terabytes (TB) per virtual disk	Allows VHDX format of virtual disks to be a maximum size of 64 TB.	Yes	Yes
Live storage migration	Allows VM storage to be moved while the VM is running.	Yes	Yes
Live VM migration	Allows VMs to be moved between Hyper-V hosts while the VM is running.	No	Yes
Hyper-V Replica	Allows VMs to be replicated periodically to another Hyper-V host for disaster recovery.	No	Yes
Microsoft RemoteFX graphics virtualization	Allows VMs to use a virtual graphics adapter to improve graphics processing in the VMs.	No	Yes
Single-root I/O virtualization (SR-IOV)	Allows more efficient access to I/O hardware devices that support SR-IOV. In most cases, 10 GB and faster Ethernet benefits from this.	64-bit VMs only	Yes
Virtual Fibre Channel	Allows VMs to access storage directly on Fibre Channel–based storage area networks (SANs).	No	Yes
Network virtualization	Allows VMs to be migrated between data centers without changing the IP configuration of the VM.	No	Yes

Installing Client Hyper-V

To use Client Hyper-V, you need to ensure that your computer meets the necessary hardware and software requirements. Most modern computers meet these requirements, but it is important to confirm.

Client Hyper-V isn't available in all editions of Windows 8 and Windows 8.1. Client Hyper-V is available only in the 64-bit version of Windows 8 Pro, Windows 8 Enterprise, and newer Windows client operating systems. Client Hyper-V isn't available in Windows 8 and Windows 8.1 consumer editions.

CHAPTER 3

The amount of memory in your computer is one factor determining how many VMs can run at one time. Your computer requires a minimum of 4 GB of physical memory to install and use Client Hyper-V. In most cases, you will want more than 4 GB of memory for running Client Hyper-V.

The exact amount of memory you require depends on the configuration of the VMs that you have running at the same time. Each running VM requires a specific amount of memory, depending on the software it is running. A single VM may require only 1 GB of memory or may require 4 GB of memory.

When a VM isn't running, it does not consume any memory. So, it is possible to have many VMs created with memory requirements in excess of physical memory but only have a few VMs running.

In many cases, you will use a local hard disk for VM storage. Most computers have a far larger local disk than is required for the operating system and applications. This leaves room for storing VMs. This is easy for individual users to manage, and if you are taking a portable computer on the road, it may be the only option.

Client Hyper-V supports all of the same storage options as Hyper-V in Windows Server 2012 R2 except for Fibre Channel. So, you have the option to store VM files on a file share (using SMB version 3) or iSCSI storage. Using network locations to store VMs can make it easier to use VMs from multiple computers. However, the VMs can't be used simultaneously by multiple computers.

CHAPTER 3

Inside OUT

VM storage performance

Storage speed is a critical component of a VM's performance. Running multiple VMs can generate a large amount of disk I/O. Most computers have inexpensive SATA drives that do not support high I/O. This can cause VMs to run very slowly.

The spinning disks in mobile computers typically are even slower than desktop computers. Consider using an SSD drive in a mobile computer with VMs. If you want to store VMs on a portable external drive, ensure that both the computer and the external drive support USB 3.0. USB 2.0 isn't fast enough to support VM storage with reasonable performance.

To use Client Hyper-V, the processor in your computer must be an x64 processor and support Second Level Address Translation (SLAT). SLAT speeds up overall memory performance. The Intel Core i3, i5, and i7 processors all support SLAT.

Inside OUT

Determining whether your processor supports SLAT

If you are not sure whether your computer supports SLAT, there are several different tools that you can use to identify SLAT support. The systeminfo command-line utility in Windows 8 and Windows 8.1 generates a report that displays whether SLAT is supported in the processor, as shown in Figure 3-2. You also can download the coreinfo tool from TechNet and use it to view processor features.

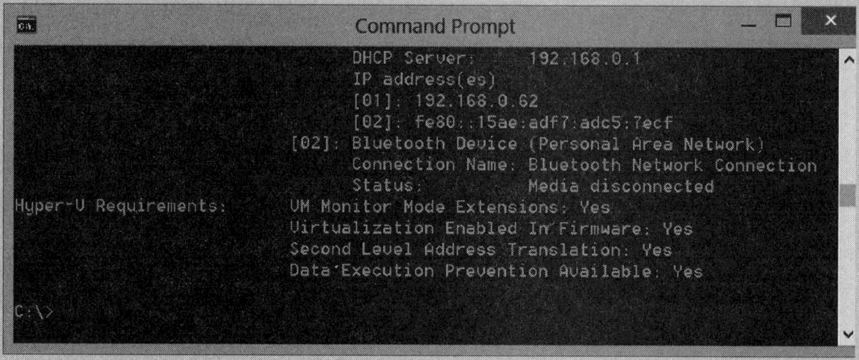

Figure 3-2 Results from systeminfo

Client Hyper-V does not require a specific processor speed. However, processor speed and the number of processor cores do make a difference in overall performance. Most modern computers have four or more processor cores, which is enough to run several VMs.

If you have a computer that meets the prerequisites for installing Client Hyper-V, you can enable the feature from Programs and Features in Control Panel. You can use the following steps:

1. Click Start, type Features, and click Programs And Features.

2. In the Programs And Features window, click Turn Windows Features On Or Off.

3. In the Windows Features dialog box, scroll down and select the Hyper-V check box, shown in Figure 3-3, and click OK.

4. When the changes are complete, click Restart Now.

5. Wait while the computer restarts and installation completes.

Figure 3-3 Enabling Hyper-V in Windows Features

In Windows 8.1, you can use Windows PowerShell to enable and disable operating system features by using the Enable-WindowsOptionalFeature cmdlet. To use this cmdlet, you must be working at a Windows PowerShell prompt that is opened with administrator permissions. You can use this cmdlet to enable the feature options that were available in the graphical interface:

- Microsoft-Hyper-V-All

- Microsoft-Hyper-V-Tools-All

- Microsoft-Hyper-V-Management-Clients

- Microsoft-Hyper-V-Management-PowerShell

- Microsoft Hyper-V

To enable Client Hyper-V by using Windows PowerShell, use the following command:

```
Enable-WindowsOptionalFeature –Online –FeatureName Microsoft-Hyper-V-All
```

You also can verify whether Client Hyper-V is installed with the following command:

```
Get-WindowsOptionalFeature –Online –FeatureName *Hyper-V*
```

Dism.exe is a command-line utility that you can use to enable and disable features in Windows 8.1. You must open the command prompt with administrator permissions to use dism.exe. To enable Client Hyper-V by using dism.exe, use the following command:

```
Dism /online /enable-feature /featurename:Microsoft-Hyper-V-All
```

When you use dism.exe to enable Client Hyper-V, it does not perform any prerequisite checks to ensure that your computer meets the necessary hardware requirements. So, it is possible to enable Client Hyper-V on a computer that does not have SLAT. However, this does not mean that Client Hyper-V will be functional. The Client Hyper-V feature will be installed, but you will not be able to create and run VMs if your computer does not meet the hardware requirements.

Hyper-V management tools

Hyper-V Manager, shown in Figure 3-4, is the primary tool for managing Client Hyper-V. Hyper-V Manager is a graphical console that provides complete administration of Client Hyper-V functionality in Windows 8.1.

Figure 3-4 Hyper-V Manager

Hyper-V Manager includes the following three panes with management information for Client Hyper-V:

- **Navigation pane**   Shows the hosts running Hyper-V to which Hyper-V Manager is connected. You can connect to multiple instances of Client Hyper-V or Hyper-V servers. Only the local computer is listed by default.

- **Details pane**   Shows detailed information about VMs on the selected host. This includes a list of VMs and status information about them. For the selected VM, you can see more detailed information about memory and networking. You also can see information about checkpoints for the selected VM.

- **Actions pane**   Shows actions that are available for managing the host and the selected VM. The host-specific actions, such as creating a new VM, also are available by right-clicking the host. The VM-specific actions, such as pausing a VM, also are available by right-clicking a VM.

When you install Client Hyper-V, it includes Virtual Machine Connection. You use Virtual Machine Connection to view the console of VMs. You also can perform some VM management tasks. In most cases, you will start Virtual Machine Connection from within Hyper-V manager, but you also can run it from the Start screen.

You can use Virtual Machine Connection to establish only one connection to the VM. If a connection already is established and a second user establishes a connection to the same VM, the first user is disconnected and the second user takes over the session.

NOTE

Both Hyper-V Manager and Virtual Machine Connection install if you enable the Hyper-V GUI Management Tools feature in Windows 8.1.

The Hyper-V module for Windows PowerShell enables you to manage Client Hyper-V by using Windows PowerShell cmdlets. Windows PowerShell enables you to configure everything that you can configure by using Hyper-V Manager and some options that you can manage only by using Windows PowerShell.

Inside OUT

Windows PowerShell cmdlets for Hyper-V

In Windows 8.1, there are almost 200 cmdlets available for managing Client Hyper-V. You can view all of the available cmdlets for managing Client Hyper-V with the following command:

```
Get-Command -Module Hyper-V
```

Cmdlets have consistent verb-noun names, so in most cases, you will know from a cmdlet name what action it will perform. Some examples are as follows:

- Cmdlets that start with "Get-" return the object property values and will not modify objects in any way.
- Cmdlets that start with "Set-" set object property values and can be used to configure objects.
- Cmdlets that start with "Disable-" disable objects.
- Cmdlets that start with "Enable-" enable objects.

The second part of a cmdlet name specifies the object type on which the cmdlet will act. Some examples are as follows:

- Get-VMHost lists Client Hyper-V computer information.
- Set-VMSwitch configures a virtual switch by setting its properties.
- New-VHD creates a new virtual hard disk file.

Each cmdlet also has parameters that you use to define specific options for that cmdlet. To identify parameters available for a cmdlet, use the Get-Help cmdlet. For easier reading, you can view the help information in a web browser instead of at the Windows PowerShell prompt by using the Online parameter. The following example shows how to view the online help information for the New-VHD cmdlet:

```
Get-Help Get-VM -Online
```

The majority of management in Client Hyper-V is simple one-time actions such as starting and turning off VMs. Actions like these typically are simpler to perform by using the graphical interface in Hyper-V Manager. Windows PowerShell is well suited for automating tasks. Also, if you are performing more complex tasks that are suitable for scripting, consider using the Windows PowerShell Integrated Scripting Environment (ISE), shown in Figure 3-5.

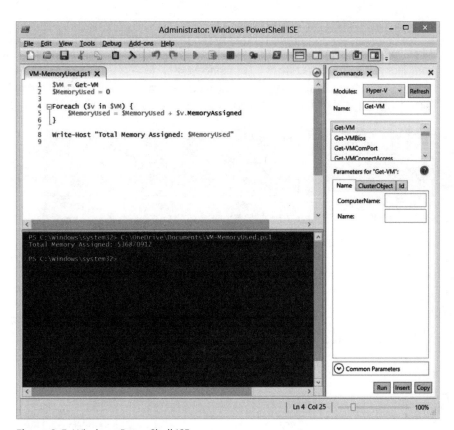

Figure 3-5 Windows PowerShell ISE

Windows PowerShell has several features that make script editing easier:

- Color-coding makes it easier to see syntax errors.

- Debugging tools make it easier to find mistakes in the script.

- The Commands pane provides help for cmdlets.

- IntelliSense is used to display context-sensitive options as you type.

- Customizable code snippets can be used to paste in frequently used code.

TIP

To use Windows PowerShell to manage Client Hyper-V, the Windows PowerShell prompt or Windows PowerShell ISE must be running as administrator. If you do not run them as administrator, the Hyper-V cmdlets are not available.

Managing virtual switches

When you have multiple physical computers that you want to connect inside the same network segment, you connect them by using network switches. Virtual switches support connectivity for VMs in Client Hyper-V. To manage virtual switches, you can use Virtual Switch Manager in Hyper-V Manager, shown in Figure 3-6, or Windows PowerShell cmdlets.

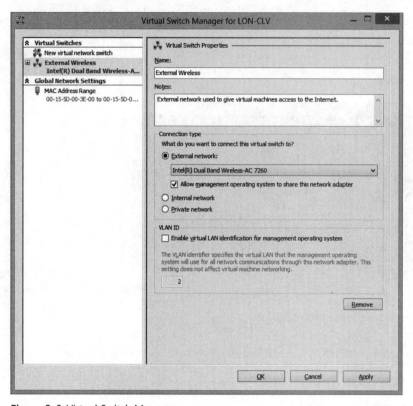

Figure 3-6 Virtual Switch Manager

When you install Client Hyper-V, no virtual switches are created by default. You need to create any virtual switches that Client Hyper-V will use. There is no limit on how many virtual switches you can create on Client Hyper-V or how many VMs you can connect to a virtual switch.

A virtual switch can be connected to:

- An external network

- An internal network

- A private network

An external network is linked to a physical network adapter in the computer running Client Hyper-V. VMs connected to an external network can access the resources on that network. For example, if the external network is linked to a gigabit network adapter card in the computer running Client Hyper-V that is connected to the corporate network, then VMs connected to the external network can access resources on the corporate network.

There is a one-to-one relationship between external networks and the number of physical network adapters in the computer running Client Hyper-V. Consequently, if you have a single network adapter in the computer running Client Hyper-V, you can have only one external network.

You connect VMs to an external network in any scenario in which you require them to have access to a physical network, such as the corporate network or the Internet. You may require VMs to have access to the corporate network if you use them for testing application and operating system updates. Internet connectivity may be required to download files from the Internet or to access cloud-based applications from within the VM.

To create an external virtual switch in Hyper-V Manager, perform the following procedure:

1. In Hyper-V Manager, in the Actions pane, click Virtual Switch Manager.

2. In the Virtual Switch Manager window, in the navigation pane, select New Virtual Network Switch.

3. In the Create Virtual Switch area, click External and click the Create Virtual Switch button.

4. In the Virtual Switch Properties area, in the Name box, type *NameOfNetwork*. You want this name to be descriptive so that it is easy to identify. For example, if this virtual switch will be linked to your wireless network adapter, a suitable name might be External Wireless.

5. In the Notes box, you can type a detailed description of the virtual switch.

6. In the Connection Type area, click External Network and select the physical network adapter to which you want the external network linked.

7. (Optional) To allow the computer running Client Hyper-V to also continue using the specified physical network adapter, select the Allow Management Operating System To Share This Network Adapter check box. In most cases, you will select this option.

CHAPTER 3

8. (Optional) To define a VLAN ID for the management operating system on the external network, select the Enable Virtual LAN Identification For Management Operating System check box and then enter the value of the VLAN ID. This option is required only if your network is configured to require VLAN configuration.

9. To finish creating the virtual switch, click Apply and click Yes to acknowledge the warning.

10. When the configuration is complete, click OK.

When you create an external virtual switch, the physical network adapter you select is no longer available to the host operating system for network activity. That is, the host operating system can no longer send network packets directly over that network adapter. The existing network adapter still appears in the list of network connections, shown as Wi-Fi in Figure 3-7, but that network adapter has no network configuration options. For example, you can't configure an IPv4 address for it. You still can configure driver options for the physical network adapter.

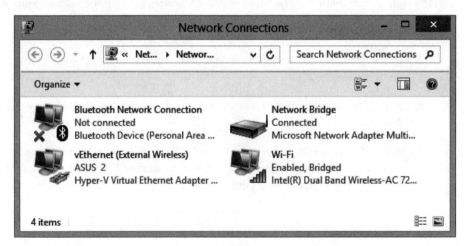

Figure 3-7 Network connections after creating an external virtual switch

If you selected Allow Management Operating System To Share This Network Adapter, then the network configuration options are all available on a new virtual network adapter that has been created. The virtual network adapter is named vEthernet (*NameOfExternalSwitch*). If you want to modify network configuration for the host operating system, you do it in the properties of the virtual network adapter. If the network adapter you selected for the external virtual switch is a wireless network, then a network bridge is created to support connectivity. If you didn't select Allow Management Operating System To Share The Network Adapter, then the virtual network adapter does not appear.

Inside OUT

Why a network bridge is required for wireless networks

When you configure a wired network adapter as an external network, the VMs communicate on the wired network without their packets being modified. Specifically, the media access control (MAC) address of the virtual network adapter is used as the source MAC address in packets sent on the wired network. This is possible because Client Hyper-V configures the wired network adapter to use promiscuous mode, which allows packets using any destination MAC address to be accepted. When not in promiscuous mode, a network adapter drops packets with a destination MAC address that does not match its own MAC address.

On a wireless network, you authenticate to a wireless access point. When using Client Hyper-V, the authentication occurs in the host operating system, and the source MAC address associated with the authentication is that of the wireless network adapter in the host. Packets with a MAC address not associated with an authenticated connection are dropped. This means that network packets from a VM with a different MAC address would be dropped.

Bridging network traffic resolves this problem. As packets move from a VM through the bridge, the source MAC address in the packet is replaced with the MAC address of the wireless network adapter. The bridge maintains a mapping table and translates incoming packets back to the correct MAC address for delivery.

➤ For more information about the requirement for a bridge when using wireless networks, see Bringing Hyper-V to "Windows 8" on the MSDN website at *http://blogs.msdn.com/b/b8/archive/2011/09/07/bringing-hyper-v-to-windows-8.aspx*.

CHAPTER 3

If you have VMs for testing purposes that only need to communicate with one another, you can use a private virtual switch or an internal virtual switch. In both cases, VMs connected to these networks can communicate only with other VMs on the same network. They do not have Internet connectivity or access to the corporate network. This makes private and internal virtual switches well suited to creating small test environments with multiple VMs. For example, you could create a VM that runs a web-based application and use another VM to access and test the application.

The only difference between private and internal virtual switches is whether the host operating system can communicate on the network. A private network is completely isolated from the host operating system. The VMs can communicate only with other VMs on the same network.

This is useful for a completely isolated test environment. By creating multiple private virtual switches, you can have multiple isolated test environments running at the same time.

An internal network allows the management operating system to communicate on the network with the VMs and creates a virtual network adapter to support this. Using an internal network is useful when you want the management operating system to access VMs to copy files or use applications.

TIP

You can use an internal network and provide VMs with access to the Internet if you use the Internet Connection Sharing (ICS) feature on the host. ICS performs network address translation to support sharing connectivity to an external network.

The Hyper-V module for Windows PowerShell includes cmdlets that you can use to create and manage switches. Some examples are listed below.

To create a new internal virtual switch named InternalTest:

```
New-VMSwitch -Name InternalTest -SwitchType Internal
```

To obtain a list of external virtual switches on the local computer:

```
Get-VMSwitch -SwitchType External
```

To change the type of a virtual switch:

```
Set-VMSwitch -Name InternalTest -SwitchType "Private"
```

To rename a virtual switch:

```
Rename-VMSwitch -Name InternalTest -NewName "Private Test"
```

To remove a virtual switch:

```
Remove-VMSwitch "Private Test"
```

Creating virtual machines

A VM represents a virtual computer in a virtualization environment. Virtual computers have components similar to those of physical computers. However, virtual computers can use only components that are part of a Client Hyper-V virtualization infrastructure. Client Hyper-V can present devices to a VM in the following two ways:

- **Emulated devices**   Client Hyper-V presents an emulated device to a VM as if it is actual hardware. Emulated devices present standard and well-known functionalities that are universal to all devices of that type. This means that almost any operating system supports them. Emulated devices are available when a VM starts, and a VM can start from them. These emulated devices include integrated device electronics (IDE) controllers and legacy network adapters.

- **Hyper-V-specific devices**   Client Hyper-V does not present Hyper-V–specific devices to the VM as actual hardware. It presents them to the operating system on the VM as a functionality that the device driver can use. Newer operating systems such as Windows 8.1 support such functionality by default when running in VMs. For other operating systems, you need to install integration services to support Hyper-V–specific devices. Hyper-V–specific devices are not available during startup, and you can't start a virtual computer from them.

When you create a VM, you specify a variety of configuration information. Table 3-2 describes the information you can specify during VM creation.

Table 3-2 VM configuration information required during creation

Item	Description
Name	Each VM is given a name to identify it. This name is independent of the computer name, but it can be the same.
	Use a name that is meaningful so that it is easy for you to identify the purpose of the VM.
Location	Specifies the file system location where all of the VM files will be stored. The default location is C:\ProgramData\Microsoft \Windows\Hyper-V. A folder for the VM is created in the specified folder.
	The files for VMs can be very large. To avoid running out of space on your C drive, you should consider storing VMs in an alternate location. Storing VMs on a separate physical disk can increase performance.
Generation	Specifies whether a VM is generation 1 or generation 2. Generation 2 VMs have new features, such as the ability to boot from a SCSI controller. If you want to use a generation 2 VM, you must install Windows Server 2012 or newer or a 64-bit version of Windows 8 or newer to the VM. After creating a VM, you can't change its generation.
Memory	Specifies the amount of physical memory that is allocated to the VM from the host. This memory needs to be sufficient to allow the operating system and applications in the VM to function properly. You can assign a static amount of memory or use dynamic memory, which expands as required.

CHAPTER 3

Network connection	By default, a new VM is created with a single network adapter that can be connected to a virtual switch. The type of virtual switch to which you connect the VM is based on the purpose of the VM. If necessary, a VM can have multiple network adapters.
Virtual hard disk location	Each VM must have at least one virtual hard disk. The default option is to create a new dynamically expanding virtual hard disk. You can select an existing virtual hard disk if you already have prepared one. For example, you could create a virtual hard disk with Windows 8.1 already installed and updated and copy that to create new VMs.
Operating system installation options	Specifies whether to install an operating system later, from an ISO image, or from a network installation server. In most cases, you choose to install the operating system later. These options do not actually install the operating system; they configure the boot order for VM, and if an ISO image was selected, they mount the ISO image to a virtual DVD drive in the VM.

To create a VM in Hyper-V Manager, perform the following procedure:

1. Open Hyper-V Manager and in the Actions pane, click New and then click Virtual Machine.

2. The New Virtual Machine Wizard appears. Click Next.

3. On the Specify Name And Location page, shown in Figure 3-8, in the Name text box, type the name of your VM.

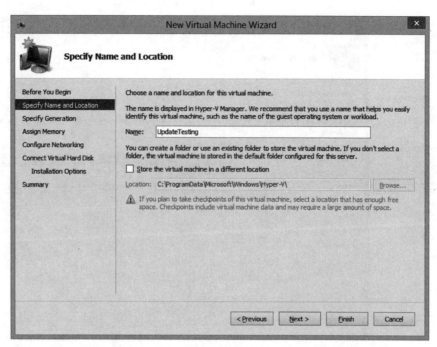

Figure 3-8 New Virtual Machine Wizard, Specify Name And Location page

4. (Optional) If you want to specify an alternate location for the VM files, select the Store The Virtual Machine In A Different Location check box and then, in the Location box, type the location and click Next.

5. On the Specify Generation page, shown in Figure 3-9, select if you want to create a generation 1 or generation 2 VM and then click Next.

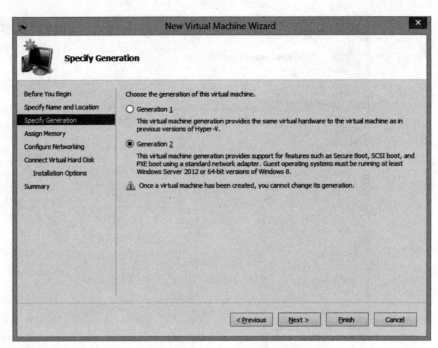

Figure 3-9 New Virtual Machine Wizard, Specify Generation page

6. On the Assign Memory page, shown in Figure 3-10, in the Memory box, type the amount of memory you want to assign the VM.

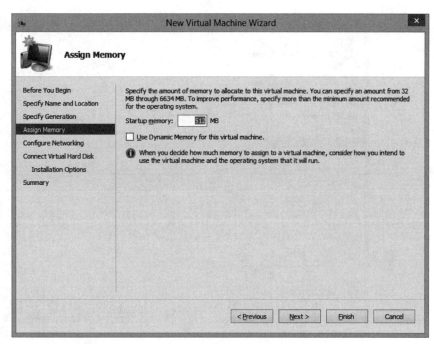

Figure 3-10 New Virtual Machine Wizard, Assign Memory page

7.   (Optional) If you want to use Dynamic Memory, select the Use Dynamic Memory For This Virtual Machine check box and click Next.

8.   On the Configure Networking page, shown in Figure 3-11, in the Connection list, select the appropriate network switch and then click Next.

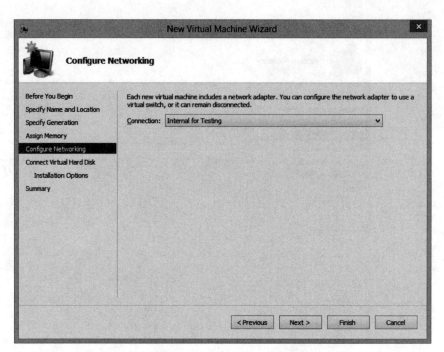

Figure 3-11 New Virtual Machine Wizard, Configure Networking page

9.   On the Connect Virtual Hard Disk page, shown in Figure 3-12, select Create A Virtual Hard Disk or Use An Existing Virtual Hard Disk and then click Next.

CHAPTER 3

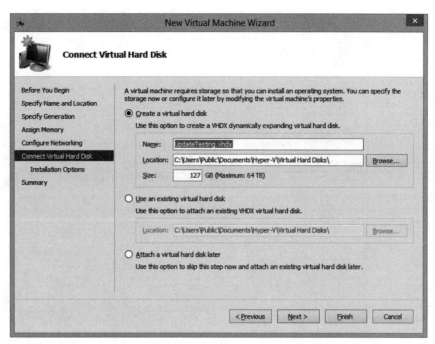

Figure 3-12 New Virtual Machine Wizard, Connect Virtual Hard Disk page

10. On the Installation Options page, shown in Figure 3-13, select where you want to install an operating system from on the VM and then click Next. In most cases, you will select to install the operating system later.

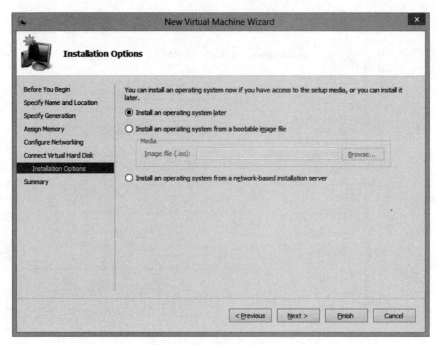

Figure 3-13 New Virtual Machine Wizard, Installation Options page

11. On the Completing The New Virtual Machine Wizard page, click Finish.

You also can use the New-VM cmdlet to create a VM from Windows PowerShell. Table 3-3 shows the important parameters for the New-VM cmdlet.

Table 3-3 New-VM cmdlet parameters

Parameter	Description
Name	Specifies the name of the VM.
Path	Specifies the file system path for storing the VM's files.
Generation	Specifies the generation of the VM. Valid values are 1 or 2.
MemoryStartupBytes	Specifies the memory assigned to the VM. If not specified, the default value is 512 MB.
NewVHDPath	Specifies the path of a new VHD that is created and attached to the VM.
NewVHDSizeBytes	Specifies the size of the new VHD that is created and attached to the VM. By default, the VHD is a dynamically expanding VHD with a maximum size of 127 GB.
VHDPath	Specifies the path to an existing VHD that will be attached to the new VM.
SwitchName	Specifies the name of the virtual switch to which the adapter for the VM will be connected.

The following example shows how to create a VM by using the New-VM cmdlet:

```
New-VM –Name UpdateTesting –Path D:\VM –Generation 2 –MemoryStartupBytes 2GB –NewVHDPath
D:\VM\UpdateTesting\UpdateTesting.vhdx –NewVHDSizeBytes 127GB –SwitchName "Internal For
Testing"
```

Virtual machine settings

In most cases, after creating a VM, you want to do additional configuration of it. Figure 3-14 shows the settings for a generation 1 VM in Hyper-V Manager. To view the settings for a VM in Hyper-V Manager, right-click the VM and click Settings or select the VM and, in the Actions pane, click Settings.

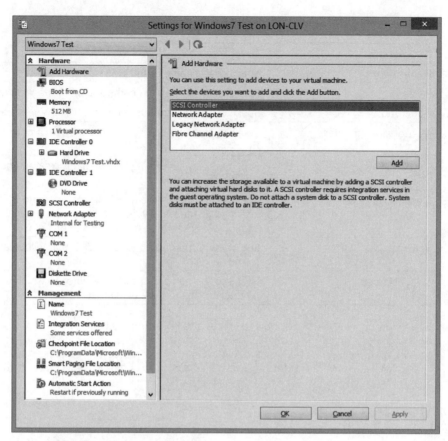

Figure 3-14 Settings for a generation 1 VM

At the top of the list of virtual machine settings is the Add Hardware option. When this option is selected, you can add SCSI controllers, network adapters, legacy network adapters, and Fibre Channel adapters. Table 3-4 describes the hardware in a generation 1 VM.

Table 3-4 Generation 1 hardware components

Component	Description
BIOS	Specifies the startup order of boot devices. The default order is CD, IDE, legacy network adapter, and floppy.
Memory	Specifies the amount of memory that is assigned to a VM.
Processor	Specifies the number of virtual processors that are available to a VM. Resource control information about balancing processor utilization also is configured here.
IDE controller	Connects IDE virtual disks and DVD drives to a VM. Generation 1 VMs have two IDE controllers. Devices that are connected to IDE controllers can be used to start a VM.
SCSI controller	Connects SCSI virtual disks to a VM. Generation 1 VMs can't start from a VHD attached to a SCSI controller. In addition, the paging file for Windows must be on a disk attached to an IDE controller.
Network adapter	Connects a VM with a virtual switch. This type of adapter can't be used for PXE booting in generation 1 VMs.
Legacy network adapter	Connects a VM with a virtual switch. Legacy network adapters are emulated, which means that they are available during startup, and generation 1 VMs can use them for PXE. In addition, legacy network adapters are more compatible with legacy operating systems for which integration services are not available.
COM port	Configures a virtual COM port to communicate with a physical computer through a named pipe. Note that this can't be employed to use physical serial devices connected to the host.
Diskette drive	Connects virtual floppy disks to a VM. A virtual floppy disk is a small file with the vfd extension.

The Management section also lets you configure the settings listed in Table 3-5. These settings are similar in generation 1 and generation 2 VMs.

CHAPTER 3

Table 3-5 Management settings for a VM

Component	Description
Name	Specify the name of a VM and add notes about it.
Integration Services	Enable services that Client Hyper-V will offer to a VM. To use any of the services, integration services must be installed and supported on the VM operating system.
Checkpoint File Location	Specify the folder in which checkpoint files for a VM will be stored. You can modify this location until the first checkpoint is created. A checkpoint is a copy of a VM at a specific point in time.
Smart Paging File Location	Specify the folder in which the Smart Paging file for a VM will be created, if necessary. A Smart Paging file is created when a VM is started and not enough physical memory can be allocated to the VM. The Smart Paging file is used as a temporary memory space, much like virtual memory on a physical computer.
Automatic Start Action	Specify whether to start a VM automatically after the Client Hyper-V computer restarts and how long after Client Hyper-V is running to start the VM.
Automatic Stop Action	Specify the state in which to place a VM when the Client Hyper-V computer shuts down.

Generation 2 virtual machines

Generation 2 VMs are a new feature in Hyper-V for Windows Server 2012 R2 and Windows 8.1. All Hyper-V VMs created before Windows Server 2012 R2 and Windows 8.1 are generation 1 VMs. Generation 2 VMs have a few additional features and a simplified hardware configuration.

The new features supported by generation 2 VMs are

- **PXE boot**   Generation 2 VMs can perform a PXE boot for operating system installation from a standard network adapter. In generation 1 VMs, you need to use a legacy network adapter for PXE boot, which has poorer performance.

- **Boot from SCSI**   Generation 2 VMs can boot from a SCSI disk or a SCSI virtual DVD. In generation 1 VMs, it isn't possible to boot from SCSI devices. Generation 1 VMs require IDE devices to boot.

- **UEFI firmware support**   Generation 2 VMs use UEFI firmware to start the boot process. This is typical on modern physical computers. In generation 1 VMs, BIOS firmware is used to start the boot process.

- **Secure Boot**   Generation 2 VMs have Secure Boot enabled by default. Secure Boot is a function of UEFI firmware and helps prevent unauthorized software from running during the boot process. If you are running a Linux-based operating system in a generation 2 VM, you need to disable Secure Boot, because the Linux operating systems are not trusted.

Whenever possible, generation 2 VMs simplify the hardware model, and the result is lower resource utilization by the VM. The following hardware has been removed from generation 2 VMs:

- **IDE controllers**   No longer required because SCSI is fully supported for all operations.

- **BIOS boot**   Removed because it no longer is required by current operating systems.

- **Legacy network adapter**   Removed because it no longer is required for PXE boot.

- **Floppy controller**   Removed because it no longer is commonly used. You can use an ISO file mounted to a virtual DVD drive as an alternative to a virtual floppy disk.

- **Hardware emulation for keyboard, mouse, and video**   Replaced with software-based devices for lower resource utilization.

- **Emulated system devices, such as PCI bus and programmable interrupt controller**   Removed because they no longer are required.

Not all operating systems can be used in generation 2 VMs. The operating system needs to support UEFI firmware and must not require any legacy hardware support. The Windows operating systems that are supported for generation 2 VMs are 64-bit versions of Windows 8 and Windows 8.1, Windows Server 2012, and Windows Server 2012 R2. Some Linux and FreeBSD distributions also are supported.

> ➤ For more information about Hyper-V support for Linux and FreeBSD, see
> Linux and FreeBSD Virtual Machines on Hyper-V on the TechNet website at
> *http://technet.microsoft.com/en-ca/library/dn531030.aspx.*

Controlling virtual machines

Each virtual machine maintains its own state within Client Hyper-V. When a VM is started, it begins the boot process and loads the installed operating system. After the operating system loads, it interacts with the virtual hardware that is configured for the VM, and you can connect to it and work with it as you would a physical computer.

CHAPTER 3

Each VM can be in one of the following states:

- **Off**   A VM that is stopped does not consume any processing, memory, or disk I/O on the host machine, and it exists in a state similar to a physical computer that is powered off.

- **Starting**   When you start a VM, it remains in the starting state for a few moments while required resources are checked and assigned to the VM. After this resource check and assignment occurs, the starting state changes to running.

- **Running**   A VM is in its normal operable state when the state Running is displayed. A running VM responds to keyboard and mouse input and shows whatever information is being sent to the VM's display adapter when you are connected to the VM.

- **Paused**   When a VM is paused, it maintains its allocation of host-computer resources, such as memory, but it stops processing within the VM. This is similar to putting a physical computer in a sleep state, but the operating system is unaware that the VM is paused.

- **Saved**   When a VM is in the saved state, its current operating state is saved to the hard disk, and it stops consuming host-computer resources until you start it and put it in a running state. When you save a VM, the contents of memory are saved to disk as a file that is the same size as the allocated memory. This file is read back into memory when you restart the VM. When a Client Hyper-V computer restarts or goes into hibernate or sleep mode, VMs that are running enter the saved state.

TIP

Storing a VM in a saved state typically makes it faster to start than a full boot process. However, if you have many saved VMs, the memory contents stored on disk can consume a significant amount of disk space. Balance the need for fast starts with disk utilization.

In most cases, to use a VM, you want to connect to the VM and view the desktop. You can connect to a VM if you select the VM and then click the Connect button on the toolbar. Alternatively, you can right-click the VM and then click Connect in the shortcut menu.

The basic connectivity to a VM allows to you to interact with the desktop of the VM as if you were sitting at the console of a physical computer. When you move the mouse within the window showing the VM, the mouse movement and keyboard input are passed to the VM. The default view is a window, as shown in Figure 3-15.

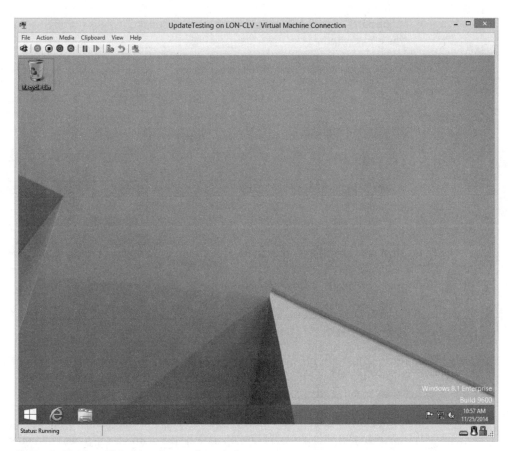

Figure 3-15 Virtual Machine Connection window

If your screen resolution is high enough, using the windowed mode for controlling a VM is simpler. In the windowed mode, you have access to the menus and toolbar at the top of the window. This removes the need to remember shortcut keys for controlling a VM. Also, it generally is easier to switch between multiple VMs when each has its own window rather than a full screen.

The menu and toolbar in the Virtual Machine Connection window are shown in Figure 3-16. The menu options provide the following capabilities:

- **File**   Access and edit the settings for the VM.

- **Action**   Perform actions such as start and turn off a VM. Each option in this menu also exists in the toolbar.

- **Media**   Access settings for the DVD drive to mount and eject ISO images.

- **Clipboard**   Take a full screenshot of the VM screen or type text from the clipboard on the host computer.

- **View**   Toggle in and out of full screen mode.

- **Help**   View help information and the version of Virtual Machine Connection.

Figure 3-16 Virtual Machine Connection menu and toolbar

The toolbar buttons, from left to right, have the following functions:

- **Ctrl+Alt+Del**   Used to pass Ctrl+Alt+Del to the VM. This is required because when you press Ctrl+Alt+Del, it is passed to the host computer regardless of whether you are in the VM. You can use the key sequence Ctrl+Alt+End as an alternative to this button when in full screen.

- **Start**   Starts the VM from a stopped state.

- **Turn Off**   Turns off the VM regardless of its current state. This is the equivalent of turning off the power on a physical computer. You typically shut down the operating system of a VM rather than turning it off.

- **Shut Down**   Shuts down the VM operating system and then turns off the VM. If you do not manually shut down the VM operating system, this is the preferred method for stopping a VM.

- **Save**   Saves the state of the VM, including memory contents, for restart later.

- **Pause**   Pauses the VM to stop processing.

- **Reset**   Resets the VM, similar to pressing Reset on a physical computer. This isn't desirable in most cases when an operating system is running.

- **Checkpoint**   Creates a checkpoint that enables you to restore the VM back to that point in time.

- **Revert**   Reverts the VM back to the previous checkpoint. All changes since the previous checkpoint are lost.

- **Enhanced Session/Basic Session**   Toggles connectivity between a basic session and an enhanced session. Enhanced Session Mode provides additional features by using Remote Desktop Protocol (RDP) to connect to the VM.

Inside OUT

Enhanced Session Mode

Enhanced Session Mode in Virtual Machine Connection uses the Remote Desktop Connection (RDC) feature in VMs and establishes a full Remote Desktop session to a VM. This means that local resources such as smart cards, printers, drives, USB devices, and any other supported Plug and Play devices can redirect to VMs. You also can use a shared Clipboard for copying content to VMs or even copy files to VMs even if the VM does not have network connectivity.

To use Enhanced Session Mode, the VM operating system must be either Windows 8.1 or Windows Server 2012 R2. In addition, the user account that is used to log on to the VM must have permission to connect remotely to the VM. This permission is given to local administrators by default.

If the requirements for Enhanced Session Mode are met, it is used automatically. Enhanced Session Mode is enabled by default in Client Hyper-V, but it can be disabled in the Hyper-V settings by unchecking the Allow Enhanced Session Mode check box in the Enhanced Session Mode Policy. It also can be disabled in user-level Hyper-V settings, as shown in Figure 3-17. To access these settings in Hyper-V Manager, right-click the host and click Hyper-V Settings.

CHAPTER 3

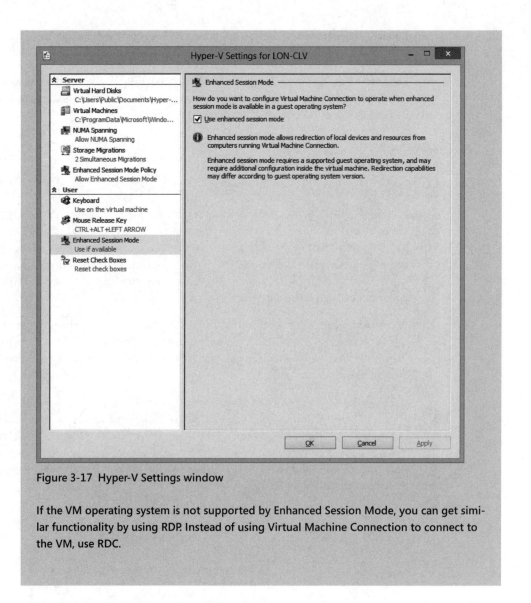

Figure 3-17 Hyper-V Settings window

If the VM operating system is not supported by Enhanced Session Mode, you can get similar functionality by using RDP. Instead of using Virtual Machine Connection to connect to the VM, use RDC.

Managing virtual machine files

When you create a VM, you can choose the location where you store the files. You may want to move VM files to an alternate location to free up disk space or as a backup. Client Hyper-V has functionality to move existing VM files and export/import VMs.

You can move VM files anytime you need to reorganize where VM files are stored. You might do this to put all VMs into a new subfolder or to move VMs to a second drive where you have more storage.

As shown in Figure 3-18, there are three move options in the wizard:

- **Move All Of The Virtual Machine's Data To A Single Location**   This option moves all of the VM configuration data and virtual hard disks to a single folder.

- **Move The Virtual Machine's Data To Different Locations**   This option enables you to select the VM data that you want to move to a new location. You can choose from Current Configuration, Checkpoints, Smart Paging, and each individual virtual hard disk. For each of the items selected, you are prompted for a folder to which to move the data.

- **Move Only The Virtual Machine's Hard Disks**   This option enables you to select which virtual hard disks to move to a specified folder.

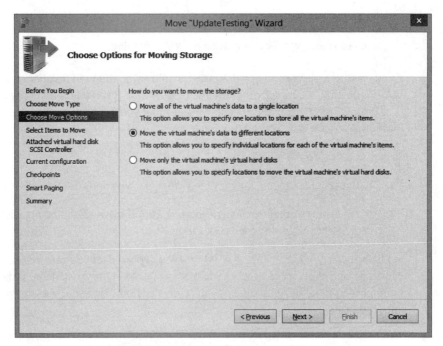

Figure 3-18 Move Wizard, Choose Options For Moving Storage page

To move all VM files to a single location, perform the following steps:

1. In Hyper-V Manager, right-click the VM and click Move.

2. In the Move "*virtualmachine*" Wizard, on the Before You Begin page, click Next.

3. On the Choose Move Type page, click Move The Virtual Machine's Storage and click Next. In Client Hyper-V, this is the only available option. On a server-based Hyper-V host, you also have the option to Move The Virtual Machine.

4. On the Choose Options For Moving Storage page, click Move All Of The Virtual Machine's Data To A Single Location and click Next.

5. On the Choose A New Location For Virtual Machine page, click Browse, select the appropriate folder, click Select Folder, and then click Next.

6. On the Summary page, click Finish.

TIP

You can move VM files even when the VM is running.

If you want to make a copy of a VM rather than moving the VM files, then you can export the VM. It is possible to just copy the VM files of a VM that is turned off and import them in a new location, but using the export function ensures that you get all of the necessary files in a single location. Also, you can export a running VM.

To export a VM, do the following:

1. In Hyper-V Manager, right-click the virtual machine and click Export.

2. In the Export Virtual Machine dialog box, click Browse, select the appropriate folder, click Select Folder, and then click Export.

In Client Hyper-V, you can import a VM that was exported, or you can import a VM that was copied as long as all of the necessary files are available. Hyper-V Manager provides a wizard for importing VMs. The wizard helps you resolve any problems that you encounter during the import process.

As shown in Figure 3-19, there are three options available when importing a VM:

- **Register The Virtual Machine In-Place (Use The Existing Unique ID)**   This option creates a VM using the files in the existing location.

- **Restore The Virtual Machine (Use The Existing Unique ID)**   This option copies the VM files back to the location from which they were exported and creates a VM using the copied files. This option effectively functions as a restore from backup.

- **Copy The Virtual Machine (Create A New Unique ID)**   This option copies the VM files to a new location that you specify and creates a new VM using the copied files.

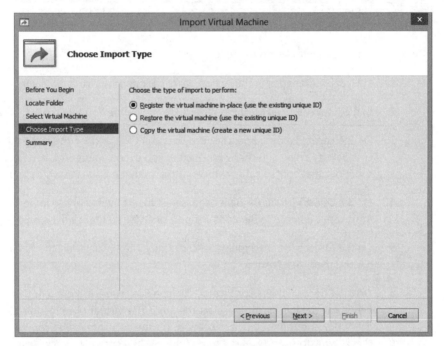

Figure 3-19 Import Virtual Machine Wizard, Choose Import Type page

Inside OUT

Unique ID for VMs

Each VM on a Hyper-V host has a unique ID. Hyper-V uses this unique ID to identify each VM because multiple VMs can have the same name. No two VMs on the same Hyper-V host can have the same unique ID.

> When you import VMs by using the Register In-Place or Restore options, the imported VM is created with the same unique ID that it had when it was exported. These two options are useful in backup and restore scenarios to ensure that you don't accidentally restore multiple copies of the same VM. If you attempt to import a VM and there is a duplicate unique ID, then the process fails and the existing VM isn't affected.
>
> If you want to create multiple copies of a VM, you should use the copy option. The copy option creates a new unique ID for each VM during the import. This can be useful if you have used Sysprep to prepare an image and want to make multiple copies of the exported VM to create a complex environment with multiple servers or client computers.

To copy an exported VM, do the following:

1. In Hyper-V Manager, in the Action pane, click Import Virtual Machine.

2. In the Import Virtual Machine Wizard, on the Before You Begin page, click Next.

3. On the Locate Folder page, click Browse, select the folder containing the VM files, click Select Folder, and then click Next. If you exported the VM, you need to select the subfolder that contains the VM files rather than the folder to which you exported.

4. On the Select Virtual Machine page, select the VM you want to import and click Next. In most cases, a single folder contains only one VM, so there will be only one VM to select.

5. On the Choose Import Type page, click Copy The Virtual Machine (Create A New Unique ID) and then click Next.

6. On the Choose Folders For Virtual Machine Files page, if you do not want to store VM files in the default locations, select the Store The Virtual Machine In A Different Location check box and then select the locations for the virtual machine configuration folder, checkpoint store, and Smart Paging folder. When complete, click Next. The default shared location for these files is suitable for use by multiple VMs because individual folders are created in this location based on the unique ID of each VM.

7. On the Choose Folders To Store Virtual Hard Disks page, click the Browse button, select a storage location for the virtual hard disks, click Select Folders, and click Next. If you attempt to import the same VM multiple times into the default location, you will experience an error because the virtual hard disks are not stored in unique subfolders and each import copies the virtual hard disk without renaming it. To resolve this issue, create individual folders to store the virtual hard disks.

8. On the Summary page, click Finish.

TIP
If you do a copy import of the same VM multiple times, the name of each imported VM is the same. Rename the VMs soon after import so that you are clear on their purpose.

Processing

Each VM is allocated one or more virtual processors. Within a VM, a virtual processor behaves similarly to how a physical processor behaves in a computer. However, a virtual processor is single core. There is no concept of multiple cores for virtual processors in Client Hyper-V. If the VM runs multithreaded applications or multiple applications, it may be beneficial to allocate multiple virtual processors to that VM.

There is no direct relationship between the number of physical processor cores in the Hyper-V host and the number of virtual processors that you can assign to multiple VMs. From a performance perspective, it is recommended that you don't assign more than twice the number of physical processor cores.

The maximum number of virtual processors that you can assign to a single VM is determined by the guest operating system and the number of logical processors in the host. You can never assign a single VM more virtual processors than the number of logical processors in the host. For example, a computer with four physical cores and Hyper-Threading enabled would have eight logical cores. Windows Server 2008 R2 Service Pack 1 and later can be assigned 64 virtual processors, but practically, it is more common to assign 2 to 4 virtual processors to a VM.

➤ For more information about the number of virtual processors supported by various guest operating systems, see Supported Windows Guest Operating Systems for Hyper-V in Windows Server 2012 R2 and Windows 8.1 on the TechNet website at *http://technet.microsoft.com/en-ca/library/dn792027.aspx.*

Regardless of the number of virtual processors allocated to a VM, you can control the percentage of host processing power allocated by using resource control, shown in Figure 3-20. In this example, the host system has a single processor with two physical cores and four logical cores. Two virtual processors have been assigned. In this scenario, two virtual processors can be up to 50 percent of the overall processing capacity of the four logical cores.

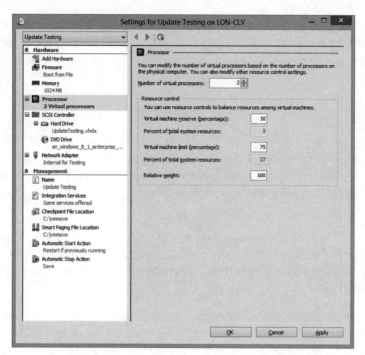

Figure 3-20 Processor settings for a VM

The Virtual Machine Reserve is the percentage of the VM's total processing power that is reserved to be available for that VM. In this example, 10 percent of the VM's total processing power is equal to 5 percent of the host computer's processing power. So, overall, 5 percent of the host's processing power is reserved for this VM.

The Virtual Machine Limit specifies a maximum percentage of a logical core that a VM can consume. In this example, a 75 percent limit means that this VM can consume up to 75 percent of two logical cores, which is 37.5 percent of the total processing capacity of the host.

The Relative Weight is used to allocate processing capacity when you have more virtual processors allocated to VMs than exist in the host. For example, you could run three VMs, each with two virtual processors, for a total of six virtual processors assigned. In a computer with only four logical cores, the Relative Weight is used to divide the real processing capacity among the running VMs. A VM with a weight of 200 is allocated twice as much processing capacity as a VM with a weight of 100.

Dynamic memory

Physical computers have a static amount of memory that does not change until you shut down the computer and add physical RAM. The experience with VMs is the same when you do not configure them to use Dynamic Memory. VMs are assigned a static amount of memory while they are running.

Static memory allocation can result in inefficient use of memory in Hyper-V hosts. A VM configured with static memory uses that amount of host memory, whether it is required or not. For example, a Windows 8.1 VM could be allocated 6 GB of memory but only be using 2 GB of memory. This results in 4 GB of host memory being allocated when it isn't required.

Dynamic memory allows the amount of memory allocated to a VM to increase or decrease based on the needs of the guest operating system. When more memory is required, Hyper-V allocates more memory to the VM. When a VM has excess unused memory, Hyper-V reduces the memory available to the VM. This results in more efficient memory allocation on the host and allows you to run more VMs on a host. You can configure VM memory usage on the Memory Settings page for each VM, as shown in Figure 3-21.

Figure 3-21 Memory settings for a VM

The memory settings you can configure are as follows:

- **Startup RAM**   Use this setting to configure the amount of memory that will be available to the VM at startup. If Dynamic Memory isn't enabled, the VM uses this amount of memory whenever it is running.

- **Enable Dynamic Memory**   Use this setting to configure the VM to use Dynamic Memory. If you enable this setting, the following three options become available:
    - **Minimum RAM**   Use this option to set the minimum amount of memory that the VM can use while it is running. The VM can't use less than this amount. You can decrease this value while the VM is running.
    - **Maximum RAM**   Use this option to set the maximum amount of memory that a VM can use while it is running. The VM can't use more than this amount. You can increase this value while the VM is running.
    - **Memory Buffer**   Use this option to specify the percentage of memory that Client Hyper-V should reserve as a buffer. Client Hyper-V uses the percentage and the current memory demand to determine an amount of memory for the buffer.

- **Memory Weight**   Use this option to specify how to prioritize memory availability for the VM compared to other VMs that are running on the same physical computer.

As with most other VM settings, you can't modify VM memory settings while the VM is running. If Dynamic Memory already is enabled, you can decrease VM minimum RAM settings and increase maximum RAM while the VM is running.

Integration services

Integration services are software installed in guest operating systems to make them Hyper-V–aware. When integration services are installed, the guest operating system has device drivers that are specific to Hyper-V. This allows the guest operating system to use Hyper-V–specific devices such as the VMBus and synthetic network adapters. Without integration services, guest operating systems can use only emulated hardware, which has lower performance.

Guest operating systems with integration services installed also have access to services provided by Hyper-V. As shown in Figure 3-22, the services can be individually enabled and disabled. In most cases, all services will be enabled. In Windows-based guest operating systems, integration services are installed as services.

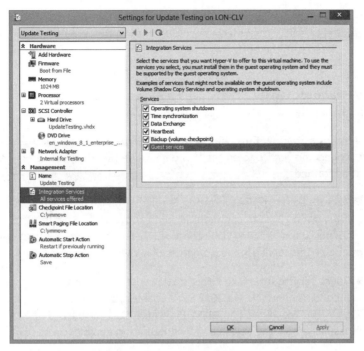

Figure 3-22 Integration services settings for a VM

By default, newer operating systems that are virtualization-aware already include integration services. You can install integration services in older guest operating systems if they are not included. Integration services are provided only for supported guest operating systems. Supported operating systems for Hyper-V in Windows 8.1 include:

- Windows XP with Service Pack 3 or newer client operating systems

- Windows Server 2003 or newer server operating systems

- Various versions of Linux and FreeBSD

The services installed in a Windows-based guest operating system are:

- **Hyper-V Guest Shutdown Service**   This service enables you to shut down the guest operating system in VMs by using the Hyper-V management tools. This removes the need to log on to the guest operating system to shut it down.

- **Hyper-V Time Synchronization Service**   This service synchronizes the time on the VM with the time on the Hyper-V host. If the guest operating system is getting time from a domain, you may want to disable time synchronization.

- **Hyper-V Data Exchange Service**   This service enables registry keys in the HKLM \SOFTWARE\Microsoft\Virtual Machine portion of the registry in guest operating systems to be shared with the host. This is used to provide general information about the VM to the host. It also can be used by software developers.

- **Hyper-V Heartbeat Service**   The Hyper-V host uses this service to verify that a guest operating system that is running in a VM is responding to requests.

- **Hyper-V Volume Shadow Copy Requestor**   When a host-based backup is performed, the host triggers this service to ensure that data within the VM is consistent before the backup is performed.

- **Hyper-V Remote Desktop Virtualization Service**   This service enables the Remote Desktop Virtualization Host to communicate with and manage VMs that are part of a Virtual Desktop Infrastructure (VDI) collection. There is no corresponding option to enable or disable this service in the properties of a VM.

- **Hyper-V Guest Service Interface**   This is a new integration service in Hyper-V for Windows 8.1 and Windows Server 2012 R2. It enables you to copy files to and from a VM through Virtual Machine Connection. Previous to this version of Hyper-V, you could copy only a small amount of text to a VM without using network connectivity.

Inside OUT

Updating integration services

When you apply updates to a Hyper-V host, you need to evaluate whether integration services needs to be updated in the VMs. Older versions of integration services will continue to work properly in most cases but may have performance or stability issues. There is no automated method for updating integration services in Hyper-V. Unless you have an automated software deployment solution such as Microsoft System Center Configuration Manager, you need to update each VM manually.

To update integration services for a Windows 8.1 VM, do the following:

1. Connect to the VM and sign in as a user account with administrator permissions.

2. In the Virtual Machine Connection window, click Action and click Insert Integration Services Setup Disk. This mounts the vmguest.iso image to the VM.

3. If autorun is enabled, integration services setup begins automatically. If autorun isn't enabled, right-click the DVD drive and click Install Hyper-V Integration Services.

4. In the User Account Control window, click Yes.

5. Complete the steps in the wizard to install an updated version of integration services. If the current version of integration services already is installed, a message appears stating that the computer already is running the current version of integration services.

The next version of Hyper-V in Windows 10 simplifies updates for integration services by making them available through Windows Update and Windows Server Update Services (WSUS). This means that you can automatically update integration services without any on-premises automatic update structure.

Managing virtual hard disks

VMs are configured with virtual hard disks to allow them to store data. Virtual hard disks are a file that is stored on a physical hard disk. The VM is configured to use the virtual hard disk file. In the VM, the virtual hard disk appears just as a physical hard disk does for a physical computer. The virtual hard disk can be partitioned and formatted just as a physical disk can.

In generation 1 VMs, virtual hard disks can be attached to the VM by using an IDE controller or a SCSI controller. The boot drive and paging files must be attached to an IDE controller. There is a limit of two devices per IDE controller and a limit of two IDE controllers per VM. So, using only IDE limits you to a maximum of four storage devices (virtual hard disks and DVD drives).

There is no technical advantage to using IDE controllers; it was just a requirement for generation 1 VMs. In fact, there is a small performance boost when using SCSI controllers in generation 1 VMs. Some other advantages of using SCSI controllers are the following:

●   There can be up to four SCSI controllers in a VM and up to 64 storage devices on each SCSI controller for a total maximum of 256 storage devices.

●   Virtual hard disks can be added to and removed from a VM while it is running.

Virtual hard disk formats

The original format for virtual hard disks supported in older virtualization technologies was the VHD file. This type of virtual hard disk still is supported in Hyper-V for Windows 8.1. VMs originally created using this disk format can be moved to Client Hyper-V. The main limitation of VHD files is that they are limited to 2 TB.

The VHDX format for virtual hard disks was introduced in Hyper-V for Windows 8 and Windows Server 2012. This type of virtual disk isn't compatible with older virtualization technologies. In Client Hyper-V, you can create VHD and VHDX virtual hard disks as shown in Figure 3-23.

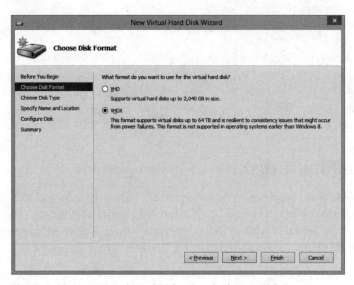

Figure 3-23 New Virtual Hard Disk Wizard, Choose Disk Format page

The VHDX format has the following advantages over the VHD format:

- Support for larger virtual hard disks, up to 64 TB

- Better resilience to corruption during events such as power outages

- Improved performance on large sector disks (standard for hard disks produced starting in 2011)

- Improved performance for dynamically expanding drives

- Support for dynamically trimming drives with unused allocated space

TIP

For new VMs, you always should use the VHDX format unless you expect the VM to be moved to an older virtualization technology that does not support the VHDX format.

Inside OUT
Pass-through disks

Client Hyper-V also supports the use of pass-through disks for VM storage. A pass-through disk allows you to mount a physical hard disk attached to the Hyper-V host directly to a VM without creating a VHD or VHDX file.

In older virtualization technologies that do not support the VHDX format, pass-through disks were used to provide access to disks larger than 2 TB. In some cases, they also provided performance benefits. With the performance improvements and increased size of the VHDX format for virtual hard disks, pass-through disks are seldom required.

Pass-through disks can be useful for Client Hyper-V to attach USB storage from the host directly to the VM. In this way, you can provide a VM with access to files such as application installation files when there is no network connectivity available and the installation files are not in an ISO.

Fixed and dynamically expanding disks

When you create a new virtual hard disk, you have the option to create it as a fixed-size disk or as a dynamically expanding disk, as shown in Figure 3-24. A fixed-size virtual hard disk is created on the physical hard disk as a VHD or VHDX file that has a size matching the size of the contents that can be stored in the fixed-size virtual hard disk. For example, if you create a 100 GB fixed-size disk, then a 100 GB VHD or VHDX file is created on the physical hard disk.

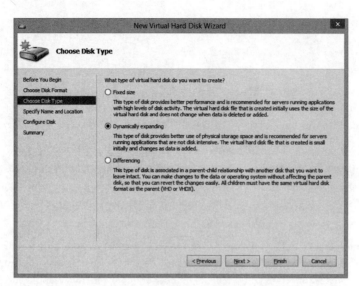

Figure 3-24 New Virtual Hard Disk Wizard, Choose Disk Type page

A dynamically expanding disk is created as a small VHD or VHDX file that can expand up to the full size specified for the virtual hard disk. For example, if you create a 100 GB dynamically expanding VHDX file, the initial size of the file is only 4 MB. As data is added to the virtual hard drive, the VHDX file expands to store that data, up to the maximum size of 100 GB.

The following are some considerations for fixed and dynamically expanding disks:

- **It is faster to create dynamically expanding virtual hard disks**   When you create a virtual hard disk, the space needs to be allocated on the physical hard disk. A fixed-size virtual hard disk needs to allocate much more physical space at creation time than a dynamically expanding disk does.

- **Dynamically expanding virtual hard disks are more space efficient**   Fixed-size virtual hard disks contain large amounts of unused space. This unused space in the fixed-size virtual hard disk is allocated on the physical hard disk and unavailable for other VMs or other purposes. Dynamically expanding virtual hard disks do not contain significant unused space because they only expand to accommodate data that is placed in them.

- **Dynamically expanding VHDX files have similar performance to fixed-size virtual hard disks**   When using VHD-format virtual hard disks, there is a significant performance advantage to using fixed-size virtual hard disks over dynamically expanding virtual hard disks. Dynamically expanding virtual hard disks in the VHDX format have similar performance to fixed-size virtual hard disks. The New Virtual Hard Disk Wizard defaults to using fixed-size for VHD-format virtual hard disks and dynamically expanding for VHDX-format virtual hard disks.

- **Dynamically expanding VHDX files can shrink dynamically**   Dynamically expanding VHD files would expand, but they would never contract to eliminate unused space in the VHD file. A VHDX-formatted virtual hard disk can dynamically shrink to free up physical hard disk space when there is unused white space in the VHDX file.

Differencing disks

A differencing virtual hard disk is a virtual hard disk that is linked to another virtual hard disk in a parent-child relationship. The parent virtual hard disk sometimes is referred to as a base disk, because it is the starting point and never changes. The differencing disk starts empty, and all disk changes are added to the differencing disk. The differencing disk is configured as a virtual hard disk in the VM.

A differencing virtual hard disk stores changes for the parent disk and provides a way to isolate changes without altering the parent disk. When you use a differencing virtual hard disk, you can access all the data from the parent disk, and changes you make only write to the differencing virtual hard disk, not to the parent disk. In other words, reads for modified data are served from the differencing virtual hard disk, and reads of all other data are served from the parent virtual hard disk. Metadata is used in both cases to determine from where data should be read, which results in differencing virtual hard disks having slower performance than fixed-size or dynamically expanding virtual hard disks. Differencing virtual hard disks must use the same format as the parent disks—either VHD or VHDX.

A differencing virtual hard disk expands dynamically as data that is intended for the parent disk writes to the differencing virtual hard disk. The base/differencing relationship is based on the integrity of the base disk. Any change made to the parent disk invalidates all differencing virtual hard disks that are linked to that parent. The parent disk is specified when you create the differencing virtual hard disk, as shown in Figure 3-25.

CHAPTER 3

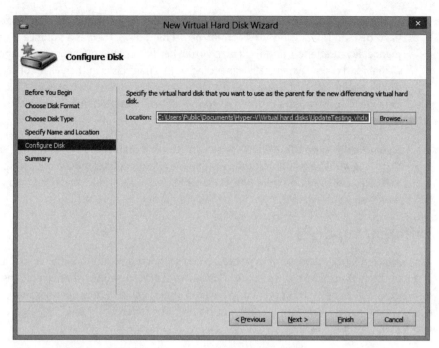

Figure 3-25 New Virtual Hard Disk Wizard, Configure Disk page

If you move a parent virtual hard disk, the differencing disk can't be used, because the dif-ferencing disk is linked to the parent at a location that no longer exists. You can reconnect the differencing virtual hard disk to the parent by inspecting it. When you inspect the differencing virtual hard disk, you are given the option to identify the new location of the parent, as shown in Figure 3-26.

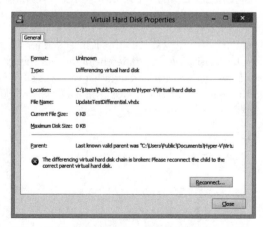

Figure 3-26 Option to reconnect differencing disk

Despite the slower performance of differencing disks, they can be useful for Client Hyper-V in scenarios in which your disk space is limited. For example, if you are using an SSD hard disk to increase performance, it typically is much smaller than a spinning hard disk. Let's say that you need to create 5 or 10 Windows Server 2012 R2 VMs for testing various scenarios.

The core operating system files of each Windows Server 2012 R2 installation are about 10 GB. You could create one parent virtual hard disk with the base installation of Windows Server 2012 R2 that is sysprepped. Then, create a differential disk from that parent for each VM. If you are creating 10 VMs, using differencing disks means that the core operating system files are stored only once instead of 10 times. As a result, about 90 GB of disk space is saved.

Creating virtual hard disks

You can create virtual hard disks for Client Hyper-V in Hyper-V Manager and by using Windows PowerShell. Within Hyper-V Manager, you can create new virtual hard disks from the Actions pane or when adding a virtual hard disk to a VM. In both cases, Hyper-V Manager opens the New Virtual Hard Disk Wizard.

To create a new dynamically expanding VHDX virtual hard disk in Hyper-V Manager, perform the following steps:

1. In Hyper-V Manager, with the Hyper-V host selected in the navigation pane, in the Actions pane, click New and then click Hard Disk.

2. In the New Virtual Hard Disk Wizard, on the Before You Begin page, click Next.

3. On the Choose Disk Format page, click VHDX and then click Next.

4. On the Choose Disk Type page, click Dynamically Expanding and then click Next.

5. On the Specify Name And Location page, in the Name box, type the name of the new VHDX file.

6. In the Location box, type or browse to the folder in which you want create the new VHDX file and then click Next.

7. On the Configure Disk page, click Create A New Blank Virtual Hard Disk, type the appropriate size in the Size box, and then click Next.

CHAPTER 3

TIP

The Configure Disk page also gives you the option to copy the contents of a physical disk or an existing virtual hard disk to the virtual hard disk that you are creating. These options are seldom used. If you use either of these options, it can take significant time to copy the data.

8.   On the Summary page, click Finish.

To create a new virtual hard disk by using Windows PowerShell, you use the New-VHD cmdlet. Table 3-6 shows some of the parameters that you can use with the New-VHD cmdlet.

Table 3-6 New-VHD cmdlet parameters

Parameter	Description
Path	Specifies the location and name of the virtual hard disk file that is being created. This is required.
Fixed	Specifies that a fixed-size virtual hard disk is being created.
Dynamic	Specifies that a dynamically expanding virtual hard disk is being created.
Differencing	Specifies that a differencing virtual hard disk is being created.
ParentPath	Specifies the location of the parent for a differencing virtual hard disk
SizeBytes	Specifies the size of the virtual hard disk to be created. You can specify the unit. If not specified, the unit defaults to bytes.

NOTE

There is no parameter for the New-VHD cmdlet to specify whether the format is VHD or VHDX. The format is determined from the file name in the path that you provide.

The following example creates a new 100 GB dynamically expanding VHDX-format virtual hard disk:

```
New-VHD –Path D:\VM\TestMachine\TestMachine.vhdx –Dynamic –SizeBytes 100GB
```

Editing virtual hard disks

After a virtual hard disk has been in use for a period of time, you may find that you need to edit the virtual hard disk to meet new requirements. You can do this via the Edit Virtual Hard Disk Wizard shown in Figure 3-27. Start the Edit Virtual Hard Disk Wizard from the Actions pane in Hyper-V Manager.

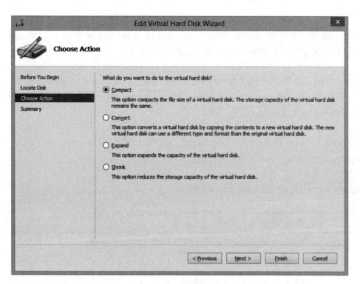

Figure 3-27 Edit Virtual Hard Disk Wizard

You can use the Edit Virtual Hard Disk Wizard to:

- **Compact a VHD file**   If you have a dynamically expanding VHD-formatted virtual hard disk that has unused white space, you can compact it to shrink the size of the VHD file on disk. You also can compact a differential disk with unused white space. This option isn't relevant for VHDX-formatted dynamically expanding virtual hard disks because they dynamically shrink when there is white space.

- **Convert a virtual hard disk**   You can convert an existing virtual hard disk to a new type if needed. You specify the format (VHD or VHDX) and type (fixed or dynamically expanding), but not the size. The wizard creates a virtual hard disk with the format and type that you specify and then copies the contents of the existing virtual hard disk into the new virtual hard disk. To perform this action, you need sufficient physical disk space to have the old and new virtual hard disks exist at the same time.

- **Expand a virtual hard disk**   If you determine that a fixed or dynamically expand-ing virtual hard disk does not have enough capacity, you can expand it. For example, if you created a 60 GB disk that is now almost full, you can expand it to 120 GB. You can expand a virtual hard disk while the VM is running.

- **Shrink a virtual hard disk**   If you have created a fixed or dynamically expanding vir-tual hard disk that is larger than necessary, you can shrink the virtual hard disk capacity. To do this, there must be unpartitioned space at the end of the disk. This may require you to shrink existing partitions in the VM. This option isn't available for VHD-formatted virtual hard disks.

CHAPTER 3

- **Merge**   Use this option to merge a differencing disk with its parent to create a single virtual disk. The content from the differencing disk is added to the parent. Don't perform this action if you have multiple differencing disks using the same parent.

- **Reconnect**   You can reconnect a differencing disk to its parent disk if the parent disk has been moved or renamed. The option only appears when the link from the differencing disk to the parent is broken.

You also can edit virtual hard disks by using Windows PowerShell cmdlets. Table 3-7 lists several cmdlets that you can use .

Table 3-7 Cmdlets for editing virtual hard disks

Cmdlet	Description
Resize-VHD	Use to expand or shrink a virtual hard disk.
Convert-VHD	Use to convert virtual hard disks to a new format or type.
Optimize-VHD	Use to compact a virtual hard disk.
Merge-VHD	Use to merge a differencing disk with its parent.
Test-VHD	Use to verify that a virtual hard disk does not have any problems.
Set-VHD	Use to update the parent path of a differencing disk.

Storage Quality of Service

By default, each VM that runs on Client Hyper-V can use as much disk throughput as the disk subsystem can provide. If you're running a single VM, this usually isn't an issue. However, when you are running multiple VMs and any of them run storage-intensive applications, performance of the disk can drop dramatically.

In older versions of Client Hyper-V in Windows 8, it was not possible to limit I/O operations per second (IOPS) per VM. If a VM had an application that was storage-intensive, and if there was a large number of read and write operations to the storage, the VM could monopolize the Client Hyper-V computer, and other VMs would have slower access to storage. In Windows 8.1, Client Hyper-V includes an option to configure Quality of Service (QoS) parameters when VMs access the storage so that you can provide enough IOPS to each VM.

You can configure storage QoS for each virtual hard disk. By specifying the maximum IOPS value on the Advanced Features page of the virtual hard disk, you can balance and throttle the storage I/O across VMs and prevent a VM from consuming excessive storage I/O operations, which could affect other VMs. You also can configure the minimum (reserved) IOPS value and receive a notification when the IOPS for that virtual hard disk is below the configured value. QoS management settings are effective as soon as you configure them on the Advanced Features page of the virtual hard disk. In addition, the VM metrics infrastructure updates with storage-related parameters so that you can monitor the performance and chargeback for used resources.

To configure QoS for a virtual hard disk, take the following steps:

1. In Hyper-V Manager, right-click the VM using the virtual hard disk and click Settings.

2. In the Settings window for the VM, in the left pane, expand the virtual hard disk and click Advanced Features.

3. In the right pane, select the Enable Quality Of Service Management check box.

4. In the Minimum box, type the minimum IOPS that you want reserved for the virtual hard disk.

5. In the Maximum box, type the maximum IOPS that you want the virtual hard disk to use.

6. Click OK.

Managing checkpoints

Checkpoints are a Hyper-V feature that you can use to create a point-in-time snapshot of a VM and then revert to it if needed. In previous versions of Hyper-V, this feature was called Snapshots, and you still can see references to Snapshots in Windows 8.1.

The primary benefit of checkpoints in Client Hyper-V is that you can use them to create hierarchies of changes, and then you can revert to them at any time. Checkpoints can be useful in some scenarios, such as when testing Windows operating system updates or training environments.

You need to be careful when using checkpoints for any type of integrated system. This is because in an integrated system, changes are made to multiple computers at the same time. This means that if you have a test environment built in Client Hyper-V, you may need to take checkpoints of all computers in the test environment rather than just the computer on which you are making changes. For example, let's say you have a test environment with a domain controller and a member server on which you are going to install applications. When you install an application on the member server, the application updates Active Directory on the domain controller. To be able to revert from this properly, you need to create a checkpoint on both the domain controller and the member server before installing the application. If you revert to a snapshot on the member server but not on the domain controller before the application installation, then Active Directory changes are made already and the application installation may fail on your next attempt.

You can create a checkpoint by using any of the following methods:

- In Hyper-V Manager, right-click a VM and then click Checkpoint (or, in the Action pane, click Checkpoint).

- In Virtual Machine Connection, click Checkpoint in the Action menu.

- In Windows PowerShell, run the Checkpoint-VM cmdlet and then specify the VM for which you want to create a checkpoint.

You can create checkpoints for either stopped or running VMs.

How checkpoints are created

Checkpoints consist of several files that represent the complete state of a VM at a certain moment in time. Because you can't modify a previous state, checkpoints are read-only, and you can't modify one after you create it. You can only view a checkpoint, change its name, or delete it.

When you create a checkpoint, Client Hyper-V performs the following procedure in the background:

1. Pauses the VM.

2. For each virtual hard disk that the VM is using, Client Hyper-V creates a differencing virtual hard disk, configures it to use the VM's virtual hard disk as a parent, and then updates VM settings to use the created differencing virtual hard disk.

3. Creates a copy of the VM configuration file.

4. Resumes running the VM.

5. Saves the content of the VM memory to disk.

Because a VM is paused before a checkpoint is created, you can't create a checkpoint of a VM that is in a paused state. As the VM resumes, while the memory is saving to the disk, Client Hyper-V intercepts memory changes that have not yet written to the disk, writes the memory pages to the disk, and then modifies the VM memory. Creating a checkpoint can take considerable time, depending on the VM memory, physical disk speed, and what is running on the VM. However, the process of checkpoint creation is transparent, and a VM does not experience any outage.

A VM checkpoint consists of the following files:

- VM configuration file (*.xml)

- VM saved state file (*.vsv)

- VM memory contents (*.bin)

- Checkpoint differencing virtual hard disks (*.avhd)

Client Hyper-V creates a saved state file and a memory content file for a VM only if a checkpoint is created while the VM is running, not if the VM is turned off. The VM memory contents file is the size of the memory that has been allocated to the VM.

The location of VM checkpoint files is configured for each VM and, by default, is the location where the VM configuration is stored. When you create the first checkpoint, Client Hyper-V creates a Snapshots subfolder and stores checkpoint files there. You can modify the location of the checkpoint files only until the first checkpoint is created. After this, the checkpoint file location setting is read-only. You can modify this setting only after deleting all checkpoints or by using the Move Wizard.

Using checkpoints

You can take more than one checkpoint of a VM. In fact, you can have a hierarchy of checkpoints. Then you can go back and apply any checkpoint that you have for a VM to access it in that state. To view the checkpoints created for a VM, as shown in Figure 3-28, select the VM in Hyper-V Manager.

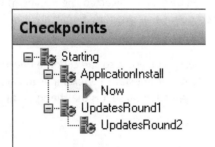

Figure 3-28 VM checkpoints in Hyper-V Manager

When you select a checkpoint, you have the following options available in the Actions pane of Hyper-V Manager:

- **Settings** This option opens the VM settings in effect for that checkpoint. All of the settings are read-only because you can't change a configuration that was used in the past. The only settings that you can modify are the checkpoint name and the notes that are associated with the checkpoint.

- **Apply** This option applies a checkpoint to a VM, which means that you return the VM to the state in which it existed when the checkpoint was taken. When you apply a checkpoint, any changes in the VM since the last checkpoint was made are lost. Before applying a checkpoint, Client Hyper-V prompts you to create a new checkpoint of the current state to avoid possible data loss.

- **Export** This option exports a VM checkpoint, which creates an exact copy of the VM at the moment you created the checkpoint.

- **Rename** This option renames a checkpoint to provide information about the state of a VM when you created the checkpoint. The checkpoint name is independent of the checkpoint content, and, by default, it contains the date and time of checkpoint creation. You can provide names that are more descriptive than the date and time to remember the purpose of each checkpoint.

- **Delete Checkpoint** This option deletes a checkpoint. Use this option if you no longer want to be able to revert a VM to the state in which it was when you created the checkpoint.

- **Delete Checkpoint Subtree** This option deletes the selected checkpoint and any checkpoints that originate from it. Checkpoints that originate from it are listed below it in the Checkpoint pane.

When you right-click a VM with at least one checkpoint, you also can click the Revert option. This returns a VM to the checkpoint previous to its current state. For example, in Figure 3-28, if you revert, the checkpoint ApplicationInstall is applied because it is the checkpoint previous to Now in the tree of checkpoints.

Considerations for using checkpoints

When you use checkpoints, you should consider the following:

- **Each checkpoint creates a differencing virtual hard disk**   When you create a checkpoint of a VM, the VM is configured with a differencing virtual hard disk even if it previously used a fixed-size virtual hard disk. Differencing virtual hard disks might perform more slowly than normal disks because they need to read from the two files (base and differencing).

- **Checkpoints require additional storage space**   If you create a checkpoint of a running VM, it also contains a VM memory snapshot. Creating multiple checkpoints can use up a large amount of storage space.

- **Checkpoints do not replace backups**   Although you can use checkpoints to revert a VM to an earlier point in time, you should not consider them backups. Even if you use checkpoints, you should perform regular backups for any data that is considered important.

- **If you no longer need a checkpoint, you should delete it**   However, this can cause merging of differencing virtual hard disks. In Windows 8.1, the merging process happens asynchronously in the background while the VM is running.

- **A VM is limited to 50 checkpoints**   In reality, there should never be a need to use 50 checkpoints. Practically speaking, performance of the differencing disks likely will suffer severely long before you reach 50 checkpoints. The number of checkpoints also may be limited based on the available storage.

- **Understand how installed applications react to checkpoints**   To ensure that the applications in your test environment function properly, make sure you understand how application updates and time changes affect all VMs.

- **Randomness of cryptographic applications can be reduced**   If randomness data is generated immediately after restoring a checkpoint, the VM will be in the same state and may generate the same "random" data.

Inside OUT

Optimizing VM performance

In a server-based implementation of Hyper-V, a lot of planning goes into the design of the system to ensure that sufficient resources are available to run the VMs with adequate performance. Often, Client Hyper-V is implemented on the fly without much planning. This can result in poorly performing VMs. Use the following guidelines when implementing Client Hyper-V:

- Use dynamic memory to optimize memory allocation.

- Ensure that each VM has sufficient memory to prevent paging file utilization, which increases disk I/O.

- Use fast disks, preferably SSD drives, to ensure sufficient disk I/O.

- Using multiple hard disks can increase disk I/O, but a single SSD drive is still faster.

- Use differential disks to minimize storage utilization when the same operating system is used for multiple VMs.

- Minimize the use of checkpoints to avoid impacting disk performance and storage utilization.

CHAPTER 4

Planning and implementing App-V

Virtualization usage has been expanding throughout the last several years. Although many IT administrators are now familiar with desktop and server virtualization, application virtualization is a lesser-known technology that is expanding rapidly. Simply put, application virtualization is a technology that delivers applications to computing devices in isolated containers without the need to perform a standard application installation on each computing device.

App-V provides a new way to deliver applications to users, a new way to centrally manage applications, and additional application capabilities for complex environments. Virtualizing applications, when appropriately planned and implemented, is an effective supplement to desktop and server virtualization and can help organizations move closer to cloud computing.

Overview of App-V

Microsoft Application Virtualization (App-V) is Microsoft's application virtualization technology. It is part of the Microsoft Desktop Optimization Pack (MDOP). MDOP is available to Microsoft Software Assurance customers and to Microsoft MSDN subscribers. It is a suite of desktop optimization applications that help IT administrators deploy, manage, and troubleshoot desktop computing environments. The newest version, at the time of this writing, is App-V 5.0 Service Pack 3.

Benefits of App-V

You know that App-V is Microsoft's application virtualization technology, and you have an idea of how to access it. But, to fully appreciate it, you should have a good understanding of its capabilities. The core capabilities that you can deliver with App-V are the following:

- **Run multiple versions of applications at the same time**   You can use App-V to run different versions of applications concurrently on the same computer. For example, it's possible to run Internet Explorer 9, Internet Explorer 10, and Internet Explorer 11 concurrently if they all are set up as App-V applications; otherwise, you can't run multiple versions of Internet Explorer side by side on the same computer. It's also possible to use App-V in conjunction with Remote Desktop Services (RDS). This allows users to run applications side by side on Remote Desktop Session Host (RD Session Host) servers.

- **Minimize application conflicts**   Sometimes two or more applications conflict with one another because of dynamic-link library (DLL) or application programming interface (API) conflicts. When you deliver these applications as App-V applications, however, there isn't a conflict because each App-V application runs in its own isolated environment.

- **Simplify application removal**   App-V applications do not install locally, which makes it easier to remove them. Clean removal isn't always possible with applications that install directly on Windows-based clients, even if an application has been designed to remove all files and settings when it uninstalls. Virtualized applications are removed easily after a user signs out from a computer.

- **Simplify application upgrades**   Instead of upgrading a locally installed application on all computers in your organization with a hotfix, service pack, or new version, the modular nature of virtualized applications means that you can replace one version of an application with an updated version with less effort. You only need to update an application on the App-V server(s), and clients receive the latest version of the application from the publishing server the next time they launch the application.

- **Minimize license-compliance risks**   App-V has application metering functionality that enables you to detect every use of a virtualized application to ensure license compliance.

- **Scale infrastructure**   You can add publishing servers to an App-V deployment as necessary to ensure that service levels are maintained as demand grows.

- **Take advantage of client hardware resources**   Even though App-V applications do not install locally, they can use a local computer's processor and RAM resources. In environments where client computers have adequate hardware resources, this can create a better experience for users than running applications on an RD Session Host server would.

- **Allow users to use roaming applications**   If applications stream with App-V rather than install locally, users can sign in to any computer that has an App-V client and quickly access their applications. You also can configure App-V to work with user virtualization to allow users to have application settings and data for App-V applications that roam across client computers.

- **Give users quick access to their applications**   Imagine a scenario in which a user needs to have an application installed. In many environments, a routine application installation requires several steps, such as copying the installation files to the client computer, manually performing the installation, manually performing application updates, and cleaning up the installation files. With App-V, you can just add the users to a group, and they can immediately run the application through App-V.

Differences between standard and virtualized applications

In a traditional IT environment, applications are installed on each computing device. For this discussion, we'll refer to the traditional installed application as a standard application. During a standard application installation, the computing device is modified to meet the application's requirements. For example, a common installation of a standard application would include the following steps:

The application's files are copied   During the installation, the installer copies the necessary application files to a specified folder. During this process, the files often are uncompressed first.

The registry is modified to support the application   Most applications add to the registry to support the installation and running of the application. In addition, it's common for existing registry keys and values to be modified to support automatic application startup on boot and to set any required dependencies.

DLL files are registered   Often, .dll files must be registered during the installation.

Permissions are configured   You often need to set permissions to configure which user(s) can run the application, which profiles the shortcuts are added to, and which users can modify configuration files.

Shortcuts are added to the device   Many applications add a shortcut to the Start screen, desktop, and taskbar. Additionally, it is common for applications to add a tray icon for quick user access.

App-V applications, which are virtualized, aren't installed onto computing devices. Instead, they are packaged for deployment. In App-V, packaging an application for deployment is known as sequencing an application. Later in this chapter, we'll discuss sequencing further. For now, let's examine the differences between an App-V application deployed to a comput-ing device and a standard application installed locally on a computing device. For applications deployed with App-V, the following characteristics highlight the different methods by which applications interact with the computing device:

App-V applications run in their own isolated environment   This reduces application con-flicts and application crashes impacting other applications or the operating system and pro-vides the foundation to allow multiple versions of applications to run at the same time.

CHAPTER 4

App-V applications use a virtual registry   This reduces installation difficulties and application conflicts and improves the stability of a client computer because applications aren't sharing a single registry.

App-V applications use virtual file systems   This reduces conflicts by ensuring that applications don't overwrite shared files.

App-V applications use virtual services   This also reduces conflicts because virtual services do not have dependencies on other non-virtual services and provide isolation from other virtual services.

App-V applications are installed by being packaged and delivered to computing devices. App-V applications only need to be updated once, by updating the application's package on the App-V server. By reducing the number of times you have to install and update an application, you can greatly reduce the number of hours required to manage your application infrastructure.

Placing and functionality of the virtualization engine

Virtual applications require access to resources on a host computer. Access typically uses a system request that a virtualization engine needs to intercept. The engine provides functions for capturing an application's system call and manipulating it where needed.

Interception in user mode

Applications run in user mode and perform operations on system services that reside in kernel mode. When an interception occurs in user mode, the virtualization engine must be placed over the native API layer. Some applications call the functions of the native API directly instead of by using Windows API.

One advantage of the user mode strategy is that the virtualization engine doesn't have to filter between system calls of different applications. The virtualization engine only works with an application that it built for the virtual environment.

Interception in kernel mode

In contrast, if the virtualization engine operates in kernel mode, it can intercept all system calls before they reach Windows executive services. The advantage is that it is easy to loosen the isolation of applications and let them share the same virtual environment. This enables you to create dependencies between packages, similar to working with middleware or plug-ins. However, the agent that builds the virtual environment must install natively on a computer to gain the required privileges for an interception in kernel mode. In this case, all applications that run on the host machine are affected. Furthermore, the virtualization layer captures system calls from all applications and must filter the processes to respond to every call correctly.

App-V implements a hybrid approach by identifying the locations of resources that the application requires. While the application is running, the virtualization engine ensures that function calls are modified only if they request a path inside the virtual file system or a key inside the virtual registry. When the engine runs in kernel mode, it also must check which package to consult to find the rules, because it will receive function calls from several running applications that belong to different packages.

The virtualization layer must intercept and redirect requests to the file system and registry to virtual counterparts that contain the files and keys that belong to a certain application. To decide which function calls to intercept and which to handle as usual, the virtualization layer needs rules. These rules generate when the App-V Sequencer, which collects all the files and registry keys that the installer creates or modifies, monitors an application's installation. Then, at the application's runtime, the virtualization engine ensures that function calls are modified only if they request a path inside the virtual file system or a key inside the virtual registry.

Application virtualization infrastructure

The infrastructure technologies of an App-V deployment are extensive, based on the deployment model that you choose. They work together to provide the complete suite of App-V technologies. It is important to familiarize yourself with all of the technologies, the typical life cycle of a virtual application, the deployment models, and some of the characteristics of packages and content packages.

App-V application life cycle

To effectively manage your virtual application infrastructure, you need to plan for the life cycle of your virtual applications. Without an effective life cycle, you may end up with application sprawl—a situation in which you have too many applications to manage. To avoid this, you should spend ample planning time designing and documenting an operational framework for your virtual application life cycle. In this section, we'll discuss the four phases of the virtual application life cycle: sequencing, publishing and deployment, updating, and termination.

Application sequencing

The App-V Sequencer is one of the primary applications of an App-V deployment. You use it to create virtual application packages. Then, you deploy the packages to your App-V clients. It is important to consider the following before you begin deploying the sequencer and sequencing applications:

- **Prerequisites**   If the computer that runs the sequencer isn't running Windows 8 or newer or Windows Server 2012 or newer, then it must have the following software installed prior to installing the sequencer. Note that the App-V client installation automatically will install the Visual C++ prerequisites.

  - Visual C++ Redistributable Package for Visual Studio 2013

  - Visual C++ 2005 Redistributable

  - Microsoft .NET Framework 4

  - Windows PowerShell 3.0

  - Microsoft KB2533623 hotfix

- **Windows 8 or newer or Windows Server 2012 or newer**   If the computer that runs the sequencer is running Windows 8 or newer or Windows Server 2012 or newer, it already has the prerequisite software.

- **Match the hardware and software**   The computer that runs the sequencer should have a hardware and software configuration that matches the App-V client computers. For example, if all of your App-V client computers run Windows 8.1, you should install the sequencer on similar computer hardware that runs Windows 8.1.

- **Use a virtual machine**   When possible, use a virtual machine (VM) as the computer that runs the sequencer. This allows you to take a snapshot of the VM prior to sequencing an application. Then, after you finish sequencing an application, you should revert the VM to the snapshot. This allows you to sequence an application with the same baseline configuration, which minimizes issues. Although the sequencer will allow you to sequence multiple applications without reverting the sequencer to a baseline configuration, it will warn you that you may encounter issues.

- **Multiple sequencers**   If you have multiple operating system versions running the App-V client, you seriously should consider having multiple sequencers. This enables you to sequence applications on the same operating system to which you will deploy or stream the applications.

Application publishing and deployment

After you sequence an application, you need to publish it and deliver it to the clients. Publishing a virtual application makes the application available to App-V clients. Before the actual publishing process, you need to be aware of the different methods that you can use based on the type of App-V deployment you have.

CHAPTER 4

Stand-alone deployment model

In the stand-alone model, you need to add the App-V package of the application to clients. You can do this by using the Add-AppVClientPackage Windows PowerShell cmdlet. For example, if you have an App-V package named 7-Zip.appv located at \\tt-util-01\share\7-Zip.appv, you can run the following command to add the package:

```
Add-AppVClientPackage -Path \\tt-util-01\share\7-Zip.appv
```

After running the command, the output will show the details of the package added. In fact, the output is the same as if you were to run the `Get-AppVClientPackage -Name 7-Zip` Windows PowerShell command. The output is shown in Figure 4-1.

```
PackageId            : 30252a91-5cc5-419a-bcfb-645c942df001
VersionId            : 5c57388f-d692-49f0-a609-25dcb6e3e690
Name                 : 7-Zip
Version              : 0.0.0.1
Path                 : \\tt-util-01\share\7-Zip.appv
IsPublishedToUser    : False
UserPending          : False
IsPublishedGlobally  : False
GlobalPending        : False
InUse                : False
InUseByCurrentUser   : False
PackageSize          : 4872031
PercentLoaded        : 10
IsLoading            : False
HasAssetIntelligence : False
```

Figure 4-1 Adding a package

In the output, notice that the IsPublishedToUser property is set to False. This is an important detail because while it is set to False, the user won't see or be able to use the virtual application. After you've added the package, the client will begin receiving the files that make up the package. The data will be stored locally on the client. You can look at the %ProgramData%\App-V directory to see data from the package.

The next step is to publish the application. However, you can't publish an application until the application has been added to the client. Once you are ready to publish, you can use the `Publish-AppVClientPackage` Windows PowerShell cmdlet. For example, if you added a package named 7-Zip, you can publish it to the client by running the following Windows PowerShell command:

```
Publish-AppVClientPackage -Name 7-Zip
```

Once you run that, the output will be similar to when you added the package. The key difference is that the IsPublishedToUser property will be updated to a value of True, as shown in Figure 4-2.

CHAPTER 4

```
PackageId            : 30252a91-5cc5-419a-bcfb-645c942df001
VersionId            : 5c57388f-d692-49f0-a609-25dcb6e3e690
Name                 : 7-Zip
Version              : 0.0.0.1
Path                 : \\tt-util-01\share\7-Zip.appv
IsPublishedToUser    : True
UserPending          : False
IsPublishedGlobally  : False
GlobalPending        : False
InUse                : False
InUseByCurrentUser   : False
PackageSize          : 4872031
PercentLoaded        : 20
IsLoading            : False
HasAssetIntelligence : True
```

Figure 4-2 Publishing a package

After you publish the package, the application becomes available to the user. If shortcuts are configured for the package, they will begin to be displayed after publishing the package.

Full infrastructure model

In the full infrastructure model, the publishing process is a bit more automated, especially when you are dealing with a large number of virtual applications. The high-level process to publish an application is shown below. Note that the first step involving Group Policy is a one-time step in a new full infrastructure model and would not need to be performed for each application that you want to publish.

1. Create a new Group Policy Object (GPO) and modify the App-V–related GPO settings for your environment. Link it to the computers that have the App-V client software. At a minimum, you should configure an App-V publishing server in the GPO so that App-V clients will automatically be configured for a publishing server.

2. Add the application package on the App-V management portal. Configure the settings based on your environment. At a minimum, you need to ensure that the users have access to the application and that the application is published. You can configure access by right-clicking the application and then clicking Edit Active Directory Access.

3. Publish the application. To publish an application from the management portal, right-click it and then click Publish. You also can publish an application by using Windows PowerShell. For example, to publish an App-V package named 7-Zip, you can run the `Publish-AppvServerPackage –Name 7-Zip` command.

4. Sync the clients or wait for the next automatic sync. To immediately sync a client with an App-V publishing server named TT-UTIL-01, run the `Sync-AppvPublishingServer –Name TT-UTIL-01` Windows PowerShell command.

Configuration Manager model

If you use App-V and Configuration Manager to manage and deliver applications, then the steps to publish an application are different from other App-V models. The following high-level steps describe the process of publishing by using Configuration Manager.

1. In the Configuration Manager console, create a new application.

2. On the General page of the Create New Application Wizard, configure the application type to be Microsoft Application Virtualization (App-V) Client 5.0. Then, browse to the location of the .appv package that you want to publish. Also, ensure that the user and deployment .xml configuration files are in the same location as the .appv file. By default, the name of the user configuration file is <app>_UserConfig.xml. For example, if the name of the .appv file is 7-Zip.appv, then the name of the user configuration file is 7-Zip_UserConfig.xml. By default, the name of the deployment configuration file is <app>_DeploymentConfig.xml. For example, if the name of the .appv file is 7-Zip.appv, then the name of the deployment configuration file is 7-Zip_DeploymentConfig.xml.

3. Complete the Create New Application Wizard by specifying application details or maintaining the default values.

4. Distribute the application to Configuration Manager distribution points so that clients can obtain the application from the nearest distribution point.

5. Deploy the application to clients. You can deploy the application as a streaming application if you have a full infrastructure App-V deployment model. Otherwise, you can opt for the download and execute method. Each method has pros and cons. See *http://technet.microsoft.com/en-us/library/jj822982.aspx* for more information on the two deployment methods.

Application update

One ongoing maintenance task that you'll need to perform is updating applications. An application update, sometimes called an application upgrade, occurs when a software company releases a newer version of the application. Often, companies release newer versions of software to fix security issues or provide new or enhanced functionality. In a standard application deployment, in which applications are installed on every computer, you need to perform the update on every computer. In a virtualized application deployment, in which applications are packaged and delivered by App-V, you only need to update the packaged application on the App-V Sequencer and then update the distribution method with the updated package.

To update an existing App-V application with the App-V Sequencer, perform the following steps:

1. Run the App-V Sequencer on the client computer that you use for sequencing.

CHAPTER 4

2. Click the Modify An Existing Virtual Application Package option, shown in Figure 4-3.

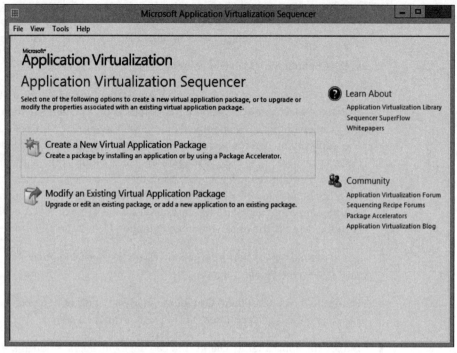

Figure 4-3 App-V Sequencer

3. On the Select Task page, shown in Figure 4-4, keep the Update Application In Existing Package option selected and then click Next.

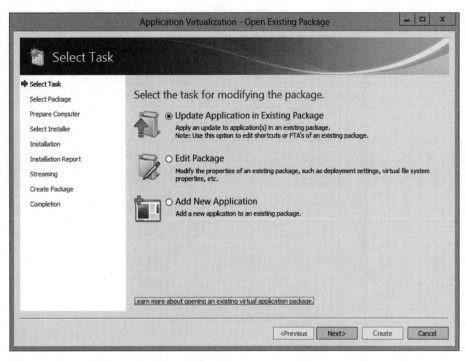

Figure 4-4 App-V Sequencer Select Task page

4. On the Select Package page, shown in Figure 4-5, click Browse and navigate to the existing App-V package file (.appv), click the file, click Open, and then click Next.

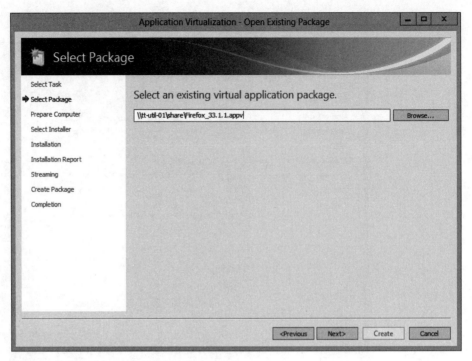

Figure 4-5 App-V Sequencer Select Package page

5. On the Prepare Computer page, shown in Figure 4-6, if the computer is ready to create a package, click Next. If issues are listed, remediate the issues if necessary and then click Refresh until the computer is ready to create a package. Click Next.

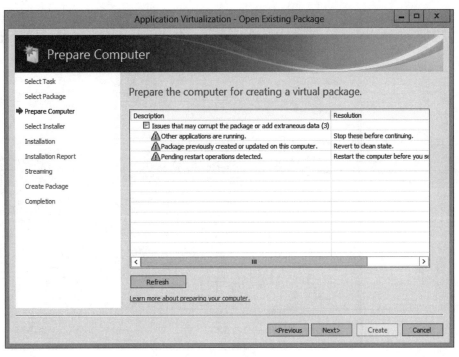

Figure 4-6 App-V Sequencer Prepare Computer page

6. On the Select Installer page, shown in Figure 4-7, click Browse and navigate to the install file for the application update. Click the installer file, click Open, and then click Next.

CHAPTER 4

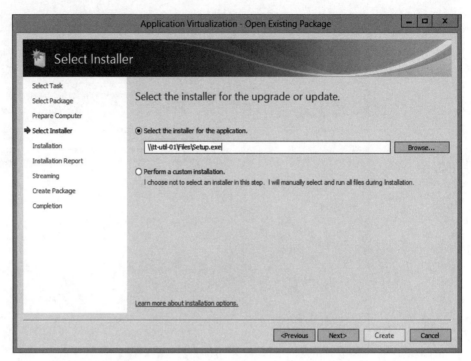

Figure 4-7 App-V Sequencer Select Installer page

7. The application update installation will begin. Update the application based on the installation program. When finished, select the I Am Finished Installing check box, as shown in Figure 4-8, and then click Next.

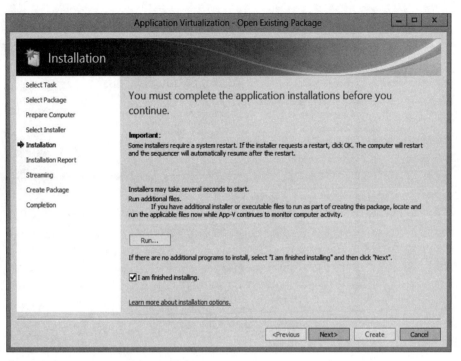

Figure 4-8 App-V Sequencer Installation page

8. On the Installation Report page, shown in Figure 4-9, if the update was successful, the App-V wizard should report that there weren't any issues detected. Click Next.

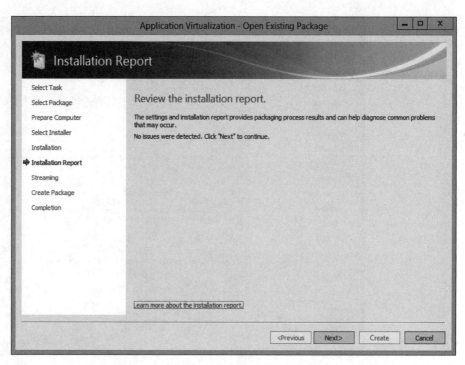

Figure 4-9 App-V Sequencer Installation Report page

9. On the Prepare For Streaming page, shown in Figure 4-10, click Run All. Then, perform any needed first-run application configurations. When finished, close the updated application and then click Next in the App-V wizard.

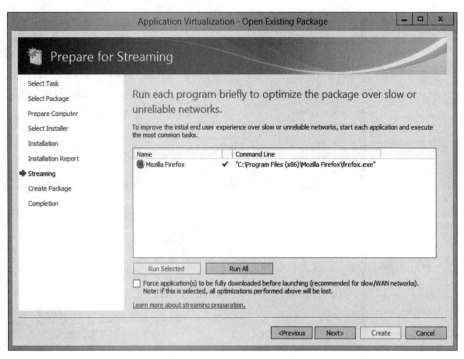

Figure 4-10 App-V Sequencer Prepare For Streaming page

10. On the Create Package page, shown in Figure 4-11, enter a location to save the updated application package and then click Create.

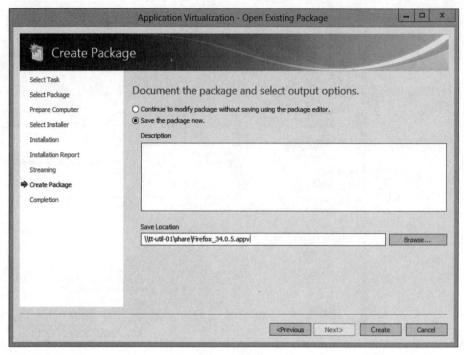

Figure 4-11 App-V Sequencer Create Package page

11. After the package creation completes, click Close. Next, you need to make the updated .appv package available to publishing servers, App-V clients, or Configuration Manager, depending on your App-V deployment model.

Application termination

As part of your routine application maintenance, you'll need to temporarily and permanently remove applications from your environment. Sometimes, you'll need to remove applications from specific users. Other times, you'll need to permanently remove an application from all of your users. You should understand the options available to you for handling these tasks. Let's look at a few scenarios and walk through the process.

Removing an application from a small number of users

There are many situations in which you will need to remove an application from one user or a small group of users. For example, if you were running end user pilot testing for a new application, you may want to remove users after they've completed their testing. There are multiple methods for doing this, but we'll focus on one of the most common methods in an environment with the App-V full infrastructure deployment model. In this model, you should be assigning application access based on Active Directory Domain Services (AD DS) security groups. When it is time to remove one or more users, the simplest method is to remove those users from the security group. The virtual application remains available in App-V, but only for users with the appropriate access rights. In situations in which you are completely and permanently removing an application from all users, you have a few options:

In the App-V Management Console, you can delete the application by right-clicking it and then clicking Delete, as shown in Figure 4-12.

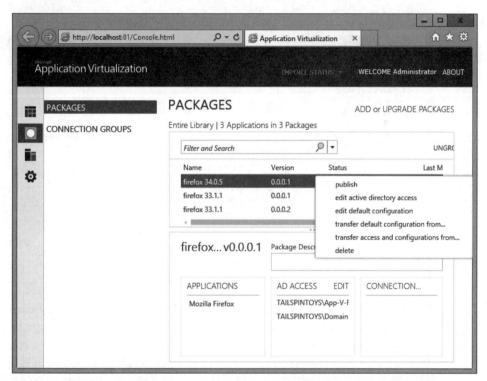

Figure 4-12 App-V Management Console showing Packages workspace with two published applications

From that point on, new App-V clients can't launch the deleted application. Users who already have the application or have used the application will still see it and be able to launch it. You should be aware of a couple of things that cause this. You delete apps from the App-V Management Server. The publishing server, by default, refreshes the list of published applications every 10 minutes. Clients get the list of applications from the publishing server. This 10-minute refresh occurs even if the management server and publishing server run on the same server! Even if you sync the App-V client with the publishing server immediately following an application deletion, it won't matter because the publishing server isn't yet aware that the application was deleted. In most production environments, this 10-minute refresh cycle is okay. However, if you need to reduce the amount of time between refreshes or manually perform an immediate refresh, you have the following options:

On the publishing server, stop the AppVPublishing application pool, shown in Figure 4-13, in Internet Information Server (IIS).

Figure 4-13 IIS application pools for App-V

Then, start the AppVPublishing application pool. This kicks off an immediate refresh of the published apps. Thereafter, you should perform a client sync to complete the removal process. Otherwise, you must wait until the next client sync.

Alternatively, you can adjust the refresh intervals in the registry on the publishing server. To do this, go to the HKEY_LOCAL_MACHINE\SOFTWARE\Microsoft\AppV\Server\PublishingService key and reduce the value of the PUBLISHING_MGT_SERVER_REFRESH_INTERVAL entry. The default is 600 seconds. You can reduce it to something much smaller, such as 10 seconds, as shown in Figure 4-14.

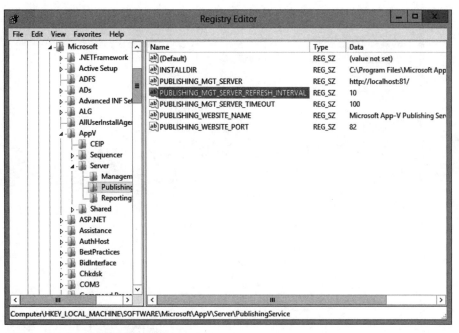

Figure 4-14 App-V publishing registry values

App-V technologies

An App-V 5.0 deployment includes a number of technologies, some of which must be present in all App-V 5.0 models, and some of which are used by only specific App-V deployments. These technologies are the management server, publishing server, management server database, reporting server, reporting server database, Sequencer, and App-V client.

From the Feature Selection page of the Microsoft Application Virtualization (App-V) Server 5.0 Setup Wizard, you can select which servers and databases you want to install, as shown in Figure 4-15.

CHAPTER 4

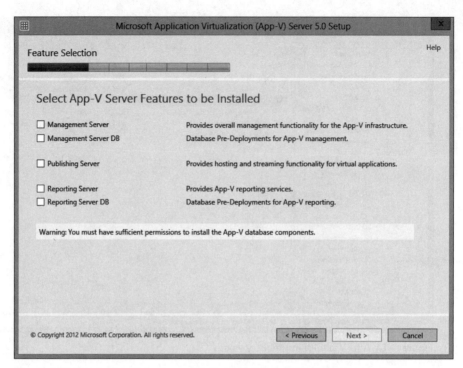

Figure 4-15 The Feature Selection page showing the available App-V server features

Management server and management server database

The management server hosts a Microsoft Silverlight–enabled web application that App-V administrators use to manage an App-V infrastructure. When you use App-V 5.0, all management occurs through the web console or Windows PowerShell, unlike previous versions of App-V. A computer must have Silverlight installed to access the console.

You can use the management server to work with the following objects:

- **Packages**   You can import packages in the App-V file format, which uses the .appv file extension. You then can publish the packages to App-V publishing servers. You also can use the console to configure package security. In Figure 4-16, the management console shows the Packages workspace with a couple of published applications.

- **Connection groups**   Connection groups make it possible for virtual applications to interact with one another. You also can use the console to configure security for connection groups.

- **Publishing servers**   You can authorize publishing servers. You perform this task from the Servers node. You must specify publishing servers in the *domain\computername* format.

- **Administrators**   You can add and manage App-V administrators. Administrators are able to import and publish packages, configure connection groups, and add publishing servers.

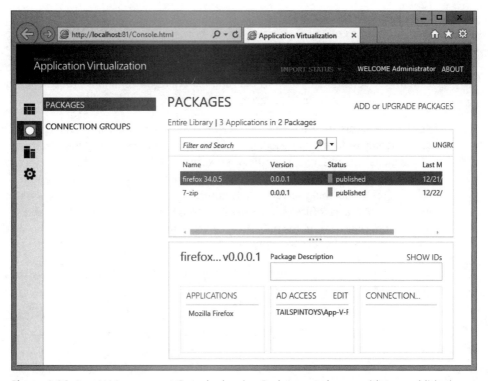

Figure 4-16 App-V Management Console showing Packages workspace with two published applications

The management server database stores the App-V configuration and data settings. The database is hosted on a Microsoft SQL Server instance that is running SQL Server 2008 Service Pack 2 (SP2), SQL Server 2008 R2, or SQL Server 2012. You should install the management server database separately from the management server, and if you do, you need to deploy the database first and then specify its location when you deploy the management server.

Publishing server, sequencer, and App-V client

The publishing server is a web server, built on IIS, which hosts and deploys applications for App-V clients. In previous versions of App-V, a publishing server was called a streaming server.

You deploy App-V applications to a publishing server in the App-V full infrastructure model by using the App-V Management Server console or by using Windows PowerShell.

You can deploy a management server and a publishing server on the same computer. You also can deploy a publishing server on a separate computer as long as you already have deployed an existing management server. This is different from previous versions of App-V, in which it was possible to deploy App-V streaming servers without having deployed a management server.

Previous versions of App-V streamed applications by using the Real-Time Streaming Protocol (RTSP). App-V 5.0 applications stream from a publishing server by using HTTP, HTTPS, or SMB. When you configure a publishing server, you specify a TCP/IP port that is used to stream applications. You subsequently use this port address when you configure Group Policy for use with App-V clients so that clients can access published App-V applications.

Publishing servers are useful in environments that have multiple geographic locations and are connected by wide area network (WAN) links. If you have the App-V full infrastructure model with a management server, publishing server, and database server at the headquarters office, clients outside the headquarters office likely would have a degraded experience compared to having App-V publishing servers locally at their office. In this case, you should deploy publishing servers at branch offices so that clients at those branch offices would be able to receive applications directly from the publishing server in the branch office, rather than across a WAN link from a publishing server in another office.

You can configure a client with the addresses of up to five publishing servers when you use Group Policy, as shown in Figure 4-17.

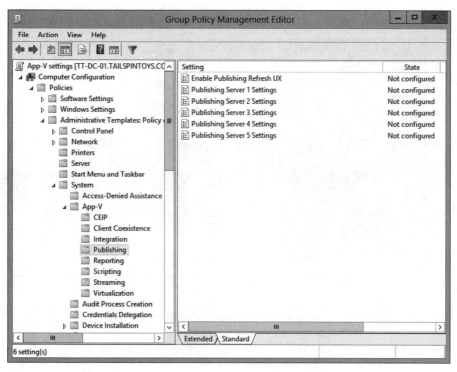

Figure 4-17 GPO settings for publishing

When configuring Group Policy to support clients in branch offices, provide the address of both the local publishing server and a second publishing server to use in case the local publishing server fails. The diagram in Figure 4-18 represents an App-V environment with a headquarters office and two branch offices. Each App-V client is configured to use the local App-V publishing server in its local office and also is configured with a secondary App-V publishing server in an alternate site.

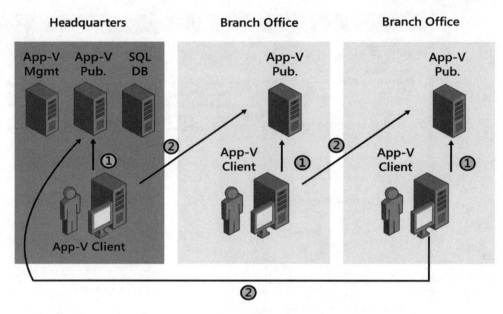

Figure 4-18 App-V environment with multiple publishing servers

You can use the Sequencer to create applications that can run under the App-V client. You should sequence an application on a Sequencer that is configured on the operating system on which the application will run. This helps minimize compatibility issues for your virtualized applications.

The App-V 5.0 Sequencer can install only on computers that run Windows 7 Service Pack 1 (SP1), Windows Server 2008 R2 SP1, Windows 8, Windows 8.1, Windows Server 2012, or Windows Server 2012 R2. In most cases, you should configure a client operating system as a sequencer. This is because most of your virtualized apps likely will be on a client operating system.

The App-V Sequencer has the following requirements:

- Windows 7 Service Pack 1 (SP1), Windows Server 2008 R2 SP1, Windows 8, Windows 8.1, Windows Server 2012, or Windows Server 2012 R2

- Microsoft .NET Framework 4 or 4.5

- Windows PowerShell 3.0 or newer

- Update for Windows KB2533623

The App-V client must be installed on computers before those computers can run virtualized applications. The App-V client supports both x86 and x64 operating system architectures:

- On x86 operating system architecture, only x86 applications are supported.

- On x64 operating system architecture, both x86 and x64 applications are supported.

You need to deploy a separate App-V client on RD Session Host servers. We look at that client in an upcoming section in this chapter titled "App-V for Remote Desktop Services client."

Reporting server and reporting server database

The App-V reporting server, an optional feature, is the built-in reporting feature that you can use for reporting on virtual application usage. The reporting server records the following information:

- Application use, including launch status, startup times, and shutdown times

- Client information such as the host name, client version, operating system version and type, processor architecture, and operating system service pack level

- Package information, such as the package name, version, source, and the percentage cached

You configure the address of the reporting server when you use App-V Group Policy settings, as shown in Figure 4-19. Clients forward data to this address, which the reporting server then forwards to the reporting server database. You can install the reporting server separately from the reporting server database, though if you do this, you already must have deployed the database on another server.

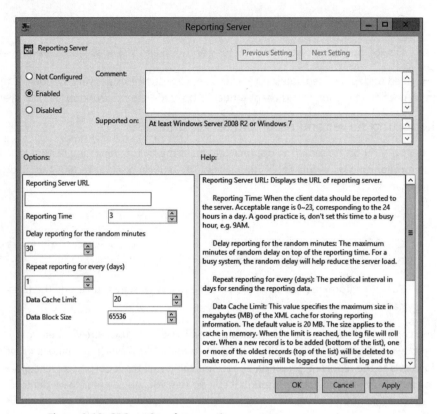

Figure 4-19 GPO settings for reporting

The reporting server database stores all the information that is forwarded to the reporting server. The instance that hosts the reporting server database must meet the same requirements as the instance that hosts the management server database. You can host both databases on the same server. You don't have to install SQL Server Reporting Services to deploy an App-V reporting server, but it is helpful because the App-V product doesn't include report generation.

App-V deployment models

There are three deployment models that you can use to deploy App-V. Each model and its characteristics are described below:

- **Full infrastructure model** This is the most complete deployment of App-V and also is the most commonly deployed model. It offers the most services and functionality and has the largest footprint. The key technologies of the full infrastructure deployment are the App-V Management Server, the App-V Publishing Server, the App-V client, and an

App-V Sequencer. SQL is required on the back end, and the solution ties into AD DS. Optional technologies are the reporting server and associated reporting database. This model offers streaming of applications without requiring a System Center Configuration Manager environment. An example of a typical full infrastructure model deployment is shown in Figure 4-20.

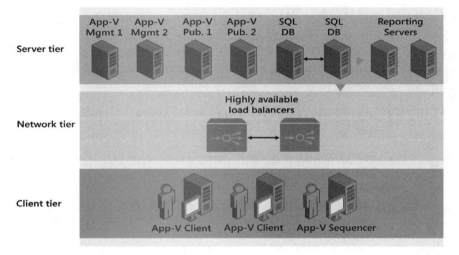

Figure 4-20 Technologies of a typical full infrastructure model

- **App-V integration with Configuration Manager model**   This is an implementation of App-V that, at a minimum, includes App-V clients, an App-V Sequencer, and System Center Configuration Manager 2012 or later. The App-V Management Server isn't part of this deployment model, the App-V Publishing Server isn't part of this deployment model, there isn't a desktop configuration service, and you can't track licensing or perform metering. The desktop configuration service is used by App-V clients to find out information about available virtual applications. This deployment model doesn't require SQL or AD DS, but it requires System Center Configuration Manager, which enables you to stream App-V applications from Configuration Manager distribution points and automatically deploy the App-V client to computers.

- **Stand-alone deployment model**   This is a small implementation of App-V. This deployment model has only App-V clients and an App-V Sequencer, which enables you to create .appv files or .msi files for delivery via a separate application delivery solution such as Group Policy or network file shares. The .appv files and the .msi files can be run only by the App-V client. This model isn't used often but can be valuable for a test environment or an environment with a lot of users who do not routinely connect to the network.

App-V packages

An App-V package comprises several files that have specific functionality. The primary package file is the .appv file that contains the captured assets and state information. Additional files provide custom integration information for publishing applications, detailed sequencing reporting, and, optionally, sequencing templates and package accelerators. You can use the following files to provide custom integration:

- The .appv file contains the captured files and state from the sequencing process in a single file. This file includes the architecture of the package file, publishing information, and registry settings in a tokenized form that can reapply to a machine and to a specific user on delivery.

- The .msi file is used in stand-alone deployments or, optionally, when deploying by using Configuration Manager or other deployment platforms.

- The _DeploymentConfig.xml file contains default publishing parameters for all applications in the package, and it can be modified to support customization.

- The _UserConfig.xml file allows customization of publishing parameters for specific domain users. You can customize items such as shortcuts and file associations with this config file.

- The Report.xml file contains diagnostic information, how sequencing is done, and what files are excluded from a package. It also contains the messages that are displayed in the Sequencer after you finish sequencing an application.

- The .cab file is an optional package accelerator file that speeds up the creation of sequenced virtual application packages.

- The .appvt file is an optional Sequencer template file that retains commonly reused Sequencer settings.

Contents of an .appv package

An .appv file is a compressed file that contains the contents of a virtual application package. It is based on the Open Packaging Conventions standard. It is used to store a combination of XML and non-XML files in a single entity. You can view .appv file contents by renaming the file with a .zip extension and exploring its contents.

The following list describes the primary .appv file contents:

- **StreamMap.xml**   Contains Feature Block 0, also named the Publishing Feature Block.

- **PackageHistory.xml**   Contains information about the origin of a package, for example, which user sequenced the package, on which machine, and at what time.

- **FilesystemMetadata.xml**   Contains a list of the files that are part of the application and were captured during the sequencing.

- **AppxManifest.xml**   Metadata for a package that contains everything that is needed to publish.

- **Registry.dat**   A mountable .dat file containing the registry that was captured as part of the package.

- **Root**   Contains the file system for the virtualized application that was captured during sequencing.

Planning App-V infrastructure

When introducing a new technology, such as App-V, planning and designing the infrastructure are fundamental to a successful implementation. As we'll discuss in this section, a reliable App-V environment depends heavily on the design and infrastructure. The process for implementing application virtualization is flexible and scalable, with larger deployments requiring more planning and different technologies.

Some key areas of interest when planning your App-V infrastructure include the following:

- The App-V infrastructure requirements

- The various App-V deployment models

- Sizing and performance

- High availability and disaster recovery

App-V infrastructure requirements

Before deploying App-V in your environment, you must ensure that the supporting infrastructure is in place and configured. App-V 5.0 has the following infrastructure requirements:

- **Active Directory Domain Services**   AD DS is required for authentication and authorization of applications and connection groups. AD DS is needed only if you plan to deploy an App-V server, such as in a full infrastructure deployment model.

- **Installation service account**   A service account in AD DS is required for the initial installation of the App-V server, presuming that your deployment is a full infrastructure model. This account needs Read permission to query AD DS and local Administrators group access on the server on which you perform the App-V installation. Following the installation of the management server, you can transition this to a security group in

AD DS, allowing you to easily add users who require administrative access to the management console.

- **Package repository**   This is the location where package files will be stored for delivery to App-V clients.

The servers in an App-V environment have the following requirements::

- **Management server**   Supported on Windows Server 2008 R2 with SP1 and newer. It requires the following technologies:

  - Microsoft .NET Framework 4.0 or newer

  - Windows PowerShell 3.0

  - Microsoft Visual C++ 2010 SP1 Redistributable Package (x86/x64)

  - Microsoft SQL Server 2008 Standard, Datacenter, or Developer edition (32-bit or 64-bit) or newer

- **Reporting server**   Supported on Windows Server 2008 and newer. It requires the following:

  - Microsoft .NET Framework 4.0 or newer

  - Microsoft Visual C++ 2010 SP1 Redistributable Package (x86/x64)

  - Windows Web Server with the IIS role installed

  - Common HTTP Features (static content and default document)

  - Application Development (ASP.NET, .NET Extensibility, ISAPI Extensions, and ISAPI Filters)

  - Security (Windows Authentication, Request Filtering)

  - Management Tools (IIS Management Console)

  - 64-bit ASP.NET

  - Microsoft SQL Server 2008 Standard, Datacenter, or Developer edition (32-bit or 64-bit) or newer

- **Publishing server**   Supported on Windows Server 2008 and newer. It requires the following:

  - Microsoft .NET Framework 4.0 or newer

  - Microsoft Visual C++ 2010 SP1 Redistributable Package (x86/x64)

  - Windows Web Server with the IIS role installed

  - Common HTTP Features (static content and default document)

- Application Development (ASP.NET, .NET Extensibility, ISAPI Extensions, and ISAPI Filters)

- Security (Windows Authentication, Request Filtering)

- Management Tools (IIS Management Console)

- 64-bit ASP.NET

Although the design of an App-V environment is very flexible, certain scenarios are not supported:

- Installation on domain controllers isn't supported for any App-V server technology.

- Installation isn't supported on Server Core installations of Windows Server.

- App-V 5.0 can't be installed on a system that has a previous version of the App-V Management Server.

- Microsoft SQL Server Express as a database engine isn't supported.

App-V deployment possibilities

Distributing virtual applications requires the App-V client software on the target computer. As you design your server infrastructure, you'll need to review the four main deployment models that we introduced earlier in this chapter. Each model has its own strengths, and the model you choose will determine which type of server infrastructure you deploy.

App-V full infrastructure model

The full infrastructure model provides all of the management server capabilities that App-V offers, including application streaming, authentication, security, licensing, and metering.

When planning for the full infrastructure model, you'll need AD DS and Microsoft SQL Server. The App-V Management Server should be on the same LAN segment hosting the database. Publishing servers are used in this model to publish content from a file server share to a distributed environment's remote locations by providing streaming capabilities close to the clients that are using the applications. This reduces latency and improves the end-user experience.

System Center 2012 Configuration Manager–integrated model

If you have an existing System Center 2012 Configuration Manager infrastructure, or you are looking to implement one, you can leverage Configuration Manager to distribute virtual applications in the same way that you distribute traditional application packages. You can add virtual applications to a Configuration Manager environment by using the same Create Application Wizard, as shown in Figure 4-21.

CHAPTER 4

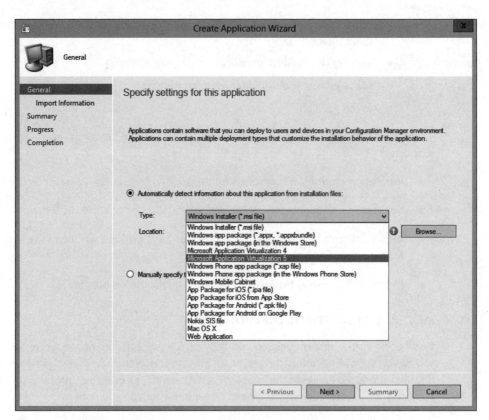

Figure 4-21 Configuration Manager Create Application Wizard

Many of the advanced capabilities that are available for managing a traditional application—such as using task sequences and building queries in collections to define which devices are targeted—also are available for a virtual application. You can target both users and computers to deliver an application in a more intelligent way, expanding on capabilities of the App-V full infrastructure model. For example, when you use a primary device as one of the possible rule requirements, you can identify which deployment type is used based on whether the user is working on his or her primary device.

The Configuration Manager–integrated model requires both the App-V client and the Configuration Manager client on each managed system. It doesn't use any server technologies of the full App-V infrastructure to deliver virtual applications; instead, it uses existing Configuration Manager distribution points to deliver the virtual application to client devices. Note that some reporting capabilities aren't available in the integrated model when compared to the full infrastructure model. For example, if you use local delivery where clients download and execute the application, you only can report if the application has been used and the last application usage time. In the full infrastructure model with reporting, you can report the number of times an application has been used.

Application delivery to a Configuration Manager client works differently from the App-V full infrastructure scenario. In the full infrastructure model, the App-V client manages its own content, and it can refresh instantly against the publishing server. In the Configuration Manager–integrated scenario, the Configuration Manager client manages the App-V client.

Configuration Manager supports two types of delivery methods for virtual applications:

- **Streaming delivery**   You can enable streaming delivery on Configuration Manager distribution points. This option streams a virtual application to a client through HTTP or HTTPS.

- **Local delivery**   This delivery first uses the Configuration Manager client to download all the files needed for the application through Background Intelligent Transfer Service (BITS). After downloading the files, the package fully loads into the App-V client cache.

Electronic software distribution model

The electronic software distribution (ESD) model is ideal for environments in which you prefer to leverage an existing software distribution solution. In this case, most distribution systems can use the virtual .msi file produced by the App-V Sequencer for delivery with an .appv package.

Planning considerations for the ESD model include the following:

- **Existing software distribution system**   An existing software distribution system that can recognize and distribute .msi packages to client devices.

- **App-V Sequencer**   A system deployed in your environment with the App-V Sequencer installed for building and managing virtual applications.

- **Windows PowerShell**   The ability to deploy a script that contains the App-V client module for Windows PowerShell cmdlets. This provides the ability to add and publish packages in ESD mode.

- **Connection groups**   Designating connection groups (grouping one or more App-V packages to enable interaction with one another) requires manually creating a connection group XML file and deploying it by using a custom Windows PowerShell script.

- **Group Policy**   Having Group Policy available simplifies the task of configuring the App-V client. Alternatively, a manual or scripted configuration is possible through the Windows Registry. In Figure 4-22, a GPO named App-V settings provides several App-V settings to computers.

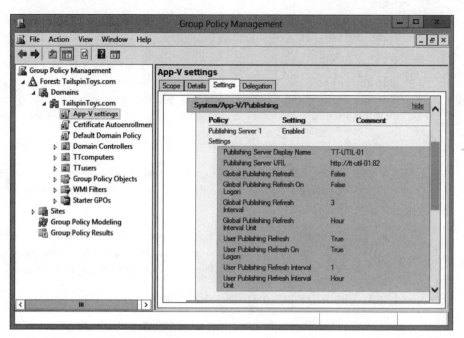

Figure 4-22 App-V GPO settings

Stand-alone deployment model

The App-V stand-alone model consists of the App-V Sequencer and an App-V client, and it requires no additional App-V infrastructure. The Sequencer has an option to create a virtual .msi file during the sequencing process. The virtual .msi file invokes Windows PowerShell commands and then publishes and loads the application to the App-V client cache.

The App-V Sequencer packages publication information, shortcuts, and the installation routines into an .appv file package, and the Sequencer generates virtual .msi files that you can execute manually. When executed, the installer adds the virtual application package to the App-V client and configures publication information to load applications from a local location rather than stream them across a WAN.

Stand-alone deployments require an App-V client on the computers, which allows a virtual .msi file to publish and load virtual applications or enables management through Windows PowerShell. You don't configure an App-V client to connect to any App-V server.

The stand-alone delivery scenario enables an organization to deploy virtual applications in situations where no servers are available to support other deployment methods for virtual applications. Use stand-alone deployments in the following scenarios:

- There are remote users who can't connect to an App-V infrastructure.

- Software management systems, such as Configuration Manager or another electronic software distribution system, already are in place.

- Network bandwidth limitations prevent electronic software distribution. In this case, you can use virtual application delivery on physical media.

Because the stand-alone model employs an .msi file, you can distribute the file if you use an existing software distribution infrastructure, such as GPOs, shared folders, optical media such as CDs and DVDs, USB flash drives, or others.

Service disruption impact

One of the common design steps in implementing App-V is to make the infrastructure highly scalable, which limits the impact of service disruption. The App-V infrastructure is highly dependent on AD DS. Therefore, it is recommended that you carefully plan your AD DS architecture to avoid unwanted service disruptions.

It's important to point out that from a client perspective, once an application is loaded on a computer, that device can run the application independently from the server. A previously published package can have different states on client computers:

- **Not Available**   In this state, the package isn't registered or isn't available on the client.

- **Registered**   In this state, the package is registered to the computer, but it still is not registered for the user.

- **Published**   In this state, the application is registered and published on the client, and the user can start using it.

- **Partially Loaded**   In this state, the application can be started because the client already has downloaded the initial feature block. Depending on which portion is missing, the rest of the files can download over the network, so the file server repository is the critical technology that provides that functionality.

- **Fully Loaded**   In this state, the application downloads and extracts entirely onto a client machine, and it can be used in an offline scenario.

The following areas will be a concern if the virtual applications aren't configured to fully load on the client machine or aren't already published on the publishing server:

CHAPTER 4

- **File server repository**   The most critical technology that influences an application's functionality will be the file server repository. Storage availability and AD DS will need extra planning considerations in this scenario.

- **Management server**   If the management server or the management database is down, adding new packages, updating existing packages, or managing connection groups won't be possible.

- **Publishing server**   Publishing server failure affects the ability to make changes to the publishing list that clients previously received, which is for non-persistent Virtual Desktop Infrastructure (VDI) and RDS scenarios.

- **Reporting server**   Reporting server or reporting database failure isn't critical to running App-V applications; the only functionality that might not work is reports that a client sends about usage statistics for virtual applications, which are stored in the reporting database.

Functional and physical placement

Organizations might plan different App-V infrastructure deployments based on their needs. When you start to plan for your App-V environment, you should try to answer the following questions to help with your design and implementation:

- Are there requirements that all roles must live on a single server? Decide whether you want to combine or cohost functionality.

- Do you need centralized or decentralized roles in a distributed environment?

- What are the requirements for high availability?

- Are the virtualized application users located in all of your office locations?

- Is your virtualization environment able to virtualize your entire App-V deployment?

Based on the answers to these questions, there are several design scenarios:

- **Small and midsize deployments**   For small and midsize scenarios, which commonly address an environment with a small number of users and few packages in a single geographical site, you might cohost all of the roles on a single server.

- **Midsize and large deployments**   For midsize and large deployments, which commonly require a flexible and scalable environment, you might consider a more complex design in which all services implement individually. In this scenario, every connection addresses a virtual IP address and machine name, and no services cohost on any given computer.

- **Distributed deployments**   For distributed deployments, which commonly need to support a large number of users in different locations with many different requirements, you should implement a scenario that can address locations with no datacenter and weak Internet connectivity. For this type of design, all configuration data that is stored in a management database should be located in a major datacenter. Because the management server communicates with the management database, it should be located close to the SQL server because SQL communication is time-sensitive and network-sensitive. The file server repository share that holds the application should be located close to clients, and interval refreshes can be adjusted according to the actual network capabilities.

- **High availability deployments**   In this scenario, you must have two identical machines (physical or virtual) that are configured in NLB mode (or behind a third-party hardware load balancer), where the following services are installed:

  - App-V management
  - App-V publishing
  - App-V reporting

Even if you don't start with a highly available environment, you should consider using load balancing. It can simplify scaling out later and provide some additional capabilities such as drainstopping a server.

It is recommend that you host the SQL Server database separately from the App-V services. This consideration is made for performance, security, and scalability. For highly available designs, you should consider implementing a SQL Server cluster.

Sizing and performance

Actual sizing and performance planning depends on multiple factors, such as scaling an App-V infrastructure properly to lower the round-trip response time and providing proper package optimization for streaming across slow networks.

Round-trip response time on a publishing server is the time that is needed for the publishing server to receive a successful package metadata update from the management server. Round-trip response time on a client is the time the App-V client computer takes to receive a successful notification from the publishing server.

If you have increased internal demand, you can implement an additional management server behind your load balancers.

Often, users might demand external scalability based on the location you must support. A design should include a content repository in each location to provide conveniently located packages to clients. Additionally, you might consider implementing a publishing server and a management server to lower the round-trip response time on clients. Capacity planning should be included to evaluate future demands in planned growth to meet expected performance levels.

A few factors influence round-trip response time on a publishing server. Some of these include the number of:

- Publishing servers that make simultaneous requests.

- Connection groups that are configured on a management server.

- Access groups that are configured on a management server.

- A single management server can simultaneously respond to up to 320 publishing servers with a round-trip response time of approximately 40 seconds; a single management server with fewer than 50 publishing servers results in a round-trip response time of less than 5 seconds.

- The number of connection groups starts to influence round-trip response time after more than 400 are created.

- The number of access groups increases the round-trip response time as it grows.

The number of publishing servers that simultaneously connect to a management server does not influence central processing unit (CPU) utilization and SQL database transactions per second; batches per second are identical, regardless of the number of publishing servers.

For App-V, reporting server capacity planning should focus on the number of clients that simultaneously send reporting information to a reporting server. Round-trip response time increases linearly with an increased number of clients. For example, round-trip response time is 2.6 seconds with 500 clients and 5.2 seconds with 1,000 clients.

Capacity planning for the publishing server influences the round-trip response time on an App-V 5.0 client computer to send a publishing refresh request and to receive a response.

The following are the main factors that influence capacity planning of an App-V publishing server:

- The number of clients that simultaneously connect to a single publishing server.

- The number of packages in each refreshThe network bandwidth between clients and the publishing server.

- A publishing server with a dual-core processor can respond to up to 5,000 clients that simultaneously request refreshes. From 5,000 through 10,000 clients, a publishing server should have a quad-core processor at minimum. Increasing the number of packages increases response time by 40 percent, and network bandwidth has a major influence on response time. For example, clients that run on slow networks—less than 1.5 megabits per second—will have a significantly slower response time than the same number of clients that run on LAN networks.

High availability for App-V

You should plan for a highly available App-V infrastructure in organizations where App-V is important. The high availability strategy for the App-V infrastructure depends on the App-V deployment model, because different procedures and settings for high availability are needed for different App-V deployment models.

Stand-alone deployment model

The stand-alone deployment model only requires an App-V Sequencer and client computers that have an installed App-V client. In the stand-alone deployment model, the App-V Sequencer is used only when a new application needs to be sequenced. Because the App-V Sequencer installs only when a new application needs to be sequenced, it isn't necessary to make the Sequencer highly available. If you stream from a central share, this share can deploy on a clustered file system or on an NLB web farm. In cases where you require access to sequencing, even in a disaster recovery (DR) scenario, you can deploy multiple sequencing computers.

App-V full infrastructure model

From a planning perspective, the App-V full infrastructure model requires the most attention. Because there are a multitude of technologies with differing high availability models, you should spend time looking at the options available and decide which one makes the most sense for your environment. The following are some questions that you should answer to help you plan for high availability:

- Does the reporting service need to be highly available?

- Does the sequencing computer need to be highly available?

- Are there infrastructure technologies outside App-V that may impact the high availability of App-V, such as load balancers, switches, virtualization servers, or storage?

- Which secondary site should each office use in the case of a publishing server failure at the office?

The answers to the above questions will help you plan the services, the number of servers required, and the high-level design of your highly available environment.

The App-V full infrastructure model stores all configuration and application information in the management server database and stores all utilization data in the reporting server database,

CHAPTER 4

so each of these databases is a single point of failure in this model. Therefore, when you are configuring the App-V full infrastructure model to be highly available, you need to ensure that the management server database and the reporting server database remain accessible. You can do this by deploying these two databases on an instance that is installed on a highly available VM or on a clustered SQL Server instance.

App-V 5.0 supports multiple management, reporting, and publishing servers. You can configure the App-V 5.0 management and reporting server databases to work with multiple management servers and reporting servers by using a security group when specifying the computer account location during setup. At any time, you can add publishing servers to an existing App-V full infrastructure model deployment.

Consider Figure 4-23, which shows what can happen when the application team provides high availability for its services but another team isn't engaged in the project and is unaware of potential impacts.

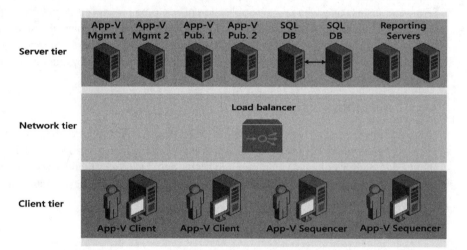

Figure 4-23 A diagram of an App-V full infrastructure deployment model

In the diagram above, although all of the App-V technologies are highly available, there is only one load balancer. It represents a single point of failure. Instead of this scenario, the availability of all services on which App-V is dependent should match the App-V availability.

Integrated Configuration Manager model

For the integrated Configuration Manager model to be made highly available, you should look at all of the options to meet your high availability requirements and figure out if any infrastructure changes are required:

- Are highly available VMs available in your environment? If so, you can use one or more for your Configuration Manager servers.

- Is your existing SQL environment highly available?

- Is the storage that the virtual environment uses highly available?

- Do you have distribution points in all of the locations to which you plan to deliver virtual applications? If so, you need to plan for scenarios in which a distribution point becomes unavailable. In environments with an existing Configuration Manager deployment, it isn't unusual to have sites with a single distribution point. You should consider multiple distribution points if your requirements include immediate access to virtual applications, especially for new App-V clients.

- You also may want to look at the overall high availability of the Configuration Manager environment. Is there an existing hierarchy with a central administration site?

Similar to other App-V deployment models, you should look at all aspects of your environment and ensure that all of the services involved are configured for high availability.

> ➤ For more information about high availability in Configuration Manager, see the
> "Planning for High Availability with Configuration Manager" website at
> *http://technet.microsoft.com/en-us/library/hh846246.aspx*.

Disaster recovery

A disaster recovery plan should include a proper backup of critical technologies to respond to a service outage. In addition, regular testing of restore operations will help ensure that the backups are functional and that the operational procedures are adequate to recover from a disaster. At a minimum, an App-V infrastructure backup should protect the management database and the package repository that contains the App-V packages. Outside App-V, you should ensure that the services on which App-V depends also are backed up and restored first after a disaster. For example, you need to ensure that AD DS, SQL, Server virtualization, and the core networking services are up and running before you can successfully recover App-V.

In an App-V backup and recovery scenario, each role has different requirements:

- A management server does not hold any unique data other than the registry configuration of the database source, so you can easily re-create this role in case of a disaster.

- A publishing server contains a registry value that indicates the host name of the management server to contact and a cached copy of the latest publishing data, which you need to back up.

- The reporting server has a registry value that indicates the name of the reporting database.

There are two different scenarios for recovery procedures:

- If a server that contains all of the roles fails, administrators should perform standard image recovery procedures that are defined by organizational policy. This often means restoring the VM or physical server to the most recent backup.

- If an App-V service fails, administrators should perform a recovery by installing the App-V technologies and prerequisites, such as installing and configuring Internet Information Services (IIS) and installing SQL Server on the database server.

When you restore the management server, it enables this service to become operational as soon as the service can contact the App-V database. When you complete the restoration of publishing servers, client requests will be serviced as soon as the service contacts the publishing servers (from 1 to 10 minutes). After the App-V services are restored, the reporting server starts accepting client connections.

Deploying App-V infrastructure

After you determine which application virtualization model to use, you need to deploy the appropriate roles to support that model. In most production environments, you should host the management server database and the reporting server database separately from the management server and the reporting server. It isn't uncommon to see the management database and reporting database also separated, depending on the database infrastructure you have. Before a deployment, you need to understand the order in which to deploy App V technologies. In this section, we will explain the following:

- App-V infrastructure requirements

- Installing management databases

- App-V Management Server configuration

- App-V Publishing Server deployment and configuration

- App-V for Remote Desktop Services clients

- Integrating App-V with System Center Configuration Manager

App-V infrastructure requirements

The technologies of App-V should be deployed in a specific order. If you deploy all roles on the same server when you deploy the App-V full infrastructure model, the installation wizard automatically deploys them in the correct order. If you deploy the roles on more than one server, you should deploy them in the following order:

1. Management server database

2. Management server

3. Publishing server

4. Reporting server database (optional)

5. Reporting server (optional)

When you configure management server database settings, you need to specify the security account of the computer that will access the database. This can be a security group account or the computer account of the server that will function as the management server. When you install a management server separately, you need to specify the instance location and credentials that will be used to access the management server database.

When you deploy a publishing server, you need to specify the network address of the management server. You can't deploy a publishing server without having a management server already deployed, unless you deploy all of the roles at the same time.

You must deploy a reporting server database before deploying a reporting server. The reporting server doesn't have dependencies on any other services in the App-V full infrastructure model.

You don't need to install the App-V Sequencer when deploying the App-V full infrastructure model. However, it is a good idea to deploy a sequencer as soon as possible to begin testing the deployment. The App-V client usually is the last application to be deployed.

Installing management databases

The management server stores all of the configuration data in an App-V management database, which includes all application metadata, the deployment configuration, the relationships, and the security assignments. The management server only communicates with the management database, and it is the first technology that should be installed in the App-V full infrastructure model. When you add management servers for a scalable deployment, you only need to allow Read and Write permissions to the database. You don't have to provide additional configurations.

CHAPTER 4

The minimum supported database platform is Microsoft SQL Server 2008 R2 Standard, Enterprise, Datacenter, or Developer edition (32-bit or 64-bit). The Developer edition should not be used in a production environment. Additional prerequisites include the installation of the following:

- .NET Framework 4 (Full Package)

- Microsoft Visual C++ 2010 SP1 redistributable package (x86)

- Windows Server 2008 or newer

In the deployment scenario in which you install all of the technologies on the same computer, the App-V server setup GUI-based installation first installs the App-V management database and then installs the management server and the publishing server. Finally, if selected, the reporting database and reporting server are installed.

If you are implementing scalable deployment, you should run the GUI installation on a server that hosts the management database because remote SQL database creation isn't supported in the installer.

As an alternative, you can install the SQL database when you execute SQL Server scripts that are extracted from the server setup, as shown in Figure 4-24. SQL Server scripts extract from the setup with the following command: `appv_server_setup.exe /layout /layoutdir=c:\ extract`.

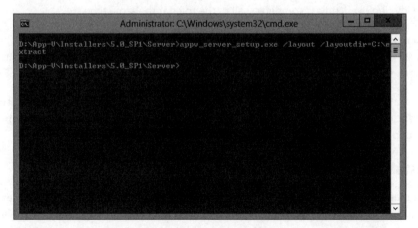

Figure 4-24 Example appv_server_setup.exe command

In the destination folder, you must modify two of the six scripts to provide the appropriate Read and Write permissions for the domain accounts or domain groups that you need to manage an App-V infrastructure. The first modification must be done to the Permissions.sql script to replace the entry for [ManagementDBWriteAccessAcountSid] and for [Management-DBWriteAccessAcountName] with the security identifier (SID) and the name for the domain group that requires Write permissions to the database. This group should include the App-V administrator account and all management servers in the environment. If you use the same account for installation and App-V administration, then you should use the same entries for [ManagementDBPublishAccessAcountSid] and [ManagementDBPublishAccessAcountName]. Otherwise, you should enter the correct SID and name for the installation account. In Figure 4-25, the Permissions.sql file has been modified and is ready for use.

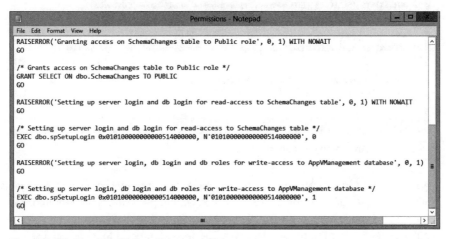

Figure 4-25 An example Permissions.sql file

Modification of the second script, Database.sql, is optional and has to be done only if you plan to replace the default database name AppVManagement with a unique name. In Figure 4-26, the Database.sql file has been updated to create a database named CustomDB.

CHAPTER 4

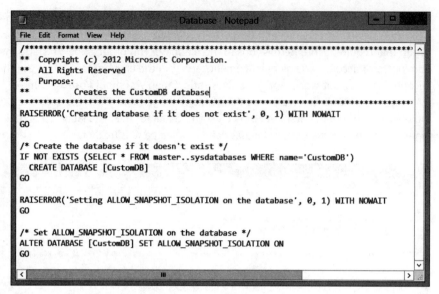

```
/******************************************************************************
** Copyright (c) 2012 Microsoft Corporation.
** All Rights Reserved
** Purpose:
**          Creates the CustomDB database
*******************************************************************************
RAISERROR('Creating database if it does not exist', 0, 1) WITH NOWAIT
GO


/* Create the database if it doesn't exist */
IF NOT EXISTS (SELECT * FROM master..sysdatabases WHERE name='CustomDB')
  CREATE DATABASE [CustomDB]
GO


RAISERROR('Setting ALLOW_SNAPSHOT_ISOLATION on the database', 0, 1) WITH NOWAIT
GO


/* Set ALLOW_SNAPSHOT_ISOLATION on the database */
ALTER DATABASE [CustomDB] SET ALLOW_SNAPSHOT_ISOLATION ON
GO
```

Figure 4-26 An example Database.sql file

A SQL Server administrator must run prepared SQL scripts against a computer that is running SQL Server that will host the database. SQL Sysadmin permissions are required. You can run the script if you first open the SQL Server Management Studio console and run it as a query, but you need select the proper database. The second method that you can use is the **OSQL** command-line application. "The switches /E, /i, and /d are case-sensitive. Reporting database setup is identical to a management database and can be done with the App-V setup installer, or it can be pre-created with SQL scripts. The following commands can be used:

```
OSQL -E -i database.SQL

OSQL -E -d MS_Appv5_Management -i CreateTables.sql

OSQL -E -d MS_Appv5_Management -i CreateStoredProcs.sql

OSQL -E -d MS_Appv5_Management -i UpdateTables.sql

OSQL -E -d MS_Appv5_Management -i insertversionInfo.sql

OSQL -E -d MS_Appv5_Management -i Permissions.sql
```

App-V Management Server configuration

An App-V Management Server provides a centralized location to manage an App-V 5.0 infra-structure for delivering virtual applications to both an App-V client and an RDS (formerly Terminal Services) client. Unlike previous versions of App-V, a web application that runs on Silverlight manages the App-V 5.0 infrastructure. You configure this web application's address when you install a management server. The installation of an App-V Management Server creates a dedicated IIS website, for which you can specify the name during the installation setup. By default, it is called the Microsoft App-V Management Service. The App-V Management Service will be configured to listen on a dedicated port number, which can be provided during setup.

App-V server features can install on multiple servers to provide scalability and high availability; however, all App-V server features would need a common way to be accessed, such as by using a load balancer. Each management server node needs connectivity to the database on the computer that is running SQL Server. If a single server hosts multiple technologies, they can use different ports, or you can configure them to share a single port.

Preinstallation tasks include configuring appropriate user and administrative groups that can install and administer a management server. A management server requires that an IIS server is installed and configured to be trusted for delegation. If you plan to support Secure Sockets Layer (SSL) for connectivity to a management server, you also need a server certificate that is issued from either an internal or a public certification authority.

Installing an App-V Management Server at the command line requires elevated privileges. You can display the installation parameters, shown in Figure 4-27, by running the following command:

```
appv_server_setup.exe /?
```

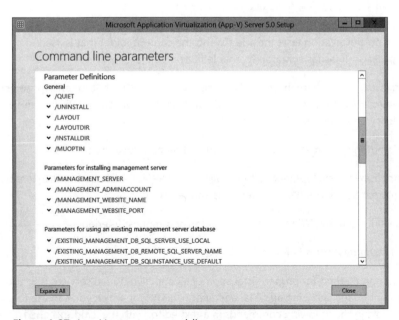

Figure 4-27 App-V setup command-line parameters

CHAPTER 4

The following commands provide an example of an App-V Management Server installation, as shown in Figure 4-28. You can verify the output of the installation in the log file appv_server _datatime.log in the %temp% directory.

```
appv_server_setup.exe /quiet /management_server /MANAGEMENT_ADMINACCOUNT="Adatum
\AppVAdmin" /MANAGEMENT_WEBSITE_NAME="Microsoft App-V Management
service" /MANAGEMENT_WEBSITE_PORT="80" /EXISTING_MANAGEMENT_DB_REMOTE_SQL_SERVER
_NAME="SQLSRV.adatum.com " /EXISTING_MANAGEMENT_DB_SQLIN STANCE_USE_DEFAULT
/EXISTING_MANAGEMENT_DB_NAME="AppVManagement"
```

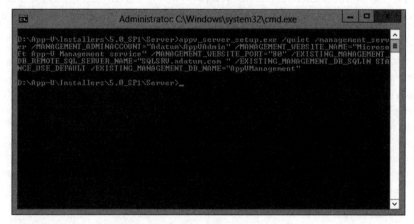

Figure 4-28 Command-line setup of an App-V server

Common postinstallation tasks include sharing the content folder that is used to store the App-V package. It also is common to enable firewall rule exceptions.

You can install a management server by using a very basic GUI, but for enterprise deployment, we recommend script-based installation. Management servers and publishing servers have a dependency on IIS with the following features:

- Common HTTP features: static content and default document

- Application development features: Microsoft ASP.NET, Microsoft .NET Extensibility, and Internet Server API (ISAPI) extensions and filters

- Security features: Windows authentication and request filtering

- Management tools features: IIS Manager

One common method for proper installation of IIS and all required services is to use the Deployment Image Servicing and Management (DISM) tool, which you can use to create a script by saving the following commands in a text editor with the .cmd extension:dism /Online /Enable-Feature /FeatureName:IIS-ApplicationDevelopment ^

```
/FeatureName:IIS-ASPNET /FeatureName:HS-commonHttpFeatures ^

/FeatureName:Iis-DefaultDocument /FeatureName:Iis-DirectoryBrowsing ^

/FeatureName:Iis-HealthAndDiagnosti cs ^

/FeatureName:HS-Httpcompressionstatic ^

/FeatureName:HS-HttpErrors /FeatureName:HS-HttpLogging ^

/FeatureName:HS-HttpTracing /FeatureName:HS-lSAPiExtensions ^

/FeatureName:HS-ISAPiFilter ^

/FeatureName:Iis-LoggingLibraries /FeatureName:HS-ManagementConsole ^

/FeatureName:Iis-Managementservice /FeatureName:HS-NetFxExtensibility ^

/FeatureName:IIS-Performance /FeatureName:ns-RequestFiltering ^

/FeatureName:HS-RequestMonitor /FeatureName:HS-Security ^

/FeatureName:Iis-staticcontent /FeatureName:Iis-webserver ^

/FeatureName:HS-webserverManagementTools ^

/FeatureName:HS-webserverRole /FeatureName:Iis-windowsAuthentication ^

/FeatureName:WAS-ConfigurationAPl /FeatureName:WAS-NetFxEnvi ronment ^

/FeatureName:WAS-ProcessModel /FeatureName:WAS-WindowsActivationservice ^
```

A management server has the following requirements:

- 1-gigahertz (GHz) or faster x64 processor; two cores Intel Xeon 2.0 GHz or faster recommended

- 2 gigabytes (GB) or more of RAM; 4 GB of RAM recommended

- 200 megabytes (MB) of free disk space (does not include content); 40 GB recommended

- Windows Server 2008 R2 SP1 or newer.NET Framework 4 Extended

- .NET Framework 3.5.1 Features (or 4.5)

- Visual C++ 2010 SP1 Redistributable Package (64-bit)

- Visual C++ 2010 SP1 Redistributable Package (32-bit)

- Silverlight

- Windows PowerShell 3.0

CHAPTER 4

App-V publishing server deployment and configuration

When you deploy an App-V publishing server, you must specify the location of an existing App-V Management Server. This is different from previous versions of App-V, in which it was possible to deploy a stand-alone streaming server without having to configure a management server.

Publishing servers function as distribution points for virtualized applications when you use the App-V full infrastructure model. Applications stream from these servers to clients. The entire application doesn't need to stream before a user can start interacting with it; therefore, you won't need as much bandwidth as you would with other deployment methods. Nonetheless, you still need to provision adequate bandwidth for the connection between a publishing server and the client.

To install a publishing server by using a GUI installer, you must follow the same steps as installing the management server. You have to point to an existing management server, and if these two roles coexist on the same computer, you must choose a different port for the website.

When you perform a command-line installation, you can use the help that the installer provides, which presents examples and definitions that construct the following command:

```
appv_server_setup.exe /?
```

You can use the following commands to perform publishing server installation at the command line:

```
appv_server_setup.exe /quiet /publishing_server

/PUBLISHING_MGT_SERVER=http://lon-svr1.adatum.com

/PUBLISHING_WEBSITE_NAME="Microsoft Appv Publishing service"/PUBLISHING_WEBSITE_PORT="80
"/EXISTING_MANAGEMENT_DB_REMOTE_SQL_SERVER_NAME="SQLSRV.adatum.com" /EXISTING_MANAGE-
MENT_DB_SQLIN STANCE_USE_DEFAULT /EXISTING_MANAGEMENT_DB_NAME="AppVManagement"
```

As a best practice, when you install on the same server as the management server, use port 80 for the publishing server and an alternate port for the management server.

After you deploy both the management server and the publishing server, you need to configure them with appropriate firewall rules to provide management and client connectivity.

A publishing server is a web application that is hosted on IIS, and any configuration changes can be done through IIS Manager or by using the HKLM\Software\Microsoft\APPV \Server\PublishingService\PUBLISHING_MGT_SERVER registry settings to point to the protocol and port that establish connectivity with the App-V Management Server. The PUBLISHING_MGT_SERVER_REFRESH_INTERVAL registry setting specifies how often a publishing server queries a management server for packages. The default value is 600 seconds (10 minutes), and for testing purposes, you can shorten the interval to propagate changes to clients more quickly. Any registry changes will become effective when the application pool restarts or IIS restarts.

You also can configure management server settings in IIS and the registry, as shown in Figure 4-29.

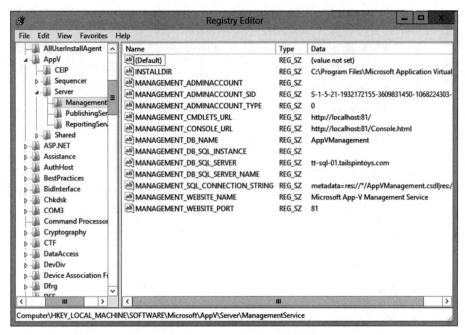

Figure 4-29 App-V registry settings for the management server

`HKLM\Software\Microsoft\APPV\Server\ManagementService` contains configuration data for a management server. From this registry location, you can identify or change a connection string to the management database *(MANAGEMENT_SQL_CONNECTION_STRING)* or identify the port and name for the management website.

In addition to the registry, some configuration settings are stored in the files in the *INSTALLDIR*. The AdminGroup.xml file contains information to recover access to an App-V console when you remove the last administrator from the console.

A publishing server has the following requirements:

- 1 GHz or faster x64 processor; two cores Intel Xeon 2.0 GHz or faster recommended

- 2 GB or more of RAM; 4 GB of RAM recommended

- 200 MB of free disk space (does not include content); 40 GB recommended

- Windows Server 2008 R2 SP1 or newer.NET Framework 4 Extended

- Visual C++ 2010 SP1 Redistributable Package (32-bit)

- Windows PowerShell 3.0

- The Web Server role with the following features:

  - Common HTTP features: static content and default document

  - Application development features: ASP.NET, .NET Extensibility, ISAPI extensions and filters

  - Security features: Windows authentication and request filtering

  - Management tools features: IIS Manager

App-V for Remote Desktop Services client

App-V 5.0 has a separate, special client that makes it possible to run virtualized applications on RD Session Host servers. With this client, you can run applications on RD Session Host servers that might not otherwise run on an RD Session Host server.

The App-V for RDS client has the following system requirements:

- 1.4 GHz or faster x86 or x64 processor

- Windows Server 2008 R2 SP1 or Windows Server 2012

- .NET Framework 3.51 and 4 (Full)

- Windows PowerShell 3.0

- Microsoft KB2533623 (Windows Server 2008 R2)

- Visual C++ 2008 redistributable (if installing by using an executable file)

You must configure Windows Server 2008 R2 or Windows Server 2012 as an RD Session Host server before you install the App-V for RDS client.

You can use the App-V for RDS client with the App-V full infrastructure, stand-alone, and Configuration Manager–integrated models. The App-V for RDS client uses the same Group Policy settings as the normal App-V client.

Integrating App-V with System Center Configuration Manager

The Configuration Manager–integrated model requires that you have an existing Configuration Manager or newer deployment. This model allows you to deploy sequenced App-V applications as one of many different application deployment types.

Before deploying sequenced App-V applications, you should configure App-V client software as an application that you can deploy. You then can specify the App-V client as a requirement when deploying any sequenced App-V application.

You can create the App-V client as an application by performing the following procedure:

1. Copy the App-V client installation file, corecli_amd64.msi or corecli_i386.msi, to a shared folder. In the Configuration Manager console, in the Software Library workspace, under the Application Management node, click Applications.

2. On the ribbon, click Create Application.

3. On the General page of the Create Application Wizard, set the type to Windows Installer (*.msi file) and then click Browse.

4. Browse to the shared folder where you copied the App-V client installation file. Finish the wizard and then click Close.

To create an App-V application in Configuration Manager, perform the following procedure:

1. In the Configuration Manager console, in the Software Library workspace, under the Application Management node, click Applications.

2. On the ribbon, click Create Application.

3. On the General page of the Create Application Wizard, set the type to Microsoft Application Virtualization 5 and then click Browse to go to the network location that hosts the file in .appv file format.

4. Finish the wizard and then click Close.

CHAPTER 4

Planning and deploying App-V clients

Overview of App-V client configuration

After you have a functional App-V deployment, your next focus will be on the client side. You need to understand how the App-V client works, especially before you begin deploying it to all of your client computers. Thereafter, you need to begin planning for the client deployment. You should assess the different deployment options and choose the deployment strategy that works best in your environment.

Finally, you will need to focus on managing the clients. After the clients are deployed, you will need to manage individual clients and manage clients in groups. You must be very familiar with Group Policy and Windows PowerShell to effectively manage the clients.

App-V desktop client

The App-V client for App-V 5.0 is a client computer application that is supported only on Windows 7 with Service Pack 1 (SP1) and Windows 8. With Service Pack 2 for App-V 5.0, the client also is supported on Windows 8.1. There is a 32-bit and a 64-bit client application available. Outside the client computers, the only way to provide virtual application functionality for other clients, such as tablets, smartphones, or other operating systems, is to use a Remote Desktop Services (RDS) environment. With RDS, you can deploy the RDS client to the RDS servers and bring App-V functionality to RDS-supported computing devices.

Requesting and executing the application

To access a virtual application on a computer with the App-V client, open the application by double-clicking a shortcut or open an associated document with registered file type extensions. For example, if the application in question is Microsoft Word, you can double-click a Word document to start the Word application. In a full infrastructure deployment, applications usually are published to users by using the publishing server. However, you also can access applications by manually publishing them on an individual computer, as described in the "Application publishing and deployment" section in Chapter 4, "Planning and implementing App-V."

The following steps explain the application request process:

1. You start an application by opening a document that will invoke file type extensions or by clicking the application shortcut.

2. The App-V client then verifies the existence of the DeploymentConfig.xml, UserConfig.xml, and Manifest.xml files in the user catalog. This will assign the application to a specific user and will initiate the process of starting the application.

3. The App-V client will check in the registry to verify that the path is registered for the package.

4. An appropriate virtual environment is created from the Manifest.xml and deployment configuration files. All App-V subsystems load, and the application starts.

5. Any additional files in the package store will stream on demand if required by App-V.

6. After the publishing refresh process, the user starts an App-V application. The App-V client prepares the virtual environment, and then the initial streaming downloads the manifest and the primary feature block so that the application is ready to start.

Isolating the application

One of the primary features of App-V is the ability to isolate a virtual application from other applications and from the operating system. An application is made up of one or more of the following objects:

- **Files**   Files can be executable files, configuration files, or other files that are part of the application.

- **Registry values**   Registry values are used to configure an application's look and feel and to control the behavior of the application, such as startup mode.

- **COM objects**   COM objects are associated with applications and must be registered.

In a standard application environment, Windows has one file system, one registry, and one COM object registration area. In an App-V environment, virtual applications are isolated so that the application's resources (files, registry values, COM objects) aren't readily available to other applications. In many cases, this isolation is a good thing because it reduces application conflicts, provides a stable environment, and increases security. In other situations, applications must see one another's objects and interact closely. For example, if you have an application that has plug-ins, the plug-ins need access to the application's resources. For those situations, App-V has connection groups. Connection groups allow you to group applications to eliminate the isolation. There is additional information about connection groups in Chapter 6, "Managing and Administering Application Virtualization."

How the App-V client accesses applications

To access an application, the App-V client communicates directly with the publishing server, assuming that you have a full infrastructure deployment of App-V. From the Microsoft App-V 5.0 Client UI, shown in Figure 5-1, you can click Update to receive new or updated virtual applications.

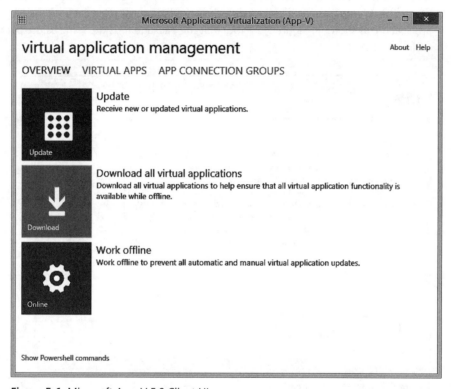

Figure 5-1 Microsoft App-V 5.0 Client UI

During that update process, the client runs the following Windows PowerShell commands in order:

```
Get-AppvPublishingServer | Sync-AppvPublishingServer

Get-AppvClientPackage

Get-AppvClientConnectionGroup

Get-AppvPublishingServer
```

After the update process, the parts of the apps that are needed to launch are delivered to the client immediately. At that point, you can launch applications while the rest of the application files are delivered via streaming, as needed.

Storage locations for App-V client data

All application content is stored in a cache area located at %SYSTEMDRIVE%\ProgramData \App-V. Each virtual application has a top-level folder named after the package ID of the application, as shown in Figure 5-2. Note that the package ID is the same as the package GUID.

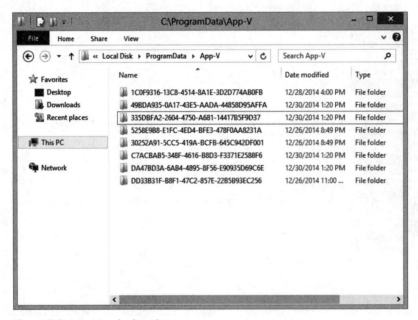

Figure 5-2 App-V cache location

By running the Get-AppvClientPackage Windows PowerShell command on a client, you can see the storage location of the virtual applications. Below is the output from one application. Note that the package ID matches one of the folders in Figure 5-2.

```
PackageId        : da47bd3a-6ab4-4895-8f56-e90935d69c6e

VersionId        : b0476a66-d0cf-40aa-8f88-a03a22af0b69

Name             : PuTTY 0.63

Version          : 0.0.0.1

Path             : \\tt-util-01\share\PuTTY 0.63.appv
```

```
IsPublishedToUser      : True

UserPending            : False

IsPublishedGlobally    : False

GlobalPending          : False

InUse                  : False

InUseByCurrentUser     : False

PackageSize            : 4047572

PercentLoaded          : 37

IsLoading              : False

HasAssetIntelligence : True
```

The path shown above, \\tt-util-01\share\PuTTY 0.63.appv, is the location of the .appv file. In this case, the file is located on a file share. You also can host the .appv file on a web server for access over HTTP. In that case, the path would show a URL such as http://tt-util-01 /Firefox_34.0.5.appv.

In addition to the App-V application content, there are several other locations with which you should be familiar. The App-V client uses these locations, shown in Table 5-1, to support the running of App-V virtual applications.

Table 5-1 App-V client important locations

Name	Location	Description
Package store	%ProgramData%\App-V	Default location for read-only package files.
Machine catalog	%ProgramData%\Microsoft\AppV \Client\Catalog	Contains per-machine configuration documents.
User catalog	%AppData%\Microsoft\AppV \Client\Catalog	Contains per-user configuration documents.
Shortcut backups	%AppData%\Microsoft\AppV \Client\Integration \ShortCutBackups	Location where previous integration points are stored. It is used for preexisting shortcuts if a package is later removed.
Copy-on-write (CoW) roaming	%AppData%\Microsoft\AppV \Client\VFS	Writable roaming location for package modification

CHAPTER 5

CoW local	%LocalAppData%\Microsoft\AppV\Client\VFS	Writable non-roaming location for package modification.
Machine registry	HKLM\Software\Microsoft\AppV	Contains package state information including a virtual registry for machine or globally published packages (machine hive).
User registry	HKCU\Software\Microsoft\AppV	Contains user package state information including a virtual registry.
User registry classes	HKCU\Software\Classes\AppV	Contains additional user package state information.

Below is additional information on these common storage locations:

- **Machine catalog**   The machine catalog stores integration points that are available to all users if the package is published as "global" or to a specific user if the UserDeploymentConfiguration.xml file exists in the machine catalog. The machine catalog includes the following files:

  - Manifest.xml

  - DeploymentConfiguration.xml

  - UserManifest.xml (globally published package)

  - UserDeploymentConfiguration.xml (globally published package)

- **User catalog**   The user catalog contains configuration settings for each user. These are used during the publishing and startup phases and contain the following two files:

  - UserManifest.xml

  - UserDeploymentConfiguration.xml

- **Shortcut backups**   Shortcut backups is the location that backs up shortcuts and integration points.

- **CoW files**   When modifications to files for App-V applications are required, these changes occur in a different location from the package store to preserve the ability to repair the applications. These locations are called copy-on-write (CoW).

- **Package registry**   An App-V client provides registry access for a virtual application during the adding phase of the package, when a copy of Registry.dat is created at %ProgramData%\Microsoft\AppV\Client\VREG\{Version GUID}.dat. This allows easy removal of the package because an actual hive file in the package is never used. Starting an application will create registry data, which is shared across all users on a computer. The location of the registry data is HKEY_LOCAL_MACHINE\SOFTWARE\Microsoft\AppV\Client\Packages\{PackageGuid}\Versions\{VersionGuid}\REGISTRY. User-specific settings are located at HKCU\Software\Microsoft\AppV\Client\Packages\PackageGuid\Registry \User.

Asset folder

In previous versions of App-V (anything older than 5.0), there was an asset folder that usually was assigned a drive letter of Q. When you sequenced applications, you installed them in a folder on the Q drive. That was a best practice, although some administrators also sequenced applications to the C drive. With App-V 5.0, there isn't a Q drive, and you can choose where to install and sequence applications. Often, the standard program installation directory is the best choice. In App-V 5.0, you can explore the App-V–related folders with native applications such as File Explorer.

Extension points

Extension points can be shortcuts, file type associations (FTAs), COM object associations, or environment variables. They are used for integrating with the operating system and providing capabilities similar to standard applications. App-V has the following subsystems available for integration:

- Shortcut subsystem

- FTA subsystem

- COM subsystem

- Software Clients subsystem

- Application Capabilities subsystem

- URL Protocol Handler subsystem

- App Path subsystem

- Virtual Applications subsystem

Extension points have been expanded in App-V 5.0. One of the features available in the Software Client extension point enables you to register applications for use as default applications in Windows. Once registered, the virtual applications can be set as the default applications. The supported application types for this feature are web browsers, email clients, instant messaging clients, media players, and virtual machines of Java (Java VMs).

How shortcuts work in App-V

In App-V prior to Version 5.0, shortcuts to virtual applications relied on an open software description (OSD) file (an .xml file that defines aspects of virtual application behavior) and a launcher application (sfttray.exe). The launcher was responsible for launching all virtual applications. In App-V 5.0, the reliance on an OSD file and the sfttray.exe application has been removed. Now, App-V shortcuts point to the .exe of the application itself. In Figure 5-3, you can see an example of an App-V shortcut. The location of the target and the folder in which to start are in the %SYSTEMDRIVE%\ProgramData\App-V structure.

Figure 5-3 App-V shortcut

In the "Managing App-V client properties" section later in this chapter, we discuss how to manage shortcuts.

App-V 5.0 and OSD files

As part of the updated feature set for App-V 5.0, the .osd file has been removed. The functionality that the .osd file and the sfttray.exe application provided has been built into the App-V client software. As mentioned earlier, this means that virtual application shortcuts point directly at the virtual application executable file.

Planning for App-V 5.0 shared content store

The shared content store is a feature in App-V 5.0 that enables the App-V client to stream packages from the source (HTTP URL or SMB UNC path) without having to cache the bulk of the packages on the client. It is a client-side setting. The shared content store feature replaces the shared cache feature in App-V 4.6. The shared content store has the following characteristics:

- **It reduces the amount of disk space use on the client**   This disk space reduction doesn't provide a lot of value for modern physical computing devices because of the very large disk drives used in client computers. However, in a virtual desktop environment or an RDS environment, the reduction in disk space is multiplied by many factors and thus provides really good value.

- **It reduces conflicts**   In multiuser environments such as RDS environments, there are risks of conflicts when multiple users are using the same apps, same files, and/or same cache. By using the shared content store, you can reduce the risk of conflicts.

- **It can be enabled during the App-V client setup or anytime thereafter**   You can enable the shared content store after installation by using the following methods:

    - Run the `Set-AppvClientConfiguration -SharedContentStoreMode 1` Windows PowerShell command. Then, reboot. Packages published after the enabling and reboot won't be completely downloaded to the client.

    - Set the value of the HKEY_LOCAL_MACHINE\SOFTWARE\Microsoft\AppV\Client \Streaming\SharedContentStoreMode key to 1. Then, reboot. Packages published after the enabling and reboot won't be completely downloaded to the client.

- **It works in a stand-alone App-V environment without a management and publishing server**   It also works in the full infrastructure and integrated App-V environments.

In most environments, setting and maintaining the App-V client configuration is performed best by using Group Policy. The same holds true for the shared content store setting because it is a client-side configuration. In Figure 5-4, the shared content store feature is set to Enabled in a Group Policy Object (GPO) setting.

CHAPTER 5

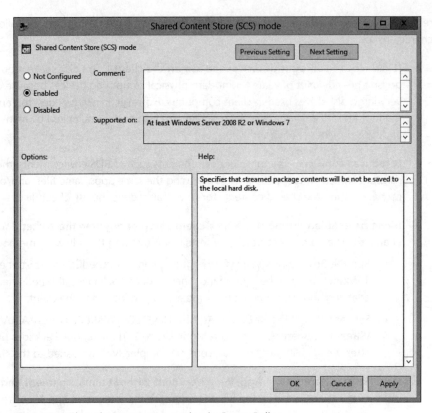

Figure 5-4 Shared content store setting in Group Policy

In Figure 5-5, an App-V client's local App-V folder size is shown with the shared content store disabled.

Figure 5-5 App-V local folder size without shared content store

In Figure 5-6, an App-V client's local App-V folder size is shown with the shared content store enabled. Note the difference in the folder size compared to the folder size shown in Figure 5-5.

Figure 5-6 App-V local folder size with shared content store being enabled

Inside OUT

Shared content store considerations

The shared content store should be considered only when the packages and the clients are connected by LAN-style connectivity. In other words, use the shared content store when there is a local high-speed network with low latency and enough bandwidth to handle the total number of simultaneous App-V clients. In addition, the packages should be stored on high-performing storage such as a SAN or NAS. With the shared content store enabled, there is a bigger load placed on the package source (often a SAN), so it is important to assess the impact and ensure that the environment is sized appropriately for your planned deployment.

Methods for deploying the App-V client

There are four ways to deploy the App-V client. You should understand these deployment options so that you can use the appropriate deployment method for your environment.

Manual deployment

A manual deployment is an installation in which an administrator double-clicks an installation file and clicks through the installation wizard until the installation is complete. In some cases, such as with Windows 7 clients, an administrator will have to ensure that the clients meet the prerequisites of the App-V client software. The prerequisites are discussed in the "Installing and configuring the App-V client" section later in this chapter. For Windows 8 and Windows 8.1 clients, you can install the App-V client without any additional software because the prerequisites are built into the operating systems. The steps to perform a manual installation on Windows 8.1 are shown below.

1. Insert the installation media. In this case, we are using the MDOP 2014 R2 DVD.

2. Navigate to the DVD drive, double-click the App-V folder, double-click the App-V 5.0 SP3 folder, dou ble-click the Client folder, and then double-click the appv_client_setup. exe installation file.

3. In the Microsoft Application Virtualization (App-V) Client Setup window, click Install.

4. On the Software License Terms page, click I Accept The License Terms and then click Next.

5. On the Use Microsoft Update To Help Keep Your Computer Secure And Up-To-Date page, select your preference for updates and then click Next.

6. On the Customer Experience Improvement Program page, select to join the program or not to join the program and then click Install.

7. On the Setup Completed Successfully page, click Close.

GPO deployment

Another option for deploying the App-V client is using Group Policy. Using Group Policy is usually a better choice than a manual deployment because it reduces the administrative overhead for the deployment. The benefits of a GPO deployment are as follows:

- **The deployment is automated**   Instead of manually clicking through the installation wizard, you can use Group Policy to install the App-V client automatically on computers. First, you need to extract the .msi installation file from the appv_client_setup.exe file from the installation media. You need to do this because Group Policy software distribution only supports the deployment of .msi installation files. To extract the .msi files to C:\temp\client, run the appv_client_setup.exe /Layout /LayoutDir=c:\temp\client from the folder that contains appv_client_setup.exe. From there, you will need to customize the .msi or use a command or script to perform the installation. This will enable you to have the end user license agreement accepted automatically during the deployment.

CHAPTER 5

- **You can target specific computers for installation**   You don't have to install the client on all domain-joined computers. By using security filtering or Windows Management Instrumentation (WMI) filtering on the GPO, you can target specific computers. In addition, you can easily install the client on newly deployed computers by adding the computers to a security group or specific OU location. Although this is better than a manual deployment, there is limited control, management, and reporting such as what is available in Configuration Manager.

- **You can automate the removal of the App-V client**   Group Policy enables you to install software. It also enables you to uninstall software. Thus, if you needed to remove the client from 100 computers, Group Policy easily could perform that task, removing the need for an administrator to manually uninstall the client on 100 computers.

Organizations that do not have a robust software distribution solution such as Configuration Manager should consider a deployment using Group Policy.

System Center 2012 Configuration Manager deployment

If you have Configuration Manager in your environment and use it for application deployment, then you should consider using it to deploy the App-V client, too. It provides the most feature-rich installation options and automation of all of the App-V client deployment methods. However, if you don't currently have Configuration Manager in your environment, an upcoming need to deploy the App-V client isn't a sufficient reason to deploy Configuration Manager. In the upcoming section titled "Installing the client with Configuration Manager," we walk through the installation steps.

Deployment by imaging

For organizations that use computer images to deploy new computers and refresh old computers, you can add the App-V client to the images. This ensures that the App-V client is installed on all of the computers, and it is a viable solution for organizations that do not have a robust software distribution environment. You should be aware of the following characteristics of deployment by imaging:

- **The App-V client version is tied to the image**   By tying the client to the image, you will have to update the image each time a new client version is released. If you add a lot of applications to your image, you can create extra administrative overhead maintaining images and applications. Many organizations are trying to move toward thin images whereby few, if any, applications are added to the image. Instead, applications are being added as part of the post-imaging process, which provides added flexibility and faster image deployments.

- **All computers will have the App-V client**   In many organizations, only certain departments have or use App-V. By making the App-V client part of the image, you may end up with the software installed on many computers on which it won't be used. This is one of the reasons that organizations are moving toward thin images, which help you install only what is needed for those who need it. This strategy helps keep computers running optimally.

- **All computers will have the same configuration**   When you add the App-V client to the image, each computer will have the same configuration for the client. They also will have the same client version. Some environments need to have different App-V settings for different departments. For example, you may want the engineering department to use App-V publishing servers in the engineering building. Or you may want the sales and marketing team to use the shared content store, while other departments shouldn't use it. Although you can configure these settings by using a GPO, you also can configure them as part of the client installation. So, depending on your environment, this may not be an issue.

App-V client for Remote Desktop

There are two App-V clients. One is the standard client that is used on App-V client computers. The other client is made specifically for RDS servers. You have to use the correct client version based on the target computer. For RDS environments, using the App-V client enables applications to stream to the RDS servers and thus to the clients. This is beneficial because you don't have to maintain the same applications individually across an entire RDS farm.

The installation wizards of the standard App-V client and the App-V client for RDS are identical. The only difference is that you use the appv_client_setup.exe installation file on the installation media for standard App-V clients, but you use the appv_client_setup_rds.exe installation file on the installation media for RDS servers. In the upcoming section titled "Installing App-V for Remote Desktop Services clients," we walk through the details of the installation.

Installing and configuring the App-V client

The App-V client is available on the Microsoft Desktop Optimization Pack (MDOP) installation media as an executable file. How you deploy an App-V client depends on the state of your App-V installation. In new installations of App-V, you can deploy an App-V client by using your organization's application deployment infrastructure or any of the following application deployment technologies:

- **Microsoft Intune**   Intune is a suitable deployment strategy for clients that rarely connect directly to your organization's network.

- **Group Policy**   App-V clients can be deployed by using a Group Policy software deployment.

CHAPTER 5

- **System Center 2012 R2 Configuration Manager**   You can configure an App-V client as an application or a package in Configuration Manager. After you configure an App-V client as an application, you can configure it as a dependency when you deploy other App-V applications.

- **Operating system image**   In many organizations, the App-V client is built into an operating system image with other clients, such as System Center 2012 Configuration Manager Service Pack 1 (SP1), System Center 2012 R2 Data Protection Manager, and System Center 2012 R2 Endpoint Protection.

You also can use these deployment methods to upgrade existing App-V clients. For example, an organization that has deployed the App-V 4.6 client to all devices can upgrade the client directly to the App-V 5.0 Service Pack 3 (SP3) client.

You also can deploy App-V clients manually, or you can run installation files by using a script. This method requires a substantial effort from an administrator and isn't a suitable strategy for large enterprise environments. Manual deployment of App-V clients might be necessary when working with individual devices in troubleshooting situations.

If you use Active Directory Domain Services (AD DS), a Group Policy software deployment is a good choice. You can use a GPO for deploying client software to selected computers or users.

Inside OUT

Consider Configuration Manager

Large organizations would benefit from using Configuration Manager. With Configuration Manager, you can schedule software installation to occur at a particular time. You also can automate the client installation if you use thin images by creating post-imaging deployment tasks. You can use precise computer targeting that allows you to target computers that meet specific conditions, such as having specific hardware or software, or computers that are online from a specified network location. Finally, you have access to Configuration Manager reporting, which can provide detailed deployment information for your application deployments.

Prerequisites for App-V client installation

Before installing an App-V client, you should be aware of the recommended hardware and software prerequisites for the App-V desktop client and the App-V client for RDS.

In general, the requirements are similar; both clients have two installer files. To install the App-V desktop client, you need an executable file named appv_client_setup.exe, and to install the App-V client for RDS, you need an executable file named appv_client_setup_rds.exe. Both installers can be used on 32-bit and 64-bit operating systems, but if you want to have more control or to perform advanced customization during setup, you should extract the content from the executable files to get two separate Windows Installers. For example, to extract the .msi files from the .exe, run the following command:

```
Appv_client_setup.exe /Layout /Layoutdir=c:\temp
```

The result of this command is two separate Windows Installers for 32-bit and 64-bit operating systems in the specified output directory:

appv_client_MSI_x64.msi

appv_client_MSI_x86.msi

Setup checks for the following prerequisite software:

- Windows 7, Window 8, or Windows 8.1

- Microsoft .NET Framework 4 or .NET Framework 3.51 (only relevant for computers that run Windows 7 because Windows 8 comes with Microsoft .NET Framework 4.5, which replaces Microsoft .NET Framework 4)

- Windows PowerShell 3.0 (only relevant for computers that run Windows 7)

- KB2533623 (only relevant for computers that run Windows 7)

- Microsoft Visual C++ 2005 Redistributable Package or newer (if using an .exe file for deployment)

An App-V client does not require CPU or RAM capacity beyond what is needed for the operating system.

Client hardware requirements

The following list displays the minimum supported hardware configuration for App-V 5.0 client installation:

- Processor, 1.4 gigahertz (GHz) or faster 32-bit (x86) or 64-bit (x64) processor

- RAM, 1 gigabyte (GB) (32-bit) or 2 GB (64-bit)

- Disk, 100 megabytes (MB) for installation, not including the disk space that is used by virtualized applications

CHAPTER 5

Supported operating systems

The following operating systems support the App-V 5.0 client:

- Windows 7 with SP1, 32-bit and 64-bit.

- Windows 8, 32-bit and 64-bit.

- Windows 8.1 requires an App-V 5.0 Service Pack 2 (SP2) or newer client., 32-bit and 64-bit

Installing the client by using Configuration Manager

Large organizations might prefer to use Configuration Manager to automate application deployment and management in an App-V enterprise environment. You can schedule software installation to occur at a particular time by using this method.

Configuration Manager can deliver App-V applications to clients in two ways: streaming delivery and local delivery (download and run). The default option when creating a new streaming package is to download content from a distribution point and run it locally.

Deploying an application by using the streaming delivery method enables an App-V client to download a virtual application to an App-V cache through HTTP or Hypertext Transfer Protocol Secure (HTTPS). Initially, only shortcuts deploy for a streamed application. Then, applications copy to a client's App-V cache when a user starts the application. This method works best when clients have a consistent, high-bandwidth connection. If a client's device is offline when the user first tries to run the application, the attempt will fail because the App-V client is unable to contact a distribution point.

Deploying an application by using the local delivery (download and run) method causes the Configuration Manager client to download an application to its own client cache by using standard distribution point functionality, which includes using Background Intelligent Transfer Service (BITS). When you run the App-V application, the App-V client streams the assets into the App-V cache. However, instead of getting the files from a server, it retrieves them from the local Configuration Manager client cache. This means that the application is available even if the client device is offline, but the local delivery application can consume up to twice the hard drive space of the streaming delivery application.

Configuration Manager adds support to manage App-V 5.0 applications. Configuration Manager uses publicly documented interfaces to interact with App-V client software. All integrations implement by using the following methods:

- **Windows PowerShell**   Configuration Manager uses the App-V client module for Windows PowerShell to manage App-V objects, including virtual applications, connection groups, and dynamic configuration files.

- **Configuration Manager client**   The Configuration Manager client determines the appropriate download or streaming location (distribution point), as with any application.

- **Windows Management Instrumentation (WMI)**   Configuration Manager uses an App-V client's WMI classes to query and report on the status of virtual applications that reside on the computer.

- **Software metering**   Software metering rules in Configuration Manager monitor application usage.

Creating an application for the App-V client

In Configuration Manager, click the Software Library workspace. Then, in the left pane, expand Application Management, right-click Applications, and then click Create Application. The Create Application Wizard will display the General page, shown in Figure 5-7. Select the option to Manually Specify The Application Information and then click Next.

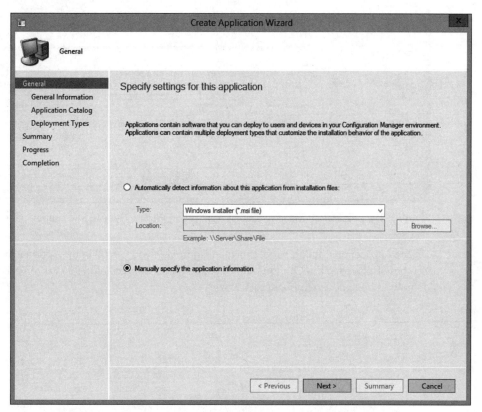

Figure 5-7 Configuration Manager Create Application Wizard, General page

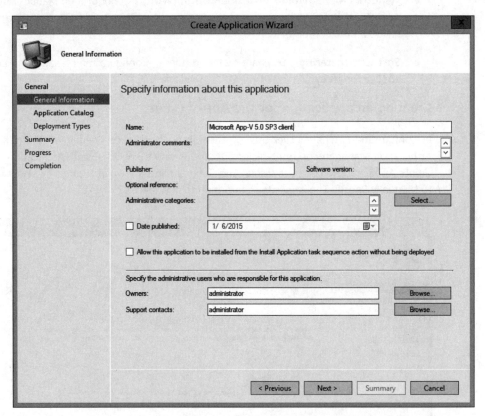

The Create Application Wizard, shown in Figure 5-8, will then display the General Information page. Enter the name of your application and enter the optional information in the other fields and then click Next.

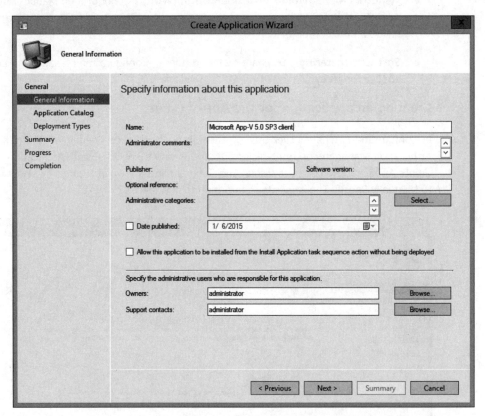

Figure 5-8 Configuration Manager Create Application Wizard, General Information page

On the Application Catalog page, shown in Figure 5-9, you can fill in the optional information, which is displayed in the Configuration Manager application catalog, or you can accept the defaults. When you are finished, click Next.

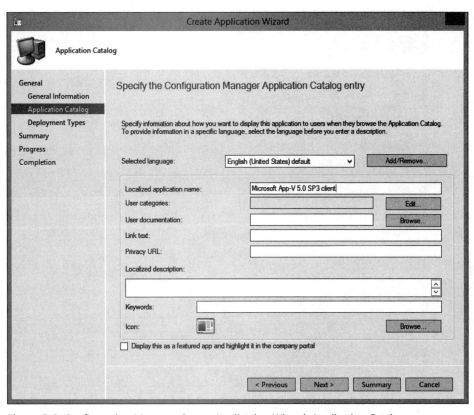

Figure 5-9 Configuration Manager Create Application Wizard, Application Catalog page

On the Deployment Types page, shown in Figure 5-10, click Add. This will run the Create Deployment Type Wizard.

CHAPTER 5

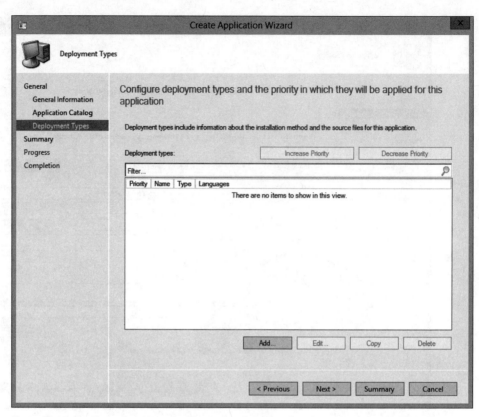

Figure 5-10 Configuration Manager Create Application Wizard, Deployment Types page

On the General page of the Create Deployment Type Wizard, shown in Figure 5-11, select the option to Manually Specify The Deployment Type Information and then click Next.

CHAPTER 5

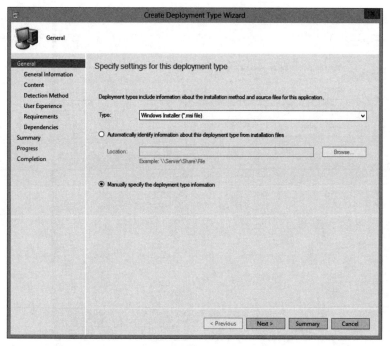

Figure 5-11 Configuration Manager Create Deployment Type Wizard, General page

On the General Information page, shown in Figure 5-12, enter a name such as App-V 5.0 SP3 Client Deployment. This page also allows you to provide additional comments or languages that could assist in identifying and documenting the deployment type.

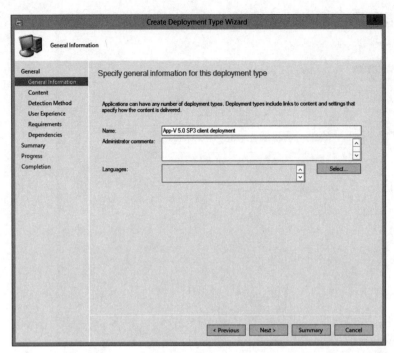

Figure 5-12 Configuration Manager Create Deployment Type Wizard, General Information page

On the Content page, shown in Figure 5-13, specify the universal naming convention (UNC) path of the network location to store the deployment type's content. You also can configure other options such as keeping the cache content persistent and enabling the clients to share the content with other clients on the same network. Additionally, the full CLI command can be specified for the target devices.

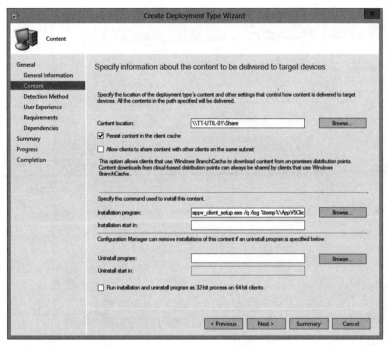

Figure 5-13 Configuration Manager Create Deployment Type Wizard, Content page

On the Detection Method page, you can add a clause to detect applications that are already present. Once you add a clause, the Detection Rule window, shown in Figure 5-14, is displayed. From there, specify the desired setting type from the Setting Type drop-down menu. You can choose File System, Registry, or Windows Installer File.

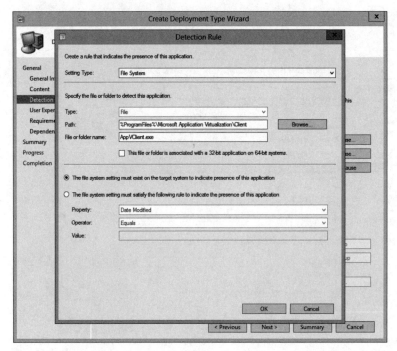

Figure 5-14 Configuration Manager Create Deployment Type Wizard, Detection Rule window

The User Experience page, shown in Figure 5-15, provides the configuration options for how the end users will view the result and whether they must be present at the computer.

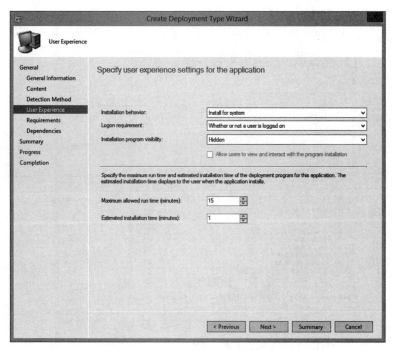

Figure 5-15 Configuration Manager Create Deployment Type Wizard, User Experience page

The Requirements page allows you to create a requirement for your deployment. When you create a requirement, the Create Requirement window, shown in Figure 5-16, is displayed. Requirements provide methods of configuring conditions that must be met for the deployment to proceed.

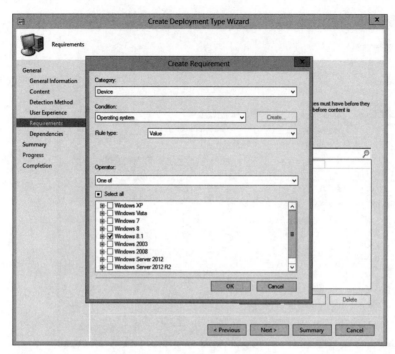

Figure 5-16 Configuration Manager Create Deployment Type Wizard, Create Requirement window

The Dependencies page, shown in Figure 5-17, allows you to configure other software dependencies that must be preinstalled before the deployment type is attempted. The dependency configuration also allows you to specify whether a dependency should be installed automatically to remediate any issues that are detected.

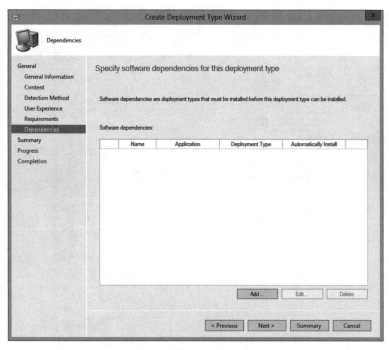

Figure 5-17 Configuration Manager Create Deployment Type Wizard, Dependencies page

The Summary page, shown in Figure 5-18, provides a summary of all of the configuration options that you specified in the Create Deployment Type Wizard. To proceed with the settings shown, click Next.

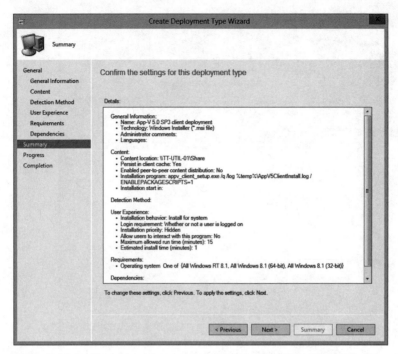

Figure 5-18 Configuration Manager Create Deployment Type Wizard, Summary page

The wizard will create the deployment type and report back any problems that were encountered during the process. Thereafter, the Completion page, shown in Figure 5-19, will be displayed.

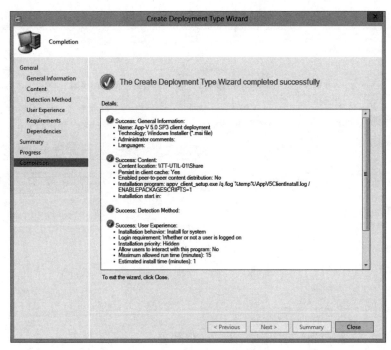

Figure 5-19 Configuration Manager Create Deployment Type Wizard, Completion page

After the deployment type information is specified, you will see the deployment type in the Create Application Wizard window, as shown in Figure 5-20. Click Next to continue.

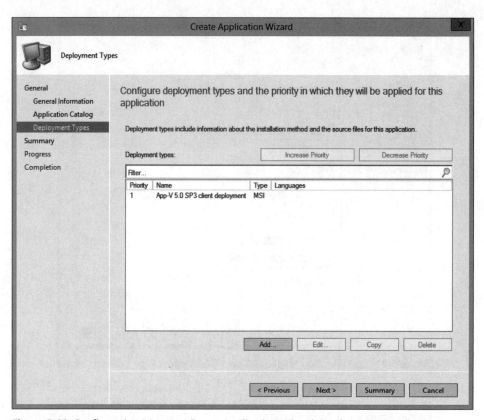

Figure 5-20 Configuration Manager Create Application Wizard, Deployment Types page

Then, the Summary page will be displayed, as shown in Figure 5-21. Review the settings and then click Next.

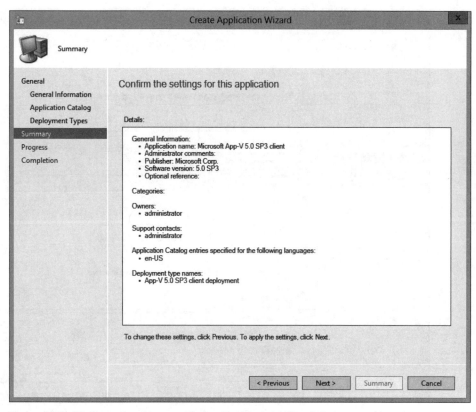

Figure 5-21 Configuration Manager Create Application Wizard, Summary page

After the creation of the application, the Completion page, shown in Figure 5-22, will be displayed.

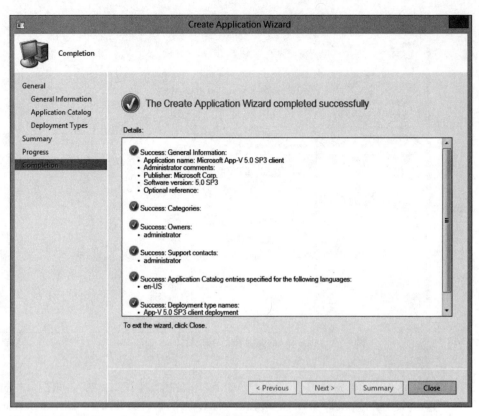

Figure 5-22 Configuration Manager Create Application Wizard, Completion page

There are two additional tasks that you need to perform to deploy the application to your Configuration Manager clients:

1. **Distribute the content to your distribution points.** In Configuration Manager, right-click the application and then click Distribute Content. Specify the distribution points or distribution point groups to which you want to distribute the content during the wizard.

2. **Deploy the application.** In Configuration Manager, right-click the application and then click Deploy. Walk through the wizard to choose the collection that you will target and the deployment options, such as the date, time, and user experience.

Installing the App-V for Remote Desktop Services client

The following operating systems support the App-V 5.0 client for RDS:

- Windows Server 2008 R2 Standard, Windows Server 2008 R2 Enterprise, and Windows Server 2008 R2 Datacenter with SP1

- Windows Server 2012

- Windows Server 2012 R2, which requires an App-V client 5.0 SP2 or newer client

Before installing the client for RDS, Remote Desktop Services roles must already be installed. The client for RDS is supported in a stand-alone App-V environment, an integrated App-V deployment, or a full infrastructure App-V deployment.

The installation process for the App-V client for RDS is straightforward and uses a standard installation wizard. Before you begin, go to the command prompt and run the `change user /install` command. This will put the RDS server into installation mode, which reduces issues when installing applications on an RDS server. Then, launch the appv_client_setup_rds.exe executable file and click the Install button, as shown in Figure 5-23.

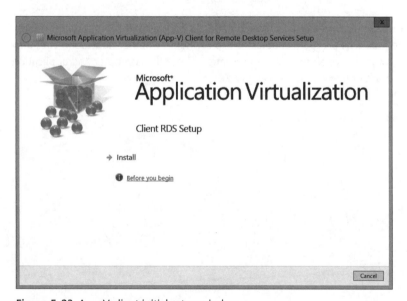

Figure 5-23 App-V client initial setup window

The next screen of the wizard is the Software License Terms page, shown in Figure 5-24. You must accept the terms to continue the installation.

CHAPTER 5

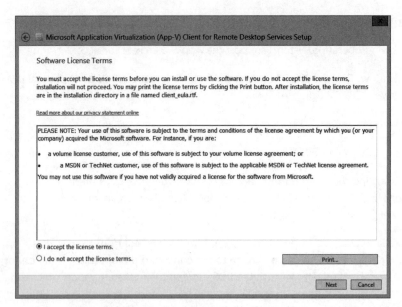

Figure 5-24 App-V client setup, Software License Terms page

The next page displays the Customer Experience Improvement Program information, as shown in Figure 5-25. The program enables you to configure whether non-identifying information can be sent to Microsoft to collect information about the computer and application. Select your program option and then click Install.

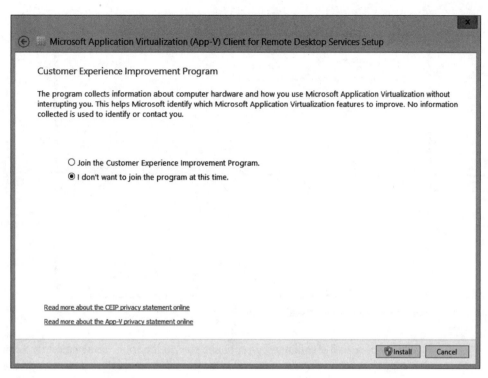

Figure 5-25 App-V client setup, Customer Experience Improvement Program page

The App-V client for RDS will be installed. After it has been installed successfully, a confirmation screen, the final screen of the wizard, will appear, as shown in Figure 5-26.

CHAPTER 5

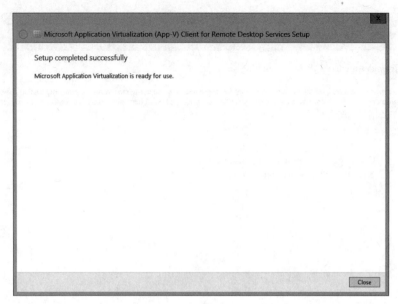

Figure 5-26 App-V client setup completion

Finally, go back to the command prompt and run the `change user/execute` command so that the server is back in execution mode, which is the standard mode when you aren't installing applications.

Configuring the App-V client for stand-alone mode

Stand-alone deployments do not need a management server, a management server database, or a publishing server.

In the stand-alone deployment model, you use the App-V Sequencer to create sequenced App-V applications as virtual application packages. You then deploy those sequenced applications in the same way you would deploy other applications in .msi file format—for example, by using Group Policy, Intune, Configuration Manager, or another application deployment technology. In App-V 5.0, you can deploy a package in a stand-alone deployment without any additional infrastructure technologies by using Windows PowerShell, which is an easy way to test package functionality before a mass deployment. The process for delivering an application consists of two main steps: adding and publishing.

To add a package, use the Windows PowerShell `Add-AppvClientPackage` cmdlet. For example, to add a package for Microsoft Office Excel Viewer, which is located in the Packages \Excel folder, you would use the following command:

```
Add-AppvClientPackage -path c:\packages\excel\excelviewer.appv
```

Adding a package will register an application for the computer, but it won't make the package available for the user or computer. The next step is to publish the package by using the Windows PowerShell `Publish-AppvClinetPackage` cmdlet, which requires you to specify at least the name of the package. For example:

```
Publish-AppvClientPackage -name ExcelViewer
```

To get the package name, you can run the `Get-AppvClientPackage | Select Name` command. The previous example command publishes a package to the current user. You also can publish an application globally, which will make the application available for all users. You can combine the steps in a single command, for example:

```
Add-AppvClientPackage -path c:\packages\excel\excelviewer.appv |
Publish-AppvClientPackage
```

In some situations, you might need to add and publish a different version of a package. In that case, use the `Publish-AppvClientPackage` cmdlet with the following parameters: PackageID, VersionID, and DynamicUserConfigurationFile. For example:

```
Publish-AppvClientPackage -name ExcelViewer -version 1 -DynamicUserConfiguration
c:\content\policies\ExcelViewer.xml
```

This will publish version 1 of a package to all users on a computer, and it will apply the dynamic configuration policy file.

To identify all of the packages that are assigned for a specific user, you can use the `Get-AppvClientPackage` cmdlet.

Unpublishing a package removes the assignments for a particular user, but it does not remove the package from a computer. To unpublish, use the following command:

```
Unpublish-AppvClientPackage "ExcelViewer"
```

To remove the package from a computer, you can use the following command:

```
Remove-AppvClientPackage "ExcelViewer"
```

Inside OUT

Removing packages

By default, cached packages are stored in the %PROGRAMDATA%\App-V folder. Administrators only have Read access to the cached files, even though at first glance it appears that administrators have Full Control permissions to the folder structure. I have had a customer change the file and folder permissions and ownership of the cached App-V data to manually remove cached packages. However, on the client from which the files and folders were manually removed, some files and folders weren't able to be deleted. Thereafter, the client began experiencing difficulty syncing with the publishing server. To avoid serious issues with the client, avoid changing ownership and permissions on the files to manually delete them. Instead, use the Remove-AppvClientPackage cmdlet to remove packages.

App-V and Virtual Desktop Infrastructure (VDI) solution

You can integrate App-V into a Microsoft Virtual Desktop Infrastructure (VDI) environment. However, there are special considerations to ensure that the two technologies work seamlessly and efficiently. There are two types of VDI environments:

- **Session-based VDI**   Session-based VDI provides shared desktops and virtualized applications (with RemoteApp). Session-based VDI relies heavily on the Remote Desktop Session Host (RD Session Host) servers to provide the functionality. In situations without App-V in which applications can't be installed on the same RDS server, you often have to deploy servers specifically for applications. For example, let's say that you want to provide Internet Explorer 10 and Internet Explorer 11 to users. Two different versions of Internet Explorer aren't supported on a single server. You have to deploy Internet Explorer 10 to one server and Internet Explorer 11 to a different server. Based on the number of users and the high availability requirements, you soon may have small server farms just for those applications. When you add other applications that conflict with one other, it becomes an administrative burden.

- **VM-based VDI**   VM-based VDI provides users with their own VM. The VMs can be pooled, which allows users to use any available VM in the pool. Pooled VMs are referred to as stateless because they do not maintain the operating system state. Or, the VMs can be personal, which allows changes to the operating system to be saved. Personal VMs are referred to as stateful VMs and provide users with an experience similar to their physical client computer. However, this solution is expensive and cost-prohibitive for many organizations. You can use user state virtualization to save some operating system settings and data, but applications aren't saved.

App-V 5.0 and third-party production integration

App-V 5.0 supports and integrates with several third-party products to enhance functionality of application delivery and management. Below are a couple of the most popular third-party products that integrate with App-V, along with an overview of the integrated solution.

- Citrix XenApp and XenDesktop   Citrix provides VM solutions and virtual application solutions. Both of these solutions integrate with App-V. The primary benefits of integrating the Citrix applications with App-V are the following:

  - **Virtual applications can be accessed from multiple operating systems**   Citrix supports Windows operating systems and Mac and Linux operating systems. By integrating App-V with Citrix, your App-V applications can be accessed by all of the operating systems supported on the Citrix platform.

  - **User settings can roam among devices and locations**   When you integrate App-V with Citrix, you can take advantage of the roaming features in Citrix. Roaming allows users to start a virtual application on one device. Later, the users can go to a different location, use a different device, and continue their virtual application session right where they left off.

- **AppSense**   AppSense offers several applications that integrate with App-V, including Environment Manager and Application Manager. The following are benefits of integrating AppSense solutions with App-V:

  - They provide precise user control so that you can control the environment based on where a user is, the time of the day, and the type of device being used.

  - They provide user settings and personalization to users regardless of the computing device that they are using. This is an enhancement to Microsoft's User Experience Virtualization.

Benefits of App-V and VDI integration

There are several benefits of integrating App-V with a Microsoft VDI environment. Some of the benefits are specific to a VM-based VDI, while other benefits are specific to a session-based VDI. The list below represents some of the key benefits:

- **Reduce the number of RDS servers**   Earlier in this section, we talked about having to separate applications that conflict with one another. This results in a larger number of RDS servers than in an environment without application conflicts. By using App-V in a VDI environment, you can deploy the applications by using App-V and reduce the number of RDS servers. App-V supports a much wider pairing of applications that conflict.

- **Reduce the total amount of storage required**   Each VM, whether a back-end RDS server, a virtualization host, or a client computer VM, takes up storage space. Additionally, applications take up storage space, especially when they are installed on hundreds or thousands of computers. App-V helps bring down the total amount of storage required because the total number of computers is reduced and the application footprint is reduced drastically.

CHAPTER 5

- **Reduce the number of images**   In many environments without App-V, you must have multiple images to meet the requirements of each department. For example, you might have an engineering image that has all of the engineering-related applications. You'd also have a corporate image that has all of the general applications, such as a productivity suite and an antivirus client. With an App-V client integrated into the VDI environment, you can use a single image and deliver apps virtually.

- **Reduce the total cost of ownership**   You can reduce your overall costs based on the savings from a reduced server footprint, reduced storage use, and a reduced number of images.

Building images with App-V

One of the decisions that you have to make is how to deploy the App-V client. We've already discussed the various deployment options. Now, we will take a closer look at the considerations for installing the App-V client into your images.

First, there are two options for your images. The first option is to install the App-V client into the image. The second option is to deploy the App-V client after an image is deployed. To provide users with immediate access to virtual applications, you should install the App-V client in the image. However, some organizations have standardized on a thin image and try to avoid adding any more applications to their images.

App-V options for image creation

There are three options to consider when you install the App-V client into your images:

- **Pre-publish App-V applications**   By pre-publishing App-V applications, you will have the shortcuts and FTAs on the image. However, the applications won't be cached as part of the image.

- **Pre-publish App-V applications and pre-cache App-V applications**   By pre-caching App-V applications along with pre-publishing the App-V applications, you will have the shortcuts, FTAs, and applications present on the image. This option presents the best user experience because performance is increased by the presence of the cached applications.

- **Use shared content store mode**   As mentioned in the section earlier in this chapter titled "Planning for App-V 5.0 shared content store," the shared content store offers multiple benefits. From the image creation perspective, you can use the shared content store instead of pre-publishing and pre-caching applications. This is the simplest approach, but it should be considered only in high-performing environments because the user experience can be degraded if any aspect of the infrastructure isn't well suited for the shared content store.

Troubleshooting App-V client installation

The most common App-V client installation issue occurs when a computer does not meet the App-V client prerequisites, but there are other installation issues. Table 5-2 displays common installation error codes associated with the App-V 5.0 and newer clients.

Table 5-2 Common App-V installation error codes

Error code	Description	Resolution
1670	Unsupported operating system.	Install the client on a supported operating system.
1671	RDS feature isn't enabled.	Add RDS role.
1672	Windows PowerShell 3.0 or later isn't installed.	Install Windows PowerShell 3.0 or later.
1673	The .NET 4.0 Full Client isn't installed.	Install the .NET 4.0 Full Client.
1674	App-V 4.6 SP1 or older is installed.	Uninstall existing App-V client.
1677	Visual C++ 2010 Runtime isn't installed.	Install Visual C++ 2010 Runtime.

As with many problems, you should look at all of the available log files to help you trouble-shoot issues. Your first stop should be the Windows Event Log. App-V clients have a dedicated set of App-V logs under Applications And Services Logs, as shown in Figure 5-27.

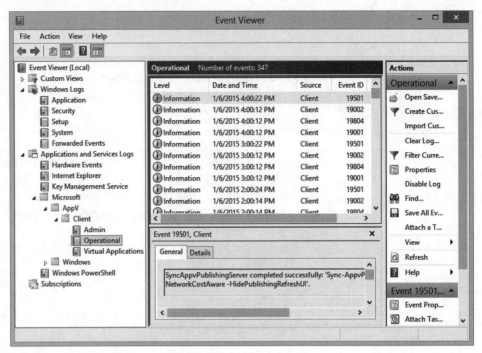

Figure 5-27 App-V client event logs

The Admin log often is filled with error messages. When troubleshooting, the Admin log is a good place to start. If you need additional information, the Operational log is quite verbose. It contains a large number of informational messages that will help you deduce what the client was doing at a given date and time. The Virtual Applications log usually is empty. When troubleshooting, however, it is a good idea to look through all three of the logs and combine the information to figure out your next steps.

Sometimes, you will need more information than what you find in the three App-V logs. Fortunately, there are a number of additional logs available. Most of them are debug logs that are disabled by default. To see the additional logs, open the Event Viewer, click the View menu, and then click Show Analytic And Debug Logs, as shown in Figure 5-28.

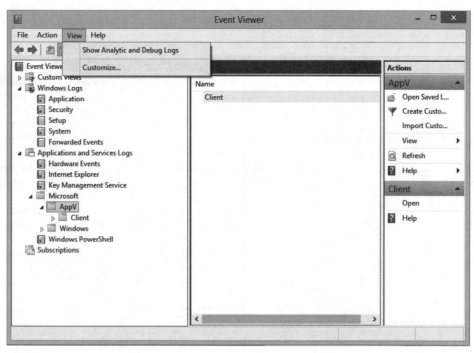

Figure 5-28 Enabling App-V debug logs

After you configure the Event Viewer to show the additional logs, a large number of new logs will be displayed, as shown in Figure 5-29.

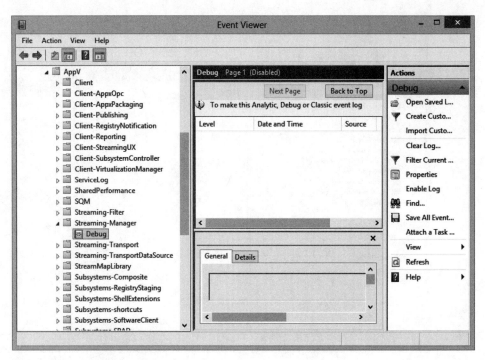

Figure 5-29 App-V debug logs

Under each of the new logs, there is a Debug log. However, the debug logs are disabled by default. To enable the logs, right-click the desired debug log and then click Enable Log, as shown in Figure 5-30.

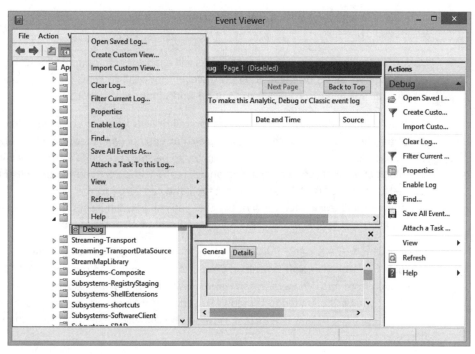

Figure 5-30 Enabling App-V debug log

TROUBLESHOOTING

Debug logging

You should only enable debug logs when troubleshooting. Enabling debug logs should be considered a temporary administrative configuration because the additional logging can cause reduced performance on a computer. Additionally, debug logging, depending on the configuration, can take up a large amount of disk space and eventually cause the system to experience serious issues if the system disk runs out of space. For App-V, all the debug logs are set to a small maximum size of about 1 MB. That is helpful from a disk space perspective. However, the logs also are configured, by default, to not overwrite events. That means when they fill up, new events won't be written. Sometimes, this isn't desired in a troubleshooting scenario.

Managing App-V client properties

Once you have the App-V client deployed in your environment, the next step is understanding how to manage those clients. Each environment has different needs, and it isn't uncommon for those needs to change over time. To effectively manage your App-V clients, you will need

CHAPTER 5

to be familiar with the App-V Client Management UI application, Group Policy, and Windows PowerShell.

Understanding how each of these tools works will enable you to optimize for future growth and change. As things progress, you may discover that certain clients require unique configurations. You will need to know which solution works in those situations.

The App-V Client Management UI Application will provide you with some basic information about the client, such as which applications are currently downloaded and which ones are part of a connection group. You also have the ability to perform certain tasks, such as initiating the download of an application or repairing an application. It is worth noting that all of the actions you perform in the App-V Client UI application also can be performed by using Windows PowerShell. In fact, you'll notice that you can you can perform more management actions from Windows PowerShell than you can from the UI application.

Starting with App-V 5.0 SP2, the App-V Client UI application is a separate download that is available from the Microsoft Download Center. You can download the App-V 5.0 Client UI application from *http://www.microsoft.com/en-us/download/details.aspx?id=41186*. Without the client, you will be limited to Windows PowerShell for all of your management tasks. For administrators, this usually is sufficient. However, for end users, the UI application provides the best user experience.

To utilize all of the available actions from within the App-V Client UI application, you must have administrative access on the computers running the App-V client.

To access the App-V Client UI application, perform the following steps:

1. On the computer running the App-V client, click Start and then select Microsoft Application Virtualization Client. If you don't see it in the Start menu, type Microsoft App and click the client from the search results.

2. In the Microsoft Application Virtualization Client, click the tab that you want to review. Each tab will provide a unique set of options:

3. **Overview**   The Overview tab provides you three basic functions. These are shown in Figure 5-31:

    Update   This action will force a connection to the publishing server for receiving new packages.

    Download All Virtual Applications   This action will download a copy of all available virtual applications so they are available for offline use.

    Work Offline   This action puts the App-V client in offline mode, preventing any further virtual application updates.

CHAPTER 5

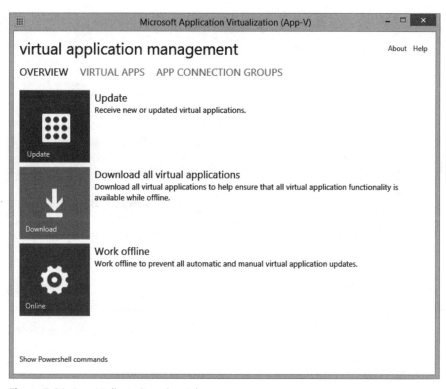

Figure 5-31 App-V client, Overview tab

4. **Virtual Apps**   The Virtual Apps tab displays all of the available virtual applications and their current status and provides a few basic management actions. These are shown in Figure 5-32:

Download   This action gives you the option to download specific virtualized applications for offline use.

Repair   This action triggers a repair of the user state for the particular virtual application.

CHAPTER 5

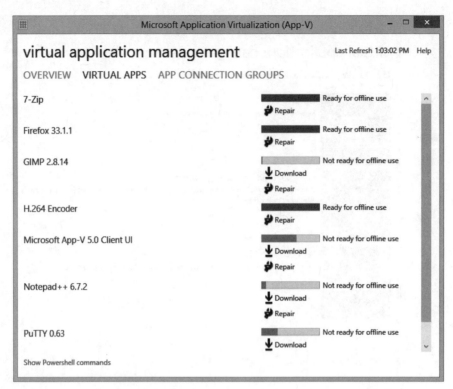

Figure 5-32 App-V client, Virtual Apps tab

5. **App Connection Groups**   The App Connection Groups tab displays all of the available grouped applications and their current status and provides the same basic management actions as the Virtual Apps tab. These are shown in Figure 5-33.

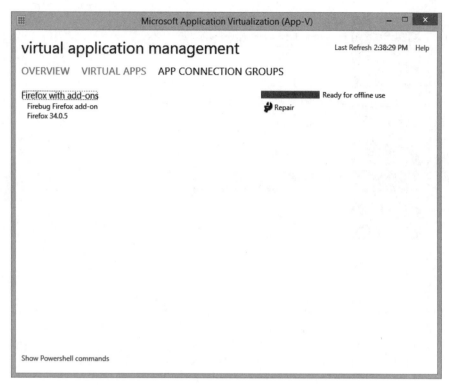

Figure 5-33 App-V client, App Connection Groups tab

Each of the tabs on the Microsoft Application Virtualization Client gives you the option to view the corresponding Windows PowerShell commands. The commands can be viewed by clicking the Show PowerShell Commands link at the bottom of each page. Output of some Windows PowerShell commands is shown in Figure 5-34.

CHAPTER 5

Figure 5-34 App-V client displaying the Windows PowerShell commands

Managing virtual applications

The Microsoft Application Virtualization Client provides you one method for interacting with applications. Let's take a closer look at this.

On the Overview tab of the Microsoft Application Virtualization Client, you have the option to update. Clicking Update will trigger a connection with the publishing server to update the list of available applications. This action is helpful when new packages are published.

On the Virtual Apps tab, you have the option to download and repair listed applications. The download action is pretty self-explanatory. You click this option if your applications aren't set up to download automatically or if you want to download a single application for offline use. The repair option triggers a few actions. It resets the virtualized application extensions and associated user state. This effectively restores the application to its original build state. When initiating a repair, it is important to note that any user customizations associated with that application also will be reset.

Managing file type associations

FTAs provide registered extensions between the operating system and the virtualized applications. For example, a .docx file will open an appropriate App-V application such as Microsoft Word when a user opens a file that has that extension. FTAs also might include alternate methods called shell integrations to start applications for different purposes, such as viewing, editing, and printing. Similar to shortcuts, you can enable or disable them by setting a value in a configuration file.

You can edit the default FTAs during the sequencing of an application, as shown in Figure 5-35, by selecting the Shortcuts And FTAs tab. You can create new associations by right-clicking File Type Associations and then clicking Add File Type Associations.

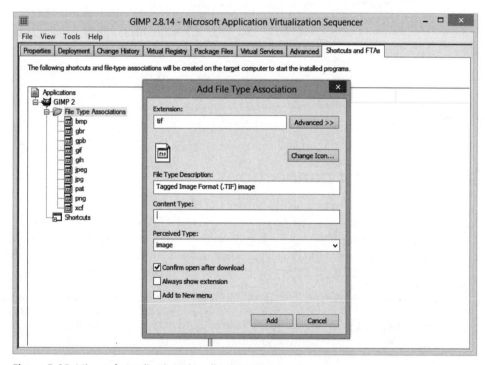

Figure 5-35 Microsoft Application Virtualization Sequencer

Alternatively, you can customize file type associations by setting a value in the configuration file. In the following example, which is a partial.xml file, the extension with the name .debug will invoke an application with the name wordpad.exe:

```
<FileTypeAssociations Enabled="true">

<Extensions>
```

```
<Extension Category="AppV.FileTypeAssociation">

    <FileTypeAssociation>

        <FileExtension MimeAssociation="true">

            <Name>.debug</Name>

            <ProgId>wordpad.DocumentMacroEnabled.12</ProgId>

            <PerceivedType>document</PerceivedType>

            <ContentType>application/vnd.ms-wordpad.document
            .macroEnabled.12</ContentType>

            <OpenWithList>

                    <ApplicationName>wordpad.exe</ApplicationName>

            </OpenWithList>

            <OpenWithProgIds>

                    <ProgId>wordpad.8</ProgId>

            </OpenWithProgIds>

        </FileExtension>
```

Managing server connections

Based on various factors, such as latency and client performance, you may need to add publishing servers or adjust various connectivity options to improve the user experience. To do so, you need to be familiar with the Windows PowerShell commands. The Add-AppvPublishing-Server cmdlet is used to assign a publishing server to the client. For example, to add a publishing server named tt-util-05 to your client, run the following command:

```
Add-AppvPublishingServer -URL http://tt-util-05.tailspintoys.com:80 –Name tt-util-05
```

After running this command, you will see output similar to the following:

```
Id : 2

SetByGroupPolicy : False

Name : tt-util-05

URL : http://tt-util-05.tailspintoys.com:80

GlobalRefreshEnabled : False

GlobalRefreshOnLogon : False

GlobalRefreshInterval : 0
```

```
GlobalRefreshIntervalUnit : Day

UserRefreshEnabled : True

UserRefreshOnLogon : True

UserRefreshInterval : 0

UserRefreshIntervalUnit : Day

The returned Id - in this case 1

Set-AppvPublishingServer is used to assign values
```

The values reported back refer to the various refresh intervals associated with this publishing server. You can adjust these settings by using the Set-AppvPublishingServer cmdlet. For example, to enable global refresh and global refresh on logon, run the following command:

```
Set-AppVPublishingServer -ServerID 1 -GlobalRefreshEnabled 1 -GlobalRefreshOnLogon 1
```

Using Windows PowerShell to configure the App-V client

App-V has added Windows PowerShell cmdlet support to its 5.0 release. This enhancement gives administrators the ability to perform tasks and automate routine activities, such as adding a new package, publishing packages, and granting access to an application.

It is important to note that all App-V PowerShell cmdlets require opening Windows PowerShell with elevated privileges.

If the system on which you are working has the App-V 5.0 client installed, then the App-V client module for Windows PowerShell will be imported already. You can confirm this by running the following command, as shown in Figure 5-36:

```
Get-Module -All | FL
```

CHAPTER 5

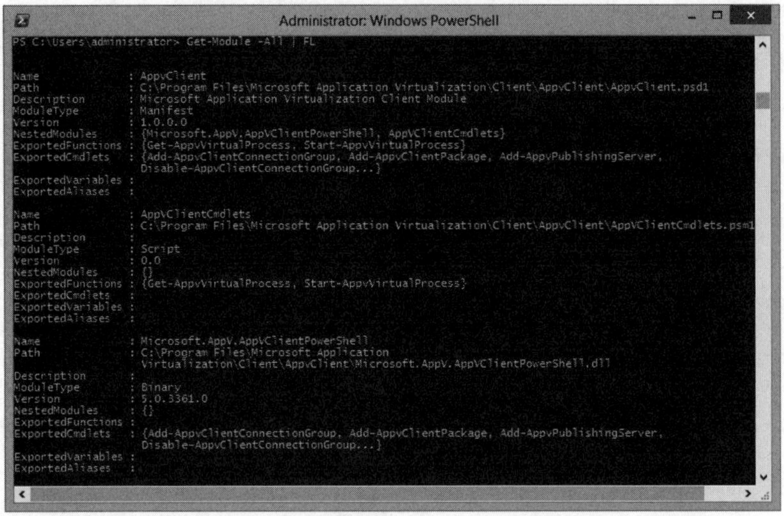

Figure 5-36 Windows PowerShell displaying App-V modules

If the AppVClient module isn't listed, you can import it manually using the following steps:

1. First, you may need to enable the RemoteSigned execution policy for Windows PowerShell. To do so, run the following command:

```
Set-ExecutionPolicy RemoteSigned
```

2. Next, import the AppVClient module by running the following command:

```
Import-Module AppVClient
```

Once the AppVClient module is imported, you can display all the Windows PowerShell cmdlets that are part of the module by using the following command, as shown in Figure 5-37:

```
Get-Command -Module AppVClient
```

Figure 5-37 Windows PowerShell displaying the cmdlets that are part of the AppVClient module

With the assortment of available cmdlets, you have the flexibility to perform all App-V management tasks by using Windows PowerShell. Let's take a look at some of the fundamental management tasks an administrator will perform and how to accomplish them by using Windows PowerShell.

One of the tasks an App-V administrator will perform is adding App-V packages to clients, especially in environments that don't have a publishing server. To do this, you can use the Add-AppvClientPackage cmdlet. For example, to add the 7-zip.appv package from a shared folder named Share on a server named tt-util-01, you run the following command:

```
Add-AppvClientPackage –Path \\tt-util-01\Share\7-Zip.appv
```

Next, you need to publish the package to make it available. To do this, you need to use the Publish-AppvClientPackage cmdlet, as follows:

```
Publish-AppvClientPackage – Name 7-Zip
```

You can combine the two commands into a single command to add and publish the package globally:

```
Add-AppvClientPackage –Path \\tt-util-01\Share\7-Zip.appv | Publish-AppvClientPackage
-Global
```

CHAPTER 5

Using Group Policy to manage the App-V client

Another option for managing your App-V client configuration includes using Group Policy. You can import the App-V ADMX templates, which enable you to configure client settings for App-V clients.

To install and begin using the App-V 5.0 ADMX templates, perform the following steps:

1. Download the latest App-V 5.0 ADMX templates. You can download them from www.microsoft.com/en-us/download/details.aspx?id=41183.

2. On the computer on which you manage Group Policy, copy the template .admx file to the following directory: %SYSTEMDRIVE%\Windows\PolicyDefinitions. Or, if you have a Central Store, copy the template to the PolicyDefinitions folder there.

3. On the same computer, copy the .adml file to the following directory: %SYSTEMDRIVE% \Windows\PolicyDefinitions\en-US. Or, if you have a Central Store, copy the .adml file to the directory in the Central Store.

4. After you have copied the files, open the Group Policy Management Console to create a GPO for your App-V 5.0 clients. In the GPO, you can find the App-V settings at the Computer Configuration/Policies/Administrative Templates/System/App-V node.

Inside OUT

Creating a Central Store for Group Policy

When administrators work with Group Policy administrative templates, they often experience difficulties such as having to modify certain GPOs from specific computers, encountering errors when trying to modify GPOs on some computers, and being unable to locate some administrative template settings from certain computers. All of these issues stem from not having a Central Store for Group Policy. Without a Central Store, administrative template files are stored on each computer that you use to manage GPOs, assuming that you copied the administrative template files to all of those computers. A Central Store centralizes administrative template files to a location that automatically is synchronized with all domain controllers. Additionally, all of the Microsoft Group Policy management tools automatically use the Central Store. This means that you can place the App-V administrative template files into the Central Store once and then be able to modify App-V GPO settings from any domain-joined computer by using the Group Policy management tools.

To create a Central Store for Group Policy in a domain named tailspintoys.com, perform the following steps:

1. Sign into a domain controller, open File Explorer, and navigate to \\tailspintoys .cocm\\SYSVOL\tailspintoys.com\Policies.

2. Create a new folder named PolicyDefinitions in the Policies folder.

3. In File Explorer, navigate to the %SYSTEMROOT%\PolicyDefinitions folder on the domain controller.

4. Copy all of the files and folders in the %SYSTEMROOT%\PolicyDefinitions folder to the \\tailspintoys.cocm\\SYSVOL\tailspintoys.com\Policies\PolicyDefinitions folder.

5. Copy the App-V administrative template files and any other administrative template files that you use to the \\tailspintoys.cocm\\SYSVOL\tailspintoys.com \Policies\PolicyDefinitions folder.

6. After replication, all of the administrative template files will be stored on each domain controller, and you can begin taking advantage of the Central Store.

The available App-V policies are divided into the following eight nodes, as shown in Figure 5-38:.

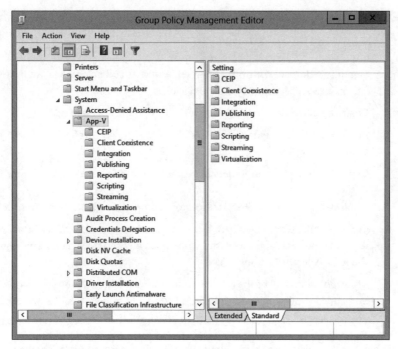

Figure 5-38 Group Policy Management Editor

- **CEIP**   The policies in this node configure settings that are related to joining the Microsoft Customer Experience Program (CEIP).

- **Client Coexistence**   The policies in this node enable automatic migration of packages that were created using a previous version of App-V.

- **Integration**   The policies in this node specify the file paths in a user profile that do not roam with a user profile when used with App-V. You also can use the policies in this node to configure the location of symbolic links to the current version of a published package.

- **Publishing**   The policies in this node specify the location of a publishing server and whether the client UI notifies a user when a publishing refresh is taking place.

- **Reporting**   The policies in this node specify the location of an App-V reporting server.

- **Scripting**   The policies in this node configure whether scripts that are defined in a package manifest configuration files should run.

- **Streaming**   The policies in this node configure settings related to package streaming to clients.

- **Virtualization**   The policies in this node configure dynamic virtualization of supported shell extensions, browser helper objects, and ActiveX controls. They also configure a list of process paths that are candidates for using virtual technologies.

Autoload

Autoload is a mechanism for controlling whether an application will be configured to load all client package files into cache. This option gives you the ability to decide which applications are cached automatically for offline use, which applications cache after first use, and which applications never cache.

In environments with mobile users, Autoload commonly will be configured to fully cache all available virtual applications. Streaming is then done locally instead of from a network file share.

The Autoload settings are stored in the registry under the following path:

HKEY_LOCAL_MACHINE\SOFTWARE\Microsoft\AppV\Client\Streaming\AutoLoad

The Autoload entry can have one of three values:

- 0 = Automatically load nothing into the cache1 = Automatically load previously used applications into the cache (default)

- 2 = Automatically load all published applications into the cache, regardless of whether they have been used previouslyAlternatively, you can configure the Autoload settings by using Windows PowerShell. For example, to configure a client so that all published applications are automatically loaded into the cache, run the following Windows PowerShell command:

```
Set-AppvClientConfiguration –Autoload 2
```

Registry settings for the App-V client

The App-V 5.0 client stores its configuration data in the registry, as shown in Figure 5-39. You easily can troubleshoot a client configuration if you familiarize yourself with the layout of the data and know which data is stored in the registry. In addition, you can configure many client settings just by changing registry entries on the client computer. This can be useful in troubleshooting scenarios.

CHAPTER 5

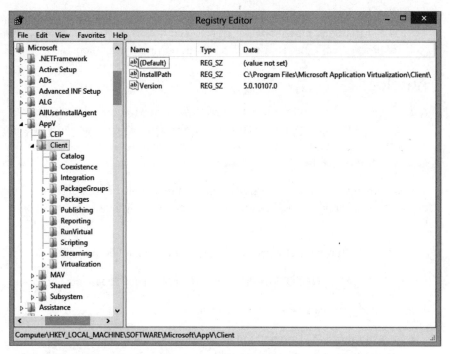

Figure 5-39 Windows Registry

App-V client information is stored in the registry in the keys that are outlined in Table 5-3. You can use the registry values to configure a client or to validate a client's configuration. Table 5-3 displays the App-V–related registry keys and their primary function.

Table 5-3 App-V client registry keys

Registry LOCATION	Function
HKEY_LOCAL_MACHINE\SOFTWARE\Microsoft\AppV\Client	Common App-V client settings
HKEY_LOCAL_MACHINE\SOFTWARE\Microsoft\AppV\Client\Streaming\PackageInstallationRoot	Directory where all new applications and updates will install
HKEY_LOCAL_MACHINE\SOFTWARE\Microsoft\AppV\Client\Streaming\AutoLoad	Specify how App-V should automatically load new packages
HKEY_LOCAL_MACHINE\SOFTWARE\Microsoft\AppV\Client\Streaming\SharedContentStoreMode	Enable or disable Shared Content Store mode
HKEY_LOCAL_MACHINE\SOFTWARE\Microsoft\AppV\Client\Publishing\Servers\{Number}\Name	Name of a publishing server

HKEY_LOCAL_MACHINE\SOFTWARE\Microsoft\AppV\Client \Publishing\Servers\{Number}\URL	URL of a publishing server
HKEY_LOCAL_MACHINE\SOFTWARE\Microsoft\AppV\Client \Publishing\Servers\{Number}\GlobalEnabled	Enable a global publishing refresh
HKEY_LOCAL_MACHINE\SOFTWARE\Microsoft\AppV\Client \Publishing\Servers\{Number}\GlobalLogonRefresh	Trigger a global publishing refresh at sign-in
HKEY_LOCAL_MACHINE\SOFTWARE\Microsoft\AppV\Client \Publishing\Servers\{Number}\GlobalPeriodicRefreshInterval	Specify or disable the publishing refresh interval
HKEY_LOCAL_MACHINE\SOFTWARE\Microsoft\AppV\Client \Scripting\EnablePackageScript	Enable scripts defined in a package manifest

As mentioned a few times previously, there also is a virtual registry. It doesn't store configuration data for the client; it is used as a virtual registry for virtual applications.

TROUBLESHOOTING

Examining the virtual registry

With App-V 5.0 and later, you can extract the virtual registry directly from an .appv file. This enables you to use the Registry Editor to browse through the virtual registry of a virtual application. This can be helpful in troubleshooting situations. To look through the virtual registry of a virtual application, perform the following steps:

1. Rename the .appv file to a .zip file.

2. Open the .zip file and extract the Registry.dat file.

3. Open Registry Editor and then navigate to HKEY_CURRENT_USER.

4. Right-click HKEY_CURRENT_USER, click New, and then click Key. Name the key TEMP.

5. Click the new TEMP key to highlight it. Then, click File and then click Import. In the Import Registry File window, change the file type to Registry Hive Files.

6. Browse to the Registry.dat file, click it, and then click Open.

7. In the Confirm Restore Key window, click Yes.

8. When completed, click OK.

9. Now you can browse the TEMP key, expand REGISTRY, and then view the virtual registry entries under the MACHINE and USER keys.

10. When finished, delete the TEMP key.

Be sure that you do not import the Registry.dat file to an existing registry key, because this could create major issues.

CHAPTER 5

Managing and administering Application Virtualization

There are several technologies of an application virtualization environment. As an administrator, you will spend the majority of your time managing and maintaining the environment. The primary technologies with which you will work on a day-to-day basis are the App-V Management Console, packages, and reporting. Thus, you should be familiar with the inner workings of them.

As with many other Microsoft infrastructure technologies, there are two ways to manage and maintain an environment. The primary method, at least historically, is the GUI-based management tools. The secondary method, which has grown in popularity, is Windows PowerShell. App-V provides GUI-based management tools, but you quickly will realize that Windows PowerShell provides the same, or better, management capabilities. You should spend time working with Windows PowerShell for App-V because it will provide a better administrative experience for some administrative tasks, especially repetitive tasks or tasks targeted toward a large number of servers.

Using the Application Virtualization Management Console

The App-V Management Console is a central place for managing application and connection groups. The App-V Management Console is a web-based console that runs on an App-V Management Server, and it can be accessed from a computer that has the Microsoft Silverlight application installed.

To connect to the App-V Management Console, open Internet Explorer and type the address of the server that hosts the management server and the port that is defined during the installation—for example, *http://tt-util-01.tailspintoys.com:81/console.html*.

The App-V Management Console is organized into four tabs:

- **Overview**   On this tab, you can get more information about the App-V Sequencer, get a direct link to the Package library, or directly access the section for adding a new publishing server package.

- **Packages** This tab consists of two sections: packages for adding and managing application packages and connection groups for connecting interrelated virtual applications.

- **Servers** On this tab, you can add publishing servers.

- **Admin** On this tab, you can identify App-V administrators. You also can add Active Directory users or groups to manage an App-V infrastructure.

By default, all three of the App-V services (management, publishing, and reporting) have an associated website in Internet Information Services (IIS), as shown in Figure 6-1.

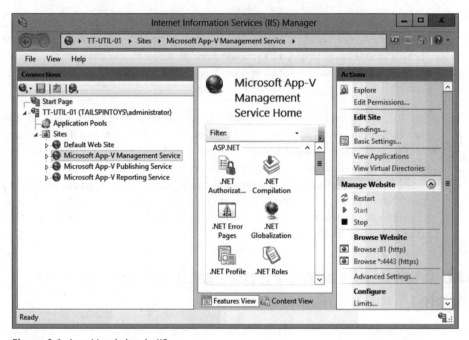

Figure 6-1 App-V websites in IIS

By default, each of the websites uses Hypertext Transfer Protocol Service (HTTP). You can increase security by using HTTPS instead. After you obtain a Secure Sockets Layer (SSL) certificate, you can add a binding for HTTPS to enable administration over HTTPS, as shown in Figure 6-2.

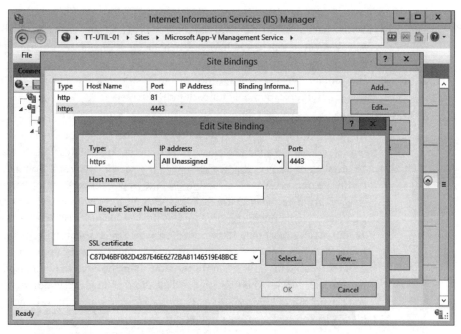

Figure 6-2 Adding an HTTPS binding

By adding HTTPS to all of the sites, you also can increase security for the connection from client machines to the publishing server and for App-V reporting users.

Inside OUT

SSL certificates

In many organizations, the management server, publishing server, and reporting server are located on separate servers. Additionally, many organizations have multiple publishing servers. Instead of using a unique SSL certificate for every service or every server, you can minimize the total number of SSL certificates by using the following options:

- **Wildcard certificate**   You can use a wildcard certificate, which secures communication to any fully qualified domain name in your domain. In this case, you could use a single certificate for everything. This is a good option if you want to reduce the administrative effort required to acquire and maintain certificates. In a high-security environment, you can enhance security by using separate certificates and certificates that secure communication only to a desired fully qualified domain name.

- **Server-based certificate**   You can use a single certificate for each server in your App-V environment. If you have one management server, two publishing servers, and one reporting server, you would need a total of four certificates. This is a good option in a high-security environment because the certificates would secure communication only for each individual server.

- **Load-balanced environment**   In a load-balanced environment, you can use a single SSL certificate for each server type. For example, if you have two publishing servers behind a load balancer, you can use a single SSL certificate that would be installed on each of the two servers. In this scenario, you still would need one certificate per server type, assuming that the App-V services are located on separate servers. If you plan to use load balancers in your environment, make sure that you research the encryption options the vendor supports. In some cases, a vendor may support only SSL termination, which means that the communication to the load balancers is encrypted but the communication from the load balancers to the back-end servers is not encrypted. In many environments, especially high-security environments, it's a good idea to maintain encryption throughout. You can do this by using an SSL pass-through configuration or by re-encrypting load-balanced traffic before sending it to the back-end servers.

The following is a list of common tasks that you can perform by using the App-V Management Console:

- Add or upgrade a package

- Manage package permissions

- Publish a package

- Search for a package

- View and edit default package configurations

- Delete a package

- Transfer permissions and package configurations to another package

- Manage administrators

- Register and unregister publishing servers

Managing App-V administrators

There are two types of users who access an App-V environment: users and administrative users. Users consume App-V services. Administrative users are responsible for some or all of the management and maintenance of an App-V environment.

In App-V, there is only one type of administrative user, known as an App-V administrator. An App-V administrator has full administrative control of App-V. You can add and remove App-V administrators by using the App-V Management Console. In Figure 6-3, a group named App-V Global Admins is being added as an administrator.

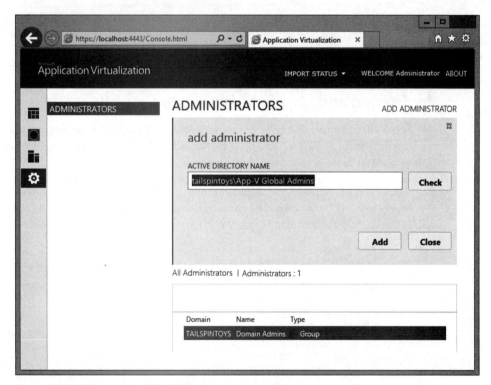

Figure 6-3 Adding an App-V administrator

In addition to administrative control of App-V, App-V administrators may need administrative access to the following services:

- **SQL Server databases**   There are two databases that can be part an of App-V environment: AppVManagement and AppVReporting. App-V administrators may need administrative access to those databases for maintenance, troubleshooting, and disaster recovery.

- **Windows local administrative access**   In troubleshooting scenarios, App-V administrators may need to perform operating system tasks that require local administrative access. Such tasks could be examining the security event log, adding extra disk space, and installing software on a new server.

- **Group Policy administrative access**   In most enterprise environments, App-V clients are configured and managed by using Group Policy Objects (GPOs). App-V administrators may need to create and modify GPOs for App-V clients. You can grant administrative control of specific App-V GPOs to App-V administrators. This is preferred over granting App-V administrators management over all GPOs or adding App-V administrators to a more powerful group, such as Domain Admins.

Many enterprises have written policies dictating how administrative access is granted. In large organizations, administrative tasks often are spread among multiple teams. For example, there may be a client services team that handles all client computer–related GPOs.

Registering and unregistering servers

The App-V Management Server synchronizes with App-V publishing servers. You can register multiple publishing servers to the App-V Management Console to enable you to manage multiple publishing servers.

Each publishing server that is registered in the App-V Management Console is displayed in the Servers tab. The Servers tab shows the registered servers and the date and time of the last publishing attempt, as shown in Figure 6-4.

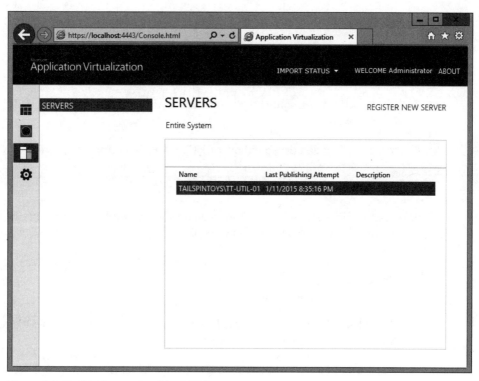

Figure 6-4 Registering an App-V publishing server

To register a new publishing server, perform the following steps:

1. Go to the App-V Management Console.

2. Click the Servers tab.

3. On the Servers tab, click Register New Server.

4. In the Server Name text box, add the name of the server. Be sure to insert the domain name before the server name. For example, if you are adding a server named TT-UTIL-01 in a domain named tailspintoys.com, you would need to specify the server as tailspintoys\tt-util-01.

5. Click the Check button. If the server is found, it will be displayed in a drop-down list under the Server Name text box. Click the server name.

6. Add a description in the Description text box, if desired.

7. Click the Add button to complete the registration process.

CHAPTER 6

To unregister a publishing server, perform the following steps:

1. Go to the App-V Management Console.

2. Click the Servers tab.

3. On the Servers tab, right-click the server that you want to unregister and then click Unregister Server.

4. In the confirmation dialog ribbon, click Confirm to complete the process.

Managing application packages

App-V packages are a foundational item in an App-V environment. Without packages, you can't stream a virtualized application to clients. A package is made of the following technologies:

- **Virtual registry file**   The virtual registry file, registry.dat, is used to enable an isolated virtual registry for an application.

- **XML files**   There are several XML files in a package. The XML files hold the configuration of the package and applications.

- **Application files**   The application files are in a folder named Root and are identical to the application files that you would have on a computer in a standard application installation.

You manage application packages by performing the following administrative tasks:

- **Create a new package**   You use the App-V Sequencer to create new packages.

- **Move the package to a repository**   After you create a new package, you need to move it to a shared network folder or a web server where clients and the management server can access it.

- **Add the package to the management server**   In a full infrastructure deployment with a management server, you need to add the package to the management server so that you can publish it and make it available to clients.

- **Grant access to the package**   After you add a package to the management server, you can grant access to it by adding groups to the application in the App-V Management Console.

- **Publish the package**   The final step in managing applications is publishing the package, either on a client or on a management server. By publishing a package, you make it available to clients.

From the management server, you can manage most aspects of a package by using the right-click menu. From the Packages tab, right-click any of the packages listed to view the menu, shown in Figure 6-5.

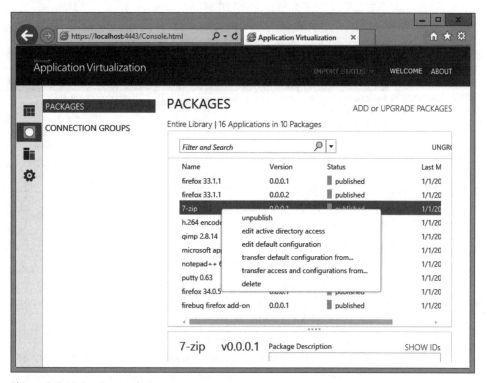

Figure 6-5 Managing packages

The right-click menu provides several routine administrative tasks with which you should be familiar:

- **Publish and unpublish**   The publishing and unpublishing process is straightforward. Right-click a package and then click Publish or Unpublish. The package's status will be updated to reflect the current status. In Figure 6-5, the packages show a status of Published.

- **Edit Active Directory access**   To grant users access to a package, click Edit Active Directory Access and then add users or groups. It's recommended that you use groups because they simplify the provisioning and deprovisioning of access. Figure 6-6 shows the access configuration for the Foxit Reader package. The App-V Core Apps group has access to the package.

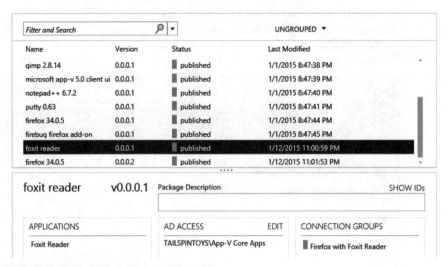

Figure 6-6 Managing package access

- **Edit default configuration**   There are several configuration areas that you can edit when you click Edit Default Configuration:

    - **Applications**   A package can contain more than one application. You can choose which applications are enabled in a package by modifying the Applications section of a package in the default configuration.

    - **Shortcuts**   You can configure three things in the Shortcuts section: enable or disable shortcuts for the package, add a new shortcut, and modify an existing shortcut.

    - **File Types**   In this section, you can view the existing file type associations that are set during the sequencing. Figure 6-7 shows the file type associations of the Gimp package.

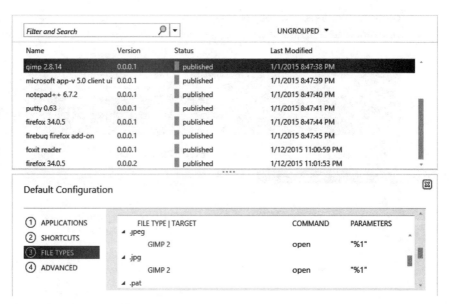

Figure 6-7 Managing file type associations

- **Advanced**   In the Advanced section, you can export the package configuration to an .XML file or import an existing configuration from an .XML file, which would overwrite the existing configuration. This is handy when you want to duplicate the configuration of one package on another.

Later in this chapter, in the section titled "Managing management servers by using Windows PowerShell," we show you how to perform some of these management tasks by using Windows PowerShell.

Connection groups

Each package, by default, is isolated from the operating system and from other packages. This isolation results in reduced conflicts. However, sometimes you need to virtualize separate applications that need to communicate with one another and share configuration information. Connection groups take separate virtualized applications and group them together to allow them to communicate and share configuration information. One of the most common uses of a connection group is to pair a primary application, such as a productivity tool, and an application plug-in—for example, Microsoft Outlook and a third-party email archiving plugin.

You manage connection groups on the Packages tab of the App-V management portal. The Packages tab has a Connection Groups section. There, you can add new connection groups, remove existing connection groups, edit existing connection groups, publish and unpublish

CHAPTER 6

connection groups, and copy existing connection groups to create a new connection group with a new version number. You can see an existing connection group in Figure 6-8.

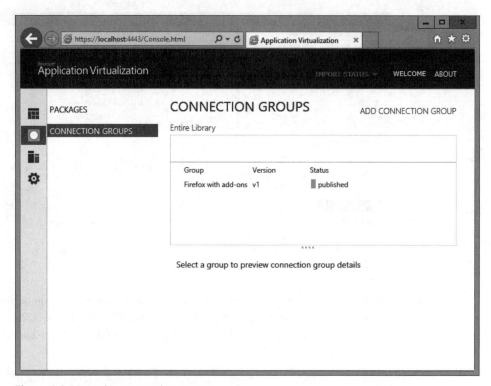

Figure 6-8 Managing connection groups

TROUBLESHOOTING

Investigating connection group issues

If a connection group stops functioning, consider the following questions immediately:

1.   Did a package get added or removed from the group?

2.   Did any of the packages in the group get upgraded?

If the answer to either of those questions is yes, then the connection group has to be upgraded to fix it. When planning for package upgrades, always check connection group membership and plan accordingly.

Managing management servers by using Windows PowerShell

In addition to managing and maintaining your App-V environment by using GUI tools, you can use Windows PowerShell. Three modules provide App-V–related cmdlets: AppVClient, AppVServer, and AppVSequencer. Don't forget that before you can use the cmdlets, you need to have the module loaded or import the module. By using Windows PowerShell, you can perform a wide variety of administrative tasks, some of which are outlined in detail below.

Adding and publishing packages by using Windows PowerShell

You can use Windows PowerShell to add new packages and then publish those packages. Most of the routine commands are just a single line of Windows PowerShell, especially if you are working with a single package. The first step in the process is to add the package by using the Import-AppvServerPackage cmdlet, as shown in Figure 6-9.

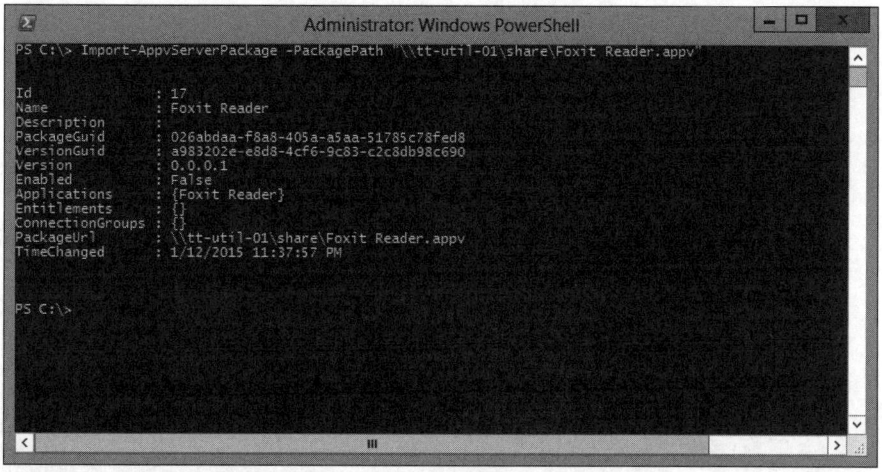

Figure 6-9 Adding a new package

In Figure 6-9, notice that there are not any entitlements and the package isn't enabled. That means that nobody has access to the package. If you publish the package, nobody would be able to use it in its current configuration. Thus, before publishing, you should grant access. You can grant an Active Directory security group access to the package by using the Grant-AppvServerPackage cmdlet, as shown in Figure 6-10.

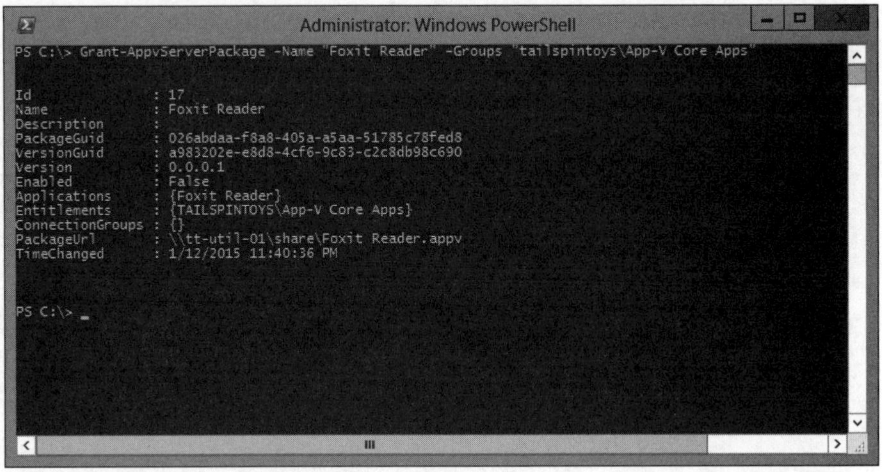

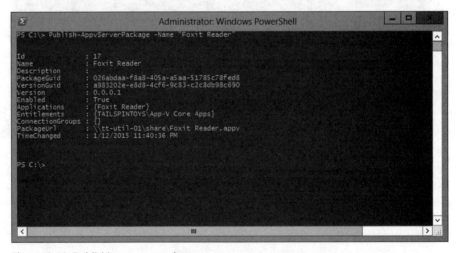

Figure 6-10 Granting access to a new package

The final step is to publish the package. Until a package is published, it's inaccessible to
App-V clients. To publish the package by using Windows PowerShell, you run the `Publish`
`-AppvServerPackage –Name "Foxit Reader"` command, as shown in Figure 6-11.

Figure 6-11 Publishing a new package

Creating and managing connection groups

You can create and manage connection groups by using Windows PowerShell. The GUI and
Windows PowerShell provide a similar experience for creating and managing one object.
However, for bulk operations, such as creating 50 connection groups, you should use

Windows PowerShell to save time and reduce administrative errors. To create a new connection group, you use the New-AppvServerConnectionGroup cmdlet, as shown in Figure 6-12.

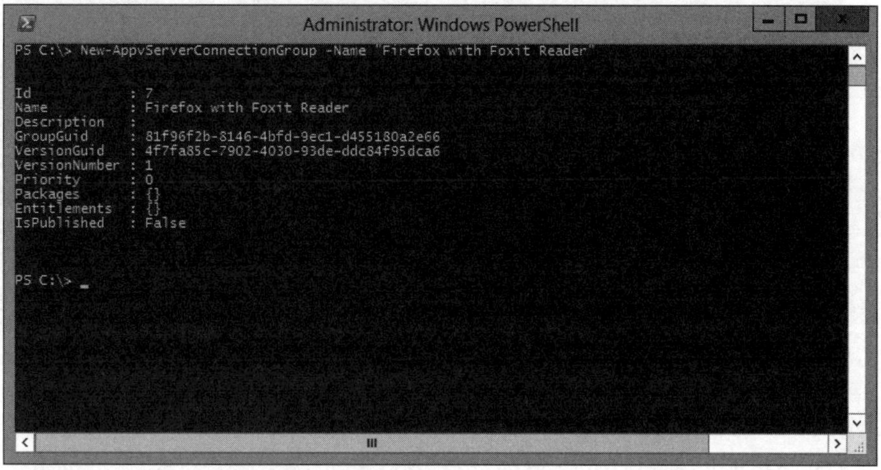

Figure 6-12 Creating a new connection group

Notice that there aren't any packages in the new connection group. A connection group has no value until at least two packages that need to communicate are in it, the appropriate security groups have been granted access to it, and it has been published.

The next step is to add packages to the connection group. To add a package named "Foxit Reader" to a connection group named "Firefox with Foxit Reader," you need to get the package and then pipe the output of that to the Set-AppvServerConnectionGroup cmdlet. The full command is `Get-AppvServerPackage -Name "Foxit Reader" | Set -AppvServerConnectionGroup -Name "Firefox with Foxit Reader"`. For connection groups, you typically need to add more than one package. In Figure 6-13, a three-line script is used to add two packages to a connection group.

CHAPTER 6

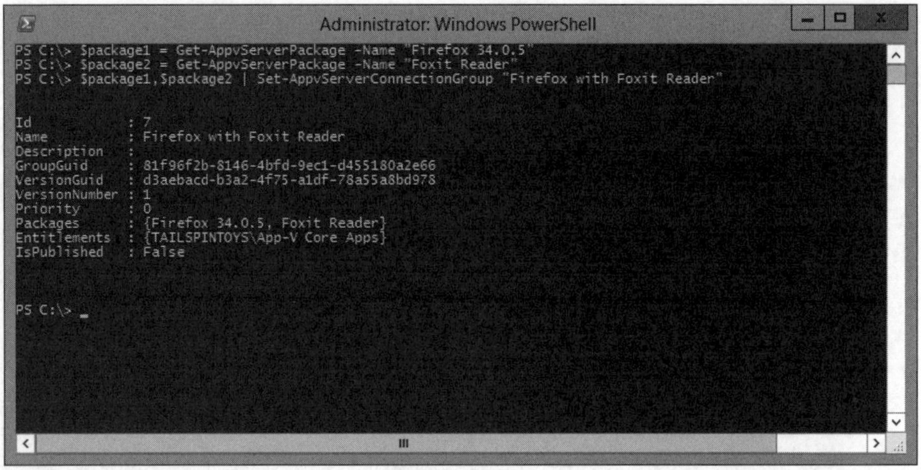

Figure 6-13 Adding packages to a connection group

Notice that the Name parameter was omitted from the Set-AppvServerConnectionGroup command. That is acceptable because the Name parameter is an optional parameter. Figure 6-13 shows the output of the command, which shows the connection group and lists Firefox 34.0.5 and Foxit Reader as being part of the connection group.

Inside OUT

Ordering packages in connection groups

The order in which you add the packages to a connection group is important. It establishes what happens if two packages in the same connection group have a configuration conflict. For example, if one package attempts to set a registry value to 1 and another package attempts to set it to 2, the order of the packages would determine which package is used for the conflicting value. In such cases, the package that was added first sets the conflicting registry value. In the management portal, you can view a connection group to list connected packages. The package on top, labeled with a 0, is the first package in the connection group. You also can view the connection group by using the Windows PowerShell Get-AppvServerConnectionGroup cmdlet. The output will show the first package added to the connection group first.

After you have a connection group and have added packages, you need to grant access to the connection group. To grant a group named "App-V Core Apps" access to a connection group named "Firefox with Foxit Reader," run the following command:

```
Grant-AppvServerConnectionGroup "Firefox with Foxit Reader" -Groups "tailspintoys\App-V
Core Apps"
```

The output of the command is shown in Figure 6-14.

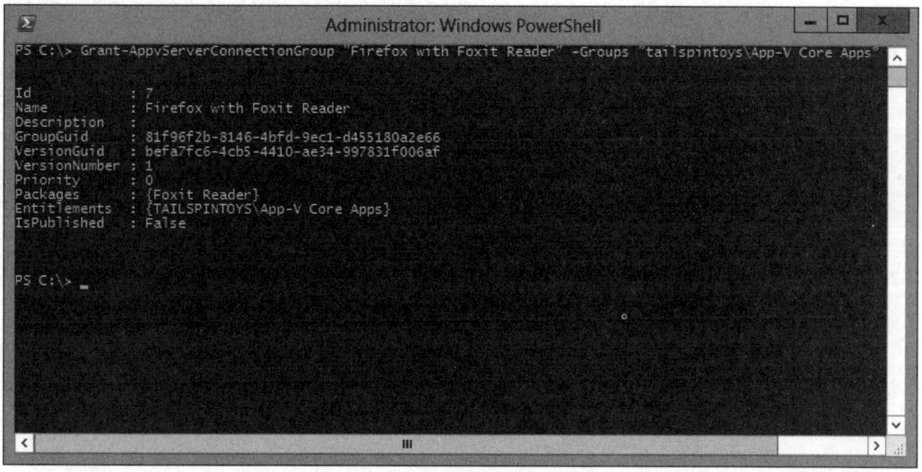

Figure 6-14 Granting access to a connection group

The final step is to publish the connection group. To publish the connection group named "Firefox with Foxit Reader," run the following command:

```
Publish-AppvServerConnectionGroup -Name "Firefox with Foxit Reader"
```

The output of the command is shown in Figure 6-15.

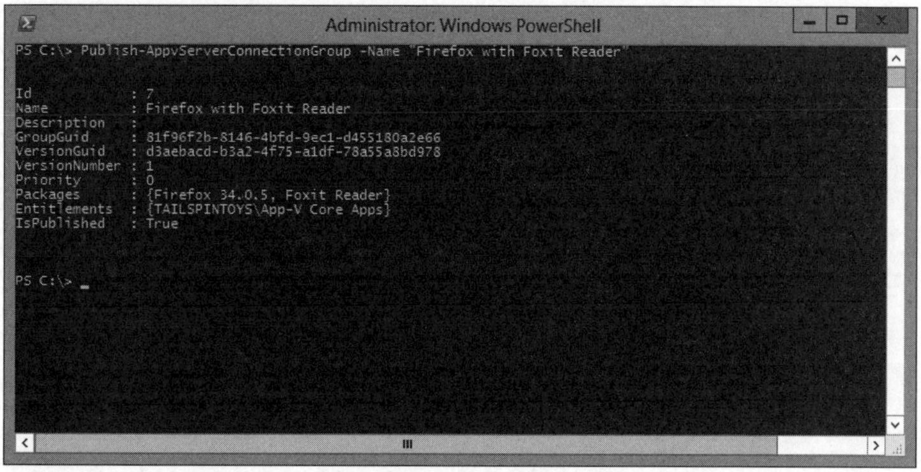

Figure 6-15 Publishing a connection group

TROUBLESHOOTING

Publishing a connection group

If you publish a connection group but users are not able to access the packages, check whether the packages are published. For users to access packages in a connection group, the connection group and all of the packages that are part of it need to be published. Additionally, the user needs to be granted access to the connection group and all of the packages that are part of it. It's a good practice to match up the entitlements of connection groups and their connected packages.

Additional Windows PowerShell management capabilities

You can manage many other aspects of App-V by using other cmdlets that are not covered in examples in this book. There are three App-V–related modules:

- **AppVServer module**   This module, available on a computer running the management server or publishing server, contains all of the cmdlets that you will need to manage the servers of a full infrastructure deployment of App-V. There are a total of 17 cmdlets to enable you to manage management and publishing tasks.

- **AppVClient module**   This module, available on computers that have the App-V client installed, contains all of the cmdlets that you will need to manage the client-side technologies. The cmdlets enable you to manage a stand-alone client or a client that is part of a full infrastructure deployment of App-V. There are a total of 30 cmdlets in the module.

- **AppVSequencer module**   This module, available on a computer running the App-V Sequencer, is the smallest module. It only offers four cmdlets. You can create new packages, create new package accelerators, expand an existing package, or update an existing package.

Tables 6.1, 6.2, and 6.3 list the cmdlets available in each App-V–related module.

Table 6-1 AppVServer module cmdlets

Cmdlet name	Description
Get-AppvServerConnectionGroup	Display the properties of a specified connection group
Get-AppvServerPackage	Display the properties of a specified package
Get-AppvServerPackageDeploymentConfiguration	Display the dynamic deployment configuration for a specified package

Get-AppvServerPackageUserConfiguration	Display the dynamic user configuration for a specified group and package
Grant-AppvServerConnectionGroup	Grant access to a connection group
Grant-AppvServerPackage	Grant access to a server package
Import-AppvServerPackage	Add a package to the server
New-AppvServerConnectionGroup	Create a new connection group
Publish-AppvServerConnectionGroup	Publish a connection group
Publish-AppvServerPackage	Publish a server package
Remove-AppvServerConnectionGroup	Delete a connection group
Remove-AppvServerPackage	Delete a server package
Set-AppvServerConnectionGroup	Add packages to a connection group; modify the priority of packages
Set-AppvServerPackage	Apply a dynamic deployment or user configuration to a package
Unpublish-AppvServerConnectionGroup	Unpublish a connection group
Unpublish-AppvServerPackage	Unpublish a server package
Update-AppvServerConnectionGroup	Modify the name of a connection group

Table 6-2 AppVClient module cmdlets and functions

Cmdlet name	Description
Get-AppvVirtualProcess	Display process information for running App-V applications
Start-AppvVirtualProcess	Run a specified program
Add-AppvClientConnectionGroup	Add a connection group to a client
Add-AppvClientPackage	Add a package to a client
Add-AppvPublishingServer	Associate the client to a publishing server
Disable-AppvClientConnectionGroup	Disable a connection group
Enable-AppvClientConnectionGroup	Enable a connection group
Get-AppvClientApplication	Display all App-V client applications
Get-AppvClientConfiguration	Display client configuration details, including whether configuration item was set by Group Policy
Get-AppvClientConnectionGroup	Display client connection groups
Get-AppvClientMode	Display whether client is in Normal mode or Shared Content Store mode
Get-AppvClientPackage	Display all client packages

CHAPTER 6

Get-AppvPublishingServer	Display all associated publishing servers
Mount-AppvClientConnectionGroup	Stream specified connection group to the local hard drive
Mount-AppvClientPackage	Load package into local hard drive cache
Publish-AppvClientPackage	Publish a client package
Remove-AppvClientConnectionGroup	Delete a client connection group
Remove-AppvClientPackage	Delete a client package
Remove-AppvPublishingServer	Disassociate client from publishing server
Repair-AppvClientConnectionGroup	Reset client connection group to original configuration
Repair-AppvClientPackage	Reset client package to original configuration
Send-AppvClientReport	Send client information to reporting server
Set-AppvClientConfiguration	Change client configuration settings
Set-AppvClientMode	Switch from Normal mode to Shared Content Store mode, or vice versa
Set-AppvClientPackage	Modify configuration of package
Set-AppvPublishingServer	Associate client with a publishing server
Stop-AppvClientConnectionGroup	Terminate shared virtual environment used by connection group
Stop-AppvClientPackage	Terminate package processes and shut down app's virtual environment
Sync-AppvPublishingServer	Sync client with publishing server to get latest packages and configurations
Unpublish-AppvClientPackage	Unpublish specified client package

Table 6-3 AppVSequencer module cmdlets

Cmdlet name	Description
Expand-AppvSequencerPackage	Expand package to local hard drive
New-AppvPackageAccelerator	Create a new package accelerator
New-AppvSequencerPackage	Create a new package
Update-AppvSequencerPackage	Update existing package to newer version

Inside OUT

Windows PowerShell and elevation

Some of the App-V cmdlets function from a standard Windows PowerShell prompt, but others require an elevated Windows PowerShell prompt. Be sure to use an elevated Windows PowerShell prompt when you use the following cmdlets:

- Add-AppvClientPackage
- Remove-AppvClientPackage
- Set-AppvClientConfiguration
- Add-AppvClientConnectionGroup
- Remove-AppvClientConnectionGroup
- Add-AppvPublishingServer
- Remove-AppvPublishingServer
- Send-AppvClientReport
- Set-AppvClientMode
- Set-AppvClientPackage
- Set-AppvPublishingServer

Modifying and upgrading published applications

Throughout the life cycle of the applications you support, you will need to make updates and modifications. This maintenance work will include everything from major version upgrades to more minor changes, such as user preferences. For an organization without application virtualization, this process can be very costly. Even with the enterprise software distribution tools, stand-alone applications can be difficult to manage.

App-V 5.0 simplifies application management. In this section, we will walk through modifying and updating applications.

Update an application

Updates to virtualized applications are handled through the App-V Sequencer. When you modify an existing virtual application package in the Sequencer, there is support for three different modification scenarios. The scenarios are shown in Figure 6-16.

CHAPTER 6

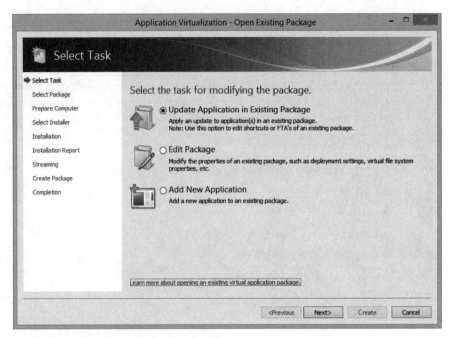

Figure 6-16 App-V Sequencer, Select Task page

Update applications in existing packages

This scenario enables you to apply updates to an existing package and seamlessly redistribute it to client computers. This method doesn't require clients to disconnect from the server. Users continue to use the currently streamed application until they disconnect. The updated version streams automatically when they reconnect.

Updating an application in an existing package is accomplished within the Sequencer. After making updates to the application, the sequencing process tags the changed blocks of code with a new version number. When clients restart the application, App-V compares the version information within the .appv file to the version on the package repository server. App-V then downloads any required blocks of code to the client.

The following procedure is an overview of the application update process in an existing package:

1.   Navigate to the package folder for the application that you are updating. Copy the package folder to the Sequencer for updating.

2.   Double-click the package's .appv file. This will start the Open Existing Package Wizard.

3. On the Select Task page, select the Update Application In Existing Package option and then click Next.

4. On the Select Package page, the .appv package will be prepopulated, as shown in Figure 6-17. Click Next to continue.

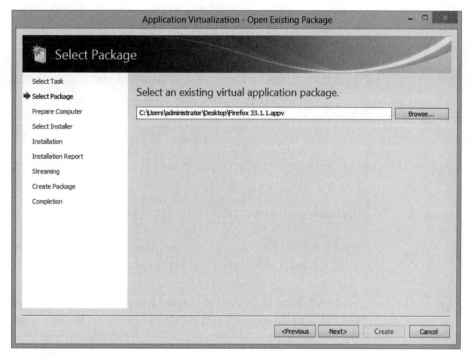

Figure 6-17 App-V Sequencer, Select Package page

5. On the Prepare Computer page, if no issues are detected or the issues can be ignored, click Next to continue.

6. On the Select Installer page, select the Select The Installer For The Application option and then browse to the installer that you need to run, as shown in Figure 6-18. Click Next to continue.

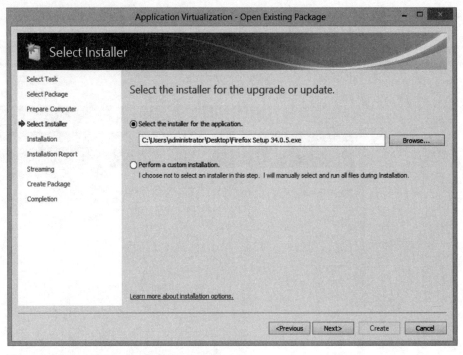

Figure 6-18 App-V Sequencer, Select Installer page

7. On the Installation page, run the installer and then select the I Am Finished Installing check box after the installation is complete, as shown in Figure 6-19. Click Next to continue.

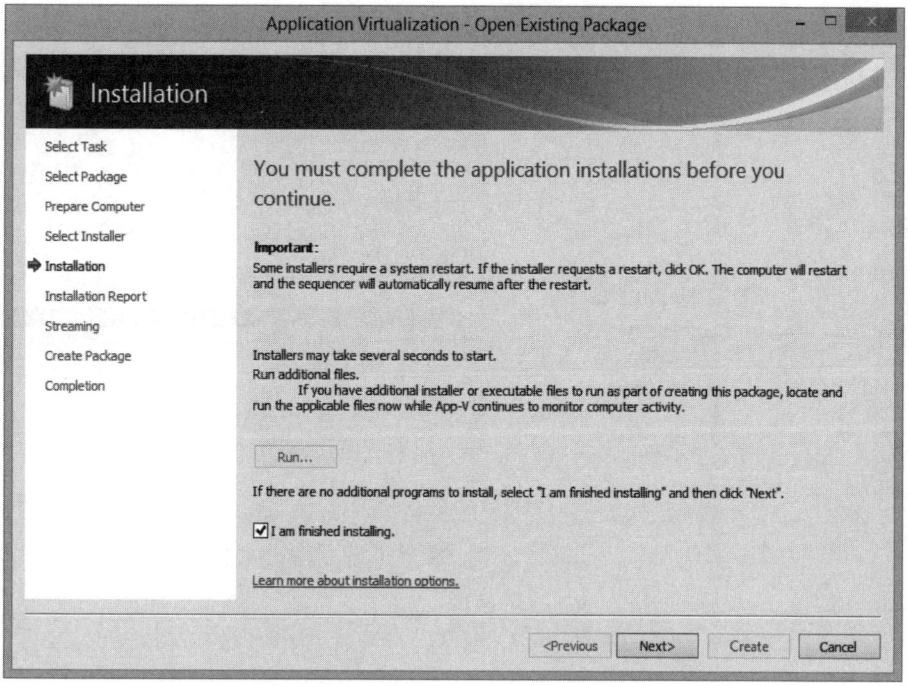

Figure 6-19 App-V Sequencer, Installation page

8. On the Installation Report page, if no issues are detected, click Next to continue.

9. On the Prepare For Streaming page, shown in Figure 6-20, click Run All to run the newly installed application(s). You should run the applications to optimize the end user experience on slow or unreliable networks. Click Next to continue.

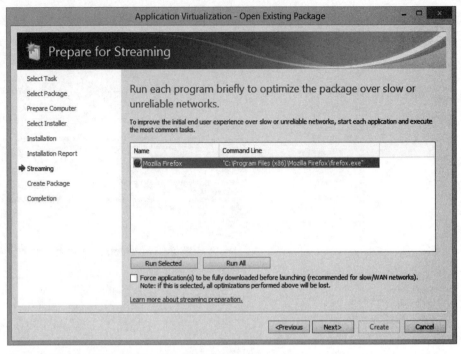

Figure 6-20 App-V Sequencer, Prepare For Streaming page

10. On the Create Package page, select the Save The Package Now option, specify the location to save the package, and then click Create. On this page, you also have the option to modify the package before saving it.

11. On the Completion page, review the notifications and then click Close.

Edit existing packages

Selecting the Edit Package option in the Sequencer enables you to make changes to an existing package without sequencing the application again. Editing a package enables you to open a package and make specific changes, such as the following:

- View associated package files

- Edit registry settings

- Review additional package settings (except operating system file properties)

- Set virtualized registry key state (override or merge)

- Set virtualized folder state

- Add or edit shortcuts and file type associations

Add a new application to a package

The Add New Application option in the Sequencer presents a similar workflow to the update procedure discussed previously because the process of adding a new application to an existing package is similar. The wizard for modifying existing App-V packages requires that you extract the existing virtual application packages on the Sequencer for updating and then installs any additional applications that will be saved in the updated package.

Copy access and configuration

After you update an application and sequence it again, you need to add the package to the App-V Management Console. During this process, you have the option to copy access and configuration data from the previous version of the package and apply it to the new package, as shown in Figure 6-21.

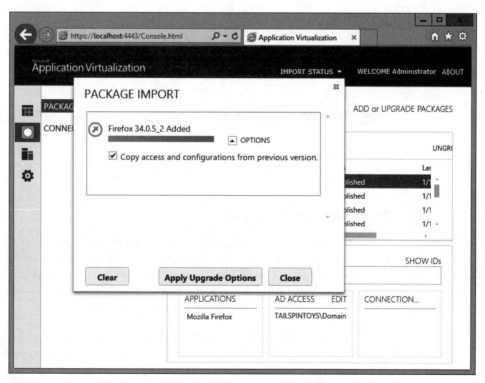

Figure 6-21 Copying access and configuration from a previous version

For example, you can import an updated version of Firefox by performing these steps:

1. Open the App-V management portal, click the Packages node, and then click Add Or Upgrade Packages.

2. Click Browse, navigate to the location of the updated package, click Open, and then click Add.

3. On the Package Import page, click Options, select Copy Access And Configurations From Previous Version, click Apply Upgrade Options, and then click Close.

4. In the list of packages, verify that a new version of the package exists and the version number has incremented up from the existing package. In this example, there now are two versions of Firefox, as shown in Figure 6-22. Publish the package to make it available to users.

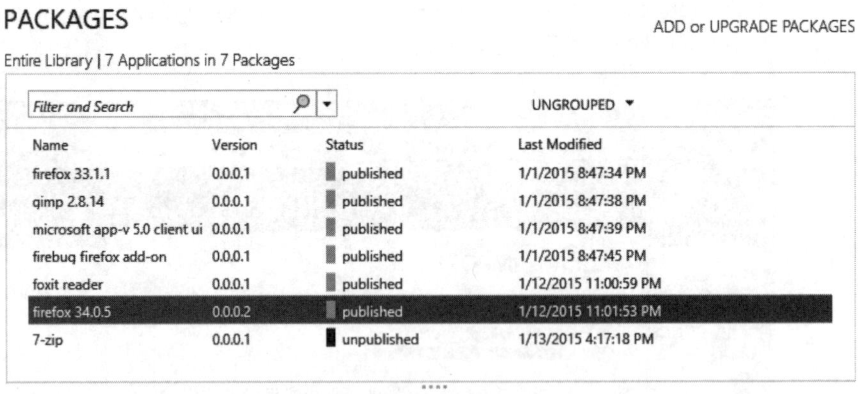

PACKAGES

ADD or UPGRADE PACKAGES

Entire Library | 7 Applications in 7 Packages

Name	Version	Status	Last Modified
Filter and Search 🔍 ▾			UNGROUPED ▾
firefox 33.1.1	0.0.0.1	published	1/1/2015 8:47:34 PM
gimp 2.8.14	0.0.0.1	published	1/1/2015 8:47:38 PM
microsoft app-v 5.0 client ui	0.0.0.1	published	1/1/2015 8:47:39 PM
firebug firefox add-on	0.0.0.1	published	1/1/2015 8:47:45 PM
foxit reader	0.0.0.1	published	1/12/2015 11:00:59 PM
firefox 34.0.5	0.0.0.2	published	1/12/2015 11:01:53 PM
7-zip	0.0.0.1	unpublished	1/13/2015 4:17:18 PM

Figure 6-22 Application Virtualization web console

Update a connection group

Connection groups enable virtual applications to communicate with one another while they run inside a virtual environment. Connection groups in App-V enable virtual applications to interact with other applications, middleware, or plug-ins that have been virtualized in separate virtual application packages. All of the packages share a virtual environment in which the virtual file system and tokenized paths merge and the registries converge.

Similar to packages, connection groups have versions. When you update a connection group (for example, by adding a package or updating an existing package), you must update the version GUID to reflect the new version. The new version is stored in the connection group XML file as the VersionId, as shown in Figure 6-23. Typically, the GUID is updated automatically, but the value can be modified manually.

Figure 6-23 App-V connection group XML file

Remove applications

When an application reaches the end of its life cycle, it's common for the App-V administrator to remove the virtualized application from all client computers. In a full infrastructure deployment of App-V, you can unpublish and delete packages from the App-V management portal. For a stand-alone deployment, you can use Windows PowerShell on each client. For this example, we use Windows PowerShell to remove Firefox, which has reached end of its life cycle on a stand-alone App-V client.

1. From an elevated Windows PowerShell prompt on the client computer, run the Unpublish-AppvClientPackage *Firefox* -Global command to remove any integrations for the user or computer. Note that the use of the wildcards means that any packages that contain the term "Firefox" will be targeted.

2. Run the Remove-AppvClientPackage *Firefox* command on the client computer to remove the local cache.

TROUBLESHOOTING
Removing applications

Sometimes, when you try to remove an application, the task will fail. Often, the failure won't pinpoint the cause of the problem. Always start by reviewing the App-V–related event log entries. A Windows PowerShell cmdlet is another good resource for pinpointing common removal problems. Run the Get-AppvVirtualProcess command to list any running virtual processes. Sometimes, a running process can impede a removal. You can kill the process(es) and then try removing the application again. To kill a process with a process ID of 3550, run the taskkill -PID 3550 command.

Edit the default configuration for a package

During the sequencing process, you have the ability to modify the default configuration of the package you are sequencing. In an update scenario, this gives you the opportunity to make several changes that may enhance the user experience for your virtualized application. From the Sequencer interface, you can make modifications, such as adding or removing file type associations, as shown in Figure 6-24. Some additional examples include the following:

- Creating and modifying registry values

- Creating and modifying shortcuts

- Creating and modifying the package contents

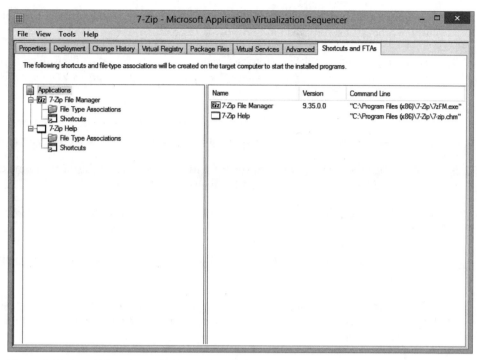

Figure 6-24 App-V Sequencer during package editing

Exporting the configuration

You can't perform all possible package configuration changes by using the App-V Management Console. Some packages require that you change the XML file manually. It's a good practice to export the current configuration to an XML file and then edit and import the changed file.

To export a package's configuration, perform the following steps:

1. In the App-V Management Console, right-click the name of the package that you want to export and then select Edit Default Configuration.

2. Click the Advanced node and then click Export Configuration.

3. Provide a location, name the XML file, and then save it.

After you export the configuration file, you can use this configuration as a backup or as a starting point to import for further customization in other packages. You also can configure the file to add or remove file type extensions or to configure some variables.

To import modified default configuration files, select Import And Overwrite This Configuration, which prompts for confirmation to overwrite the existing configuration.

For example, if you want to customize a dynamic user configuration file with an application that mounts a file share to a drive letter for a particular Active Directory Domain Services (AD DS) group, perform the following procedure:

1. Right-click the name of the package that you want to view and then select Edit Active Directory Access to view the configuration that is assigned to a given user or group.

2. Select the AD DS group that you want to customize. Select Custom from the drop-down list if it isn't already selected. A link named Edit displays.

3. Click Edit. The dynamic user configuration that is assigned to the AD DS group displays.

4. Click Advanced and then click Export Configuration. Type a file name and then click Save. You now can edit the file to configure a package for a user and then import the modified file.

By using the App-V Management Console when you import a new version of the package, you can transfer access and configuration to another version of the package. To do this, perform the following steps:

1. Select the package that you want to transfer to the new configuration.

2. Right-click the package and then select Transfer Default Configuration From or Transfer Access And Configurations From, depending on the configuration that you want to transfer.

3. To transfer the configuration, in the Select Previous Version dialog box, select the package that contains the settings that you want to transfer and then click OK.

Assignment of applications

When it comes time to assign applications, the destination often is subjective based on different requirements. In some cases, you may need an application, such as a piece of licensed software, to follow the user. In other cases, such as a PDF reader, user assignment may not be critical.

Making packages available to users and computers is a straightforward task with App-V. You can assign packages in various ways by using AD DS security groups. You have the flexibility to assign applications by user, computer, or both. In Figure 6-25, you can see the package assignment is targeted at the Domain Users group, making the assignment available to all users. Alternatively, you can create a new AD DS security group containing computer objects and target the package assignment there.

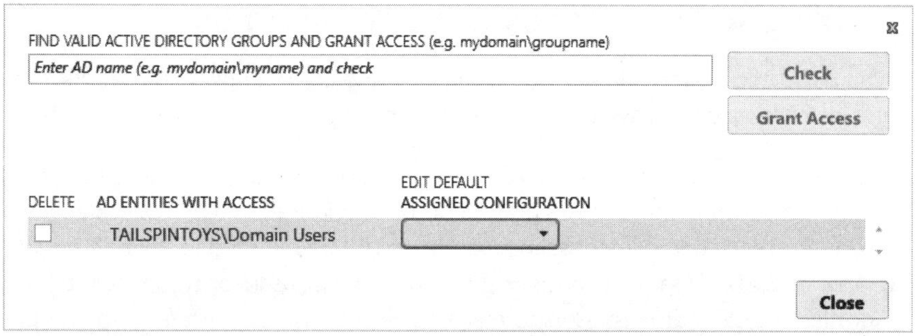

FIND VALID ACTIVE DIRECTORY GROUPS AND GRANT ACCESS (e.g. mydomain\groupname)

Enter AD name (e.g. mydomain\myname) and check

Check

Grant Access

DELETE   AD ENTITIES WITH ACCESS

EDIT DEFAULT
ASSIGNED CONFIGURATION

☐   TAILSPINTOYS\Domain Users

Close

Figure 6-25 Granting access in the App-V Management Console

Naming conventions

By establishing standards for virtual applications in your organization, you can simplify administration of the App-V environment. In addition, you can ensure that troubleshooting is smoother. In this section, we will discuss naming conventions and some good practices for maintaining your environment.

When you import a package in the App-V Management Console, each package is identified by its GUID and version ID, which helps avoid conflicts with different versions of the application. The App-V Management Console can identify different versions of a package, but to more easily navigate the App-V Management Console and locate an application package, you should consider the following common naming conventions:

- **Vendor**   For example, Microsoft

- **Application**   For example, Office

- **Version**   For example, 2013

- **Language**   For example, .en and .de

- **Operating system (OS) architecture**   For example, 32-bit or 64-bit

If you create an application package for Microsoft Office 2013, English language, packaged for 32-bit architecture, the package name would be **Microsoft_Office_2013_EN_32.**

You can use the same naming strategy when you create folders in a package repository on a file server or web server. You should place any new version of a package in a separate sub-folder to avoid overwriting configuration files and to be able to remove an older package easily.

CHAPTER 6

Enabling scripting for dynamic configuration

Dynamic configuration enables you to manage and control how virtual applications integrate into the base operating system and how the virtual packages behave on clients.

When the Sequencer creates a package, the AppxManifest.xml file and Content_Types.xml file contain extension points and integration of the configuration with the underlying operating system. For many deployment scenarios, you might be required to adjust specific configurations or to enable/disable extensions points for specific users or computers. Dynamic configuration enables administrators to make post-sequence modifications to an App-V package without making any changes to the App-V package itself.

A common example of post-sequence modification is applications that require access to a specific mapped drive that the user who is opening the application uses. Another example is disabling the mailto extension to prevent virtualized applications from overwriting the extension from other applications.

Dynamic configuration uses two .xml files that are created during sequencing:

- The dynamic deployment configuration file, PACKAGE_NAME_DeploymentConfig.xml

- The dynamic user configuration, PACKAGE_NAME_UserConfig.xml

You can use the configuration files to do the following:

- Assign scripts to run during specific package and application events

- Enable or disable a virtual subsystem, such as environment variables, registry modification, services, or fonts

- Enable or disable extensions, such as file type associations, URL protocols, or AppPaths

- Override shortcut configurations

Settings that are configured in a dynamic deployment configuration file affect all users who work on the same App-V client computer. A dynamic user configuration contains settings that apply configurations for a package to individual users who are members of AD DS groups and can override dynamic deployment configuration settings. For example, you can provide a shortcut configuration in the user deployment configuration file that will override the shortcut configuration in the deployment configuration file.

Both configuration files start with a header that is followed by a PackageID, which also exists in the manifest file. The rest of the file is the body, which includes all application extension points for application configuration.

Deployment configuration files provide configuration settings in two sections, one relative to the computer context and one relative to the user context. The settings configured in the user configuration file can override these because they provide the same capabilities as the settings in the deployment configuration files.

Machine configuration control settings typically are written to the HKEY_LOCAL_MACHINE registry keys on the virtual registry. Machine configuration control settings contains four subsections:

- **Subsystems**   These are arranged as nodes under <Subsystems>, and they contain settings that configure extensions, application capabilities, machine wide virtual registry, and machine wide virtual kernel objects.

- **ProductSourceURLOptOut**   This subsection indicates whether the URL for a package can be modified globally through PackageSourceRoot to support branch office scenarios. The default is false, and the setting change takes effect on the next start.

- **MachineScripts**   This package can be configured to execute scripts at deployment time, publishing, or removal.

- **TerminateChildProcess**   This application executable can specify which child processes will terminate when an application .exe process terminates.

User configuration control settings in the dynamic configuration file affect per-user locations for all users who receive a package. User configuration control settings contain four subsections:

- **Applications**   This setting enables you to turn on or turn off extension points for a particular application that is part of a virtual package.

- **Subsystems**   This setting controls the behavior of shortcuts, file type associations, URL protocols, AppPath, software clients such as an email client, news readers, media players, and the behavior of a Microsoft component object model (COM).

- **UserScripts**   This setting includes scripts to set up or alter the virtual environment, in addition to running scripts at deployment or removal time, before an application runs.

- **ManagingAuthority**   This setting can be used when two versions of a package, one deployed on App-V 4.6 and the other deployed on App-V 5.0, coexist on one computer.

App-V allows scripting in these dynamic configuration files to set up or alter a virtual environment, in addition to running scripts at deployment or removal time, before an application executes. Scripting also can be used to clean up an environment after an application terminates. You can make custom modifications by using any text editor or XML editor.

Script execution time can be during one of the App-V package life-cycle phases, including the following:

- AddPackage

- PublishPackage

- UnpublishPackage

- RemovePackage

- StartProcess

- ExitProcess

- StartVirtualEnvironment

- TerminateVirtualEnvironment

Before implementing dynamic configuration scripting, script processing must be enabled on your App-V clients. You can do this during the installation of the App-V client by enforcing the EnablePackageScripts option. Alternatively, you can use the following Windows PowerShell command:

```
Set-AppvClientConfiguration -EnablePackageScripts 1
```

App-V reporting

Reporting is an optional App-V feature. In large or complex environments, reporting in App-V provides administrators with a wealth of information that can be useful in upgrade and migration scenarios and during troubleshooting situations. It also adds to the administrative overhead of an App-V environment.

How App-V reporting works

App-V 5.0 provides reporting functionality to collect information from App-V clients.

Besides having clients send data to a reporting server in a full infrastructure deployment model, there are two other situations in which reporting works a little differently:

- In the System Center 2012 R2 Configuration Manager–integrated model, the Configuration Manager client sends the reporting data.

- In the stand-alone mode, data, in the form of XML files, is sent to a shared location.

In the full infrastructure model, reporting functionality depends on SQL Server Reporting Services and IIS, which must be configured for Windows authentication. If you use default steps for configuring reports, the default website is named Reports; for example, *http://tt-util-01:83/reports*.

A reporting server collects reporting data that a client sends by using an HTTP POST request. The reporting server processes the incoming data by parsing the XML data and sending the information to a reporting database.

SQL Server will run a job named ProcessAppVReportingDataJob, which can be found under SQL Server Agent\Jobs, to write data into actual application usage tables.

The reporting server will receive a successful reply from the database and then notify the App-V client that the data was successfully stored in the database. This results in an attempt on the client side to clear the current data cache.

Figure 6-26 shows the reporting flow from an App-V client.

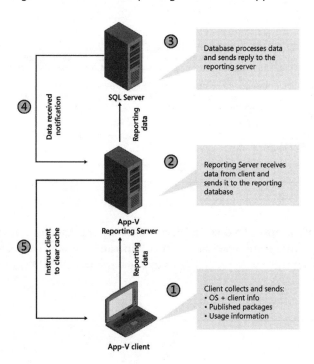

Figure 6-26 App-V reporting flow

Data collected by App-V reporting

Each App-V client communicates directly with the reporting server. You can collect software-metering information about application usage regardless of whether a client is connected to a reporting server. Collected data is stored in XML files in the %SYSTEMDRIVE%\ProgramData \Microsoft\AppV\Client\Reporting folder with a unique name. To open this location, you may need to provide administrative credentials. The following information is collected:

- **Information about the client**   The client sends the following information to the reporting server: hostname, operating system type, operating system version, service pack level, App-V client version, and processor architecture.

- **Information about packages**   The client sends the following information to the reporting server: package name, package version, package source, and the percentage of an application that is cached. Figure 6-27 shows the XML content containing package information.

```xml
<?xml version="1.0"?>
- <REPORT_DATA_CACHE>
  - <APP_RECORDS>
      <APP_RECORD LaunchStatus="00000080-00000000" Launched="2015-01-
          13T23:16:46.188Z" PackageVersion="3D565CBB-0913-43A7-B1B2-2444E7656718"
          User="TAILSPINTOYS\Administrator" Server="tt-util-01" Ver="1.0.0.0" Name="H.264
          Encoder"/>
      <APP_RECORD LaunchStatus="00000080-00000000" Launched="2015-01-
          13T23:16:50.439Z" PackageVersion="25D3DFE0-6248-4FAD-8E68-8823A9E139AA"
          User="TAILSPINTOYS\Administrator" Server="tt-util-01" Ver="6.7.2.0"
          Name="Notepad++"/>
      <APP_RECORD LaunchStatus="00000080-00000000" Launched="2015-01-
          13T23:16:56.846Z" PackageVersion="B0476A66-D0CF-40AA-8F88-A03A22AF0B69"
          User="TAILSPINTOYS\Administrator" Server="tt-util-01" Ver="0.63.0.0"
          Name="PuTTY"/>
  </APP_RECORDS>
</REPORT_DATA_CACHE>
```

Figure 6-27 XML reporting data

- **Information about usage**   The client sends the following application information to the reporting server: username, application name, application version, connection group information, the start and end times of applications, the run status, and the shutdown state.

App-V client configuration for reporting

You can configure App-V clients to meet your reporting requirements by using Windows PowerShell (often for troubleshooting or for stand-alone deployments) or by using Group Policy (typically for all but the smallest implementations). You should use Group Policy to ensure a consistent configuration across all of the clients. The following client configuration options are available:

- **Reporting Server URL**   You can set a specific reporting server by specifying the URL. For example, if your reporting server is named TT-UTIL-01 and the reporting service runs on port 83, you would set the URL to *http://tt-util-01:83*.

- **Reporting Time**   You can set the time to a number between 0 and 23. Each number represents an hour of the day. For example, 3 represents 3:00 A.M.

- **Delay Reporting**   You can set a delay so that the reporting time is staggered for clients. This helps prevent congestion if all clients try to send reporting information at the same time. You can set the delay based on minutes, and the maximum number of minutes allowed is 60.

- **Repeat Reporting**   You can set clients to report every day by setting the repeat reporting to 1. The maximum number of days allowed is 30.

- **Data Cache Limit**   Each App-V client stores reporting information in .XML files. You can set the cache limit to something other than the default of 20 megabytes (MB). The maximum size allowed is 1,024 MB.

- **Data Block Size**   The data block size is the maximum amount of data that will be transferred to the reporting server at one time. The default value is 65,536 bytes.

Figure 6-28 shows the reporting server configuration items in a GPO.

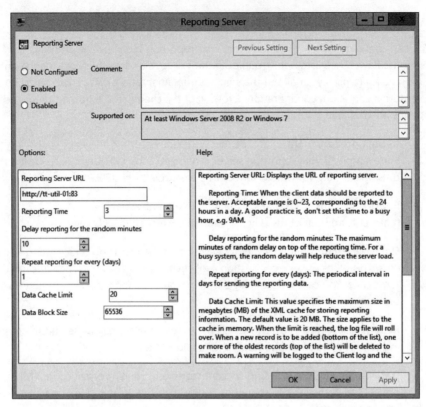

Figure 6-28 Client reporting configuration

To manually enable a client for reporting, use the following Windows PowerShell command syntax:

```
Set-AppvClientConfiguration -ReportingServerURL <url>:<port> -ReportingEnabled 1 -
ReportingStartTime <0-23> -ReportingRandomDelay <#min>
```

For example, to enable reporting for a client, setting the report server to TT-UTIL-01 on port 83 with the time of day being 3:00 A.M. and the random delay set to 10 minutes, run the following Windows PowerShell command:

```
Set-AppvClientConfiguration -ReportingServerURL http://tt-util-01:83 -ReportingEnabled
1 -ReportingStartTime 3 -ReportingRandomDelay 10
```

The random delay ensures that the client will report at the configured time and up to 10 minutes thereafter. An off-peak time and a random delay help reduce the load on the server. To send reporting data to the reporting server on demand, use the Send-AppvClientReport cmdlet, as shown in Figure 6-29.

Figure 6-29 Sending a report by using Windows PowerShell

Generating App-V reports

No predefined reports are installed by default that will display information about App-V application usage after the reporting server is installed and App-V clients are configured to send data to the reporting server. You can create your own reports if you are familiar with SQL Server Reporting Services, or you can download sample App-V reports from the Microsoft Download Center at *http://www.microsoft.com/en-us/download/details.aspx?id=42630*.

After you download App-V SQL Server Reporting Services reports, you should run App-V_SSRS_Reports.exe to extract the nine predefined App-V reports that must import to a reporting server.

To import these ready-to-use reports, you should use Report Manager by accessing the default reporting URL address; for example, *http://tt-util-01.tailspintoys.com/reports*. On the SQL Server Reporting Services home page, perform the following steps:

1. On the SQL Server Reporting Services home page, click **Upload File.**

2. Click **Browse** to locate the predefined .rdl file that contains the report and then select **OK**.

3. Repeat the procedure for every report that you plan to upload to the reporting server.

After you import the sample reports, you should see them on the Reports site, as shown in Figure 6-30.

Figure 6-30 App-V Reports site

Application sequencing

One important aspect of application virtualization is the end user experience. As the administrator, you need to ensure that your environment performs adequately and consistently so that users have a positive experience and stay productive. Of all the App-V technologies, sequencing is the most important for a positive end user experience.

There are many facets to sequencing applications. It's important to be familiar with all of the sequencing options, including the advanced sequencing features, so that you can select the appropriate method to sync your various applications for the best user experience. In this chapter, we will explore sequencing, starting with the basic features and finishing with advanced sequencing features for complex situations.

Overview of application sequencing

Several areas of sequencing contribute to the success of a virtualized application, including the sequencing computer, the Sequencer application, the method by which you install and configure an application for virtualization, and the files that make up a virtualized application. In this section, we will look at all of these areas in detail.

App-V Sequencer

The App-V Sequencer is a software application that you use to create and modify virtual applications for an App-V environment. The Sequencer installation file is on the Microsoft Desktop 2014 R2 installation media along with the server-based portions of App-V. At the time of this writing, the App-V Sequencer is at version 5.0 with Service Pack 3. The following is an overview of the Sequencer's capabilities:

- **Create new virtualized application packages** The Sequencer can create new virtual application packages by monitoring application installations. We present the steps in the sequencing process in the next section of this chapter, titled "The sequencing process."

- **Modify existing virtualized application packages**   The Sequencer can open an existing virtual application package and enables you to modify the configuration, for example, by adding shortcuts, changing icons, or even adding applications.

- **Save packages as .MSI or .APPV**   The Sequencer can save a virtualized application as an .msi file, which enables you to distribute it by using Configuration Manager or other software distribution methods. You also can save a virtualized application as an .appv file, which enables you to use the application virtually with an App-V client.

During sequencing, as part of the preparation for streaming, you can run the newly installed application, which helps optimize the package. Or, you can skip running the application and proceed with the sequencing. These options are shown in Figure 7-1.

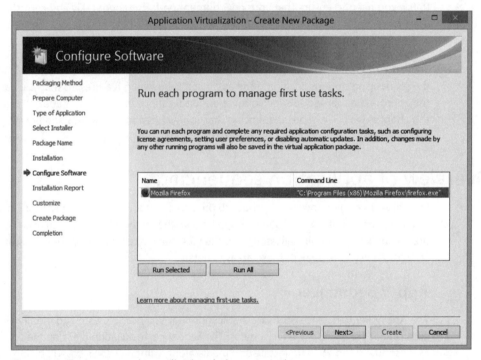

Figure 7-1 Option to run the application during sequencing

The result of skipping running the application is called Fault Streaming. Fault Streaming results in the App-V client downloading only the needed application data as it's being requested, on the fly. In many situations, skipping the optimization isn't recommended because you won't be able to configure the application settings that often are set during the first run of an application. By running the application to prepare it for streaming, the Sequencer creates a feature block map, among other tasks. A feature block map is a grouping of all of the necessary files required to publish and launch the application or to use the application in its entirety, such as using it offline. The following feature groupings store the data for virtual applications:

- **Publishing Feature Block**   The publishing feature block, also known as Feature Block 0 (FB0), is new to App-V 5.0. FB0 is a grouping of items required for publishing, such as the shortcuts, icons, metadata, and scripts.

- **Primary Feature Block**   The primary feature block, also known as Feature Block 1 (FB1), is a grouping of the application files required to launch the application.

- **Secondary Feature Block**   The secondary feature block, also known as Feature Block 2 (FB2), is a grouping of everything not included in FB0 and FB1. It contains all of the files that are not needed to start the application.

The sequencing process

Application sequencing is the process of using the App-V Sequencer application to create or modify a customized and virtualized application. The sequenced application is made to run in an App-V client environment when packaged as an .appv file or as an .msi file.

There are several steps to the sequencing process, and the steps can vary based on the options you choose as you work through the Sequencing Wizard. The following are the high-level steps of sequencing a new application:

- The App-V sequencing application is launched. You select the initial settings to begin.

- The App-V Sequencer begins monitoring for application installation changes.

- The application installation installs the application being sequenced and the Sequencer captures the changes to the system, including the addition of new folders, new files, registry entries, and environment variables, and changes to any part of the system.

- The installation finishes and is launched while the Sequencer monitors changes that occur on the first run of the application. Typical changes that occur on the first run of the application often are related to licensing, activation, registration, and initial look and feel.

- Optionally, the package settings, including shortcuts and file associations, are modified.

- The virtual application is saved and copied to the App-V application repository or another location.

CHAPTER 7

The diagram in Figure 7-2 shows the high-level steps of sequencing a typical application.

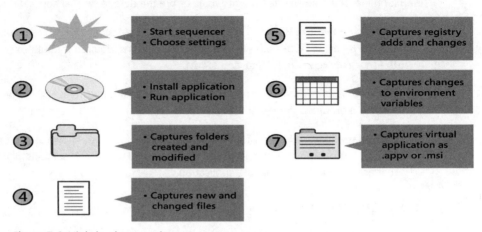

Figure 7-2 High-level sequencing steps

Items to document in a recipe

A recipe in App-V is a detailed step-by-step plan for sequencing applications. In an enterprise environment, the sequencing process is a critical part of management, and every installation detail and sequencing configuration setting is important. Because thousands of people could use your virtualized application, any details you miss could result in major issues. For administrators who are experienced with application preparation outside an App-V environment, some of the skills and techniques used there translate to an App-V environment. To maximize your chance for success, you need to focus on the complete process, including application features, application updates, post-installation steps, application usage, and App-V compatibility of applications.

Application parts

The first area to consider when planning for sequencing an application is the application features. For simple applications, all of the features may be contained in a single installation file such as setup.exe. For most environments, you likely are going to have a mix of simple applications and complex applications. Complex applications may have additional parts, such as the following:

- **Plug-ins or add-ons**   Many large or complex applications have other applications that provide additional functionality for them. For example, a web browser often has plug-ins that provide additional functionality such as ad blocking, developer tools, and antimalware services. Plug-ins or add-ons have a variety of installation methods. Some are stand-alone installers; others have to be installed by using the application. For sequencing, you should map out all of the needed plug-ins or add-ons in advance and ensure that you know the installation methods.

- **Device drivers**   Some applications install device drivers. Device drivers can't be virtualized. You still need to plan for them because they will add complexity and administrative time to the process.

- **Multiple installers**   Occasionally, you will encounter an application that has multiple installers. This can happen with large and complex suites that often are a single product with multiple applications.

Updates

In many environments, especially those that are not virtualized, administrators spend a lot of time managing application updates. A virtualized application environment should reduce the amount of administrative time needed for updating applications. One primary focus of a virtual application environment is disabling automatic updates in virtualized applications. You should disable automatic updates at the time of sequencing, if possible. Often, you can disable automatic updates during the first run of the application. During sequencing, run the application, disable automatic updates, and then proceed with the sequencing.

In a virtual application environment, you will perform application updates on the back end by sequencing. After sequencing, you will make the updated virtual applications available based on your App-V deployment. For example, if you have a full infrastructure deployment of App-V, you will import the updated application in the App-V management console and then publish it.

Post-installation steps

If an application that you are sequencing requires post-installation steps, you should perform them during the sequencing process so that they can be captured as part of the virtual package. The following is a list of common post-installation steps:

- **Accept a license agreement**   Some applications present a license when they are first launched. Make sure that you validate licensing for relevant applications prior to saving the sequenced application.

- **Set file type associations (FTAs)**   Some applications set FTAs during installation. Other applications set FTAs during the first launch of the application. You should set the preferred FTAs during sequencing.

- **Miscellaneous configuration**   You may need to disable miscellaneous application items such as tips and tricks that are presented on initial launch. Other common items that you may need to disable are activation, registration, and services that send usage data such as errors to the provider.

Application usage

App-V creates the feature block map by monitoring the launch and initial use of the application. This ensures that performance is maximized. You need to take the rights steps, however, so that the Sequencer has all of the needed information to maximize performance.

First, you need to understand how users use the application. Then, you need to perform those actions in the application while you are sequencing it. For example, if you are sequencing a web browser, you would run it, configure any post-installation steps, and then use it to visit a website, fill in a website form, and download a file. Often, applications have configuration triggers that prompt users the first time that they perform certain actions. For example, an application such as Internet Explorer may prompt a user to remember passwords after the first time the user enters a username and password on a website form. By performing the steps, the Sequencer can include the needed features in the primary feature block.

Application compatibility with App-V

Some applications are not supported for virtualization by App-V. Often, unsupported applications are unsuitable for virtualization for other reasons, too, such as having extraordinary complexity. The following are some of the applications that App-V doesn't support for virtualization:

- **Microsoft SQL Server**   You can't use App-V to virtualize SQL Server. In addition, any application that tries to install SQL Server as part of its installation isn't supported.

- **Microsoft SharePoint Server**   You can't use App-V to virtualize SharePoint. In addition, any application that tries to install SharePoint as part of its installation isn't supported.

Portions of a sequenced application

A sequenced application is made up of several files, all of which contribute to the application's functionality or configuration. You should be familiar with the files and folders that are created during the sequencing of an application, as shown in Table 7-1.

Table 7-1 Files and folders created during sequencing

File	Description
Report.xml	Contains information about files that are excluded during the sequencing process and provides diagnostic and advisory items, such as warnings or errors that are encountered during sequencing.

\<app name\>_UserConfig.xml	Contains settings that can be set for a particular user or group during application publishing. This file commonly is used to customize shortcuts and extension or FTAs for specific users.
\<app name\>_DeploymentConfig.xml	Provides global settings for published applications in a package, for example, common shortcuts or particular scripts that will run for all users.
.msi	Virtual executable file deployment, which either is used for manual deployment or can integrate with existing deployment systems such as Configuration Manager. This file isn't a stand-alone installer and requires an .appv file.
.appv	Contains the captured files and state from the sequencing process in a single file. This file includes the architecture of the package file, publishing information, and the registry in a tokenized form that can reapply to a machine and to a specific user on delivery.
.cab	Optional package accelerator file that speeds up the creation of sequenced virtual application packages.
.appvt	Sequencer template file that retains commonly reused Sequencer settings.
StreamMap.xml	The publishing feature block contains a minimum required environment for running applications.
PackageHistory.xml	Contains information about the origin of a package, for example, which user sequenced the package, on which machine, and at what time.
FilesystemMetadata.xml	Contains lists that are used to augment the file information captured under the root folder, such as empty and opaque folders.
AppxManifest.xml	Metadata for a package that contains everything you need to publish. It governs the operating system integration configuration and extension points.
Registry.dat	A mountable .dat file that contains the registry that is captured as part of a package.
Root (folder)	Contains the file system for the virtualized application that is captured during sequencing.

Planning for application sequencing

Before you begin the sequencing process, you need to perform some planning steps to ensure that your environment is ready for sequencing and that you and the other administrators understand best practices related to sequencing. In this section, we will cover the planning steps and best practices related to sequencing.

Sequencer configuration

The computer that has the App-V Sequencer installed on it is called the sequencer. Before you build and configure your sequencer, you should be familiar with the requirements and some of the best practices for the configuration.

You should install the App-V Sequencer on a client computer that runs the same operating system as the clients that will run the sequenced applications. When you are selecting the client on which to install the Sequencer, keep the following guidelines in mind:

- If applications will run on an x64 version of the Windows 7 operating system, you should sequence the applications on a computer that runs the x64 version of Windows 7.

- If you have a mix of x86 and x64 clients, you can either sequence the x86 version of an application and deploy it to both architectures or sequence the x86 and x64 versions separately.

- A computer that runs the Windows 8 operating system usually will run an application sequenced on a computer that runs the Windows 7 operating system.

- Although an application that is sequenced on a computer that runs Windows 8 usually will run when deployed through App-V to a computer that runs Windows 7, this isn't recommended because there could be issues in such situations.

The client that runs the Sequencer should have no applications installed beyond the base operating system and should be as close to an out-of-box experience (OOBE) as possible. You should not use a computer that has had applications installed and then removed, because some applications might not have been fully removed, which might affect the sequencing process. This is an important part of making sure that sequencing works correctly. Sequencing involves capturing only those modifications made during application installation; additional applications and certain services can interrupt the sequencing process, causing it to fail.

In addition to the considerations presented above, you should avoid using operating system images that include clients from antimalware applications and products such as Configuration Manager or System Center 2012 Data Protection Manager. Finally, ensure that you use the same User Account Control (UAC) settings on the Sequencer as you do on the App-V client computers.

Before performing a sequencing operation on a newly installed computer that runs Windows 8, you should disable the following services:

- Windows Defender

- Windows Update

- Windows Search

Minimum system requirements

Sequencer hardware requirements reflect the hardware of the computers on which you will deploy virtual applications. Some applications might require intensive system resources, so we recommend that the Sequencer has enough memory and a fast enough processor and hard drive.

Sequencer hardware requirements include the following:

- **Processor**   1 gigahertz (GHz) or faster. The sequencing process doesn't take advantage of multiple cores or processors.

- **Memory**   1 gigabyte (GB) of RAM or more.

- **Page file**   We recommend 500 megabytes (MB).

- **Hard drive**   30 GB minimum.

The Sequencer has the following software requirements:

- Windows 7 with SP1 (x86 or x64)

- Windows 8 (x86 or x64) or Windows 8.1 (x86 or x64)

- Windows Server 2008 R2 SP1

- Windows Server 2012

- Windows Server 2012 R2

- Microsoft .NET Framework 4 (Full Package)

- Windows PowerShell 3.0 (included with Windows 8)

- Microsoft KB2533623 (an update for Windows 7)

- Microsoft Visual C++ Redistributable Package (x86 and x64; executable file install only)

Using a virtual machine as a sequencer

You should use a virtual machine (VM) as your sequencer when feasible. This enables you to revert the sequencer to a known state before each sequencing task. In this section, we examine the process of using a VM in Hyper-V on Windows Server 2012 R2.

First, you need to have a VM created and the appropriate operating system installed. As mentioned previously, you should use the same operating system version that your App-V clients use. Once you have the operating system installed, you need to perform the recommended configurations discussed previously, such as shutting off some services and matching the UAC settings with your App-V clients. Once everything is configured, you should take a checkpoint in Hyper-V. A checkpoint, sometimes called a snapshot, is a point-in-time backup that saves the state of the virtual hard disks and the virtual hardware configuration. You can revert to a checkpoint to revert the VM to the point in time of the checkpoint. Although checkpoints, especially those taken in Hyper-V, don't replace backups, they have some real-world use cases. In Hyper-V, you can have a maximum of 50 checkpoints per VM. To take a snapshot of your VM, perform the following steps:

1. Open Hyper-V Manager.

2. Right-click the VM and then click Connect to open the Virtual Machine Connection application. This will bring you to the virtual console of the VM, as shown in Figure 7-3.

3. In the Virtual Machine Connection window for your VM, click the Action menu and then click Checkpoint.

4. In the Checkpoint Name window, type a descriptive name and then click Yes.

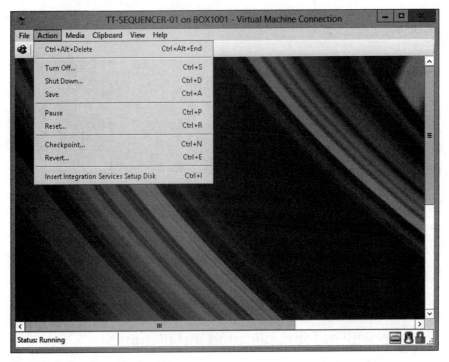

Figure 7-3 Creating a checkpoint

TROUBLESHOOTING

Hyper-V checkpoints

You also can take a checkpoint by using the Hyper-V management console. To do so, right-click a VM and then click Checkpoint. However, when you take a checkpoint from Hyper-V Manager, you can't name it with a custom name. If you have multiple check-points and don't name them, you will have to rely on the date to identify your check-points. In many cases, using a custom name for your checkpoint will save you time later when you need to revert a VM. This can be very helpful, especially in a troubleshooting or outage situation.

You also can manage checkpoints by using Windows PowerShell. However, to take advantage of the checkpoint-related cmdlets that we use in our examples, your Hyper-V server needs to run on Windows Server 2012 or Windows Server 2012 R2. Figure 7-4 shows a new checkpoint being created for a VM named TT-SEQUENCER-02 and a query of all of the checkpoints for the VM. To create the new checkpoint, you run the `Checkpoint-VM –Name "TT-SEQUENCER-02" –SnapshotName "Sequencer base"` command. To query all of the checkpoints for the VM, you run the `Get-VMSnapshot -VMName "TT-SEQUENCER-02"` command.

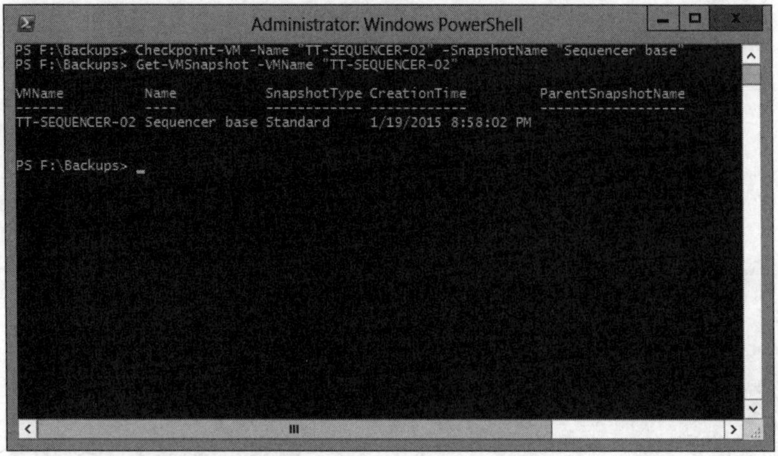

Figure 7-4 Managing checkpoints

Best practices for application installation

When you sequence an application, there are some important considerations to ensure that your virtualized application provides a good user experience. Some of these considerations are application-specific, such as a configuration that controls the application behavior. Other considerations, which we cover in this section, apply to the sequencing process. You want the virtualized application to perform adequately and provide a seamless experience for users. The following best practices are recommended:

- **Do not package temporary files**   Some applications will extract temporary installer files to a temp directory. The Sequencer will pick up those files and include them in the virtualized package. Instead, extract the temporary files to a location that isn't included in the package. You can add a location as an exclusion in the Sequencer.

- **Disable automatic application updates**   Many applications have a built-in update feature to update the application version automatically. For virtualized applications, you will control updates on the back end, as part of your App-V environment. Thus, you should disable all automatic update checks in an application during sequencing.

- **Install all needed portions during sequencing**   Some applications have multiple parts or are a suite of applications. Often, these applications perform partial installations with the most popular applications or features. When sequencing such an application, you should install all of the needed features or applications at the time of sequencing.

This is because the virtual application can't be updated from the client, and you don't want users being prompted to install an application or feature when they aren't able to do so.

- **Create a step-by-step installation document**   For each application that you plan to sequence, you should create a recipe that lists the steps needed to prepare for the installation, install the application, and configure the application. This will ensure that the sequencing process is seamless because you will know all of the steps to perform ahead of time. Administrators who are new to sequencing should practice sequencing an application several times while testing the sequenced application between each sequencing.

- **Reboot if required**   If an application installation requires a reboot, ensure that you reboot during the sequencing process. The Sequencer will continue monitoring after the reboot until the installation is complete.

Later in this chapter, in the section titled "Sequencing tasks," we walk through a step-by-step sequencing process for an application and point out some of these best practices for the application.

Inside OUT

Apps that automatically run after installation

Some applications ask you to run the application as the last step of the Installation Wizard. Often, these applications default to running immediately following the installation, so if you click through quickly, you may unknowingly run the application. To avoid this, deselect the option to run after the installation, return to the Sequencer, and then select the check box to report that the installation portion is complete. On the subsequent sequencing page, you can run the application to complete the optimization. If you don't perform these steps at the right time, the application won't be optimized for streaming. This is another configuration item that you should add to your recipes.

Best practices for package configuration

Along with the best practices for application installation, there are some best practices for creating an App-V package. The package is created during sequencing, and some of the options presented to you during sequencing form the configuration of the package. You should be familiar with the following best practices:

- **Use the application's native installation path**   During sequencing, you need to choose the primary virtual application directory. To do so, you specify the installation path for the application that you are installing during sequencing. It's a required part of the Sequencing Wizard. You should use the application's native installation path. To find the native installation path, you can run the installation program outside the sequencing process. When you get to the installation path during the process, copy the path and then cancel the installation. This is a key piece of information that you will want to add to your recipes. Thereafter, you can just paste the path into the Sequencer during the sequencing process. Note that although this is a best practice, it isn't the only viable option for the primary virtual application directory. Some administrators use an alternative method and don't experience any degradation.

- **Fill in a detailed description**   During sequencing, you should add a detailed description. The description should contain details about the package, such as the version of the application, any special installation options, the list of applications in a package, and other similar information. When you have multiple administrators or a long list of virtualized applications, the information that you put into the description will be very helpful.

- **For streaming packages, always run the application during sequencing**   If you are planning to stream an application that you are sequencing, you should run the application as part of the optimization during sequencing. The publishing feature block will be created as part of this process. This will create a better end user experience when users run the applications.

- **Don't define target operating systems unless necessary**   When you sequence an application, don't define the target operating systems unless you need to. In general, you will have more flexibility if all of the operating systems are able to run an application. There are exceptions such as Remote Desktop Services (RDS) or security. For example, if you are sequencing an application for an RDS environment, then you should define the operating system so that the application doesn't accidentally become available to client computers on which it wasn't intended to be used. In a high-security environment where you are trying to meet or exceed operational security standards or compliance mandates, you should consider defining a target operating system because it slightly enhances security.

Applications that cannot be sequenced

In some cases, an application either isn't compatible with application virtualization or presents enough problems when virtualized that you should not virtualize it. As the administrator, you should know the types of applications that are not always suitable for virtualization, such as the following:

- **An application that starts during startup**   Sometimes, applications start during a computer's startup sequence, often as part of a Windows service. App-V doesn't support these types of applications because it relies on a logged-on user to launch virtualized applications.

- **An application that installs device drivers**   Device drivers can't be virtualized. If an application installs or requires a device driver, you must install the device driver in Windows, outside App-V. This is sometimes, but not always, feasible. One exception to the device driver limitation is some user-mode device drivers that can be virtualized.

- **Internet Explorer**   Because Internet Explorer is built into Windows, it can't be virtualized with App-V. This also is true for other default Windows applications such as WordPad.

- **An application that interacts with several other applications**   App-V provides app isolation. If you use connection groups, you can group some applications so that they can communicate. However, if you have an application that needs to communicate with several other applications, it probably isn't a good candidate for virtualization. Such an application would introduce many complexities for virtualization and require extra administrative overhead.

The App-V 5.0 Sequencing Guide, available at *http://www.microsoft.com/en-us/download/details.aspx?id=27760*, contains additional information on identifying applications that may not be suitable for virtualization.

If you want to provide access to applications that don't work under App-V, consider looking at session-based desktops, which are covered in Chapter 8, "Planning and deploying session-based desktops," or RemoteApp programs, which are covered in Chapter 9, "Configuring RemoteApp programs and client connectivity."

Sequencing an application

In this section, we focus on the end-to-end process for sequencing an application. Along the way, we review some of the best practices discussed previously and put them to use as we begin sequencing applications. The sequencing process will be covered through the GUI and through Windows PowerShell. You need to be proficient in both to optimize your deployments.

Types of applications that can be sequenced

App-V supports three types of applications for sequencing. These options are presented to you after you run the Sequencer and choose the option to create a new package, as shown in Figure 7-5.

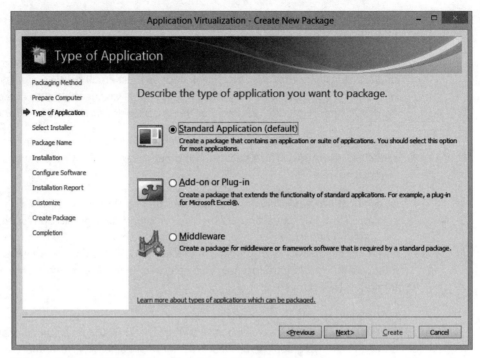

Figure 7-5 Create New Package Wizard, Type Of Application page

The types of applications that you can package are described in detail below:

- **Standard Application (default)**   This application type, which is the default type, creates a package that contains an application or suite of applications and is the most common option for most virtualized applications. Examples of the standard application type
are Notepad++, Mozilla Firefox, and WinZip.

- **Add-on or Plug-in**   This application type creates a package that extends the functionality of standard applications. You can use this option for locally installed applications
or other virtualized applications by using connection groups. Examples of the add-on
or plug-in application type are Mozilla Firefox browser add-ons and Microsoft Office
plug-ins.

- **Middleware**   This application type creates a package that a standard
application requires to run. Examples of the middleware application type are
Microsoft .NET Framework and the Java Runtime Environment.

In addition to the application types that can be sequenced, it is important to understand the
limitations of sequencing an application, as discussed earlier in this chapter in the section titled
"Applications that cannot be sequenced."

Preparing for sequencing

At this stage, you should have a good understanding of the planning steps and best practices for sequencing an application. Next, you will prepare the computer for sequencing, in line with the best practices discussed in the section titled "Planning for application sequencing" earlier in this chapter.

For this example, we will sequence applications for deployment to client computers running Windows 8.1 Enterprise x64. To ensure a smooth sequencing process and the best user experience possible for this scenario, complete the following steps for installing the Sequencer:

1. **Install the operating system**   Install Windows 8.1 Enterprise x64 on a VM that meets the minimum system requirements for the App-V Sequencer application. See the section titled "Minimum system requirements" earlier in this chapter for more information.

2. **Install patches on the sequencer**   Install all of the needed operating system patches and restart the computer. Be careful about installing optional patches, such as Silverlight. You don't want any unnecessary software installed on the sequencer. Look at Programs And Features to ensure that there aren't applications installed.

3. **Disable Services**   Disable the Windows Defender, Windows Search, and Windows Update services to avoid impacting the sequencing process:

    a.   First, open the Windows Defender application.

    b.   Click the Settings tab and then click the Administrator section in the left pane.

    c.   In the right pane, deselect the Turn On This App check box, as shown in Figure 7-6. Click Save Changes and then click Close on the confirmation window.

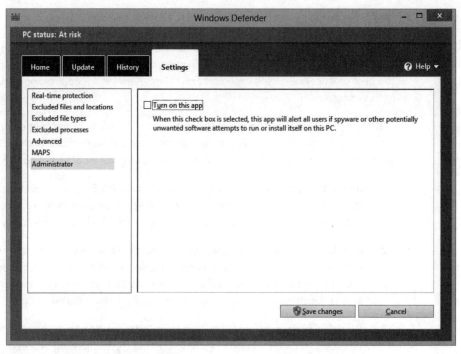

Figure 7-6 Windows Defender application

    d. Next, open the Windows Services management console.

    e. Scroll down to the Windows Defender service. Confirm the service isn't running and that the Startup Type is set to Manual.

    f. Scroll down to the Windows Search service. Right-click the service and then click Stop. Click Yes to also stop the Windows Media Player Network Sharing Service. Right-click the Windows Search service and then click Properties. Change the startup type to Disabled and then click OK.

    g. Scroll down to the Windows Update service. Right-click the service and then click Properties. Change the startup type to Disabled and then click OK.

4. **Install the App-V Sequencer**   Run the appv_sequencer_setup.exe and install the Microsoft Application Virtualization Sequencer.

5. **Create a checkpoint**   Create a checkpoint (snapshot) of the current state using the method appropriate to your hypervisor.

After completing the above tasks, you should have a functional VM for sequencing applications.

Sequencing tasks

We will now run through the tasks for sequencing an application. In the following example, we look at sequencing the Mozilla Firefox web browser.

1. Download the Mozilla Firefox installer and save it to your desktop on the sequencer. You should download the full offline installation file so that you don't have to wait for the download during sequencing and to avoid having any download activity captured during the sequencing.

2. Launch the Sequencer.

3. Click the Create A New Virtual Application Package option.

4. On the Packaging Method page, ensure that the Create Package (Default) option is selected and then click Next.

5. On the Prepare Computer page, review any issues and remediate them. In the top half of Figure 7-7, you can see that the wizard has identified that Windows Defender is active. After disabling Windows Defender, click Refresh. The Sequencer will report that it is ready to proceed, as shown in the bottom half of Figure 7-7. Click Next to continue.

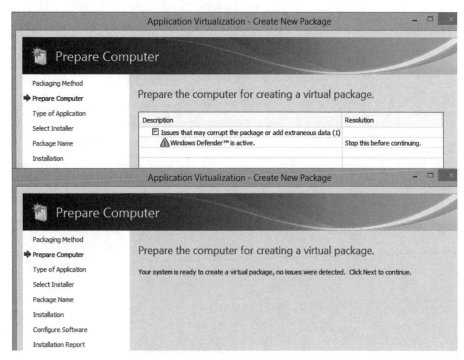

Figure 7-7 Create New Package Wizard, Prepare Computer page

6. On the Type Of Application page, select Standard Application (Default) and then click Next.

7. On the Select Installer page, shown in Figure 7-8, ensure that the Select The Installer For The Application option is selected, click Browse, select the Firefox installer, and then click Open. Click Next to continue.

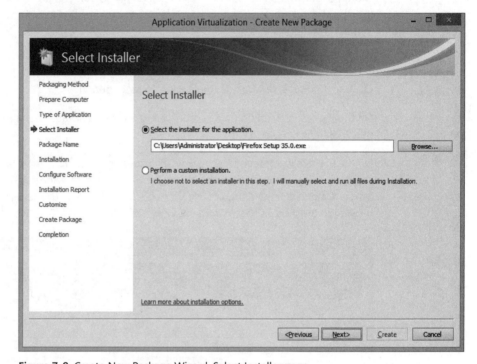

Figure 7-8 Create New Package Wizard, Select Installer page

8. On the Package Name page, enter a name for the virtual application package, as shown in Figure 7-9. Note that clicking Next will begin the installation process. Click Next to continue.

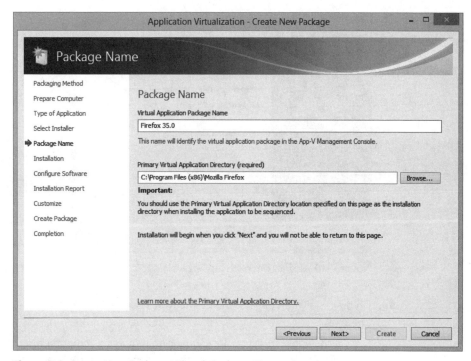

Figure 7-9 Create New Package Wizard, Package Name page

9. The Mozilla Firefox Setup page will be displayed. Chose the option to do a custom install. Leave the default destination folder but choose not to install the maintenance service. On the final page of the installer, uncheck the box for Launch Firefox Now, as shown in Figure 7-10. This application has some first-use triggers that you should capture during the Configure Software step, so we will not launch the application at this stage.

Figure 7-10 Mozilla Firefox Setup Wizard

10. On the Installation page of the Create New Package Wizard, there are three items to be aware of:

- If the application you are sequencing requires a computer restart, you can proceed with the restart, and the Sequencer will resume automatically after the reboot.

- If the application you are sequencing has multiple installers, you can start the next installer by clicking Run. Locate the next installer and then click Open to run it.

- After you've finished installing all the parts for this application, select the I Am Finished Installing check box, as shown in Figure 7-11. Click Next to continue.

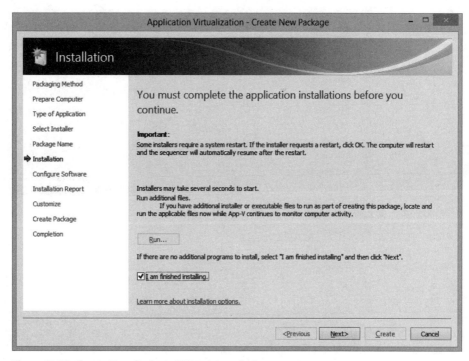

Figure 7-11 Create New Package Wizard, Installation page

11. On the Configure Software page, select the Mozilla Firefox application and click
    Run Selected, as shown in Figure 7-12. During this step, you launch the sequenced
    application, apply any custom settings, and configure first-use items.

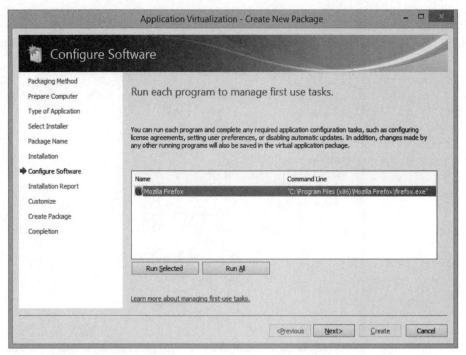

Figure 7-12 Create New Package Wizard, Configure Software page

For this Firefox example, we will configure a few items through the Sequencer during this step. Be aware that each application is different and that optimizing these settings will depend on your environment. In some cases, configuring your applications will be better handled through application-specific configuration files, registry keys, or a Group Policy Object (GPO).

a. **Import Wizard**   This is the first prompt that appears after running Firefox for the first time. We don't want to import anything into Firefox. Click the Don't Import Anything option and then click Next.

b. **Take A Quick Tour**   Firefox wants to walk you through the application settings. We don't want our users to see this. Click the Not Now option.

c. **Default Browser**   Firefox asks you to set it as your default web browser. In this case, we are opting not to make it the default browser, so select the Don't Ask Me Again check box and then click the Not Now option.

d. **Automatic Updates**   Firefox has automatic updates enabled by default. Rather than enabling automatic updates, you should deliver application updates by using updated App-V packages. Click the menu icon in the upper-right corner of the browser. Click Options, click the Advanced tab, and then click the Update sub-tab. Under Firefox Updates, click Never Check For Updates and deselect the Use A

Background Service To Install Updates check box. Click OK to apply the changes.

e.   Close Tabs   When you exit Firefox, it will confirm that you want to close all open tabs. We will opt to leave this prompt in place. Ensure that the Warn Me When I Attempt To Close Multiple Tabs option is selected and then click Close Tabs. After completing the Firefox configuration, click Next to continue. The Sequencer will collect the changes and apply them to the package.

12. On the Installation Report page, note any recorded issues. In our example, the Sequencer reported that some files were excluded from the package and suggests that you resolve this by verifying package functionality, as shown in Figure 7-13. Click Next to continue.

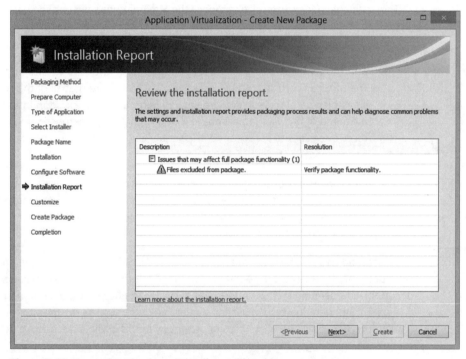

Figure 7-13 Create New Package Wizard, Installation Report page

Customizing the package

On the Customize page of the Create Package Wizard, you are presented with two options:

- **Stop Now**   Create A Basic Virtual Application Package (Default)

- **Customize**   Further Configure The Virtual Application Package
    - Optimize this package for deployment over slow or unreliable network
    - Restrict operating systems that can run this package

Continuing with the Firefox example, select the Customize option and then click Next.

The first page in the Customize section is the Streaming page. This page gives you the opportunity to tune the user experience in case of slow or unreliable networks. You can do this in one of two ways:

- **Run the application**   Select the application from the list and click Run Selected. The Mozilla Firefox web browser will launch. Make sure that all of the configuration adjustments we made earlier are applied here. Try a few common tasks like accessing the menu or browsing to a website. Confirm that they are functioning and then close the browser. In the background, the Sequencer is recording each action to optimize performance.

- **Force download**   If you are certain that streaming this application won't be suitable for your environment, you can select the option to force applications to be fully downloaded before they are launched. This will ensure the application can't be used until it is fully cached on the client computer.

The second page in the Customize section is the Target OS page. This page gives you the opportunity to isolate which operating system platforms can run this package. By default, any supported operating system can run the package. You have the option to narrow this scope to a particular operating system version and architecture, such as the 64-bit version of Windows 8.1. However, as mentioned previously in this book, it is a good practice not to limit the operating system platforms unless you have to.

The most notable item on this page is the built-in warning when you select an operating system that doesn't match the one installed on the Sequencer, as shown in Figure 7-14. This is recorded in the best practices, and the Sequencer is smart enough to warn you. When you are finished with your selection, click Next to continue.

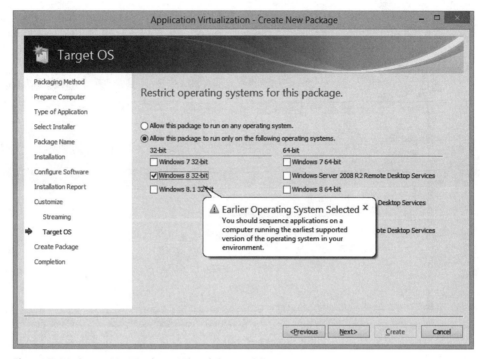

Figure 7-14 Create New Package Wizard, Target OS page

Package editor

On the Create Package page of the Create Package Wizard, you are presented with two options:

- **Continue To Modify Package Without Saving Using The Package Editor**   This launches the package editor at the end of the wizard. The package editor is composed of several tabs that enable further configuration modifications prior to saving a package.

- **Save The Package Now**   This option enables you to set a save location and create the package now.

For the Firefox example, click the Continue To Modify Package Without Saving Using The Package Editor option and then click Next. On the Completion page, click Close to complete the wizard. The package editor will start automatically.

The package editor contains eight tabs below the menu bar. You should be familiar with the available options and how to work with them.

On the Properties tab, shown in Figure 7-15, you can enter a package name, which displays in the App-V management console, and you can use the Description field to add information about a package.

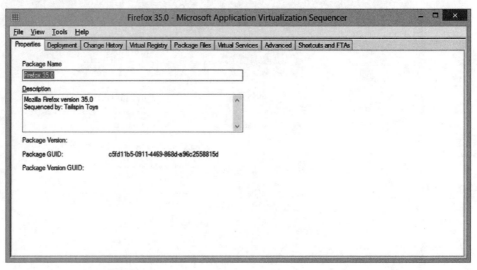

Figure 7-15 Package editor, Properties tab

On the Deployment tab, shown in Figure 7-16, you can redefine the approved operating system for this package. Note that a warning will be displayed when you select an operating system that doesn't match the Sequencer.

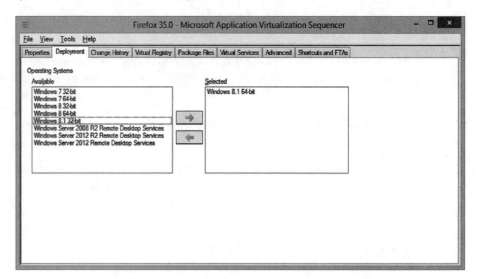

Figure 7-16 Package editor, Deployment tab

The Change History tab, shown in Figure 7-17, displays information about when a sequence was performed. This information includes the Sequencer software and the sources of the Sequencer system.

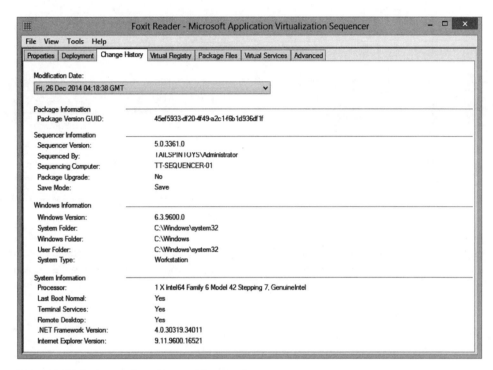

Figure 7-17 Package editor, Change History tab

The Virtual Registry tab, shown in Figure 7-18, shows the registry keys and the values that were added or adjusted during the recording phase. On this tab, you can add or modify keys. Some applications require a virtual registry to merge with local keys—or, in some situations, to override a local key—but the Sequencer usually selects the correct setting.

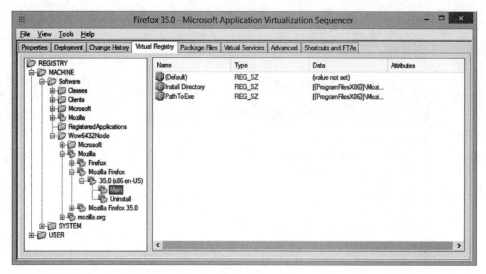

Figure 7-18 Package editor, Virtual Registry tab

The Package Files tab, shown in Figure 7-19, shows the files that were collected during the sequencing process. Similar to the virtual registry, you can add or delete files, or you can merge or override files and folders with local systems.

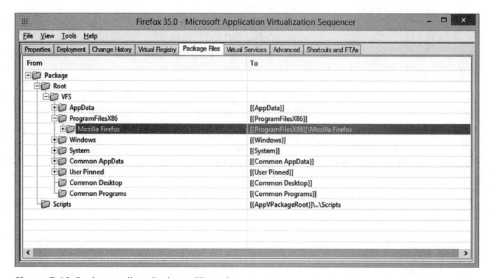

Figure 7-19 Package editor, Package Files tab

On the Virtual Services tab, shown in Figure 7-20, if the sequenced application created a service during the sequencing process, you can modify the properties of that service. For example, if you left the Mozilla Maintenance service enabled during the installation, it would be displayed on this tab. If a service is listed, you can define the startup type and dependencies or provide the credentials under which the service will run. You can't disable a virtual service on this tab. You only can disable a virtual service by using dynamic configuration files during the monitoring phase or by opening the Services.msc console and performing the appropriate action.

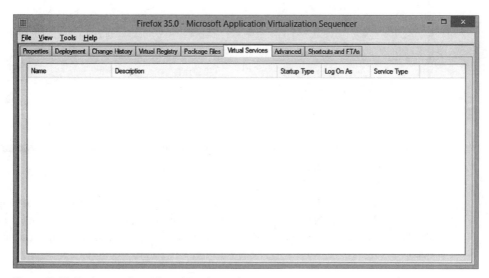

Figure 7-20 Package editor, Virtual Services tab

The Advanced tab, shown in Figure 7-21, has three configurable settings:

- **Allow All Named Objects To Interact With The Local System**   Creates named kernel objects from a virtual bubble that are visible to nonvirtualized applications

- **Allow All COM Objects To Interact With The Local System**   Creates COM objects from a virtual bubble that are visible to nonvirtualized applications

- **Allow Virtual Applications Full Write Permissions To The Virtual File System**   Allows applications in the virtual bubble write permissions to the virtual file system

CHAPTER 7

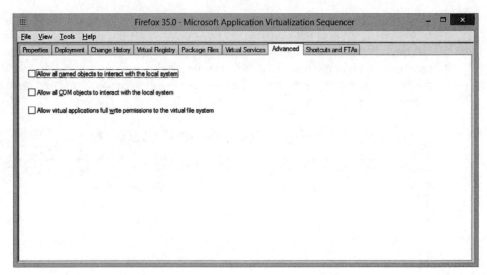

Figure 7-21 Package Editor, Advanced tab

On the Shortcuts And FTAs tab, shown in Figure 7-22, you can edit, remove, or add applications and FTAs and shortcuts that relate to the applications. A common practice is to remove shortcuts to Help and README files, including desktop shortcuts that the application installer adds.

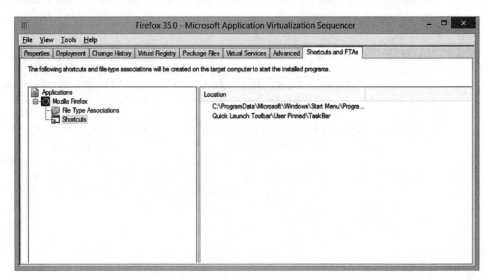

Figure 7-22 Package editor, Shortcuts And FTAs tab

Windows PowerShell

The Sequencer includes support for Windows PowerShell. All Sequencer functions must be performed in an elevated Windows PowerShell console, and the Windows PowerShell module for the Sequencer must be loaded. To load the Sequencer Windows PowerShell module, run the following command:

```
Import-Module AppVSequencer
```

You can sequence an application by using Windows PowerShell by using the New-AppVSequencerPackage cmdlet. For example, to sequence the 7-Zip application, run the following command:

```
New-AppvSequencerPackage –Name "7-Zip 9.20" –Path "C:\Packages" –Installer "C:\Users
\Administrator\Desktop\7z920-x64.msi" –PrimaryVirtualApplicationDirectory "C:\Program
Files\7-Zip"
```

For more information on sequencing applications by using Windows PowerShell, see *https://technet.microsoft.com/en-us/library/jj684300.aspx.*

Deploying Office 2013 by using App-V

Starting with App-V 5.0 SP2, support was added for virtualizing the volume license edition of Office 2013, along with activation support through a Key Management Service (KMS) server, Active Directory–based activation, and activation by using multiple activation keys (MAKs). Prior to the release of SP2, App-V could be used only with Microsoft Office 365 ProPlus or pre-2013 releases of Office such as Office 2010.

App-V provides a highly manageable experience for delivering Office volume license editions and Office 365 ProPlus. Some of the major benefits include the following:

- Support for installing Office 2013 in RDS environments

- The ability to deselect features from the Microsoft Office system at installation time

- Full integration with the local operating system

- Fast deployment and easy application of life cycle management

You can use additional add-ins with Office 2013 virtual packages, but these add-ins need to be sequenced by using the Sequencer and later need to be added in a connection group with the Office 2013 virtual package.

Office Deployment Tool for Click-to-Run

Unlike standard applications, preparing Office 2013 for App-V requires the use of a separate tool named the Office Deployment Tool for Click-to-Run, which is used instead of the App-V

Sequencer to sequence Office 2013. A special packager mode of the Office Deployment Tool (ODT) creates an Office 2013 Click-to-Run App-V package.

The following high-level steps show you how to use the Office Deployment Tool for Click-to-Run:

1. Download and run the self-extracting Office Deployment Tool for Click-to-Run from *http://www.microsoft.com/en-us/download/details.aspx?id=36778*.

2. After running the officedeploymenttool.exe and selecting the target directory, you will have two files in the specified directory:

   a. **Configuration.xml**   This file is used to specify the Click-to-Run installation and update options for the Office Deployment Tool.

   b. **Setup.exe**   This is the Office Deployment Tool executable, providing the option to download, configure, and package Office 2013.

3. Open the Configuration.xml in a text editor such as Notepad. The version of Configuration.xml included with the ODT includes some commented-out examples of supported options. It is important to remember that this tool also is used for Click-to-Run deployments, so some of the provided options are not necessary for an App-V package. In this example, we will focus on the following options:

   a. **SourcePath**   This defines the package source location where the Office 2013 binaries will be downloaded.

   b. **OfficeClientEdition**   This defines the Office 2013 architecture version.

   c. **Product ID**   This defines the product version. Note that you can have multiple Product ID tags, in case you want to add Office applications, such as Visio or Project, to the package.

   d. **Language ID**   This defines the language pack. Note that you can include multiple Language ID tags, but this will increase the size of the package.

4. In the following example, we have defined our desired configuration for an Office 2013 ProPlusVolume 32-bit installation, as shown in Figure 7-23. Update your configuration.xml and save it.

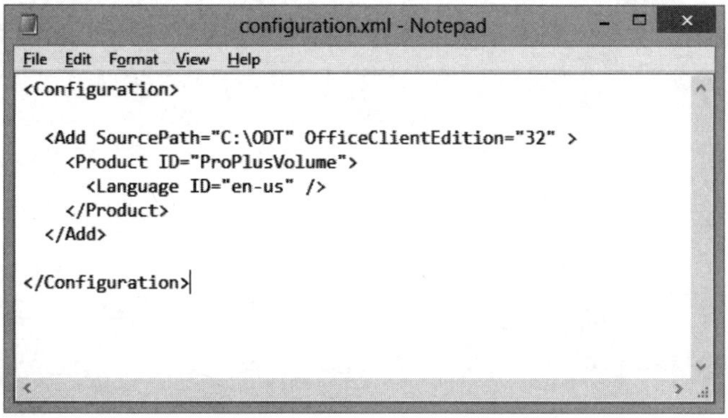

Figure 7-23 Configuration.xml

Download Office 2013

With the ODT installed and your customized configuration.xml file, you can download the Office 2013 App-V streams by taking the following steps:

1. Open an elevated command prompt and browse to the directory where you installed the ODT.

2. Run the following command to begin downloading the Office 2013 streams:

   ```
   Setup.exe /download configuration.xml
   ```

   The Office 2013 stream will begin downloading to the source path, as defined in your configuration.xml. In this example, the stream will be saved in the C:\ODT\Office folder. This process could take considerable time, depending on your Internet connection and the options defined in your configuration.xml.

3. Open File Explorer and browse to the ODT logging path. If the Logging Path tag was not changed in the configuration.xml, all logs will be saved in %temp%.

4. Open File Explorer and browse to the source path defined in the configuration.xml. Navigate through the subfolders to display the Office 2013 streams, as shown in Figure 7-24.

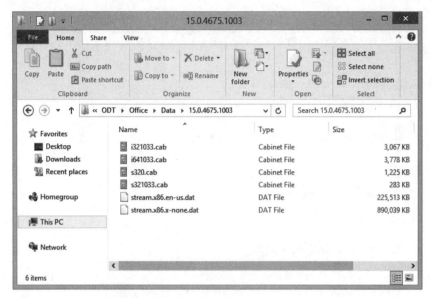

Figure 7-24 Folder showing Office 2013 streams

Inside OUT

ODT and elevation

You will use three primary functions with the ODT:

- Download
- Configure
- Package

For the configure function (/configure) and the package function (/packager), you must use an elevated command prompt. Although you can perform the download without elevation, it's a good practice to use elevation throughout so that you don't have to switch between elevated and nonelevated prompts.

Package Office 2013

After downloading the Office 2013 stream using the ODT, you can use the ODT to create an .APPV package by taking the following steps:

1. Open an elevated command prompt and browse to the directory where you installed the ODT.

2. Run the following command to begin packaging the Office 2013 streams. Note that the final option is the output directory. In this example, we will output the files into the current directory using the period symbol to represent the current directory.

    ```
    Setup.exe /packager configuration.xml .
    ```

    The amount of time this process will take depends on the performance of the computer from which you are packaging.

3. Once complete, open File Explorer and browse to the source path. You should have a new directory named AppVPackages. Inside this directory, you will find the following files, as shown in Figure 7-25:

    a. **ProPlusVolume_en-us_x86.appv**   This is the Office 2013 ProPlusVolume EN-US 32-bit App-V package.

    b. **ProPlusVolume_en-us_x86_DeploymentConfig.xml**   This is the DeploymentConfig.xml, as reviewed in Chapter 6, "Managing and administering Application Virtualization."

    c. **ProPlusVolume_en-us_x86_UserConfig.xml**   This is the UserConfig.xml. Note that this is included by default through the packager, but it isn't used in a global Office 2013 deployment. You can ignore this file.

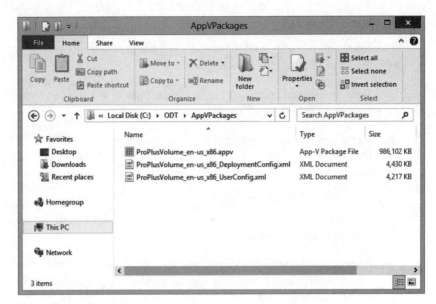

Figure 7-25 Office 2013 App-V files

Deploy Office 2013

You can deploy this Office 2013 virtual package by using any App-V deployment models discussed in Chapter 4, "Planning and implementing App-V," such as the full infrastructure model, the Configuration Manager–integrated mode, the stand-alone model, or you can publish it to the App-V client for RDS.

In the following example, we do a quick stand-alone deployment to test the Office 2013 package.

1. Copy the App-V package to a computer running an App-V client.

2. Open an elevated Windows PowerShell prompt.

3. Run the following command to import the App-V client module:

   ```
   Import-Module AppvClient
   ```

4. The APPV package includes an embedded script. Run the following command to ensure that the App-V client can execute embedded package scripts:

   ```
   Set-AppvClientConfiguration –EnablePackageScripts 1
   ```

5. Run the following command to add the APPV package and publish it globally to the App-V client:

```
Add-AppvClientPackage "C:\ODT\AppVPackages\ProPlusVolume_en-us_x86.appv" |
Publish-AppvClientPackage -Global
```

The output from this command will show that the application has been published successfully, as shown in Figure 7-26.

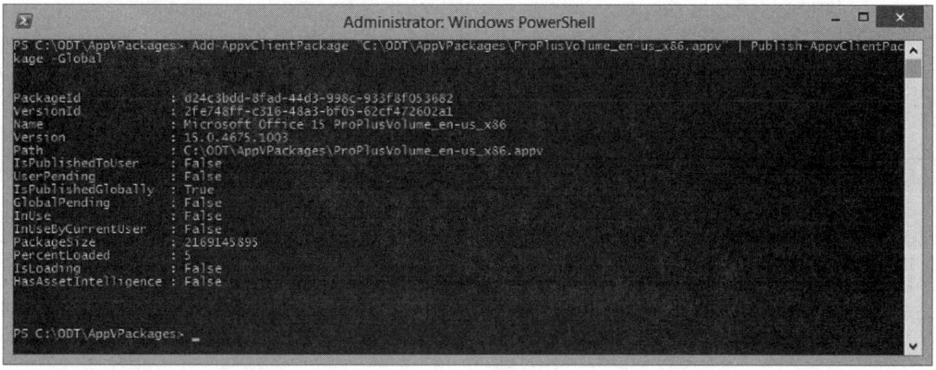

Figure 7-26 Windows PowerShell

Once they are published, you can open each of the Office 2013 applications and validate functionality. For more information on deploying Office 2013 by using App-V, see *http://support.microsoft.com/kb/2915745*.

Advanced application sequencing

When you perform sequencing tasks, some application types require special consideration. For example, you might have applications that need to sequence repeatedly with small changes. In such cases, package accelerators will speed up and simplify the overall process. Additionally, you might need to upgrade existing packages or add applications to an existing package and then run it side by side with the original package. You can use several advanced sequencing techniques for these scenarios, and this section describes how to do so.

Package accelerators

Package accelerators enable you to create an application package without monitoring an application installation; instead, package metadata from a previous sequence is used alongside the installation media to reproduce a package. Sometimes, Microsoft and other product vendors provide package accelerators to speed up and simplify the process of creating a package. The Sequencer also provides a way to create package accelerators. Package accelerators are commonly used in situations in which you want to customize specific settings of an application but don't want to go through a full application sequencing. You can reuse and share package accelerators, but be aware that they can contain sensitive information such as passwords or user-specific information.

To create a package accelerator by using the Sequencer, you need the App-V package and the application installation files or the location where the files are installed locally. For the installation files, you can use Windows Installer .msi files, .zip files, .cab files, or other necessary files and folders. Self-extracting executable files need to be extracted and then presented with a folder location during package accelerator creation.

A package accelerator will create a PackageName.cab file that contains the following:

- A manifest file

- Additional files that contain customizations, which the application added at the time of sequencing

- Files that are necessary for the virtual environment and streaming optimization

The Sequencer provides the capability to create App-V package accelerators by using Window PowerShell commands, too.

Creating a package accelerator

To create a package accelerator, perform the following steps:

1.   Open the Sequencer. Click the Tools menu and then click Create Accelerator, as shown in Figure 7-27.

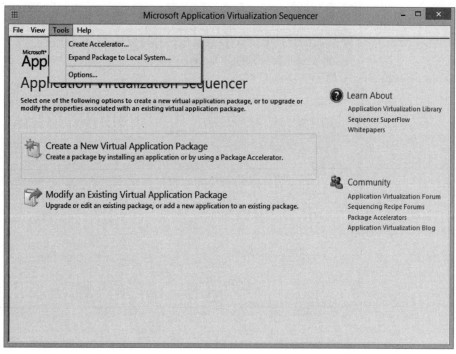

Figure 7-27 Creating an accelerator

2. On the Select Package page, shown in Figure 7-28, browse to and select the App-V package by specifying the location of the .appv file.

CHAPTER 7

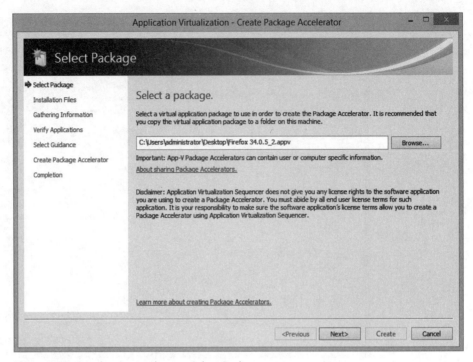

Figure 7-28 Creating an accelerator, Select Package page

3. On the Installation Files page, shown in Figure 7-29, specify the location of the installation files. It is a good practice to have the application installed on the Sequencer before you begin creating the package accelerator.

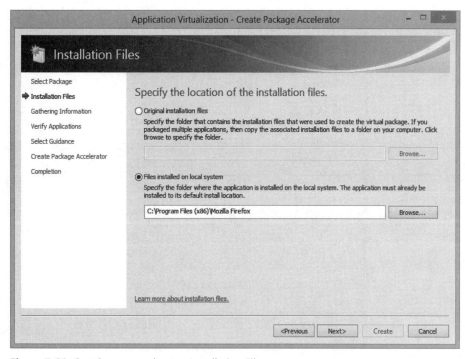

Figure 7-29 Creating an accelerator, Installation Files page

4. On the Create Package Accelerator page, shown in Figure 7-30, review any files that are not found in the location that you specified in the previous step. If some missing files are required, you can return to the previous step by clicking Previous and then copy any missing files in the location that is specified on the Installation Files page. Otherwise, click the option to remove the missing file or files and then click Next.

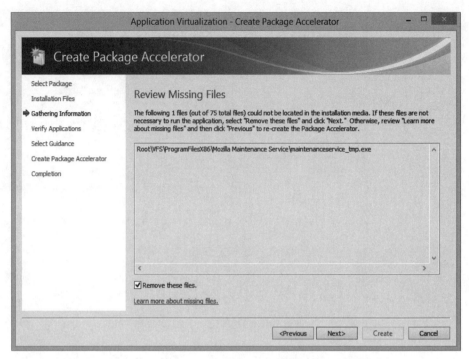

Figure 7-30 Creating an accelerator, Create Package Accelerator page 1 of 2

5. On the second page of the Create Package Accelerator section, shown in Figure 7-31, all identified files that were put into the accelerator will be displayed. On this page, you can remove unnecessary files from the accelerator. Click Next.

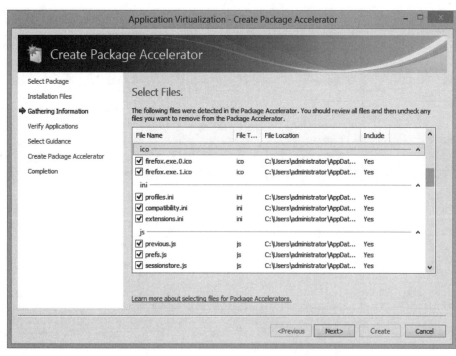

Figure 7-31 Creating an accelerator, Create Package Accelerator page 2 of 2

6. On the Verify Applications page 1 of 2, shown in Figure 7-32, the applications that were detected in the package will be displayed. In this case, only one application was detected. If more than one application is detected, and you see one that you don't want to be part of a package built from the accelerator, you can delete it before proceeding. Click Next.

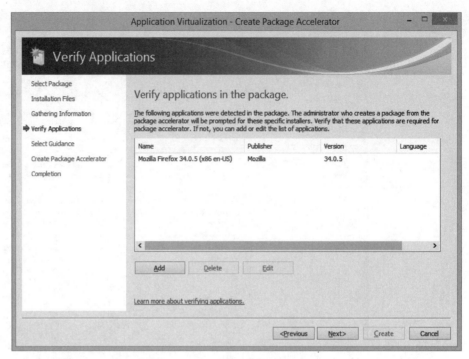

Figure 7-32 Creating an accelerator, Verify Applications page

7. On the Select Guidance page, shown in Figure 7-33, you can import .txt or .rtf files that contain instructions on how a package should be configured, required prerequisites, and some general advice for administrators to use during package creation.

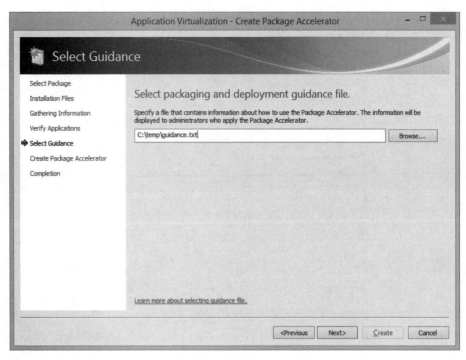

Figure 7-33 Creating an accelerator, Select Guidance page

8. On the Create Package Accelerator page, shown in Figure 7-34, specify a location to save the package accelerator as a .cab file and then click Create.

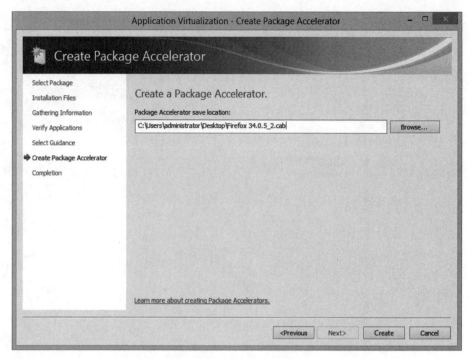

Figure 7-34 Creating an accelerator, Create Package Accelerator page

9. After the accelerator is created, click Close.

You also can use Windows PowerShell to create a package accelerator. During Windows PowerShell package accelerator creation, several parameters are required for the New-AppvPackageAccelerator cmdlet, including the following:

- **InstalledFilesPath**   Points to the location that contains the installation files

- **InputPackagePath**   Specifies the location of the package

- **Path**   Specifies the location where a package accelerator will be saved

- **AcceleratorDescriptionFilePath**   Specifies the location of the .txt file or .rtf file that contains additional guidance for package creation

- **Installer**   Points to an application's source files, if the application isn't already installed locally

The following Windows PowerShell package accelerator command creates a new accelerator for the Microsoft Excel Viewer application:

```
New-AppvPackageAccelerator –InstalledFilesPath "C:\Program Files\Microsoft Excel Viewer"
–InputPackagePath "C:\Packages\Microsoft Excel Viewer\Microsoft_ExcelViewer.appv" –Path
"C:\Packages\Microsoft Excel Viewer" –AcceleratorDescriptionFilePath "C:\SourceFiles
\guidance.txt"
```

After creating a package accelerator, you can use it, without sequencing, to create new packages. To create a package from a package accelerator, take the following steps:

1. Open the App-V Sequencing Wizard and then click
Create A New Virtual Application Package, as shown in Figure 7-35.

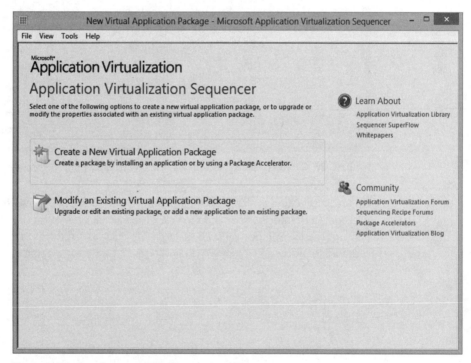

Figure 7-35 Creating a package from an accelerator

2. On the Packaging Method page, shown in Figure 7-36, click the
Create Package Using A Package Accelerator option and then click Next.

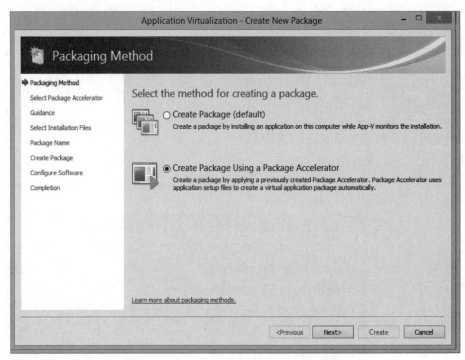

Figure 7-36 Creating a package from an accelerator, Packaging Method page

3.   On the Select Package Accelerator page, shown in Figure 7-37, specify the path to the package accelerator .cab file and then click Next. If the .cab file isn't digitally signed, a pop-up message will be displayed asking if you want to run the file. If you trust the file, click Run to proceed.

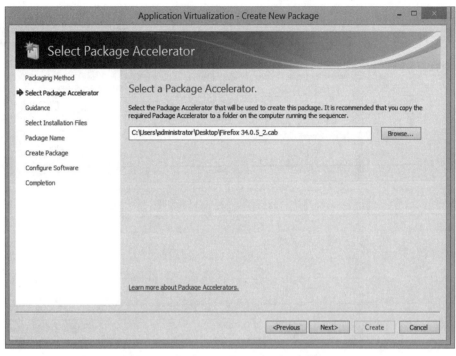

Figure 7-37 Creating a package from an accelerator, Select Package Accelerator page

4. On the Guidance page, shown in Figure 7-38, review the information from the guidance file, if any, and then click Next.

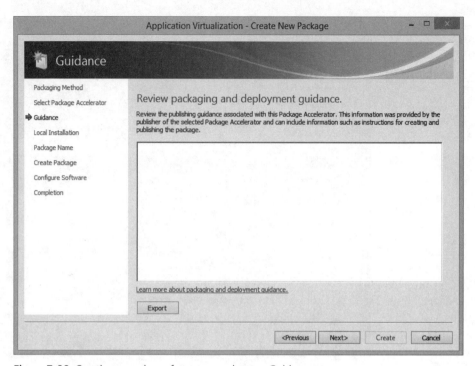

Figure 7-38 Creating a package from an accelerator, Guidance page

5. On the Local Installation page, shown in Figure 7-39, if the application is installed, select the I Have Installed All Applications option and then click Next. If the application isn't installed, you can install it at this time. Select the I Have Installed All Applications option, and then click Next.

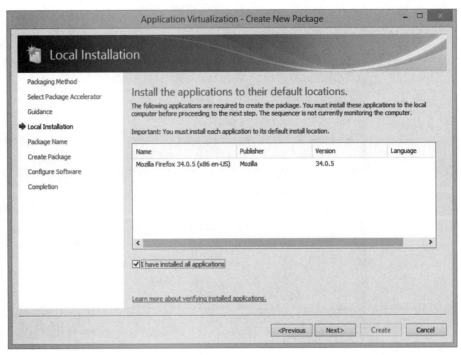

Figure 7-39 Creating a package from an accelerator, Local Installation page

6. On the Package Name page, shown in Figure 7-40, enter a name for the package and then click Next.

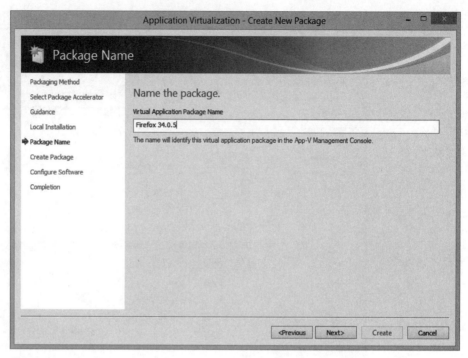

Figure 7-40 Creating a package from an accelerator, Package Name page

7. On the Create Package page, shown in Figure 7-41, enter a detailed description of the package if desired, specify the location to save the package, and then click Create. After the creation process completes successfully, click Next.

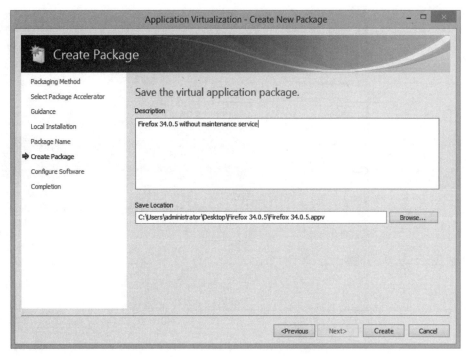

Figure 7-41 Creating a package from an accelerator, Create Package page

8. On the Configure Software page, shown in Figure 7-42, you can select the
    Configure Software option, which enables you to run the application and configure
    first-use tasks. Or, you can skip the configuration and complete the package creation
    process. To provide the best user experience, it is highly recommend that you use the
    Configure Software option.

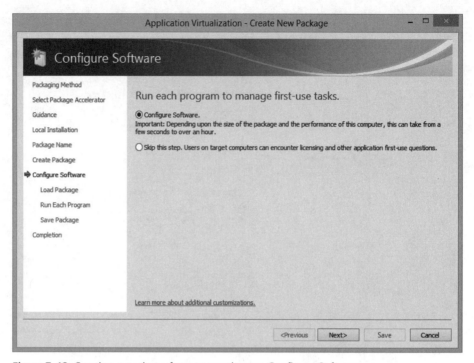

Figure 7-42 Creating a package from an accelerator, Configure Software page

9. On the Run Each Program page, shown in Figure 7-43, click Run All to run each application in the package. In this example, there is one application named Mozilla Firefox. After you click Run All, Mozilla Firefox launches. Then, you can configure some of the first-use tasks such as choosing whether to set the browser to default if you have not configured that elsewhere, such as in an application configuration file. When complete, close the application and then click Next.

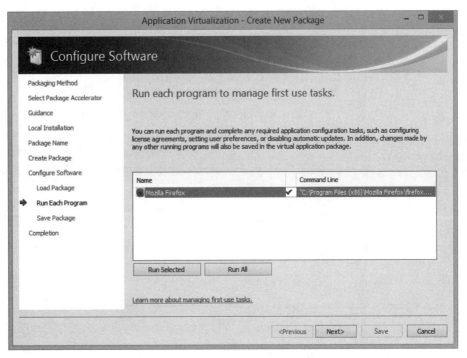

Figure 7-43 Creating a package from an accelerator, Run Each Program page

10. On the Completion page, shown in Figure 7-44, view the report and then click Close to complete the package creation process.

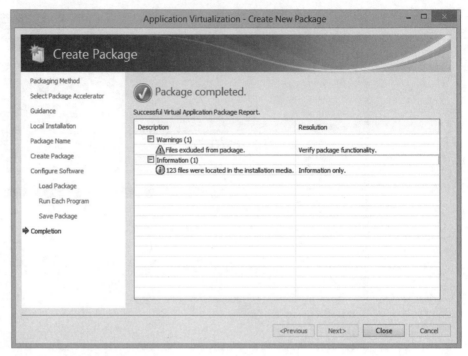

Figure 7-44 Creating a package from an accelerator, Completion page

Inside OUT

Signing .cab files

Often, IT administrators are unfamiliar with signing .cab files. Signing files usually is relegated to IT developers who often sign code or scripts. With the rise in popularity of Windows PowerShell, some IT administrators are getting a bit more exposure. From an App-V perspective, you should understand how to sign .cab files for a couple of reasons:

- **Increasing the security of your environment**   Package accelerators contain installation files, and malicious code can be embedded, especially when accelerators aren't signed.

- **Participating in public forums**   It's common to download and upload package accelerators from public community sites such as TechNet. When downloading an accelerator file, most administrators prefer to have it signed so that they have more trust in it. Similarly, if you plan to share an accelerator with the public, you should sign your accelerator file first.

There are a few ways to sign .cab files, and the methods also are applicable to signing other files and code. The following method uses tools provided by Microsoft. There are a couple of prerequisites that you need to meet:

- **SSL certificate** You need to have a certificate to sign a .cab file. Specifically, you need to have a certificate for code signing. Certificates have intended purposes, which define how they can be used. For example, you can have a certificate for server authentication that can't be used for code signing. If you intend to sign .cab files for internal company use only, you can use an internal public key infrastructure (PKI) to obtain a user-based secure sockets layer (SSL) certificate with code signing defined as the intended use. If you intend to sign .cab files for public use outside your company, however, you should use a third-party certificate that is trusted. In a nonproduction environment, you also can use a self-signed certificate.

- **Signing tool** Whether you use an internal certificate or a third-party certificate, you need a tool that will sign the .cab file. Microsoft offers a signing tool, signtool.exe. It is available in several developer-related Microsoft software development kits (SDKs), including the Microsoft Windows SDK for Windows 7 and .NET Framework 4, which you can download from *http://www.microsoft.com/en-us/download/details.aspx?id=8279*.

After you have your SSL certificate and signing tool, you can perform the following high-level steps to sign .cab files:

1. Export your certificate to a Personal Information Exchange (.PFX) file.

2. Copy the .cab file and the .pfx file to the location of signtool.exe. By default, when using the Windows SDK for Windows 7, the location of signtool.exe is C:\Program Files\Microsoft SDKs\Windows\V7.1\Bin.

3. Open an elevated command prompt and navigate to the location of all three files.

4. Run the SignTool sign /f tt-cert.pfx /p Pa$$w0rd "Firefox 33.1.1.cab" command. It will run the signing tool that uses a certificate file named tt-cert.pfx that has a password of Pa$$w0rd. It will sign a .cab file named Firefox 33.1.1cab. A message indicating success will be displayed when the signing is finished.

You also can use Windows PowerShell to create a package from a package accelerator. The following command creates a package from a package accelerator:

```
New-AppvSequencerPackage –Name "Microsoft Excel Viewer" –Path "C:\Packages"
–AcceleratorFilePath "C:\SourceFiles\Microsoft_ExcelViewer.cab" –InstalledFilesPath
"C:\Program Files\Microsoft Excel Viewer"
```

Options for updating packages

As part of your application maintenance, you sometimes will need to upgrade applications to newer versions. When you modify an existing package in the Sequencer, there is support for three different update scenarios:

- Updating an application in an existing package

- Editing an existing package

- Adding a new application

In the next few sections, we discuss each of these scenarios in detail.

Update an application in an existing package

You can apply updates to an existing package and redistribute it seamlessly to clients. This method doesn't require a server restart or a client disconnection from the server. Users continue to use the currently streamed application until they disconnect. The updated version streams automatically when they reconnect. You can take advantage of this functionality during the sequencing process by tagging changed blocks of code with a new version number. When the client starts the application, App-V compares the version information within the .appv file to the version on the package repository server and then downloads only the required blocks of code to the client.

The following steps provide an overview of the application update process for an existing package:

1. Copy the package folder of the application that you are updating from the package content location to the Sequencer.

2. Double-click the package's App-V file to open the Sequencer and select a modification task (Update Application In Existing Package, Edit Package, or Add New Application) for the package. Click Next.

3. Verify the path to the .appv file that you want to update. Click Next.

4. On the Prepare Computer page, address any issues that are listed, if applicable, and then click Next.

5. On the Select Installer page, browse to the installer that will update the application. Click Next.

6. On the Installation page, the installer will run. Proceed with the installation. The Sequencer will monitor for updates. When the installation completes, select the I Am Finished Installing check box and then click Next.

7. On the Installation Report page, review the information provided, if any, and then click Next.

8. On the Streaming page, run the applications in the package to optimize them and then click Next.

9. On the Create Package page, you can modify shortcuts further, add or remove registry settings, or reconfigure FTAs by selecting the Continue To Modify Package Without Saving Using The Package Editor option. This opens the package editor, which allows further virtual package customization. In this case, maintain the default setting, which saves the package now, specify a location to save the package, and then click Create.

10. On the Completion page, click Close to complete the process.

Edit a package

Editing a package enables you to make changes to an application package without sequencing the entire application again. By editing a package, you can make changes including the following:

- Viewing associated package files

- Editing registry settings

- Reviewing additional package settings (except operating system file properties)

- Setting virtualized registry key state (override or merge)

- Setting virtualized folder state

- Adding or editing shortcuts and FTAs

Earlier in this chapter, in the section titled "Package editor," we displayed all of the editing tabs and described the functionality available.

Add a new application

The process of adding a new application to an existing virtual application package is similar to the application update procedure. The wizard for modifying existing App-V packages requires extracting existing virtual application packages into the Sequencer for updating. Then, it installs any additional applications that will be saved in the updated package version. Because of these similarities, we won't walk through a step-by-step scenario for adding a new application in this book.

Sequencing for connection groups

Connection groups enable applications to communicate with one another while they run in a virtual environment. Connection groups in App-V enable virtual applications to interact with other applications, middleware, or plug-ins that have been virtualized in separate virtual application packages. All of the packages share the virtual environment where the virtual file system and tokenized paths merge and the registries converge. This gives you the flexibility to maintain packages independently and removes the redundancy of adding an application several times to a computer.

The most common scenario for using connection groups is when you use applications that depend on plug-ins, such as ActiveX controls, or applications that depend on middleware, such as Object Linking and Embedding Database (OLE DB) providers or Java runtime environments. For example, you may want to run Outlook 2013 and a third-party antispam add-on. These applications need to communicate with one another, and a connection group facilitates that.

Although connection groups in App-V provide extended functionality beyond traditional virtualization, they can introduce some issues when certain applications are grouped in a connection group:

- **Conflicting files or registry values**   Packages that combine in a connection group might use the same file path, which normally points to different content, or they might have registry keys and values with the same name but different content. In case of conflicts, you should identify which application should prevail by configuring the package order in a connection group. For more detail, see the App-V Team Blog post at *http://aka.ms/VirtApps/sequencing*.

- **Failure to load add-ins because of root folder dependency**   Sequencing two virtual packages that use the same root folder might prevent you from locating appropriate files when you combine packages in a connection group because root folders are not merged. One solution is to specify different primary virtual application paths during application sequencing. By doing this, you combine all the files from the package in the virtual file system, and nothing ends up in the root folder.

- **Dependency on .ini file**   Some applications require a full path for middleware or an add-in to be specified in .ini files, which might make an App-V client unable to decouple these paths or configurations from the .ini files. This might result in an application that doesn't function properly when it is used in a connection group. One solution would be to sequence all applications in a single package, but then you will lose connection group functionality. Other ways to make this application operational are to ensure that both the Sequencer and the client computers have the same configuration with matching drive letters or to use a publishing script to set the .ini file contents based on the client system.

The Sequencer provides different wizard-based workflows for creating packages that are intended for use in connection groups. Some common scenarios include add-ons or plug-ins that extend the functionality of an application. For example, you could create an add-on for a sequenced web browser or a graphic design program. When you install an add-on or plug-in, you first install the application and then add the add-on or plug-in. Another common case is a middleware application type, which enables you to sequence middleware or framework software that another sequenced application package requires. For example, a particular environment might be required to run a sequenced application. You can sequence it as middleware.

The following high-level steps represent the process to sequence plug-ins and middleware:

1. Sequence the primary application as a standard application type and then copy the package files to a network storage location.

2. Revert the sequencing VM to the base snapshot and then copy the primary application package to the sequencing VM.

3. Sequence the plug-in.

4. Create a connection group on the App-V management server to link the two packages.

Dynamic configuration and targeted scripting

Dynamic configuration enables you to manage and control the way virtual applications integrate into the base operating system and how the virtual packages behave on clients.

When the Sequencer creates a virtual package, the AppxManifest.xml file and Content_Types.xml file contain extension points and integration of the configuration with the underlying operating system. For many deployment scenarios, you might be required to adjust specific configurations or to enable or disable extension points for specific users or computers. Dynamic configuration enables administrators to make these modifications without making any changes to the App-V package itself.

A common example of post-sequence modification is some applications that require access to a specific mapped drive that the user who is opening the application uses. Another example is disabling the mailto extension to prevent virtualized applications from overwriting the extension from other applications.

CHAPTER 7

Dynamic configuration uses two .xml files that are created during sequencing:

- **The dynamic deployment configuration file, <PACKAGE_NAME> _DeploymentConfig.xml**   You can import this file into the App-V management portal to update a package's configuration by editing the default configuration for a package.

- **The dynamic user configuration file, <PACKAGE_NAME>_UserConfig.xml**   You can import this file into the App-V management portal to update a package's configuration by editing the default configuration for a package.

You can use these configuration files to do the following:

- Assign scripts to run during specific package and application events

- Enable or disable a virtual subsystem, such as environment variables, registry modification, services, or fonts

- Enable or disable extensions, such as FTAs, URL protocols, or AppPaths

- Override shortcut configurations

Settings that are configured in a dynamic deployment configuration file affect all users who work on the same App-V client computer. A dynamic user configuration contains settings that apply configurations for a package to individual users who are members of specified Active Directory Domain Services (AD DS) groups and can override dynamic deployment configuration settings. For example, you can provide a shortcut configuration in the user deployment configuration file that will override the shortcut configuration in the deployment configuration file.

Both configuration files start with a header that is followed by a PackageID that also exists in the manifest file. The rest of the file is the body, which includes all application extension points for application configuration.

Deployment configuration files provide configuration settings in two sections, one relative to the computer context and one relative to the user context. The settings that are configured in the user configuration file can override these because both of the configuration files provide the same capabilities.

Machine configuration control settings typically are written to the HKEY_LOCAL_MACHINE registry keys in the virtual registry. Machine configuration control settings contain the following four subsections:

- **Subsystems**   These are arranged as nodes under <Subsystems>, and they contain settings that configure extensions, application capabilities, machine-wide virtual registry, and machine-wide virtual kernel objects.

- **ProductSourceURLOptOut**   This subsection indicates whether the URL for a package can be modified globally through PackageSourceRoot to support branch office scenarios. The default is false, and the settings change takes effect on the next start.

- **MachineScripts**   This package can be configured to execute scripts at deployment time, publishing, or removal.

- **TerminateChildProcess**   This application executable can specify which child processes will terminate when an application .exe process terminates.

User configuration control settings in the dynamic configuration file affect per-user locations for all users who receive a package. User configuration control settings contain the following four subsections:

- **Applications**   This setting allows you to enable or disable extension points for a particular application that is part of a virtual package.

- **Subsystems**   This setting controls the behavior of shortcuts, FTAs, URL protocols, AppPath, software clients such as an email client, news readers, media players, and COM.

- **UserScripts**   This setting includes scripts to set up or alter the virtual environment before an application runs, in addition to running scripts at deployment or removal time.

- **ManagingAuthority**   This setting can be used when two versions of a package exist on the same computer, one deployed on App-V 4.6 and the other deployed on App-V 5.0.

App-V allows scripting in these dynamic configuration files to set up or alter a virtual environment before an application executes, in addition to running scripts at deployment or removal time. Scripting also can be used to clean up an environment after an application terminates. You can make these custom modifications by using any text editor or XML editor.

_DeploymentConfig.xml has triggers for user context in addition to computer context. When the desired script needs to be called or the context under which the script must run will determine the dynamic configuration file, _DeploymentConfiguration.xml or _UserConfiguration. xml, where the script is implemented.

Script execution time can be during one of the App-V package life cycle phases, including the following:

- AddPackage

- PublishPackage

- UnpublishPackage

- RemovePackage

- StartProcess

- ExitProcess

- StartVirtualEnvironment

- TerminateVirtualEnvironment

Before implementing dynamic configuration scripting, script processing must be enabled on App-V clients. This can be done during App-V client software installation by using the following Windows PowerShell command on each client:

```
Set-AppvClientConfiguration -EnablePackageScripts 1
```

In most environments, you should use Group Policy to configure scripting. There is an App-V GPO setting named Enable Package Script that you can enable to automate the configuration across the clients.

TROUBLESHOOTING

Group Policy for App-V

Administrators sometimes find themselves managing an environment that they did not design and implement. These environments often are referred to as inherited environments. Troubleshooting can be tough in inherited environments because you might not have any documentation, and you might not be familiar with the configuration. To ease the burden of troubleshooting Group Policy–related issues in an App-V environment, you should familiarize yourself with the following tips:

- **All settings are computer settings**   You can find all of the App-V–related settings in the computer configuration of a GPO. Because the settings are all computer settings, you need to ensure that the GPO's security filtering includes the App-V client computer objects. Note that the Authenticated Users group contains all of the domain computer objects.

- **Links must include the OUs that contain the App-V client computers**   You need to ensure that your App-V GPOs are linked to OUs that contain the App-V client computers, not the users.

- **Ensure that the computer settings are enabled**   Because all of the App-V settings are in the computer configuration of a GPO, you need to ensure that the computer configuration settings are enabled for the GPO. You can do this by right-clicking the GPO, clicking the GPO Status menu, and then viewing the status.

- **The GPO policy settings must be enabled**   You need to enable and configure some App-V policy settings and then test the functionality after the GPO is applied or refreshed. By default, computers update Group Policy every 90 minutes plus a random number of minutes from 0 to 30. Thus, expect an update every 90 to 120 minutes. You can restart a computer to speed up the process because Group Policy updates occur during each startup.

CHAPTER 7

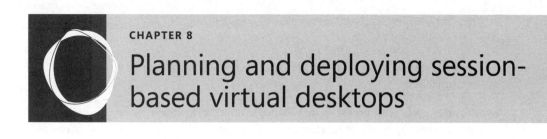

Planning and deploying session-based virtual desktops

Session-based virtual desktops are widely used by organizations to provide remote access to data and applications in a centralized and controlled environment. In Windows Server 2012 R2, Remote Desktop Services (RDS) provides the infrastructure to implement session-based virtual desktops and virtual machine (VM)–based virtual desktops.

In older versions of Windows Server, session-based desktops were provided by a feature named Terminal Services. Terminal Services had the same basic functionality for session-based desktops as RDS, but RDS has been extended with additional functionality to improve the user experience and manageability.

Understanding RDS

RDS is a Windows Server role that provides much more than just remote desktops. RDS includes six role services that enable you to create a scalable and fault-tolerant RDS deployment. You can manage an RDS deployment centrally and in the same way, regardless of the number of servers in an RDS deployment. This makes RDS very scalable.

One of the most common uses for RDS is the deployment of session-based virtual desktops. In a session-based virtual desktop, all processing is performed on a Remote Desktop Session Host (RD Session Host) server, and the results are displayed on a Remote Desktop client. The communication between the client and the RD Session Host server uses Remote Desktop Protocol (RDP).

RDP is a very efficient protocol and sends a limited amount of data over the network. This makes it possible to use RDS to provide desktops and applications for users over a LAN, from branch locations over a WAN, or over the Internet.

RDS includes the following functionality:

- **Provides users with a full desktop** Whether you use session-based virtual desktops or VM-based virtual desktops, you can provide users with access to a full remote desktop that you can access from almost anywhere if you configure the necessary infrastructure.

- **Provides users with access to applications**   You can use RemoteApp to provide users with access to applications running on an RD Session Host server. These applications run in a window just as regular applications do on users' desktops. From the user's perspective, applications delivered by RemoteApp function as if they are installed locally.

- **Allows secure remote access without using a virtual private network**   The Remote Desktop Gateway (RD Gateway) role service is used as a proxy for accessing session-based virtual desktops or VM-based virtual desktops. This is suitable for securing access from the Internet.

The Terminal Services functionality found in older versions of Windows Server had only session-based virtual desktops and applications. In Windows Server 2012 R2, you also can use RDS to deploy VM-based virtual desktops. Connectivity to the VMs is done by using RDP, just as in a session-based deployment.

Some benefits of using RDS for virtual desktops and applications include the following:

- **Easier application deployment and updates**   A typical application deployment requires you to install and update the application on each client computer. In all but the smallest environments, this requires you to implement some type of automated deployment tools for applications. With RDS, you only need to install and update applications on the central servers. This is significantly less work than installing and updating applications on individual client computers.

- **Simplified access to data and applications**   When you implement RDS, applications and their data can be accessed from anywhere. You can allow users to use applications from a computer in the office, a home computer, and mobile devices.

- **Faster access to remote data**   Access to data over a virtual private network (VPN) or WAN links often results in poor application performance. For example, an application that requires access to a SQL server may be very slow if the connectivity to the SQL server has high latency. When you use RDS, you place the central servers with the application installed close to the application data, and network latency is removed as a performance problem.

- **Higher data security for mobile users**   Without RDS, mobile users copy data onto a mobile computer and take it with them. Or, in some cases, they use a VPN to access data remotely while offsite. In both cases, there is a risk that the mobile computer could be lost or stolen and the data accessed by unauthorized users. When you use RDS for remote access to data, there is no need to copy data to the remote device. This mitigates the risk that your organization will lose control of the data.

- **Simplified client hardware management** Using RDS to provide virtual desktops reduces the effort to manage client device computers because the devices are performing much less work. Computers used to access virtual desktops become essentially disposable because the only configuration information they contain is the connection information to the remote desktop. In some cases, you may be able to extend hardware life because the client device is performing very little work.

Comparing RDS and the Remote Desktop feature

Remote Desktop is a feature in Windows 8.1 and Windows Server 2012 R2 that enables you to connect to a computer remotely and to view its desktop, just as when you sign in to that computer locally. The primary intention of the Remote Desktop feature is remote administration. That is why, when you enable the feature, by default only the administrator who enables it can connect to the remote desktop. Other users can connect to the remote desktop only if you grant them permission.

RDS is a Windows Server role that is available only in the Windows Server operating system. To deploy RDS, you need to install at least three role services and perform an additional configuration. RDS provides a similar experience to the Remote Desktop feature, but the primary intention of RDS is to enable users to have a standard remote environment that is available from any device and to use remote resources while integrating remote applications on the local user desktop. Table 8-1 compares RDS and the Remote Desktop feature.

Table 8-1 Comparing RDS and the Remote Desktop feature

RDS	Remote Desktop Feature
Can support many simultaneous users.	Desktop operating systems are limited to one simultaneous user. Server operating systems are limited to two simultaneous users.
Proper licensing must be purchased and configured.	No additional licensing is required.
Used to access a full remote desktop or remote applications (RemoteApp).	Used to access the full remote desktop.
Supports advanced features such as RemoteFX USB Redirection and multimedia redirection.	Does not support advanced features.
Requires an infrastructure of multiple servers that has been properly planned and deployed.	Is enabled on a single computer.

CHAPTER 8

RDS architecture

There are six RDS service roles that can be included in an RDS deployment. At minimum, you need to have the Remote Desktop Connection Broker (RD Connection Broker) role service, the Remote Desktop Web Access (RD Web Access) role service, and either the RD Session Host or Remote Desktop Virtualization Host (RD Virtualization Host) role service. You can install individual RDS role services, but you won't be able to manage them unless they are part of an RDS deployment. Depending on your implementation goals, an RDS deployment can include additional RDS role services, and RDS role services can be installed on multiple servers for scalability and high availability.

Windows Server 2012 R2 RDS includes the following role services:

- **RD Session Host**   This role service configures a server to provide session-based desktops and applications. Users can connect to an RD Session Host server and then run applications and use the network resources that the RD Session Host offers. RD Session Host is a required role service in a session-based desktop deployment of RDS.

- **RD Virtualization Host**   This role service integrates with the Hyper-V role in Windows Server 2012 R2 to provide VMs that can be used as virtual desktops. The RD Virtualization Host role service also monitors and reports on established client sessions to the RD Connection Broker role service. This role service is responsible for managing the VMs that function as pooled and personal virtual desktops. If VMs are in a saved state, the RD Virtualization Host role service starts the VMs to prepare them for a user connection. For pooled virtual desktops, the RD Virtualization Host role service reverts the VMs to their initial state when users sign out. The RD Virtualization Host role service is required in a VM-based deployment of RDS.

- **RD Connection Broker**   This role service manages connections to RemoteApp programs and virtual desktops, and it directs client connection requests to an appropriate endpoint. The RD Connection Broker role service also provides session reconnection and session load balancing. For example, when a user disconnects from a session and later establishes a connection, the RD Connection Broker role service ensures that the user reconnects to his or her existing session. This role service is mandatory in all RDS deployments, but it does not require large amounts of server resources.

- **RD Web Access**   This role service provides a web-based interface to RemoteApp programs, session-based virtual desktops, or VM-based virtual desktops. A webpage provides each user with a customized view of all RDS resources that have been published to that user. This role service supports organizing resources in folders, which enables administrators to group remote applications in a logical manner. It also publishes available RDS resources in an RDWeb feed, which can integrate with the Start screen on client devices. RD Web Access is a mandatory role service for each RDS deployment.

- **Remote Desktop Licensing (RD Licensing)**   This role service manages RDS client access licenses (RDS CALs) that are required for each device or user to connect to an RD Session Host server. You use RD Licensing to install, issue, and track RDS CAL availability on an RD Licensing server. You are not required to install this role service during an initial RDS deployment, but an RDS deployment without proper licensing ceases to function after 120 days.

- **RD Gateway**   This role service allows authorized remote users to connect securely to RemoteApp programs and virtual desktops from outside the organization over the Internet. An RD Gateway server acts as a proxy for external users to connect to internal RDS resources. To increase compatibility with firewalls in public locations such as hotels, RDP traffic is encapsulated in Hypertext Transfer Protocol Secure (HTTPS) packets. Access is controlled by configuring Remote Desktop connection authorization policies (RD CAPs) and Remote Desktop resource authorization policies (RD RAPs). An RD CAP specifies who is authorized to make a connection, and an RD RAP specifies to which resources authorized users may connect.

All deployment and management of RDS is done by using Server Manager, as shown in Figure 8-1. Server Manager provides an overview of all servers in an RDS deployment and a management interface for each server. RDS in Server Manager uses a discovery process to detect the role services that are installed on each machine that is added to Server Manager.

CHAPTER 8

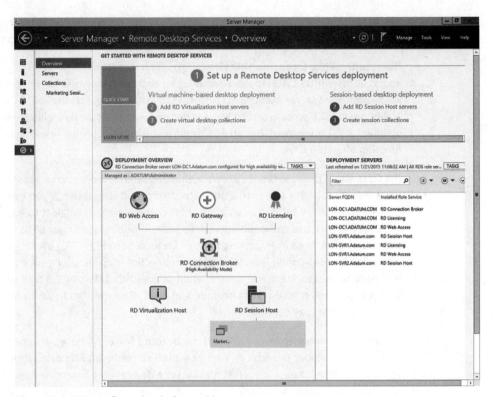

Figure 8-1 RDS configuration in Server Manager

NOTE

Legacy Remote Desktop administration tools such as
Remote Desktop Services Manager and RD Session Host Configuration,
which were used for configuring and administering RDS in Windows Server 2008 R2,
are replaced with RDS in Server Manager in Windows Server 2012 and
Windows Server 2012 R2.

Connecting to virtual desktops and RemoteApp programs

Windows client operating systems include Remote Desktop Connection (RDC), which is used to connect to virtual desktops and applications. Microsoft also provides Microsoft Remote Desktop for iOS and Android devices. All of these applications use RDP to connect to virtual desktops and RemoteApp programs.

When you use RDC to access a computer with the Remote Desktop feature enabled, you enter the IP address or DNS name of the remote computer, as shown in Figure 8-2. This type of direct connectivity doesn't work when connecting to RDS because you are connecting through the RD Connection Broker and need to be directed to a specific collection for the RemoteApp program or virtual desktop.

Figure 8-2 Remote Desktop Connection (RDC)

After you implement servers for the RDS infrastructure, you need to create collections that define what the clients are connecting to and how it is configured. There are two types of collections:

- **Virtual desktop collections**   This type of collection contains VMs hosted on RD Virtualization Host servers.

- **Session collections**   This type of collection contains RD Session Host servers that provide session-based virtual desktops or RemoteApp programs.

To connect to collections in RDS, you need to have an .rdp file with the correct connectivity information for the RD Connection Broker and the collection to which you are connecting. RDC uses the connectivity information in the .rdp file.

You can create an .rdp file manually and make it available to users. When the user opens the .rdp file, RDC launches and connects to the RD Connection Broker. This method is functional but relatively complex because you need to learn the syntax for creating .rdp files and need to update them if your infrastructure changes.

The simplest way to provide user connectivity to RDS is by using RD Web Access, shown in Figure 8-3. When users connect to RD Web Access, they are provided with a list of collections to which they have access. When they click the appropriate collection, an .rdp file with the correct configuration information is generated, and RDC launches using the information in the .rdp file. This provides a consistent access method even if the RDS deployment is modified.

CHAPTER 8

CHAPTER 8

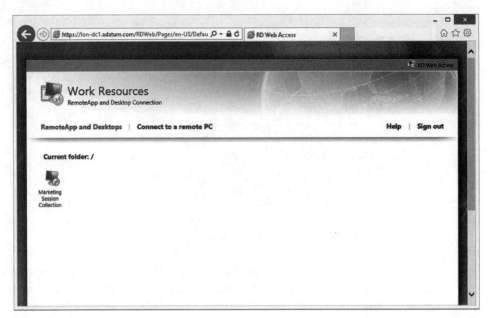

Figure 8-3 RD Web Access

The following process, shown in Figure 8-4, is used when clients connect to a session collection by using RD Web Access:

1. Users connect to the RD Web Access portal and identify the RDS resource to which they want to connect.

2. Users click the link on the RD Web Access portal for the RDS resource they want to access. This downloads the .rdp file, which contains information about the resource to which the user wants to connect.

3. RDC is launched, and it uses the information in the .rdp file to initiate a connection with the RD Connection Broker role service. After users authenticate to the RD Connection Broker role service, the RDC passes the request about the RDS resource to which the user wants to connect.

4. The RD Connection Broker role service examines the request to find an available RD Session Host server in the desired collection and sends the connection information back to the RDC client. If the request matches a session that already is established for the associated user, RD Connection Broker redirects the client to the server in the collection where the session was established. If the user doesn't have an existing session in the collection, the client redirects to the server that is most appropriate for the user

connection, based on the RD Connection Broker load balancing algorithm—for example, weight factor, fewest connections, and least utilized.

5. The RDC client establishes a session with the RD Session Host server that RD Connection Broker provided.

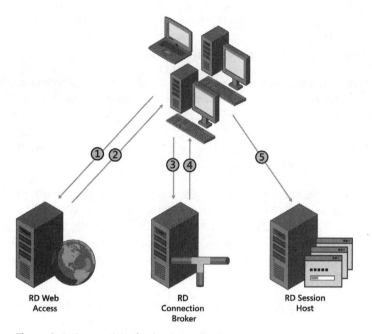

Figure 8-4 Connectivity for session collections

RDS functionality that enhances the client experience

RDC uses the RDP protocol to connect to RDS servers. The following are some of the specific features available that enhance the client experience:

- **Bandwidth reduction features**   When an RDP connection is established, various methods to reduce network bandwidth are used, such as data compression and caching. Caching enables an adaptive user experience over LANs and WANs. Clients can detect available bandwidth and adjust the level of graphic detail that is used.

- **Full desktop or application window only**   When a client connects to RDS, it can display either a full remote desktop or only the window of a remotely running application (RemoteApp program). With full desktops, users can perform remote administration or run multiple applications. However, the user must deal with two desktops: local and remote. RemoteApp programs integrate with local desktops, but they still require network connectivity to RDS.

- **RemoteApp programs that look and feel like locally installed applications**   The window displayed when you connect to a RemoteApp program looks like a locally installed application. Links to RemoteApp programs can be added to a client's Start screen. RemoteApp program icons support pinning, tabbed windows, live thumbnails, and overlay icons. RemoteApp windows can be transparent, and the content of a RemoteApp window displays while you are moving it.

- **Reconnection to existing sessions**   If a user disconnects from a remote desktop session, the user can reconnect to the session and continue to work from the point at which he or she disconnected. The user can connect from the same device or from a different client device. If a session disconnects for a different reason, for example, because network connectivity is lost, the user automatically reconnects to the disconnected session when network connectivity is restored.

- **Redirection of local resources**   Client resources such as drives, printers, the Clipboard, smart card readers, and USB devices can redirect to a remote desktop session. This enables you to use locally attached devices while working on RDS and to use the Clipboard to copy content between a local and remote desktop. You even can redirect USB devices that you plug in when the remote desktop connection already is established.

- **Windows media redirection**   This feature provides high-quality multimedia by redirecting Windows media files and streams from RDS to a client. When Windows Media Player is used in a session-based virtual desktop, the multimedia file is not rendered on the RD Session Host. Instead, the multimedia stream is redirected to the RDC client and is rendered on the client. This reduces load on the RD Session Host and provides higher quality audio and video playback on the client. If the RDC client does not have the necessary codec for the multimedia content, then the content is rendered on the RD Session Host.

- **Multi-monitor support**   This feature enables support for up to 16 monitors of any size, resolution, and layout. Applications function just as they do when you run them locally in multi-monitor configurations.

NOTE

Multi-monitor support requires RDC version 7.0 or later. This software is included with Windows 7 and later. If you are connecting to a computer running Windows 7, multi-monitor support is available only for the Ultimate and Enterprise editions. If you are connecting to a computer running Windows 8 or Windows 8.1, multi-monitor support is available only for the Professional and Enterprise editions.

- **Single sign-on (SSO)**   When users connect to RDS, they have to provide their credentials again. With SSO, a user can connect to a remote desktop or start a RemoteApp program as the user who signed in to the local computer, without reentering credentials.

- **CPU, disk, and network Fair Share**   Fair Share features are enabled by default on RD Session Host servers to ensure even resource distribution among users. One user can't monopolize resources or negatively affect the performance of other users' sessions. Fair Share can distribute network, disk, and CPU resources dynamically among user sessions on the same RD Session Host server. You can control Fair Share settings through Group Policy.

RemoteFX

RemoteFX introduces a set of enhancements to RDP that enables rich graphics and video capabilities within a remote desktop session, regardless of whether you are connecting to a session-based virtual desktop, running a RemoteApp program, or connecting to a VM-based virtual desktop. In all three cases, the user experience is almost identical to using a local physical desktop. RemoteFX is included in RDS, and you don't need to enable it explicitly unless you want to use the RemoteFX virtual graphics processing unit (vGPU) on a VM-based virtual desktop. In that case, you must add hardware to the VMs that are used for the virtual desktop.

The following is a list of some RemoteFX features:

- **RemoteFX for WAN**   This feature delivers an improved user experience over lower-speed networks, such as at a branch office, on a wireless device, or working from home over a WAN connection. RemoteFX for WAN combines the RemoteFX Adaptive Graphics feature with intelligent WAN-aware transports. TCP and UDP can be used for remote desktop connections. The protocol that is better suited for the current connection is selected automatically, and automatic detection of network conditions to adjust the encoding of content is available.

- **RemoteFX Adaptive Graphics**   This feature dynamically adapts to changing network conditions and optimizes encodings based on the content delivered. RemoteFX Adaptive Graphics use multiple codecs, which are optimized for different types of content, such as text, images, and video.

- **RemoteFX Media Streaming**   This feature provides redirection of multimedia content. When a user attempts to play multimedia content in a remote session, the content is intercepted and redirected to the client. The client receives the compressed content, decodes the content, and plays it back locally.

- **RemoteFX Multi-Touch**   This feature extends the Windows 8.1 touch experience to devices on which multi-touch is the primary means of user interaction. Windows 8.1 users are able to interact with remote desktop sessions in the same way as a local desktop, including support for multi-touch gestures and the ability to navigate between local and remote sessions by using touch.

- **RemoteFX USB Redirection** This feature enables devices to redirect at the USB level. Because of this, no device drivers are required on the client computer, and any USB device—including audio, storage, all-in-one printers, and scanners—can be redirected.

Inside OUT

vGPU for VM-Based Virtual Desktops

An RD Virtualization Host server can suffer from high processor utilization due to graphics processing in the VMs it's hosting. This occurs because the processors in the RD Virtualization Host server do the graphics processing for each VM. This can limit the scalability of the RD Virtualization Host server.

One solution for reducing processor load on the RD Virtualization Host server is to use the vGPU functionality that is available in Windows Server 2012 R2. When you use the vGPU functionality, the VMs can use a dedicated graphics processor in the RD Virtualization Host server for graphics processing. From a performance perspective, this is like putting a more advanced video card in a desktop computer.

To use vGPU on an RD Virtualization Host server, you must meet the following requirements:

- **Second Level Address Translation (SLAT) support** The processor in the RD Virtualization Host server must include support for SLAT. For Intel processors, this is called Extended Page Tables. For AMD processors, this is called Nested Page Tables.

- **Supported video adapter** The video adapter in the RD Virtualization Host server must be DirectX 11-capable with a Windows Display Driver Model (WDDM) 1.2–compatible driver. WDDM 1.2 was introduced with Windows 8.

- **Windows 7 Enterprise with SP1 or Windows 8 Enterprise** Only the Enterprise editions of Windows 7, Windows 8, and Windows 8.1 support the use of vGPU in the VM.

- **Generation 1 VMs** The vGPU functionality isn't supported for generation 2 VMs in Hyper-V. You must configure VMs as generation 1 VMs.

If you meet the requirements for using vGPU, then you can add a RemoteFX 3D Video Adapter to VMs. In the configuration for the RemoteFX 3D Video Adapter, you can configure a maximum number of monitors and maximum monitor resolution.

Remote Desktop Connection configuration options

When you connect to a virtual desktop through RDS, RDC is configured automatically by using an RDP file that is provided by the RD Web Access server. When you use RDC to connect to a server or client with the Remote Desktop feature enabled, you can configure the connectivity settings manually. The configuration options are grouped on several different tabs. Microsoft Remote Desktop for iOS and Android have similar configuration options but different user interfaces.

On the General tab, you can specify the computer to which you want to connect by using RDC and user credentials. You also can save RDC settings in a text file with an .rdp file name extension to initiate a connection later without configuring RDC settings again.

The Display tab is shown in Figure 8-5. On this tab, you can choose the size of the remote desktop window, including the option to run the remote desktop in full-screen mode. You can select to use all local monitors for a remote session, select color depth, and enable a connection bar when the remote desktop is running in full-screen mode.

Figure 8-5 Remote Desktop Connection, Display tab

The Local Resources tab is shown in Figure 8-6. On this tab, you can set remote audio settings, such as whether you want to enable remote audio playback and recording. You also can specify a location where Windows key combinations, such as Alt+Tab, are applied and whether local devices and resources in remote sessions are available. For example, you can enable the option to make the Clipboard, local drive, printers, and devices that you plug in later available in a remote session.

Figure 8-6 Remote Desktop Connection, Local Resources tab

On the Programs tab, you can specify a program that starts automatically in a remote desktop session when you connect to a remote computer. If you configure this option, when you close the program, your session is signed out automatically.

On the Experience tab, you can select a connection speed to optimize performance. You can enable different features, such as the following:

- Desktop background

- Font smoothing or visual styles in RDC

- Show window contents while dragging

By default, RDC automatically detects connection quality and configures connection quality–dependent features accordingly. On this tab, you also can configure persistent bitmap caching and automatic reconnection if a connection drops.

RDC displays the bandwidth with an icon on the connection bar (top of the window) that is similar to a signal strength meter. The meter is based only on bandwidth and does not take latency into account. The number of bars in the icon identify the bandwidth, as show in Table 8-2.

Table 8-2 RDC bandwidth values

Icon	Bandwidth
4 bars	10 megabits per second (Mbps) and higher
3 bars	2000–9999 kilobits per second (Kbps)
2 bars	512 Kbps - 19999 Kbps
1 bar	Less than 512 Kbps
No icon shown	No bandwidth detected or older remote desktop host

On the Advanced tab, you can configure server authentication and Connect From Anywhere settings. The server authentication options allow you to define what should be done if the certificate provided by the server during authentication isn't valid. By default, a warning is displayed and you have the option to continue. If desired, you can configure this setting to connect without warning or prevent connections.

The Connect From Anywhere settings allow you to configure connectivity through an RD Gateway server. You can configure the alternate credentials for authentication to the RD Gateway server and the location of the RD Gateway server.

RDS licensing

If you want to use RDS, you need to purchase additional RDS CALs for each user or device that uses RDS. This is in addition to the typical licensing that is required for desktop computers. For example, in an environment where users have desktop computers and some applications are delivered by RemoteApp, you would need the following licenses:

- Operating system license for the desktop computer

- Server licenses for the Windows-based servers that deliver the RemoteApp programs

- Windows CALs for each user or computer that accesses the Windows servers

- RDS CALs for each user or desktop that uses RemoteApp programs

- Application licenses for each user or desktop that uses RemoteApp programs

RDS CALs provide users with access to session-based virtual desktops or RemoteApp programs. Licensing for VM-based virtual desktops is slightly more complex because the operating system for the VM also needs to be licensed. If you connect to a VM-based virtual desktop from a device that is covered by a Microsoft Software Assurance agreement, then the license

CHAPTER 8

includes rights to use that same operating system in a VM-based virtual desktop. If the device isn't covered by a Microsoft Software Assurance agreement, then you need to purchase Windows Virtual Desktop Access (Windows VDA) licenses.

➤ For more information about licensing VM-based virtual desktops, see Chapter 10, "Planning and implementing pooled and personal virtual desktops."

When a client attempts to connect to an RDS deployment, the server that accepts the connection determines if an RDS CAL is needed. If an RDS CAL is required, then the server requests the RDS CAL on behalf of the client that is attempting the connection. If an appropriate RDS CAL is available, it is issued to the client, and then the client can connect to RDS.

RD Licensing manages the RDS CALs that are required for each device or user to connect to an RD Session Host server. You use RD Licensing to install, issue, and track the availability of RDS CALs on an RD Licensing server. At least one RD Licensing server must be deployed in the environment. The role service can be installed on any server, but for large deployments, the role service should not be installed on an RD Session Host server.

After an RDS installation, there is an initial grace period of 120 days. This grace period begins after the RD Session Host accepts the first client connection. If you have not installed valid licenses by the time the grace period expires, clients will not be able to sign in to the RD Session Host.

Inside Out

Licensing modes

Each RD Session Host server is configured with a licensing mode. The licensing mode determines the type of RDS CALs that an RD Session Host server requests from an RD Licensing server on behalf of a client that is connecting to an RD Session Host server. There are two licensing modes:

- **Per User**   This gives one user the right to access any RD Session Host server in an RDS deployment from an unlimited number of client computers or devices. You should use RDS Per User CALs when the same user connects to RDS from many devices.

- **Per Device**   This gives any user the right to connect to any RD Session Host server in an RDS deployment from a specific device. When a client connects to an RD Session Host server for the first time, a temporary license is issued. When the client computer or device connects to an RD Session Host server for the second time, if the license server is activated and enough RDS Per Device CALs are available, the license server issues the client computer or device a permanent RDS Per Device CAL. You should consider RDS Per Device CALs when multiple users use the same device for connecting to RDS, for example, a point-of-sale device that is used by different clerks.

A single RDS deployment can be configured with only one licensing mode. If you need a mix of Per User and Per Device RDS CALs, then you need to implement two RDS deployments.

> ## NOTE
> **A permanent RDS Per Device CAL is valid for a randomly selected number of days between 52 and 89. If the RDS Per Device CAL isn't renewed, then it is returned to the available licenses on the RD Licensing server. You can revoke RDS Per Device CALs before they expire and return them immediately to the available licenses. You are limited to revoking a maximum of 20 percent of the RDS Per Devices CALs.**

If you need to provide access to RDS for multiple external users who are not employees of your organization, then you should consider using an RDS External Connector License. An RDS External Connector License allows an unlimited number of nonemployees to connect to a specific RD Session Host. If you have multiple RD Session Host servers, you need multiple RDS External Connector Licenses in addition to any required Windows Server External Connector Licenses.

Planning infrastructure for session-based desktops

The planning for implementing RDS for session-based desktops can be fairly complex compared to other Windows-based role services. Most Windows-based role services require only one server. RDS requires at least three role services and, in most cases, the role services are spread across multiple servers. You should be aware of the functionality that each role service provides. You also should be aware of how an RDS deployment uses each role service. You need to know role service requirements and which hardware resources are most critical for each role service.

Assessing RDS infrastructure requirements

Before you implement RDS, you must determine your organization's requirements. To do so, you first must evaluate if RDS is the appropriate solution for your needs, and then you must choose between session-based and VM-based desktop deployments. If necessary, an RDS deployment can include both session-based and VM-based desktop deployments. You also must evaluate the existing server infrastructure and estimate the required server hardware, network bandwidth, client types and requirements, and connectivity needs for a successful RDS deployment.

Determine your RDS needs

To determine if RDS is an appropriate solution for your needs, you should assess and analyze the types of users, hardware, and applications in your organization. Areas of consideration include the following:

- **User types**   Do you have users in remote locations, single-task users, contractors, and other types of users who would benefit from remote applications or virtual desktops?

- **Hardware**   What client hardware currently is deployed in your organization? Would it be beneficial to move from traditional desktops to thin clients for some users? Do you allow users to bring their own devices into the organization's network? Do users wish to use mobile devices to run certain applications?

- **Application compatibility**   Can the applications run in a multiuser environment? If not, will the applications run in a virtual environment?

- **Application performance**   How do the applications perform in a remote or virtual environment? Keep in mind that many applications perform better as RemoteApp programs on RDS because processing takes place on a server.

- **Application support**   Do vendors support the applications in a virtual or multiuser environment? Do vendors provide support to multiple users?

- **Licensing**   Can the applications be licensed for a virtual or multiuser environment?

- **Business benefits**   Are there justifiable business reasons to implement this solution? Potential benefits include cost savings, reduced deployment time, centralized management, and reduced administration costs.

- **Legal requirements**   Because of financial and legal requirements, some organizations mandate that applications and data remain on-premises. RDS enables users to connect to a standard virtual desktop to use familiar applications and to work with data from almost any device, while organizational data stays in the data center.

Choosing between session-based and VM-based desktop deployments

RDS has two deployment types:

- **Session-based virtual desktop deployment**   This provides users the ability to connect to an RD Session Host and use a full desktop or run remote applications and present them on a client as if they were installed locally.

- **VM-based virtual desktop deployment**   This provides users with access to a full Windows client operating system that runs on a VM, for example, Windows 7 or Windows 8.1.

You need to decide which RDS deployment type is best for your environment based on various requirements. For example, you must consider if users must be completely isolated or if they must have administrative access. You should consider whether the applications work properly in a multiuser environment. In addition, you must consider whether you can install and run applications on Windows Server. Remember that a VM-based virtual desktop deployment typically requires a more powerful server infrastructure and more disk storage than a session-based virtual desktop deployment for the same number of users. For some applications, VM-based virtual desktops might be the only viable solution.

Generally, you should choose session-based virtual desktops if possible. Session-based virtual desktops support a larger number of users than VM-based virtual desktops on the same hardware.

Determine server hardware and network resource requirements

Once you determine the RDS deployment benefits for your organization, you must consider the hardware requirements to support your users, including the following:

- **Number of users**   How many users will use RDS, and where are they located?

- **User types**   How many users run CPU-intensive and bandwidth-intensive applications? Will you have to provide more bandwidth and server hardware to support expected usage?

- **Connection characteristics**   How many concurrent connections do you expect? Can your server and bandwidth resources handle peak usage times?

- **Application silos**   Will you have to create multiple server collections to support different applications that might not be able to run on the same server?

- **Load balancing**   Will you have to include multiple servers in a collection to spread the load among the servers? This increases available resources and provides redundancy.

- **High availability**   What is the organization's tolerance for downtime? Do you need close to zero downtime, or could your organization tolerate the time it would take to restore from backups?

- **Expansion considerations**   What are the growth expectations? At what point will new resources need to be brought online?

Determine user requirements

Another aspect to consider is user requirements. A large organization with multiple locations might have a number of mitigating factors to consider, such as the following:

- **Languages**   Organizations with a global presence need to support multiple languages. You might need to install language packs on all of your RDS servers.

CHAPTER 8

- **Profile management**   How will you store user states? Do users require the same user state when they sign in locally and to an RDS session? Which type of Windows user state virtualization will be used?

- **Printing**   Will existing printers function properly in a remote desktop environment? Will there be problems finding printer drivers to support existing printers? Is there a budget to replace older printer models?

Determine how clients access RDS

Clients can connect to RDS in various ways. You probably will need to provide different access methods for different groups of users. Areas to consider include the following:

- Will you allow users to connect over the Internet from remote locations? If so, you will need to set up an RD Gateway and obtain certificates.

- How will you handle Secure Sockets Layer (SSL) certificates—by using certificates from non-Microsoft certification authorities (CAs) or by using certificates that an internal CA issues?

Based on your assessment results, start designing your RDS deployment. You should identify RDS role services that are required and that you will deploy. You also should determine the number and hardware configuration of servers that are required, in addition to planning required storage, connectivity, and firewall configuration.

Planning for the RD Session Host role service

The RD Session Host role service provides Windows-based apps or full Windows desktops for RDS clients. This role service is mandatory for every RDS deployment that provides users with session-based desktops or RemoteApp programs. An RD Session Host server accepts incoming RDP requests, and after a client authenticates, it provides a desktop-based or application-based session to the client. An RD Session Host server is the central location where remote applications are installed, accessed, and maintained.

To plan the deployment of an RD Session Host server, you must consider the number of installed applications, the type of applications, resource use, the number of connected clients, and the type of user interaction. While connected to one RD Session Host, users might run a simple application that has low resource utilization and rarely runs, for example, an old data entry application. On another RD Session Host, users often might run a resource-intensive graphical application that requires many CPU resources, a considerable amount of RAM, intensive disk I/O operations, and that causes a lot of network traffic. If the hardware configuration on both of the RD Session Hosts is the same, the second server is considerably more utilized and can accept fewer user connections.

RD Session Host planning focuses on the number of concurrent users and the workload they generate. A server with a particular hardware configuration might support many simultaneous users or only a few, depending on their usage patterns and the applications that they are running on the RD Session Host.

The following are the main resources that you should consider when estimating RD Session Host utilization:

- **CPU**   Each remote application that users start runs on an RD Session Host and utilizes CPU resources on the RD Session Host. In an environment where many users are connected to the same host, CPU and memory typically are the most critical resources.

- **Memory**   Additional memory must be allocated to an RD Session Host for each user who connects to the RD Session Host, whether connecting to a full Windows desktop or running a RemoteApp program.

- **Disk**   Because user state typically isn't stored on an RD Session Host, disk storage usually isn't a critical resource. However, many applications run simultaneously on an RD Session Host, and the disk subsystem should be able to meet their disk I/O needs.

- **Network**   The network should provide enough bandwidth for connected users and for the applications that they run. For example, applications that use a SQL database use the network to connect to that SQL database. Also remember to consider the network bandwidth required to support the user connectivity to the RD Session Host server.

- **GPU**   Applications that are graphically intensive, especially those that include three-dimensional graphics, might require vGPU support and RemoteFX to perform well. Without such support, graphics render on the server's CPU and may limit the number of users on the RD Session Host to a relatively small number.

When estimating the required resources for an RD Session Host, you can use one of the following methods:

- **Pilot deployment**   This is a common and a simple approach. You first need to deploy RDS in a test environment and capture its initial performance. After that, you start increasing server load by increasing the number of users and monitoring response times and user feedback. You can find out how many users can connect to an RD Session Host and still have an acceptable user experience based on the number of users and the system response time. Based on the findings, you can estimate the number of servers that are needed for a production environment. This approach is reliable and simple, but it requires initial investments for the pilot deployment.

- **Load simulation**   This method also uses an initial RDS deployment in a test environment. You need to gather information about applications that users operate and how users interact with the applications. After that, you can use load simulator tools to generate various levels of typical user loads against an RDS deployment. When a load simulator tool runs, you need to monitor server utilization and responsiveness. This method is similar to the pilot deployment method, but it uses a load simulation tool instead of real users to generate user load. It also requires an initial investment, and its results depend on the initial estimation of actual user usage.

- **Projection based on single-user systems**   This method uses data that is collected from a single-user system for projecting expected utilization on an RD Session Host with multiple user sessions. This method requires detailed knowledge of applications that are used, and it usually is not very reliable because a single-user system has a different overhead than a multiuser system.

It is critical that you plan for future scalability of an RDS deployment. User needs for applications will change over time, and you need to be ready to expand your RDS deployment to meet those needs. In some cases, you may be able to scale up the capacity of the individual servers with additional processors or additional memory. Scaling up by using more powerful servers tends to be expensive. Scaling out by adding servers generally is less expensive.

Fortunately, you can scale out an RDS deployment for session-based virtual desktops and RemoteApp programs by adding RD Session Host servers. For example, if you have an RDS deployment for session-based virtual desktops that uses two RD Session Host servers, and those two servers are experiencing frequent peaks of 100 percent CPU utilization, you can add a third RD Session Host server. The RD Connection Broker then automatically load balances the connections across three servers instead of two and reduces the CPU utilization on the two existing servers.

Planning for the RD Connection Broker role service

During RDS deployment planning, you must designate a server on which to install the RD Connection Broker role service. The RD Connection Broker role service is required in each RDS deployment. It provides users with access to RemoteApp programs, session-based virtual desktops, and VM-based virtual desktops. The RD Connection Broker role service manages all aspects of session connectivity. Functions performed by the RD Connection Broker role service include the following:

- **Routes connection requests**   Determining the most appropriate RD Session Host or virtual desktop to which to send a connection request, based on a user's identity and the current load on RD Session Host or RD Virtualization Host servers.

- **Stores information about connections to VMs and sessions**   By default, connection information is stored in the Windows Internal Database (WID) on an RD Connection Broker server. By storing this information, the RD Connection Broker role service can reconnect users to the same session in an RDS deployment with multiple RD Session Host servers.

- **Configures RDS servers in the same group (collection)**   You configure settings—for example, session settings or certificates—once, and RD Connection Broker applies the settings to servers in the collection.

- **Manages VM creation and deletion**   In VM-based desktop deployments, RD Connection Broker manages VM creation and deletion for managed collections, and it assigns personal virtual desktops to users,

- **Provides information to RD Web Access servers**   The RD Connection Broker role service gathers collection information about RemoteApp programs, session-based virtual desktops, and VM-based virtual desktops.

When a user initiates a session, the session request is received by the RD Connection Broker role service, which queries the database to determine if there is an existing disconnected session for that user. If so, the user is directed to the disconnected session. If not, the RD Connection Broker role service determines the server in the collection that is best able to handle the new connection, based on the load-balancing algorithm.

Inside OUT

RD Connection Broker scalability

Performance for an RD Connection Broker server depends on the number of requests it receives in a given time frame. Users generate a load on the RD Connection Broker server only when they perform the initial connection to a RemoteApp program or a session-based virtual desktop. This makes it different from an RD Session Host server, for which performance depends on the number of simultaneous users.

A single RD Connection Broker server with four processor cores and four gigabytes (GB) of RAM can process approximately 10 connections per second with a maximum processing time of 1 second. If you are willing to increase the maximum processing time to 12 seconds, that same server can process approximately 60 connections per second. For more detailed information about RD Session Broker scalability, see the white paper "RD Connection Broker Performance and Scalability" at *http://go.microsoft.com/fwlink/?LinkID=510038&clcid=0x409*.

When you consider the number of connections per second to which your RD Connection Broker server will be subject, you need to consider peak utilization times. First thing in the morning when users arrive and after lunch likely are peak times when users are connecting.

A single RD Connection Broker server can handle a large number of connection requests, and for performance, your RDS deployment may require only one. A more critical consideration for the RD Connection Broker role service is availability.

The RD Connection Broker role service is an entry point to an RDS deployment, and it is critical that it is available all the time. If the RD Connection Broker role service isn't available, then clients can't connect to RemoteApp programs or virtual desktops, but existing connections to RemoteApp programs and virtual desktops continue to function properly. When an RDS deployment only has one RD Connection Broker server, the server represents a single point of failure. To make the RD Connection Broker role service highly available or to increase scalability, you can add RD Connection Broker servers.

➤ Configuring high availability for the RD Connection Broker role service is covered in more detail later in this chapter in the section titled "Understanding high availability for RDS."

Planning for the RD Web Access role service

The RD Web Access role service is a mandatory part of each RDS deployment, and it installs the Web server role, Internet Information Services (IIS), as its prerequisite. The benefits of RD Web Access include the following:

- From almost anywhere, authorized users quickly can access a list of available RemoteApp programs, remote desktops, and virtual desktops on a webpage.

- A list of available RDS resources publishes automatically via an RDWeb feed, and it can integrate with the Start screen on the client.

- Changes in available RDS resources update automatically on clients that have subscriptions to an RDWeb feed.

- Users can launch the RDC client from the RD Web Access portal, which enables them to connect remotely to the desktop of any computer on which they have Remote Desktop access.

- RD Web Access and RDWeb feeds are personalized and show only RDS resources for which users have permissions.

- Administrators can customize an RD Web Access portal without programming.

➤ More information about customizing RD Web Access is provided in Chapter 9, "Configuring RemoteApp programs and client connectivity."

It's important to remember that the RD Web Access role service only provides a link to launch RemoteApp programs or to connect to a Remote Desktop session. The RD Web Access role service doesn't proxy client requests. When a user connects to a RemoteApp program or a virtual desktop, the client establishes a direct connection to the target server.

Performance considerations for an RD Web Access server are similar to those for an RD Connection Broker server because the RD Web Access role service provides only initial connectivity to RemoteApp programs and virtual desktops. After users are connected to requested resources, the RD Web Access role service is no longer used. Therefore, RD Web Access server performance needs to be designed to accommodate usage at peak times like morning arrivals and after lunch. If required for high availability or scalability, you can implement multiple RD Web Access servers and load balance them.

Planning for preserving user state

In a session collection with multiple RD Session Host servers, the connections from clients are load balanced across the RD Session Host servers by the RD Connection Broker server. By default, when a user connects to a specific RD Session Host server, a local profile is created for that user on the RD Session Host server. The next time a user connects, the RD Connection Broker may direct the client to a different RD Session Host server, where a different local profile is created. Each time users sign in, they may be using a different profile on a different RD Session Host server. This means that user state information such as application configuration, Desktop configuration, Favorites, and Documents are not the same across sessions. To provide a consistent user experience, you should preserve user state across multiple RD Session Host servers.

If users have desktop computers and session-based virtual desktops, you also need to consider whether you want user state to be preserved between desktop computers and the virtual desktops. This can be complicated by the fact that session-based virtual desktops may not have the same configuration as the desktop computers, and, consequently, it may not make sense to synchronize all of the user state information. For example, synchronizing Desktops may result in desktop shortcuts appearing that point to applications that are not available on the RD Session Host servers.

Roaming profiles

Roaming user profiles can be used to synchronize user state, but they synchronize entire user profiles. This typically is not desired for session-based desktops because not all user state information needs to be synchronized between desktop computers and RD Session Host servers. If you use roaming profiles for the desktop computers in your organization and you want to ensure that roaming profiles are not used on the RD Session Host servers, then you can configure the msDS-PrimaryComputer attribute for users and enable the Download Roaming Profiles On Primary Computers Only Group Policy setting.

You also can set user properties for roaming user profiles that are specific to RD Session Host servers, as shown in Figure 8-7. If you configure the Profile Path, then a user connecting to a session-based virtual desktop uses the specified profile path rather than a roaming profile configured on the Profile tab. Effectively, the RDS user profile becomes a roaming profile used only when connected to an RD Session Host server.

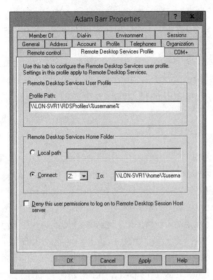

Figure 8-7 User Properties, Remote Desktop Services Profile tab

Instead of configuring individual user accounts with RDS-specific profiles, you can use Group Policy. In a Group Policy object that applies to the RD Session Host servers, you can configure settings in Computer Configuration\Policies\Administrative Templates\Windows Components\Remote Desktop Services\Remote Desktop Session Host\Profiles. There are two relevant settings:

- **Set Path For Remote Desktop Services Roaming User Profile**   Specify a UNC path for storing all user profiles. A subfolder for each user is created automatically.

- **Use Mandatory Profiles On The RD Session Host Server**   Indicates that the path specified in the Set Path For Remote Desktop Services Roaming User Profile setting contains a mandatory profile that can't be modified. When this setting is enabled, the UNC path for profiles does not contain subfolders for each user.

Folder redirection

Folder redirection also is an option for users with session-based virtual desktops. You can redirect only the folders that are suitable for use on the virtual desktops and desktop computers. Commonly redirected folders include Documents, Favorites, and AppData\Roaming.

If you use folder redirection for desktop computers and don't want folder redirection used when users sign in to the RD Session Host servers, you can use the msDS-PrimaryComputer attribute in user accounts just as you can for roaming profiles. In addition to configuring the attribute, you need to enable the Redirect Folders On Primary Computers Only Group Policy setting.

User profile disks

RDS in Windows Server 2012 and newer offers the option to configure user profile disks to preserve user state across sessions. A user profile disk is a VHDX file that is mounted to the user's profile path at C:\Users\%username% on the RD Session Host. The user profile disk is mounted during sign in. During a user's session, all changes to the profile write in his or her VHDX file, and when the user signs out, his or her profile disk is unmounted. The administrator specifies the maximum size of user profile disks and can limit which folders in a user profile are included in or excluded from a user profile disk.

User profile disks are configured individually for each session collection and can't be shared among collections. A share is specified in the collection configuration to store the user profile disks. All RD Session Host servers in the collection have access to the user profile disks in the share. This provides users with consistent user state from any RD Session Host server in the collection.

User profile disks can be used in conjunction with folder redirection and roaming user profiles. Folder redirection will reduce the size of user profile disks and allow the redirected folders to be accessed from desktop computers. Roaming user profiles are synchronized with the user profile disk.

From a server management perspective, one benefit of user profile disks is controlling the amount of data stored on the C drive of RD Session Host servers. Large user profiles stored on RD Session Host servers can cause the C drive to run low on space and cause performance issues. Because user profile disks are stored on a network share and mounted in C:\Users, the C drive never is used to store profile data.

The primary consideration when planning user profile disks is ensuring that the necessary disk space is available for network storage. To ensure that network storage is sufficient, you need to determine the average user profile size. The amount of storage that you need to allocate for user profile disks is the average user profile size times the number of users plus an allowance for growth in both the number of users and the average profile size.

User profile disks are dynamically expanding VHDX files. By default, the maximum size of a user profile disk is 20 GB, but you can set this to be larger or smaller depending on the needs of your users.

When you configure the share for user profile disks, all RD Session Host servers need to have Full Control permissions. This allows the RD Session Host servers to create and manage the user profile disks. When you configure a collection with user profile disks, these permissions are assigned automatically.

Inside OUT

Infrastructure testing prior to rollout

After you assess RDS infrastructure requirements and familiarize yourself with RDS and its role services, you should perform a proof-of-concept (POC) deployment. POC deployment is critical for a successful RDS deployment. It enables you to evaluate whether all the requirements are met and to perform a load simulation, which simulates typical user actions and validates your estimates for capacity, application workloads, and usage patterns by performing a test run in a controlled environment. During testing, you should find answers to the following questions:

- **How many users can connect, and what is an average response time?**   Can POC deployment support the expected number of RD users, and is the response time acceptable? How utilized are servers, how long do user sign-in and sign-out take, and is the user experience as expected?

- **How does the application consume system resources?**   Does it do so in accordance with documented estimates? If the application uses hardware as expected, the rest of the deployment can continue based on initial estimates. If it doesn't use hardware as expected, you must recalculate capacity requirements to ensure accurate estimates.

- **Are all of the potential user environment scenarios being tested?**   You should test the application by accessing it in all the ways a user might use it. If there are access methods that you can't replicate in a POC environment, these access methods should be implemented in a controlled manner when performing the final deployment.

- **Are the applications and hardware running as expected?**   Is additional performance tuning required? Do you need to perform any additional application configuration to run as expected in an RDS environment? Also, confirm that hardware performance is within estimated parameters.

- **Are there any unexpected changes in usage or access?**   If any part of the presentation virtualization POC deployment does not reflect your production environment, alter the POC deployment so that it is as similar as possible to your final, planned infrastructure.

Using testing to eliminate errors in a deployment is important because problems with a presentation virtualization environment are much easier to resolve during testing than during full deployment.

Windows Server 2012 R2 includes a Best Practices Analyzer (BPA) for the Remote Desktop Services server role. BPA for RDS can analyze an RDS environment and check for changes that need to be made for RDS to perform optimally. You can access BPA in Server Manager or by running the Invoke-BpaModel cmdlet.

Deploying session-based virtual desktops

RDS includes multiple role services. If you use Server Manager for RDS deployment, you should be aware that if you use role-based or feature-based installation, you can install individual RDS role services. However, if you install an RDS role service in this way, you can't manage it. If you want to manage RDS, a deployment must have at least three role services: RD Connection Broker, RD Web Access, and either RD Session Host or RD Virtualization Host. Individual RDS role services can't be managed if they are not part of an RDS deployment.

Understanding the session-based desktop deployment process

You can deploy RDS by using Server Manager or Windows PowerShell. Server Manager has the ability to install the necessary server roles, role services, and features on multiple servers that are part of an RDS deployment. All management of RDS also can be done from Server Manager.

Inside Out

Adding servers to Server Manager for RDS deployment

Server Manager can be used to manage the local server and remote servers, but you need to add the remote servers manually before they can be managed. A typical RDS deployment has multiple servers, and you should add each of the servers to Server Manager before you begin the deployment process.

To add a server to Server Manager, perform the following steps:

1. In Server Manager, click Manage and click Add Servers.

2. In the Add Servers window, on the Active Directory tab, in the Name (CN) box, type the name of the server and click Find Now.

3. Double-click the server you want add and then click OK.

The high-level steps for deploying session-based virtual desktops are as follows:

1. **Start the RDS installation**   In Server Manager, use the Add Roles And Features Wizard to select the Remote Desktop Services Installation option, shown in Figure 8-8. This option configures the wizard to collect the information necessary to perform a deployment of RDS across multiple servers.

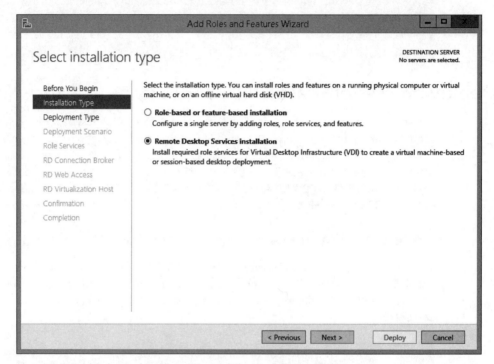

Figure 8-8 Add Roles And Features Wizard, Select Installation Type page

2. **Select the RDS deployment type**   On the Select Deployment Type page, shown in Figure 8-9, select the appropriate deployment type. The Quick Start option installs the required role services on a single server and creates a session collection with several sample RemoteApp programs (Calculator, Paint, and WordPad). You only should use the Quick Start option for testing. In most cases, you want to select the Standard Deployment option because this allows you to customize the deployment for your environment.

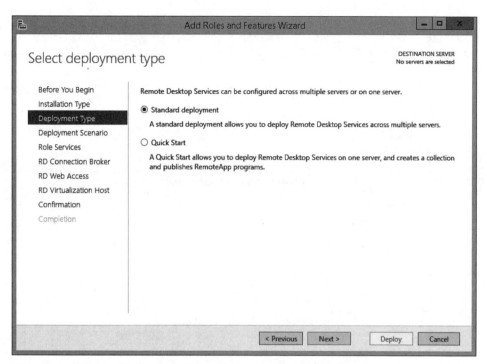

Figure 8-9 Add Roles And Features Wizard, Select Deployment Type page

3. **Select the RD deployment scenario**   On the Select Deployment Scenario page, shown in Figure 8-10, select the Virtual Machine–Based Desktop Deployment option or the Session-Based Desktop Deployment option. A VM-based desktop deployment is used to deploy personal and pooled virtual desktops on computers running Hyper-V. A session-based desktop deployment uses RD Session Hosts.

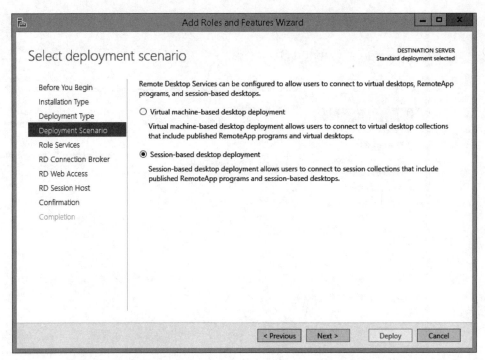

Figure 8-10 Add Roles And Features Wizard, Select Deployment Scenario page

4. **Select servers for RDS role services**   In the Add Roles And Features Wizard, select the servers on which you want to install the RD Connection Broker, RD Web Access, and RD Session Host role services. As part of making RDS highly available, you can install each role service on multiple servers. In most RDS deployments, the RD Session Host role service isn't combined with other role services. The RD Connection Broker and RD Web Access role services can be combined in smaller RDS deployments.

During the deployment, the servers on which you installed the RD Session Host role are restarted. After the installation, you can perform initial configuration of the RDS deployment. You also can add servers to the deployment. At minimum, you should add RD Licensing, because you can't connect to an RD Session Host without valid RDS CALs after the initial grace period of 120 days expires. You also should consider installing multiple instances of the RDS role services for high availability.

Inside OUT

Using Windows PowerShell to deploy RDS

You can use Windows PowerShell to deploy RDS on Windows Server 2012 or newer. In Windows Server 2012, use the New-SessionDeployment cmdlet. In Windows Server 2012 R2, use the New-RDSessionDeployment cmdlet.

➤ You can use Windows PowerShell to manage all aspects of deploying and managing RDS. For more information about cmdlets available for deploying and managing RDS in Windows Server 2012 R2, see the Remote Desktop Cmdlets in Windows PowerShell page on TechNet at *http://technet.microsoft.com/en-us/library/jj215451.aspx.*

To install a session-based deployment of RDS, perform the following steps:

1. In Server Manager, click Manage and then click Add Roles And Features.

2. In the Add Roles And Features Wizard, on the Before You Begin page, click Next.

3. On the Select Installation Type page, click Remote Desktop Services Installation and click Next.

4. On the Select Deployment Type page, click Standard Deployment and click Next.

5. On the Select Deployment Scenario page, click Session-Based Desktop Deployment and click Next.

6. On the Review Role Services page, click Next. This page provides a brief description of each role service, but there is nothing to configure. The currently logged-on account is being used to create the deployment and is displayed here as a reminder.

7. On the Specify RD Connection Broker Server page, shown in Figure 8-11, in the Server Pool box, double-click the server on which you wish to install the RD Connection Broker role service and click Next.

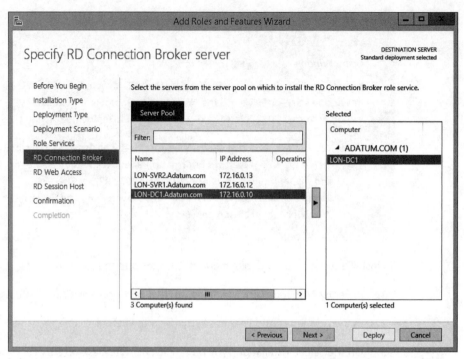

Figure 8-11 Add Roles And Features Wizard, Specify RD Connection Broker Server page

8. On the Specify RD Web Access Server page, shown in Figure 8-12, select the Install The RD Web Access Role Service On The RD Connection Broker Server check box and click Next. Alternatively, you can select another server on which to install the RD Web Access role service.

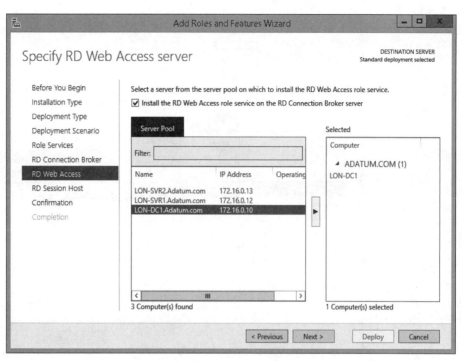

Figure 8-12 Add Roles And Features Wizard, Specify RD Web Access Server page

9.   On the Specify RD Session Host Servers page, shown in Figure 8-13, double-click the server on which you wish to install the RD Session Host role service and click Next.

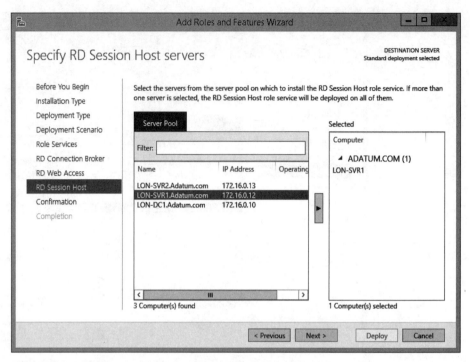

Figure 8-13 Add Roles And Features Wizard, Specify RD Session Host Servers page

10. On the Confirmation page, review the selected servers, select the Restart Destination Server Automatically If Required check box, and click Deploy.

11. On the Completion page, wait for the installation of the RDS role services to complete and click Close. If you are installing roles on the server from which you started the installation, the server may restart and require you to sign in again.

Understanding session collections

Session collections enable you to organize and control user connectivity to RDS. Each session collection contains either RD Session Host servers for session-based virtual desktops or VMs on Hyper-V for pooled or personal virtual desktops.

Collections simplify the administration process by enabling you to manage all collection members as a unit instead of managing them individually. For example, after you configure a collection with session settings, those settings automatically apply to all the servers in the collection. If you add a server to a collection, session settings also automatically apply to the added server.

When you add multiple RD Session Host servers to a collection, connections automatically are load balanced among them. The RD Connection Broker server uses the collection configuration information to identify that there are multiple RD Session Host servers and connects an equal number of clients to each. If an RD Session Host server in a collection fails, the RD Connection Broker connects all users to the remaining RD Session Host servers in the collection.

When there are multiple RD Session Host servers in a collection, they need to be configured with identical applications. Users expect the same applications to be available each time they sign in. If RD Session Host servers have different applications installed, it will appear to users that applications are randomly appearing and disappearing with each connection.

To create a session collection, perform the following steps:

1. In Server Manager, in the navigation pane, click Remote Desktop Services.

2. In Remote Desktop Services > Overview, click Create Session Collections.

3. In the Create Collection Wizard, on the Before You Begin page, click Next.

4. On the Name The Collection page, in the Name box, type the name of the collection and click Next. Make the name something that accurately describes how the collection will be used. You also can type in a more detailed description.

5. On the Specify RD Session Host Servers page, shown in Figure 8-14, double-click the RD Session Host server you want to add to the collection and click Next. Only RD Session Host servers already added to the RDS deployment appear in the Server Pool box. An RD Session Host server can be added to only one collection.

CHAPTER 8

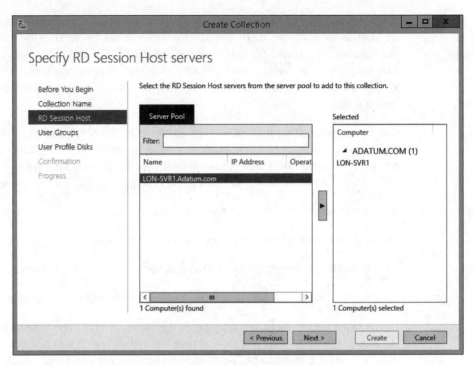

Figure 8-14 Create Collection Wizard, Specify RD Session Host Servers page

6. On the Specify User Groups page, shown in Figure 8-15, remove the Domain Users group, add the groups you want to have access to the collection, and then click Next. The Domain Users group is listed by default and would allow any user in your organization to access the collection. In most cases, you want to restrict collection access to a specific group of users.

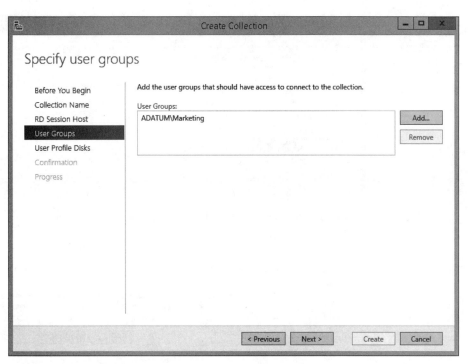

Figure 8-15 Create Collection wizard, Specify User Groups page

7. On the Specify User Profile Disks page, shown in Figure 8-16, select the Enable User Profile Disks check box if you have decided to implement user profile disks for users. If you select this option, you need to enter the UNC path where the user profile disks will be stored in the Location Of User Profile Disks box. You also need to specify a size in the Maximum Size (In GB) box.

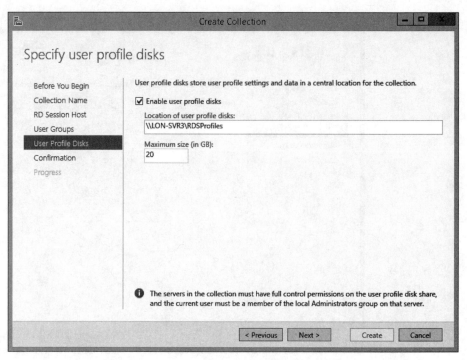

Figure 8-16 Create Collection Wizard, Specify User Profile Disks page

8. On the Confirm Selections page, click Create.

9. On the View Progress page, wait until all tasks are complete and then click Close.

Configuring session collections

The user interface for creating a session collection allows you to configure only a few of the configuration options for a session collection. After the session collection is created, you can edit the session collection and configure many more options.

To edit a session collection, perform the following steps:

1. In Server Manager, in the navigation pane, click Remote Desktop Services.

2. In Remote Desktop Services, in the navigation pane, click the collection you want to edit.

3. While viewing the collection, next to the Properties box, click Tasks and click Edit Properties.

4. In the *CollectionName* Properties window, edit the properties as required and click OK.

When you are editing the properties of a session collection, the editing window is divided into pages with groups of related options. The General page, shown in Figure 8-17, has the Name and Description that you entered during creation. The Show The Session Collection In RD Web Access check box was not available during creation. It is selected by default. Consider disabling this option during scheduled outages when you are performing maintenance on a session collection, for example, when you are upgrading an application on the RD Session Hosts in the collection.

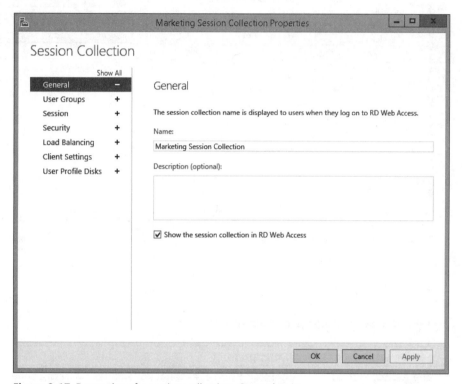

Figure 8-17 Properties of a session collection, General page

The User Groups page in the properties of a session collection allows you to configure which groups of users can connect to the session collection. This is the same as the user groups configured during creation.

The Session page, shown in Figure 8-18, has a number of settings that control session limits and temporary folders.

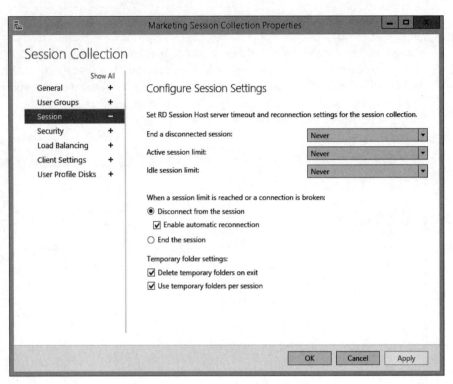

Figure 8-18 Properties of a session collection, Session page

Table 8-3 describes the session settings available on the Session page.

Table 8-3 Session settings for a session collection

Session setting	Description
End A Disconnected Session	Controls when a session is ended after a user disconnects. You can select to never end disconnected sessions or select a value ranging from one minute to five days. The default value is Never. A session is disconnected when there is a network connectivity issue or when a user closes the Remote Desktop Connection window without signing out. A disconnected session keeps all of the applications open and continues to use memory on the RD Session Host. Users can reconnect to the session and resume working where they left off, but if there are too many disconnected sessions, the RD Session Host may not have enough memory.

Active Session Limit	Controls how long an active session can be before it is disconnected or ended. To allow active sessions with no limit, select Never. To limit active sessions, select a time value ranging from one minute to five days. The default value is Never.
	Users receive a warning two minutes before the active session limit is reached. This provides users with time to save their work. An active session is one in which the user is performing a task. An active session is identified by mouse movement or keyboard input. There is seldom a need to limit active sessions, but you could limit them if you are concerned that unauthorized users are accessing a session. This will force the user to reconnect and provide authentication credentials when the limit is reached.
Idle Session Limit	Controls how long an idle session can be idle before it is disconnected or ended. To allow idle sessions with no limit, select Never. To limit idle sessions, select a time value ranging from one minute to five days. The default value is Never.
	Users receive a warning two minutes before the idle session limit is reached. This provides users with an opportunity to move the mouse or press a key to make the session active and avoid the idle session limit.
	An idle session is one in which the user isn't performing a task. An idle session is identified by a lack of mouse movement or keyboard input. Most organizations configure an idle session limit. This has a similar effect on security as having the screen lock on a desktop computer. If a session is connected but unused, it may mean that the user has left his or her connection unattended.
When A Session Limit Is Reached Or A Connection Is Broken	Controls the action that is taken when the active session limit is reached, the idle session limit is reached, or a network problem disconnects a client. You can choose Disconnect From The Session or End The Session.
	In most cases, you will select Disconnect From The Session to prevent users from losing their work when they are disconnected. When you select this option, you also can select Enable Automatic Reconnection. This allows the RDC client to reconnect automatically after short network interruptions. If you do not select this option, the users must provide authentication credentials to reconnect to their disconnected session.
	By default, Disconnect From The Session and Enable Automatic Reconnection are selected.
Delete Temporary Folders On Exit	Configures temporary folders to be deleted when a session ends. This ensures that temporary files do not consume unnecessary disk space. This option is enabled by default.

Use Temporary Folders Per Session	Configures each session for a user to have separate temporary folders on RD Session Host servers where a single user account is allowed to have multiple simultaneous sessions. This option is enabled by default to ensure that multiple sessions on an RD Session Host server do not conflict. However, it isn't relevant in most deployments because users typically are limited to a single session.

The Configure Security Settings page, shown in Figure 8-19, allows you to configure the Security Layer and the Encryption Level to use for the session. The Security Layer defines encryption methods that are used to encrypt communication between the RDC client and the RD Session Host. The available options for security layer are as follows:

- **RDP Security Layer**   This is the weakest option for the security layer. It is available to support older RDP clients. This security layer does not support the use of Network Level Authentication.

- **SSL (TLS 1.0)**   This is the strongest security layer. This security layer supports the use of network-level authentication. When this security layer is used, a certificate on the RD Session Host is used to establish the encryption channel. If the name on the certificate does not match the name used when connecting to the RD Session Host, then a warning is displayed on the client. This is supported by Windows XP SP3 and newer operating systems.

- **Negotiate**   This is the default selection for security layer. SSL (TLS 1.0) is used if available on the server and client. If SSL (TLS 1.0) can't be used, then RDP Security Layer is used.

Figure 8-19 Properties of a session collection, Configure Security Settings page

Network Level Authentication is an authentication method that requires clients to enter authentication credentials before they are connected to the RD Session Host server. The credentials are passed by the RDC client to the RD Session Host server, and if the credentials are valid, the sign-in process is performed. When Network Level Authentication isn't used, clients can connect to the RD Session Host server and interact with the sign-in screen on the RD Session Host before they are authenticated. This is a security risk because it is possible for unauthenticated clients that have access to RD Session Host servers to see recently used user names and the operating system version.

You can force all clients to use Network Level Authentication by selecting the Allow Connections Only From Computers Running Remote Desktop With Network Level Authentication check box. This is enabled by default.

The Encryption Level setting allows you to configure the number of bits used for encryption. This setting applies for both security layers, and more bits provide stronger encryption. The options for Encryption Level are as follows:

- **Low**   Uses 56-bit encryption for data sent from the client to the server. Data sent from the server to the client isn't encrypted. This option is provided to support older clients and typically isn't required.

- **High**   Uses 128-bit encryption for all data sent between the client and server. This option can be used by Windows XP and newer operating systems. This is the preferred option.

- **FIPS Compliant**   Uses encryption algorithms that are FIPS 140-1 or FIPS 140-2 compliant for all data sent between the client and server. Federal Information Processing Standards (FIPS) is a United States government standard for data encryption. This option typically isn't used unless requested specifically by an organization that needs to meet FIPS requirements.

- **Client Compatible**   Negotiates the highest level of encryption supported by the client and uses that. This is the default configuration, but it can be considered a security risk because it allows 56-bit encryption for clients that request it. Use this option only if you need to support clients that can't use 128-bit encryption.

➤ **The Configure Load Balancing Settings page in the properties of a session collection is covered later in this chapter in the section titled "High availability for RD Session Host servers."**

The Configure Client Settings page has settings for device redirection and monitors. By default, redirection is enabled for all available options. If desired, you can select to enable or disable redirection for the following:

- Audio And Video Playback

- Audio Recording

- Smart Cards

- Plug And Play Devices

- Drives

- Clipboard

- Printers

➤ **You can find more information about the client settings in Chapter 9.**

The User Profile Disks page, shown in Figure 8-20, allows you to configure all of the information entered during collection creation and to define what data is stored on the user profile disks. There are two options for user profile disks data settings:

- **Store All User Settings And Data On The User Profile Disk**   Specifies that the complete user profile is stored on the user profile disk. You can add specific folders and files within the profile to exclude.

- **Store Only The Following Folders On The User Profile Disk**   Specifies that only selected folders in the user profile are stored on the user profile disk. The folders available for selection are Contacts, Desktop, Documents, Downloads, Links, Music, Pictures, Roaming User Profile Data, and User Registry Data. You also can add specific files and folders within the profile to include.

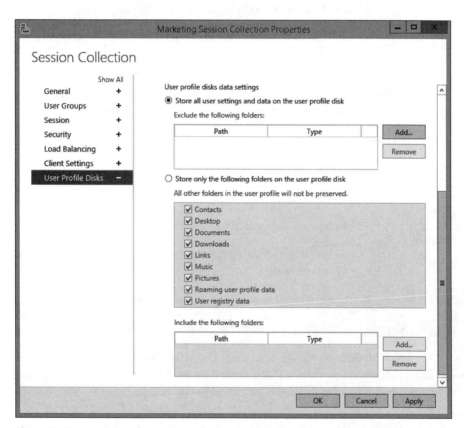

Figure 8-20 Properties of a session collection, User Profile Disks page

Configuring RD Licensing servers

The initial configuration of RDS doesn't configure licensing. However, a functional RDS deployment in production must have licensing properly configured to ensure that users can connect. To configure licensing for RDS, you need to complete the following tasks:

- Set the licensing mode

- Install an RD Licensing server

- Activate an RD Licensing server

- Install and activate CALs

To install an RD Licensing server, perform the following steps:

1. In Server Manager, in the navigation pane, click Remote Desktop Services.

2. On the Overview page, in the Deployment Overview area, click RD Licensing.

3. In the Add RD Licensing Servers Wizard, on the Select A Server page, double-click the server you want to configure as an RD Licensing server and click Next.

4. On the Confirmation page, click Add.

5. Wait until the installation is complete and click Close.

To set the licensing mode for an RDS deployment, perform the following steps:

1. In Server Manager, in the navigation pane, click Remote Desktop Services.

2. On the Overview page, in the Deployment Overview area, click Tasks and click Edit Deployment Properties.

3. In the Deployment Properties window, in the navigation pane, click RD Licensing.

4. On the RD Licensing page, select Per Device or Per User and click OK.

The Microsoft Clearinghouse is the service that is used to activate RD Licensing servers and RDS CALs. When you install an RD Licensing server, you need to activate it before it can be begin servicing clients. To do this, you use Remote Desktop Licensing Manager (RD Licensing Manager), shown in Figure 8-21. RD Licensing Manager is installed on each RD Licensing server.

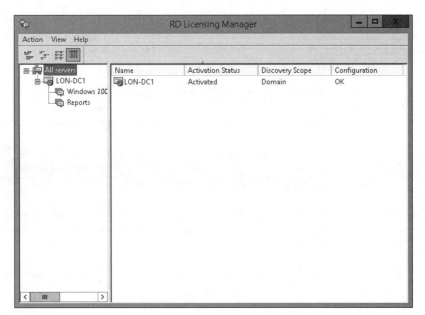

Figure 8-21 RD Licensing Manager

When you activate an RD Licensing server, you need to exchange information with the Microsoft Clearinghouse. You can choose from the following connection methods:

- **Automatic Connection (Recommended)**   Transfers the necessary information between the RD Licensing server and the Microsoft Clearinghouse over the Internet. The RD Licensing server must have connectivity to the Internet.

- **Web Browser**   Requires you to enter a Product ID at the website https://activate.microsoft.com. Then, you type the license server ID provided by the website into the Activate Server Wizard. Use this connection method if the RD Licensing server does not have access to the Internet.

- **Telephone**   Requires you to phone the Microsoft Clearinghouse and provide the Product ID for your server. You are then give a license server ID, which you need to enter into the Activate Server Wizard. Use this connection method if you have no access to the Internet.

Installing RDS CALs is a similar process to activating an RD Licensing server. The same connectivity methods to the Microsoft Clearinghouse are supported. The installation process automatically uses the method that you used when activating the server. You can change the connectivity method in the Properties of the server if required.

To activate an RD Licensing server over the Internet, perform the following steps:

1. In Server Manager, click Tools, point to Terminal Services, and click Remote Desktop Licensing Manager.

2. Right-click the licensing server and click Activate Server.

3. In the Activate Server Wizard, on the Welcome To The Activate Server Wizard page, click Next.

4. On the Connection Method page, in the Connection Method box, select Automatic Connection (Recommended) and click Next.

5. If you have not already configured the company information for your server, you are prompted to do so. On the Company Information page, enter the required company information and click Next.

6. On the next Company Information page, if desired, enter the optional information and click Next.

7. On the Completing The Activate Server Wizard page, deselect the Start Install Licenses Wizard Now check box and click Finish.

8. Right-click the server and click Review Configuration.

9. In the Server Configuration window, shown in Figure 8-22, click Add To Group.

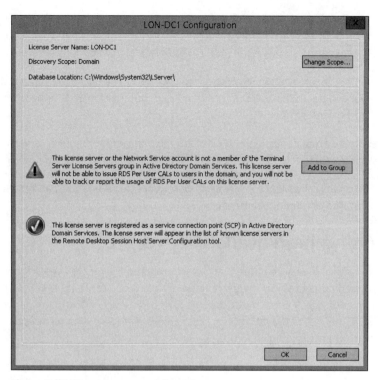

Figure 8-22 License server configuration

10. In the RD Licensing Manager window, click Continue to acknowledge the warning about requiring Domain Admin privileges.

11. In the RD Licensing Manager dialog box, click OK to acknowledge that the server has been added to the Terminal Server License Servers Group.

12. In the Server Configuration window, click OK.

To install RDS CALs over the Internet, perform the following steps:

1. In Server Manager, click Tools, point to Terminal Services, and click Remote Desktop Licensing Manager.

2. Right-click the license server and click Install Licenses.

3. In the Install Licenses Wizard, on the Welcome To The Install Licenses Wizard page, click Next.

4. On the License Program page, select the license program used to purchase your RDS CALs and click Next. Available license programs include Open License, Enterprise Agreement, Campus Agreement, and more.

5. Enter the information requested and click Next. The information requested varies depending on the licensing program used, but it will include either a license code or an agreement number.

6. On the Product Version And License Type page, enter the product version, license type, and number of RDS CALs based on your license and click Next.

7. Wait while the Microsoft Clearinghouse processes the request and the RDS CALs are installed and then click Finish.

Understanding high availability for RDS

A highly available service is one that is available almost all of the time. High availability often is expressed numerically as the percentage of time that a service is available. For example, a requirement for 99.9 percent availability allows 8.75 hours of downtime per year, or approximately 40 minutes of downtime every four weeks. With 99.999 percent uptime, the allowed service downtime is reduced to only 5 minutes per year.

To achieve high availability for a service such as RDS, you need to identify single points of failure in the infrastructure and work to eliminate them. For example, if you have only one RD Session Host server, that is a single point of failure. There will be a service outage if that server has hardware problems or is taken offline for maintenance.

To make infrastructure highly available, you need to make it redundant. For example, within a server, using mirroring (RAID 1) for disks ensures that that failure of a single hard disk does not cause the server to fail. This principle also can be applied at other levels of infrastructure such as networking, network services, and data center power. To make RDS highly available, you need multiple servers for each of the RDS role services, but not all RDS role services automatically become highly available just because you add more servers running the role service. Some RDS role services require you to implement load balancing.

Inside OUT

Redundant hardware vs. redundant servers

Within a server, two common hardware components for high availability are dual power supplies and hardware RAID cards. Combined, these options can add $1,000 to the cost of a server.

When you have highly available infrastructure with multiple servers, you can balance the high availability of components within a server with the high availability provided by having multiple servers. Instead of providing hardware redundancy in servers, you can provide the redundancy with additional servers. This can be a cost-effective way to provide high availability.

In the previous example, you could save $1,000 per server by not putting in dual power supplies and hardware RAID cards. In a large RDS deployment, if you are implementing eight RD Session Host servers, this would save $8,000 in hardware costs, which you could use to purchase two or three additional servers to provide high availability.

Most administrators want their individual servers to be highly available, but it's really the services that need to be highly available. The key to making this strategy work is providing enough redundant servers and monitoring so that you can resolve issues quickly when a server fails

Understanding load balancing

Load balancing is a technology that you can use to achieve high availability and scalability primarily for stateless services. The term *stateless* refers to workloads that respond to each request independently from previous requests and without keeping client state. For example, when a client requests a webpage, a Web server gathers all of the necessary information from the request and then returns a generated webpage to the client. When the client requests another webpage, it might request the webpage from the same Web server or from any other identically configured Web server in a load-balancing cluster.

The servers that are part of a load balancing cluster are referred to as nodes. Each node is configured with the same software so that clients can connect with any node and obtain the intended service. For example, each node would have the same website configured.

Clients connect to a virtual IP address that is used to access all nodes in the cluster. To the clients, the virtual IP address behaves the same way that an IP address configured on a physical server would. Only one cluster node responds to each client request.

If a node in the cluster fails, the remaining nodes continue to service clients. This makes a load balancing cluster highly available. Adding nodes to the cluster increases the capacity of the cluster. Adding nodes is scaling out.

Windows Network Load Balancing

Windows Network Load Balancing (NLB) is a software solution for load balancing that is included in Windows Server operating systems. NLB creates a virtual IP address that all of the nodes in the load balancing cluster share. When a request comes in to virtual IP, the request is received by all nodes, but only one node responds. The nodes determine the appropriate node to respond based on an algorithm that they all use.

The most common reason organizations consider using NLB is the cost. Because it is included in Windows Server operating systems, it is effectively free. However, there are a few drawbacks to using NLB:

- **It is not service aware**   NLB is capable of identifying when a server is no longer responding but not when a service is no longer responding. This means that some types of failures result in clients being directed to a nonresponsive service on a partially functional node.

- **Scalability is limited**   NLB supports up to 32 nodes in a cluster, but performance peaks at 8 nodes.

- **Network hardware configuration may be required**   Some network switches need additional configuration to work with NLB. This is required because multiple devices are sharing the same virtual IP address but are connected to different switch ports.

Hardware-based load balancing

Most large organizations use specialized hardware load balancers instead of using NLB. Hardware load balancers are more scalable than NLB, but they also are significantly more expensive. The least expensive hardware load balancers are about $2,000, and they can cost more than $40,000.

The configuration of a hardware load balancer varies depending on the vendor, but all of them provide the same basic functionality. The virtual IP address for the load balancing cluster is assigned to the load balancer, and the load balancer receives requests from the clients. The load balancer then forwards each request to a single node.

The load balancer is responsible for identifying failed nodes. Node failure can be identified at the node level, as NLB does, or at the service level. If service-level failure is used, the load balancer monitors the service on each node and stops sending client requests if the service stops responding.

Inside OUT

DNS round robin

An alternate method for load balancing is DNS round robin. This method is implemented entirely by using DNS records and does not require any additional software or hardware. The main concern with DNS round robin is that it can be less reliable than NLB or hardware-based load balancing.

In DNS, a host (A) record is used to identify the IP address to which a name should resolve. For example, a host (A) record identifies the IP address to which www.microsoft.com resolves. If you create multiple host (A) records for a name, then it resolves to multiple IP addresses. When a client resolves the name, the DNS server provides IP addresses from all of the host (A) records for that name. This configuration is called DNS round robin.

When a client receives multiple IP addresses from a DNS server, the typical behavior is to contact the first IP address in the list. If the first IP address in the list doesn't respond, then the client contacts the second IP address in the list. This process continues until the client successfully connects to an IP address or the list is exhausted.

The main drawback to DNS round robin is that it's unpredictable. The client is in control of the process for managing server failure and the list of IP addresses. If the software developer for the client software does not manage server failure well, then users experience poor performance. For client software that is designed to use DNS round robin, it is a simple and effective load balancing mechanism.

CHAPTER 8

High availability for RD Session Host servers

When an RDS deployment has a single RD Session Host server, that server becomes a single point of failure. When it fails, the failure will affect all users who are connected to it and who run RemoteApp programs on that server. You must consider the possibility of failure or the lack of RD Session Host server availability in your disaster recovery plan.

You can take several steps to improve RD Session Host availability. You can use reliable and redundant hardware from respected vendors to minimize the probability of hardware failure. You also should make sure that the network is reliable and that there are multiple network paths to an RD Session Host server. You should be aware, however, that failures are unavoidable, and no single server can always be available without downtime. For example, after you install Windows updates, computer restart is often required, which causes server downtime.

To make the RD Session Host server role highly available, you should have multiple RD Session Host servers in each collection. The RD Connection Broker role service automatically load balances connections to the RD Session Host servers. If the RD Connection Broker role service identifies that an RD Session Host server is unavailable, clients are not directed to the failed RD Session Host server. Clients are directed only to the remaining functional RD Session Host server.

As a best practice, all RD Session Host servers should have a similar hardware configuration. This ensures that all RD Session Host servers have similar performance and can handle a similar number of clients. The default configuration of load balancing for a collection, shown in Figure 8-23, is best suited for this scenario.

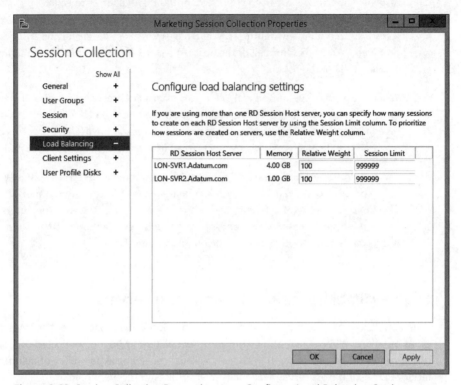

Figure 8-23 Session Collection Properties page, Configure Load Balancing Settings page

You can adjust the ratio of sessions allocated to an RD Session Host server by adjusting the Relative Weight value for that server. The default value for all servers is 100. When all servers have the same value, they all receive the same number of sessions. If you have one server with significantly better hardware and give that server a Relative Weight of 200, then it will receive twice as many sessions as a server with a Relative Weight of 100.

You also can set a Session Limit for each server. The default value for the Session Limit is 999,999, which effectively is unlimited. If you have determined that users experience performance issues when more than 80 clients are connected, then you can set a session limit of 80 to ensure that performance is satisfactory for all users.

To add a second RD Session Broker server to an RDS deployment, perform the following steps:

1.   In Server Manager, in the navigation pane, click Remote Desktop Services.

2. On the Overview page, click Add RD Session Host Servers.

3. In the Add RD Session Host Server window, on the Select A Server page, in the Server Pool box, double-click the server you want to configure as an RD Session Host server and click Next.

4. On the Confirm Selections page, select the Restart Remote Computers As Needed check box and click Add.

5. Wait until the RD Session Host role service is installed on the server and click Close.

To add an RD Session Host server to a session collection, perform the following steps:

1. In Server Manager, in the navigation pane, click Remote Desktop Services.

2. In the navigation pane, click the session collection.

3. Scroll down to the Host Servers box, click Tasks, and click Add RD Session Host Servers.

4. In the Add Servers To Collection Wizard, on the Specify RD Session Host Servers page, double-click the RD Session Host server that you want to add to the session collection and click Next.

5. On the Confirm Selections page, click Add.

6. Wait until the task is complete and then click Close.

High availability for the RD Connection Broker role service

The RD Connection Broker role service is responsible for directing clients to an available RD Session Host server. If the RD Connection Broker role service is unavailable, then users are not able to access session-based virtual desktops. Having a single RD Connection Broker server creates a single point of failure.

To make the RD Connection Broker role service highly available, you need to have multiple RD Connection Broker servers. The RD Connection Broker role service uses a SQL Server database to track sessions that have been allocated to RD Session Host servers. For multiple RD Connection Brokers servers to work together, they need to share a single SQL Server database.

NOTE

High availability for the RD Connection Broker role service in Windows Server 2012 and newer is active/active. This means that multiple RD Connection Broker servers can respond to client requests at the same time. Older implementations of the RD Connection Broker and Terminal Services (TS) Connection Broker high availability were active/passive. A second server was used only when the first server failed. This provided high availability but not scalability.

To prepare the RD Connection Broker role service for high availability, you need to do the following:

- Configure a server running Microsoft SQL Server 2008 R2 or newer. The RD Connection Broker servers must have permission to create a database on the server.

- Install the SQL Server Native Client on all RD Connection Broker servers. The RD Connection Broker servers use this to connect to the SQL database.

- Configure a static IP address on all RD Connection Broker servers. This is required to implement DNS round robin for load balancing.

- Configure a DNS round robin record for the RD Connection Broker servers. Select a name that is meaningful, such as rds.adatum.com.

Inside OUT
Configuring SQL permissions for RD Session Broker high availability

To assign the necessary permissions for RD Session Broker servers on the SQL server, perform the following steps:

1. Create a security group in Active Directory Domain Services (AD DS) and add the computer accounts for the RD Connection Broker servers.

2. Restart the RD Connection Broker server so that the new group membership takes effect.

3. On the SQL server, open SQL Server Management Studio.

4. In the Connect To Server window, verify that the correct instance of SQL server is listed and click Connect.

5. In SQL Server Management Studio, in Object Explorer, expand Security, and expand Logins.

6. Right-click Logins and click New Login.

7. In the Login – New window, on the General page, in the Login Name box, type Domain/GroupName.

8. Click the Server Roles page, select the Dbcreator check box, and click OK.

9. Close SQL Server Management Studio.

When you configure the RD Connection Broker role service for high availability, its database moves from a local WID to a computer that is running SQL Server. Even when an RDS deployment has multiple RD Connection Broker servers, SQL Server still can be a single point of failure. You should make sure that SQL Server is highly available by running it in a failover cluster.

When you configure high availability for the RD Connection Broker role service, you need to provide a Database Connection String that the RD Connection Broker servers use to connect to the SQL server. The Database Connection String has the following format:

```
DRIVER=SQL Server Native Client 11.0;SERVER=LON-SQL.Adatum.com;Trusted_
Connection=Yes;APP=Remote Desktop Services Connection Broker;Database=RDS-DB
```

There are several things to note about the Database Connection String:

- **A SQL native client version is specified**   In this example, the SQL native client version is 11.0. This is used when your SQL server is SQL Server 2012. If your SQL server is SQL Server 2008 R2, then the SQL native client version is 10.0.

- **A server name is specified**   In this example, the server name is LON-SQL.Adatum.com. In your deployment, you should specify the name of the SQL server that will be hosting the database for the RD Connection Broker servers.

- **A database name is specified**   In this example, the database name is RDS-DB. This is the name of the database that will be created for the RD Connection Broker servers to use. You can select an alternate name, but it should be a meaningful name to make it easy to identify.

To configure the RD Connection Broker role service for high availability, perform the following steps:

1.   In Server Manager, in the navigation pane, click Remote Desktop Services.

2.   On the Overview page, in the Deployment Overview area, right-click RD Connection Broker and click Configure High Availability.

3.   In the Configure RD Connection Broker For High Availability Wizard, on the Before You Begin page, click Next.

4.   On the Configure RD Connection Broker For High Availability page, shown in Figure 8-24, in the Database Connection String box, type the appropriate Database Connection String for your environment.

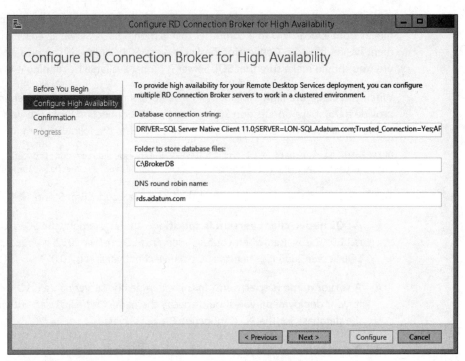

Figure 8-24   Configure RD Connection Broker For High Availability Wizard, Configure RD Connection Broker For High Availability page

5. In the Folder To Store Database Files box, type the path for the database on the SQL server. The database will be created in this location. This folder must already exist.

6. In the DNS Round Robin Name box, type the name of the DNS round robin record that you created for the RD Connection Broker servers and then click Next.

7. On the Confirmation page, click Configure.

8. On the Progress page, click Close.

After you have configured high availability for the RD Connection Broker role service, the RD Connection Broker icon in the Deployment Overview area is updated with the text (High Availability Mode). Now you can add another RD Connection Broker server by right-clicking the RD Connection Broker icon and clicking Add RD Connection Broker server. The new RD Connection Broker server will use the central SQL database that you have configured.

High availability for the RD Web Access role service

RD Web Access servers are a critical part of an RDS deployment. The RD Web Access servers are responsible for providing clients with an .rdp file that contains connectivity information to collections. If RD Web Access isn't available, then clients can't obtain the necessary configuration information to connect to session-based virtual desktops. You should make RD Web Access servers highly available.

Load balancing is used to make RD Web Access servers highly available. You can use NLB, hardware-based load balancing, or DNS round robin. If you are using NLB or hardware-based load balancing, you'll need to create a DNS record for the virtual IP address used by the load balancing cluster. For example, you could create a host (A) record for RDWeb.adatum.com that resolves to the virtual IP address. If you are using DNS round robin, then you need to create multiple host (A) records for RDWeb.adatum.com that resolve to the IP addresses of the RD Web Access servers.

To add an RD Web Access server, perform the following steps:

1. In Server Manager, in the navigation pane, click Remote Desktop Services.

2. On the Overview page, right-click RD Web Access and click Add RD Web Access Servers.

3. In the Add RD Web Access Servers Wizard, on the Select A Server page, double-click the server you want to configure as an RD Web Access server and click Next.

4. On the Confirmation page, click Add.

5. Wait until the installation is complete and click Close.

6. Configure your load-balancing solution with the IP address of the new RD Web Access server.

High availability for the RD Licensing role service

The effect of the RD Licensing role service for an RDS deployment varies, depending on the licensing mode that has been selected. When an RDS deployment is configured for Per User licensing, the RD Session Host servers contact an RD Licensing server each time a client connects. If an RD Licensing server isn't available, then users can't connect.

Per User licensing isn't enforced by RD Licensing servers. If an RD Session Host server can contact an RD Licensing server, that is sufficient to allow a connection. You are responsible for ensuring that you are in compliance with licensing requirements, but they are not enforced.

CHAPTER 8

To make an RDS deployment with Per User licensing highly available, you need to install multiple RD Licensing servers. If the first RD Licensing server is unavailable, then the second is contacted.

Allocation of RDS User CALs among the RD Licensing servers does not matter because they are not enforced. To simplify license management, you can install and activate all RDS User CALs on a single RD Licensing server.

High availability for an RDS deployment configured for Per Device licensing also requires multiple RD Licensing servers, but configuration is more complex because RDS Device CAL usage is enforced. If an RDS Device CAL isn't available, then connectivity can be blocked. Because of this, you need to consider how CALs are allocated among the RD Licensing servers.

RDS client behavior for Per Device licensing varies, depending on the state of the client:

- **First connection**   The first time a device connects, it is issued a temporary CAL that can be used only once. If an RD Licensing server is unavailable, the temporary CAL can't be issued, and new devices are unable to connect. The temporary CAL can be issued by any RD Licensing server even if no RDS Device CALs are available on that server.

- **Temporary license**   The second time a device connects, it is issued a permanent RDS Device CAL. For a device to be issued a permanent RDS Device CAL, an RD Licensing server with unallocated Per Device CALs must be available. If an RD Licensing server with unallocated Per Device CALs isn't available, then the temporary CAL remains valid for 90 days.

- **Permanent CAL**   Devices with a permanent CAL can connect to an RD Session Host when no RD Licensing server is available. Permanent RDS Device CALs are valid for 52 to 89 days and can't be renewed if no RD Licensing server is available.

- **Permanent CAL expired**   If the permanent CAL has expired and an RD Licensing server isn't available, the connection is blocked. An RD Licensing server with unused Per Device CALs must be available to issue a new permanent CAL.

The simplest way to configure high availability for the RD Licensing role service when using Per Device licensing is to put all RDS Device CALs on a single RD Licensing server. The second RD Licensing server has no CALs installed and issues only temporary licenses. In this configuration, failure of the RD Licensing server with CALs has no effect on devices with a permanent or temporary license, which typically are the majority of devices. Devices connecting for the first time are issued a temporary license from the remaining RD Licensing server without CALs. The only clients unable to connect are devices with an expired license, which should be a small number of devices.

A slightly more complex way to configure high availability for the RD Licensing role service when using Per Device licensing is to split RDS Device CALs among RD Licensing servers. Most CALs are installed on the primary RD Licensing server, but some are installed on a secondary RD Licensing server. This configuration is better because if the primary RD Licensing server fails, then CALs can be issued by the secondary RD Licensing server, and no devices should be prevented from connecting.

Splitting CALs between two RD Licensing servers is slightly more expensive because you need to purchase additional CALs for the secondary RD Licensing server. In a large deployment of RDS, this likely is worth the additional cost to avoid outages. In a small deployment of RDS, it may not be worth the cost because very few users would be affected.

When you have multiple RD Licensing servers, it is critical that you configure the RDS deployment to use the RD Licensing server you have configured with the CALs as the primary RD Licensing server.

To configure the order of RD Licensing servers, perform the following steps:

1.   In Server Manager, in the navigation pane, click Remote Desktop Services.

2.   On the Overview page, in the Deployment Overview area, click Edit Deployment Properties.

3.   In the Deployment Properties window, in the navigation area, click RD Licensing.

4.   Select the server you want to be primary, click Move Up until it is at the top of the list, and click OK.

To add an RD Licensing server, perform the following steps:

1.   In Server Manager, in the navigation pane, click Remote Desktop Services.

2.   On the Overview page, in the Deployment Overview area, right-click RD Licensing and click Add RD Licensing Servers.

3.   In the Add RD Licensing Servers Wizard, on the Select A Server page, double-click the server you want to configure as an RD Licensing server and click Next.

4.   On the Confirmation page, click Add.

5.   Wait until the installation is complete and click Close.

CHAPTER 8

Configuring RemoteApp programs and client connectivity

After you have completed the basic installation of Remote Desktop Services (RDS) and created a session collection, you can optimize the user experience further. One way to optimize the user experience is by implementing RemoteApp programs as an alternative to session-based virtual desktops. RemoteApp programs are similar to locally installed applications.

You also need to be aware of how you can optimize client connectivity. An important element of this is certificate configuration to avoid unnecessary warnings and enable single sign-on (SSO). You also can customize Remote Desktop Web Access (RD Web Access) and control device redirection.

Publishing and configuring RemoteApp programs

With RemoteApp programs, you can use RDS to make programs on a Remote Desktop Session Host (RD Session Host) server appear as if they are running on a user's local computer. RemoteApp program windows are shown on and integrated with a client's Desktop instead of being presented as part of a session-based virtual desktop. Figure 9-1 shows a RemoteApp program open on a Desktop.

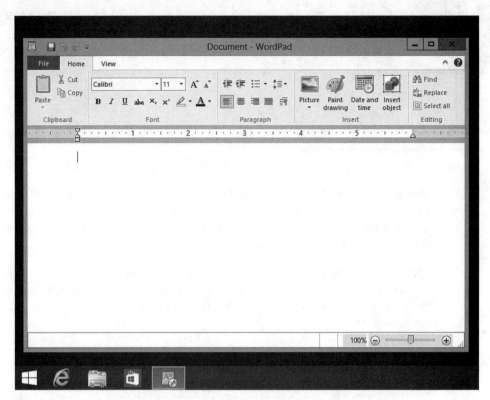

Figure 9-1 RemoteApp program open on a Desktop

Using a RemoteApp program is similar to using a local application. When you implement RDS to provide access to a few applications, RemoteApp programs generally are easier for users to understand and use than session-based virtual desktops. Users can become confused when there is a session-based virtual desktop and a local Desktop. This is particularly true if the session-based virtual desktop is used in full-screen mode.

For tablet users, working with a full session-based virtual desktop can be challenging because small tablet interfaces can make it difficult to navigate the full session-based virtual desktop and start applications. RemoteApp programs launch the program directly from the tablet to simplify the connectivity process.

Scenarios in which RemoteApp programs can be useful include the following:

- **Remote users** Users often need to access applications from remote locations, for example, when users work from home or work while traveling. RemoteApp programs allow these users to access applications over an Internet connection. Using Remote Desktop Gateway (RD Gateway) with RemoteApp programs helps secure remote access to applications without using a virtual private network (VPN). Additionally, you can allow users to access remote applications through an RD Web Access page or integrate applications on the Start screen.

- **Line-of-business application deployments**   Organizations often need to run consistent line-of-business (LOB) applications on computers and devices that run different versions of Windows operating systems and non-Microsoft operating systems. Instead of deploying LOB applications locally, you can install applications on an RD Session Host server and make them as available as RemoteApp programs.

- **Roaming users**   In some organizations, a user might work on several different computers. If users work on a computer on which an application isn't installed, they can access the application remotely through RDS.

- **Branch offices**   In a branch office environment, there might be limited local Information Technology (IT) support and limited network bandwidth. If you use RemoteApp programs, you can centralize application management and improve remote application performance in limited bandwidth scenarios.

- **Application compatibility**   When users have varying operating systems and configurations, conflicts may prevent applications from being installed locally. For example, multiple versions of an application may not coexist properly. Or an application may not be available for operating systems other than Windows. RemoteApp resolves compatibility issues by running the application on an RD Session Host instead of locally.

Understanding RemoteApp programs

A RemoteApp program is an application installed on an RD Session Host server. Remote Desktop Connection (RDC) and the RD Session Host use Remote Desktop Protocol (RDP) to redirect screen information for just the application instead of the full session-based virtual desktop. If a user runs multiple RemoteApp programs from the same session collection, the RemoteApp programs share the same session on the RD Session Host.

RemoteApp programs include the following features:

- **Start without prompts**   When you click a RemoteApp program link or tile, the program can start without any prompts or user interaction. In the background, the client establishes an RDP connection, signs in, starts the remote program, and displays its window.

- **Run in own window**   A RemoteApp program displays in its own window on a client. You can move, resize, minimize, maximize, or close the window the same way as any other application window. A RemoteApp window can show its content while you move or resize the window.

- **Start automatically based on file type associations (FTAs)**   You can start a RemoteApp program from an RD Web Access page, from the Start screen, or by double-clicking a file with an associated file name extension.

- **Display live thumbnails and allow application switching**   A RemoteApp program icon displays on the taskbar even if the program is minimized. If multiple instances of a RemoteApp program run, multiple (tabbed) program icons display on the taskbar. When you move the pointer to the taskbar icon, a live thumbnail of the program window displays. You can use a standard Alt+Tab key combination to switch between running programs, including RemoteApp programs.

- **Display notifications and dialog boxes locally**   If a RemoteApp program uses a notification area icon, this icon appears in the client's notification area. Also, RDS redirects dialog boxes and other windows from the RemoteApp program to the local Desktop.

- **Have similar icons**   RemoteApp programs have similar icons on the taskbar as locally installed applications, but they include a "Remote Desktop" symbol. You can notice a change in the status of a RemoteApp program because the icon overlay is supported. For example, Microsoft Outlook uses a letter overlay to notify the user that new email has been received.

RemoteApp programs integrate so well with the local Desktop that users may not be aware that they are running on an RD Session Host server. This enables you to integrate specific apps from an RD Session Host server with locally installed apps on a desktop computer.

Installing applications on RD Session Host servers

Whether you are providing session-based virtual desktops or RemoteApp programs, you need to ensure that apps are installed properly on the RD Session Host servers. Before you attempt to install the app in a production environment, you need to verify that it works properly when installed on an RD Session Host server. When you install the app on an RD Session Host server, you need to follow a specific installation process.

The following are some considerations for deploying apps on RD Session Host servers:

- **Suitability for multiuser environments**   This is the most important consideration for apps installed on RD Session Host servers. Historically, most end-user apps function well in multiuser environments, but this isn't always the case. Ideally, the app vendor officially will support installation on RD Session Host servers. In some cases, you may need to obtain an update from the app vendor that enables an app to run properly on an

RD Session Host server. If an app can't run on RD Session Host servers, then you'll need to install it on desktops or consider using an alternative app.

NOTE

Many apps that aren't officially supported for RD Session Host servers run properly, but the vendor hasn't done the necessary testing. You can choose to install the app anyway and accept the risk of unforeseen failures. Whether you do this depends on the organizational benefits of putting the app on RD Session Host servers versus the cost of potential failure in the future.

- **App compatibility**   You need to investigate whether apps have compatibility issues when coexisting on RD Session Host servers. Ensure that you thoroughly test apps before you put them into a production environment. You might need collections with separate pools of RD Session Host servers to run incompatible applications separately from one another.

- **App dependencies**   Install related apps or apps that have dependencies on other local apps on the same RD Session Host server. For example, all the apps in a suite such as Microsoft Office should be installed on the same RD Session Host server unless otherwise prescribed by the vendor.

- **Capacity requirements**   There are no firm numbers on how many clients a single RD Session Host server can support. Resource requirements depend on the number of apps that are being used simultaneously and the resource requirements of individual apps. Adding a new app to an RD Session Host server will increase the load on the server. Don't assume that because the number of clients remains the same, the load won't increase.

- **Licensing requirements**   The licensing requirements for apps vary widely among vendors and apps. In many cases, installing an app on an RD Session Host server means that you need to purchase licenses for every user who has access to session-based virtual desktops. In a large RDS deployment, this can be very expensive. You may be able to mitigate this by using RemoteApp programs, which can be controlled by user groups. Some vendors have specific licensing for RDS deployments.

Installing an app on an RD Session Host server is different from installing an app on a traditional desktop. RD Session Host servers operate in two modes: install mode and execute mode. You must put a server in install mode to install multiuser apps properly. In install mode, the Windows operating system ensures that appropriate registry entries and initialization (.ini) file settings are configured for an app to function in multiuser environments. After an app successfully installs, the server must be placed back into execute mode.

CHAPTER 9

The Windows Installer Service is RDS-aware. This means that Windows Installer packaged apps (.msi) automatically are installed properly. Windows Installer switches to install mode and back to execute mode as part of the installation process. Most apps are distributed as Windows Installer packages as for installation, but you should verify before installing.

If the app isn't distributed as a Windows Installer package, then you need to ensure that you install it by using the proper process. One way to install the application properly is by using the Install Application On Remote Desktop Server option in the Programs area of Control Panel, shown in Figure 9-2. This option is added to all RD Session Host servers. Using this option opens a wizard that prompts you for the location of the installation files and puts the server into install mode while performing the installation.

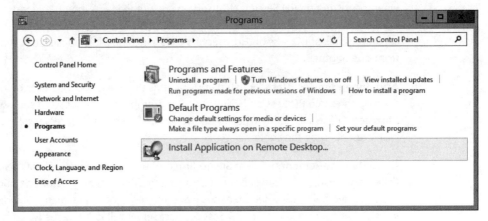

Figure 9-2 Programs area of Control Panel

Alternatively, you can use a command prompt to manually put the RD Session Host server into install mode by using the following command:

```
change user /install
```

After the RD Session Host server is switched to install mode, install the application. Then, change the RD Session Host server back to execute mode by using the following command:

```
change user /execute
```

You also can check the current server mode by using the following command:

```
change user /query
```

You also can use apps deployed by using Microsoft Application Virtualization (App-V) for session-based virtual desktops and RemoteApp programs. Using App-V can mitigate some compatibility issues and simplify application deployment and updates.

➤ For more information about using App-V with RDS, see Integrating App-V With Microsoft VDI at *http://go.microsoft.com/fwlink/?LinkID=510044.*

Publishing RemoteApp programs

Before users can access RemoteApp programs, you must publish them. Publishing configures a session collection with the information necessary for users to access the apps on the RD Session Host servers.

To publish a RemoteApp program from a session collection, perform the following steps:

1. In Server Manager, in the navigation pane, click Remote Desktop Services.

2. In the navigation pane, click the session collection from which you want to deploy RemoteApp programs.

3. In the RemoteApp Programs area, shown in Figure 9-3, click Tasks, and click Publish RemoteApp Programs.

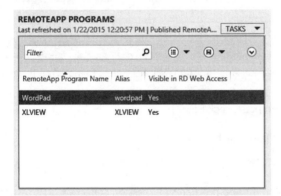

Figure 9-3 RemoteApp Programs area in Server Manager

4. In the Publish RemoteApp Programs Wizard, on the Select RemoteApp Programs page, shown in Figure 9-4, select the check boxes beside the apps that you want to publish and click Next. This list of applications is queried from an RD Session Host server in the collection. If an app you want to publish isn't listed, you can use the Add button to browse for the executable for the app.

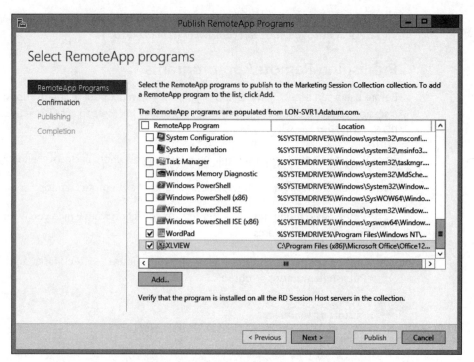

Figure 9-4 Publish RemoteApp Programs Wizard, Select RemoteApp Programs page

5.   On the Confirmation page, click Publish.

6.   On the Completion page, click Close.

NOTE

After you publish RemoteApp programs in a session collection, that session collection can be used only for RemoteApp programs. You can't provide session-based virtual desktops and RemoteApp programs from the same session collection.

Configuring RemoteApp programs

After you publish a RemoteApp program, it appears in the RemoteApp Programs area, as shown in Figure 9-3. In this area, you can see the name of the program and whether it is visible in RD Web Access. To configure a RemoteApp program, right-click the RemoteApp program and click Edit Properties.

In the properties of a RemoteApp program, on the General page, shown in Figure 9-5, you can change the RemoteApp Program Name. This value controls the name that is visible in

RD Web Access for the application. You also can choose whether to Show The RemoteApp Program In RD Web Access.

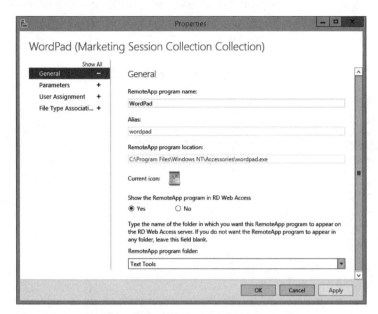

Figure 9-5 Properties of a RemoteApp program, General page

You can organize applications in RD Web Access by entering a folder name in the RemoteApp Program Folder box. Any folder name that you enter is used to generate a folder in RD Web Access in which the RemoteApp program appears. After you have entered a folder name for one RemoteApp program, it is available in the drop-down list when you edit other RemoteApp programs. This makes it easier to organize the applications in consistent folder names.

The Parameters page has settings that control which command-line parameters can be passed to the application at startup. The options are as follows:

- **Do Not Allow Any Command-Line Parameters**   Prevents any command-line parameters from being used when starting the app. This is the default.

- **Allow Any Command-Line Parameters**   Allows users to pass command-line parameters to the RemoteApp program by using a custom RDP file. This isn't recommended because it may be a security risk.

- **Always Use The Following Command-Line Parameters**   Allows administrators to set command-line parameters that are used each time the RemoteApp program is started. Use this when an app requires command-line parameters to function properly.

The User Assignment page, shown in Figure 9-6, allows you to control which users have access
to the RemoteApp program. By default, all users and groups that have access to the collection
have access to a RemoteApp program in that collection. If you choose to give specific users
and groups access to the RemoteApp program, then the allowed users must be given access
to the collection and the RemoteApp program.

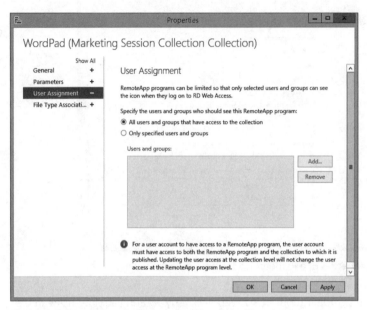

Figure 9-6 Properties of a RemoteApp program, User Assignment page

The File Type Associations page, shown in Figure 9-7, is used to define file associations that
can be configured for the RemoteApp program. If you select a file type here, then clients with
access to this RemoteApp program automatically launch the RemoteApp program when they
double-click a file with that extension. For example, if the WordPad RemoteApp program is
associated with the .docx file type, then the WordPad RemoteApp program will be launched to
edit any .docx file that is opened. FTAs for RemoteApp programs only work when the client is
using RemoteApp and Desktop Connections, which integrates with the Windows clients.

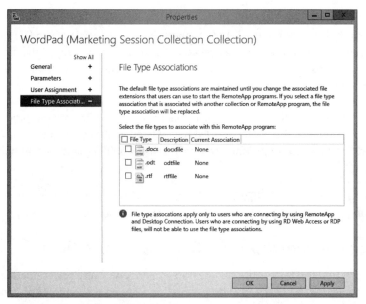

Figure 9-7   Properties of a RemoteApp program, File Type Associations page

Inside OUT

Windows PowerShell cmdlets for RemoteApp programs

As for other parts of RDS, there are Windows PowerShell cmdlets for creating and configuring RemoteApp programs. To get a list of Windows PowerShell cmdlets for RemoteApp programs, run the follow command:

```
Get-Command *RemoteApp* -Module RemoteDesktop
```

Configuring and managing client connections to RDS

Versions of RDS previous to Windows Server 2012 allowed you to create RDP files and .msi files that clients could use to initiate connectivity to session-based virtual desktops and RemoteApp programs. Starting with Windows Server 2012 R2, the two methods available for clients to initiate connections to RemoteApp programs are Desktop Connections and RD Web Access. Both of these methods obtain an RDP file from the RD Web Access server that provides the proper connection information to the RD Connection Broker and session collection.

NOTE

It technically is possible to use RDC to connect directly to a session-based virtual desktop on an RD Session Host, but a direct connection doesn't have any of the high availability or load balancing benefits of a full RDS deployment. A direct connection also is unable to use RemoteApp programs.

When users are connected to session-based virtual desktops and RemoteApp programs, it's important to configure device redirection. Device redirection allows session-based virtual desktops and RemoteApp programs to use local resources on the client, such as hard drives and printers.

You can manage connections to RD Session Hosts. One of the most useful options is shadowing. Shadowing allows you to see the user's session to help troubleshoot issues.

Configuring RemoteApp and Desktop Connections

RemoteApp and Desktop Connections is a feature in Windows 7 and newer operating systems. After you've configured RemoteApp and Desktop Connections, the RemoteApp programs available to the logged-on user are displayed in the Start screen in the Work Resources (RADC) section, shown in Figure 9-8. You can pin RDS resources to the Start screen, but not to the taskbar. You also can find RDS resources by searching on the Start screen. Integrating RemoteApp programs into the Start screen makes them more like traditional apps and consequently increases user satisfaction over accessing RemoteApp programs through RD Web Access.

Figure 9-8 Work Resources (RADC) in the Start screen

When RemoteApp and Desktop Connections are configured, users also can launch RemoteApp programs based on file type. This is called document invocation. A specific file extension is associated with the RemoteApp program, and when users open a file with that extension, the RemoteApp program is launched to open the file. This is similar to the way traditional apps function, and it also increases user satisfaction.

RD Web Access has a web feed available at *https://server/rdweb/webfeed.aspx.* RemoteApp and Desktop Connections uses the web feed as the source of data for displaying RemoteApps. Like RD Web Access, only the resources that you have permission to use are displayed.

NOTE

Each RD Web Access server is configured with a certificate to secure communication with clients. If clients do not trust the certificate, then RemoteApp and Desktop Connections fail when creating a connection.

In a domain-based environment, the simplest way to configure clients with the correct URL for the web feed is by using Group Policy. Configure the URL in the Specify Default Connection URL setting in User Configuration\Policies\Administrative Templates\Windows Components \Remote Desktop Services\RemoteApp and Desktop Connections.

For computers that aren't joined to a domain, you can configure the web feed URL manually for RemoteApp and Desktop Connections. You can supply the URL explicitly, or the configuration process can identify the URL based on the user's email address.

Identifying the web feed URL based on the user's email address is the simplest way for users to configure RemoteApp and Desktop Connections because they already know their email address. To support email-based discovery, you need to create a text (TXT) record in DNS named _msradc with a value of the URL for the web feed. For example, if the email address is adam@adatum.com and the server name for the web feed is rdweb.adatum.com, then you need to create the _msradc TXT record in the adatum.com domain with a value of *https://rdweb.adatum.com/RDWeb/Feed/webfeed.aspx.*

To configure RemoteApp and Desktop Connections manually on a client, perform the following steps:

1.   On the Start screen, type RemoteApp and then click Access RemoteApp And Desktops.

2.   In the Access RemoteApp And Desktops window, on the Enter Your Email Address Or Connection URL page, shown in Figure 9-9, in the Email Address Or Connection URL box, type the URL of the web feed or email address of the user and click Next.

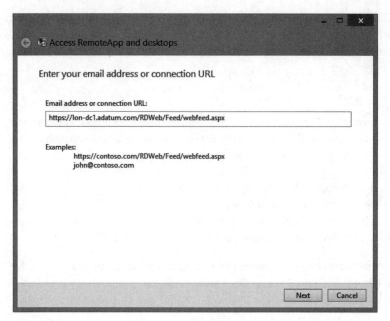

Figure 9-9 Access RemoteApp And Desktops Wizard, Enter Your Email Address Or Connection URL page

3. On the Ready To Set Up The Connection page, click Next.

4. In the Windows Security dialog box, enter your credentials and click OK. To avoid needing to enter the credentials again, select the Remember My Credentials check box.

5. On the You Have Successfully Set Up The Following Connection page, click Finish.

After you have configured a connection for RemoteApp and Desktop Connections, you can view or modify the connection in Control Panel, as shown in Figure 9-10. In this window, you can view the properties of the connection or remove it. After clicking the Properties button, you can check for updates by clicking the Update Now button.

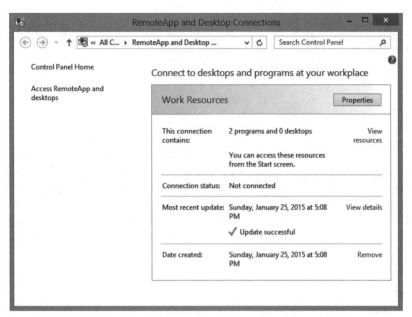

Figure 9-10 RemoteApp and Desktop Connections in Control Panel

CHAPTER 9

Inside OUT
Refreshing data for RemoteApp and Desktop Connections

When you configure RemoteApp and Desktop Connections, it collects the list of RemoteApp programs and desktops from the web feed. By default, this information is updated once a day by a scheduled task named User_Feed_Synchronization-{GUID}. If users are given access to a new RemoteApp program, they won't see it until this scheduled task runs. This also explains why the Connection Status often is Not Connected. A connection isn't created until the scheduled task is run.

In most cases, a daily update is sufficient because users typically don't need immediate access to new programs. If users do need immediate access to a new RemoteApp program, they can trigger an update from the properties of the connection from RemoteApp and Desktop Connections in Control Panel. You also can update the triggers for the scheduled task.

Customizing RD Web Access

RD Web Access automatically customizes the view of RemoteApp programs and virtual desktops based on which ones the user has permission to access. Access to these resources is configured in the properties of the RemoteApp programs and collections.

Another simple customization for RD Web Access is placing RemoteApp programs into folders. If many RemoteApp programs are available, this makes it easer for users to find specific RemoteApp programs. This is configured in the properties of the RemoteApp program.

Some organizations like to customize the look of the RD Web Access site to include their company logo or an access policy. The files for the RD Web Access site are located in C:\Windows\Web\RDWeb\Pages. The simplest modification you can make is replacing images with your own. If you make more complex modifications, you will need to fine-tune the layout of the pages. When you customize the RD Web Access pages, you need to make the same customizations on all RD Web Access servers.

> NOTE
> **When you apply updates to RD Web Access servers, it is possible that the pages you've modified will be overwritten by the update. Make sure you have a backup of the modifications you've made.**

There also are application settings for RD Web Access that you can configure in the Internet Information Services (IIS) Manager or the web.config file. You can modify the following settings:

- **PrivateModeSessionTimeoutInMinutes**   This value specifies the time after which a user has to retype his or her credentials if the user connects to the RD Web Access portal from a private computer. By default, this value is 240 minutes, which means that a user has to reauthenticate with the portal after 4 hours.

- **PublicModeSessionTimeoutInMinutes**   This value specifies the time after which a user has to retype his or her credentials if the user connects to an RD Web Access portal from a public or shared computer. By default, this value is 20 minutes.

- **PasswordChangeEnabled**   By default, this setting is set to false. If you enable it, users will be able to change their Active Directory Domain Services (AD DS) password on the RD Web Access portal, but only if their password has expired or if they must change their password at next sign-in. If neither of these prerequisites is met, users won't be able to change their password on the portal.

- **LocalHelp**   By default, this setting is set to false, which means that if a user clicks the Help link on the RD Web Access portal, he or she is directed to help information that is available on the Microsoft portal. If you set this value to true, local help information from an RD Web Access server will be used.

- **ShowDesktops**   By default, this setting is set to true, which adds a Connect To A Remote PC tab on the RD Web Access portal. On this tab, you can specify the computer to which you want to connect, remote desktop size, and device redirection settings. By using this tab, you can connect to any computer that has Remote Desktop enabled, not only to RDS resources. If you set the ShowDesktops setting to false, the Connect To A Remote PC tab is hidden from the RD Web Access portal.

- **xClipboard, xDriveRedirection, xPnPRedirection, xPortRedirection, xPrinterRedirection**   These settings control if the Clipboard, drives, supported Plug and Play (PnP) devices, serial ports, and printers redirect by default from your client computer to the remote session. By default, only Clipboard and local printers redirect. These settings apply when connecting to RDS resources and when initiating a connection from the Connect To A Remote PC tab, but you can modify them if needed.

To modify application setting for RD Web Access by using IIS Manager, perform the following steps:

1. In Server Manager, click Tools and click Internet Information Services (IIS) Manager.

2. In IIS Manager, in the navigation pane, expand the server, expand Sites, expand Default Web Site, expand RDWeb, and click Pages.

3. In the details pane, double-click Application Settings.

4. Right-click the setting you want to change and click Edit.

5. In the Edit Application Setting dialog box, in the Value box, enter the new value and then click OK.

6. Close IIS Manager.

NOTE

Changes to the Pages application take effect immediately. You don't need to restart the website. Users will see the changes if they refresh their browser.

Understanding device redirection

Device redirection is used to make resources from client devices available to a virtual desktop or RemoteApp programs. For example, device redirection can allow drive letters and printers in the client device to be accessible from within a virtual desktop or RemoteApp program. You can control which devices can be redirected from the properties of a collection, as shown in

CHAPTER 9

Figure 9-11. Allowing device redirection improves the user experience by simplifying the environment.

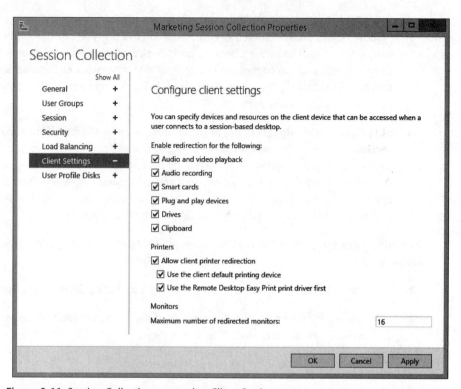

Figure 9-11 Session Collection properties, Client Settings page

Redirection can be enabled for the following:

- **Audio And Video Playback**   Enables audio generated by applications running in a remote session to be played on the local device.

- **Audio Recording**   Enables applications running in a remote session to use a microphone connected to the local device.

- **Smart Cards**   Enables applications running in a remote session to authenticate by using a smart card reader attached to the local device.

- **Plug and Play Devices**   Allows various PnP devices, typically USB, to be redirected and accessible to applications running in a remote session. For example, an application may require a USB key to be inserted to verify license compliance, or a video camera could be used for video conferencing. USB drives and USB printers aren't in this category.

- **Drives**   Allows access to local drive letters in the remote session. This allows users to save data to their local device. Some organizations disable this option because they consider it a security risk.

- **Clipboard**   Allows users to copy and paste data between the remote session and their local device. This is important to provide full integration with the Windows Desktop for RemoteApp programs. Some organizations disable this option because they consider it a security risk.

Inside OUT

PnP device redirection

PnP devices are redirected to the RD Session Host server when they are plugged in. The devices don't need to be plugged in when you start the session. For example, you can connect a USB video camera to a client device while the session is open. The USB video camera will be added to the session and accessible to applications.

Unlike some other redirection options, PnP device redirection isn't supported over multiple cascaded remote desktop connections. This typically isn't relevant for users, but it may be relevant for administrators who connect to a session-based virtual desktop and then, from that session-based virtual desktop, connect to other servers for remote administration.

Understanding printer redirection

When you connect to a virtual desktop or start a RemoteApp program, all local printers by default redirect to a remote session. This provides you with the same printer devices in the remote session as you can use locally. Printer redirection settings in a session collection are as follows:

- **Allow Client Printer Redirection**   Enables printers installed on the client device to be used in the remote session.

- **Use The Client Default Printing Device**   Configures the default printer in the session to be the same as the default printer configured on the client device. This makes printing in RemoteApp programs behave in the same way as in local applications.

- **Use The Remote Desktop Easy Print Print Driver First**   Specifies that the Remote Desktop Easy Print driver is preferred over device-specific printer drivers.

Before Remote Desktop Easy Print was available, to redirect printers you needed to install printer drivers on the RD Session Host server that matched the printer drivers installed on clients. The printer driver on the RD Session Host server would generate the print job, which would be passed to the printer on the client for printing. If the correct printer driver was not installed on the server, then the printer was not available in the remote session. Remote Desktop Easy Print was introduced in Windows Server 2008.

Another concern before Remote Desktop Easy Print was the size of the print jobs being transferred between the clients and RD Session Host servers. Because the print jobs were generated with printer-specific drivers, some of the print jobs were very large. This is because some inexpensive printers do most of the processing in Windows and send a large rendered file to the printer. Large print jobs would cause printing to be slow, and in some cases they would saturate WAN or Internet connections.

The Remote Desktop Easy Print driver provides two benefits:

- **Eliminates print driver management on RD Session Host servers**   The Remote Desktop Easy Print universal driver acts as a proxy and redirects all printing-related work to the client, even if the drivers for the local printer aren't available on the RD Session Host server. Remote Desktop Easy Print renders the print document in XPS format on the RD Session Host server and then transfers it to the client, where the local printer driver prints the document. Because an XPS document is platform-independent and you can print it on any platform, there are no cross-platform compatibility issues when using Remote Desktop Easy Print.

- **Reduces printing-related network traffic**   XPS-formatted print jobs generated by Remote Desktop Easy Print are smaller than many of the print jobs generated by printer-specific drivers. In some cases, the print job transferred between the RD Session Host and client device is reduced by over 90 percent.

NOTE

Remote Desktop Easy Print is supported by Remote Desktop Connection 6.1 and newer. This is available in Windows XP SP3 and newer.

Managing connections

When a user is connected to an RD Session Host server to access RemoteApp programs or a session-based virtual desktop, you can perform some simple management of the connection. When you are viewing a collection in Server Manager, the Connections area has a list of connections to the collection. By default, Server Manager updates this list every 10 minutes. Remember to refresh the list to get the current list of connections.

The management options for a connection are as follows:

- **Disconnect**   You can disconnect a user from a connection. Even if a session is in a disconnected state, it still runs, and the user can reconnect to the session later. By default, sessions that are in a disconnected state are never ended, but you can configure a time limit for such sessions.

- **Log Off**   You always can sign out of a remote session, but if a session is in a disconnected state, this is the only available option. Signing out closes all the applications that run in the remote session without saving changes, and it signs out the user. This removes the user session, and if a user initiates a connection again, a new connection will be established.

- **Send Message**   You can specify a message title and a message that is sent to the user who has an active remote session. A user can view only one message at a time and must acknowledge the message by clicking OK. If you send multiple messages to the same connection, the user receives the next message when he or she acknowledges the previous message.

- **Shadow**   You can enter into an active session and either view the session or take the control of it. When you select the Shadow option, by default, a user who is in the remote session is prompted for consent, which is a legal requirement in some environments. If the user refuses the request, you can't shadow that session. If you decide not to prompt for user consent, you can't use the Shadow option in a default RDS configuration. You must configure a Group Policy setting to be able to shadow a session without user consent. You should be aware that only administrators can shadow sessions. You can't delegate the ability to use the Shadow option to users who aren't members of the Administrators group.

CHAPTER 9

Inside OUT

Using Windows PowerShell to manage connections

You also can use Windows PowerShell to manage connections. The following cmdlets can be used:

- Get-RDUserSession
- Disconnect-RDUser
- Invoke-RDUserLogoff
- Send-RDUserMessage

There is no Windows PowerShell cmdlet to start shadowing a session, but you can use mstsc.exe with the SessionID option. The Get-RDUserSession cmdlet displays the sessionID.

Shadowing connections was available in RDS for Windows Server 2008 R2 but was not available in RDS for Windows Server 2012 R2. It has been added back in Windows Server 2012 R2.

➤ For more information about shadowing connections on Windows Server 2012 R2, see Windows 8.1/Windows Server 2012 R2 – RDS Shadowing is back! on TechNet at *http://go.microsoft.com/fwlink/?LinkID=510050.*

Configuring certificates and single sign-on

When you deploy RDS, each server in the deployment has a digital certificate that is used to implement Secure Sockets Layer (SSL) and prove its identity to clients. The default certificates are self-signed certificates that aren't trusted by clients. You need to change the certificates to certificates that are trusted by clients.

Inside OUT
Obtaining certificates

When you obtain a certificate from a public certification authority (CA), you need to pay the public CA for that service. The price of certificates varies widely depending on the public CA. Typical prices range from $20 to $400. Functionally, the certificates provide the same service, so there is no technical advantage to using more expensive certificates. The more expensive certificates may be considered more trustworthy by some clients and also may include insurance. A certificate obtained from a public CA is trusted automatically by all computers.

If your organization has an internal CA, the domain likely has been configured to automatically trust certificates issued by your internal CA. So, if all your clients are domain-joined computers, a certificate from an internal CA is a good choice. Now, however, many deployments of RDS include devices and external computers that aren't part of the domain and won't automatically trust a certificate from an internal CA. If your deployment of RDS might be accessed by anything but domain-joined computers, then you should get a certificate from a public CA.

When a client device accesses an RDS server, the domain name used to access the RDS server must match a name in the certificate. For example, if the domain name used to access the RD Connection Broker is broker.adatum.com, then the certificate on the RD Connection Broker servers needs to include that name. If the name isn't included on the certificate, then the connection isn't trusted and the behavior is the same as using a self-signed certificate.

You can use the following certificate types:

- **Server**   A standard server certificate has a single name. A multiserver RDS deployment will require multiple server certificates.

- **Wildcard**   A wildcard certificate allows any name in a domain. For example, *.adatum.com is valid for any name in the adatum.com domain. This type of certificate can be used on multiple servers. This can simplify certificate management.

- **Subject alternative names (SAN)**   A SAN certificate includes multiple names. You could create a SAN certificate that includes all of the names for your RDS deployment and manage only one certificate. A SAN certificate typically is less expensive than a wildcard certificate and can include names from multiple domains if required.

NOTE

A unified communications certificate (UCC) is the same thing as a SAN certificate. Different certificate vendors refer to it as either a UCC or SAN certificate.

Understanding RDS certificates

You can configure certificates for RDS deployments in Server Manager. You should not configure RDS-related certificates on individual servers, because you would need to configure them again after each change, for example, after replacing or adding a server. When you configure RDS certificates on the Manage Certificates page for the RDS deployment properties, RD Connection Broker will ensure that those certificates automatically propagate to the appropriate servers in the RDS deployment. It also will apply them after each configuration change.

There are four certificates used by RDS:

- RD Connection Broker – Publishing

- RD Connection Broker – Enable Single Sign On

- RD Web Access

- RD Gateway

RD Connection Broker - Publishing

This certificate is used when clients connect to the RD Connection Broker to be directed to an RD Session Host server. When you connect to RDS resources by using RD Web Access, the .rdp file that downloads from the portal includes the RD Connection Broker fully qualified domain name (FQDN) as a remote server. If you have configured the FQDN correctly in the

CHAPTER 9

RD Connection Broker – Publishing certificate, there is no security warning when you connect to the broker.

If you implement high availability for the RD Connection Broker role service, then a DNS round robin name is created. The certificate needs to include the DNS round robin name instead of individual server names.

The RD Connection Broker – Publishing certificate also is used for signing .rdp files that download from the RD Web Access portal. If the .rdp file isn't signed or is signed with an untrusted certificate, you need to review the connection settings and manually initiate the connection. If the .rdp file is signed, a connection automatically initiates.

NOTE

Even if RD Connection Broker is configured with a publishing certificate that clients trust, users will receive a prompt that the RemoteApp program could harm their computers. If you want to avoid prompts when starting a RemoteApp program, you need to specify trusted publishers. You can do that by configuring the Specify SHA1 Thumbprints Of Certificates Representing Trusted .rdp Publishers policy setting in Group Policy. This setting is in User Configuration\Policies\Administrative Templates\Windows Components\Remote Desktop Services\Remote Desktop Connection Client.

RD Connection Broker – Enable Single Sign On

When you initiate a remote desktop connection to an RD Session Host in a collection or start a RemoteApp program, you need to provide user credentials, even when you already have signed in with domain credentials. By configuring the RD Connection Broker – Enable Single Sign On certificate, a user's current credentials will be used for accessing the RDS resource, and the user won't have to reenter credentials. This certificate should have the RD Connection Broker FQDN in its common name. You can use the same certificate as for RD Connection Broker – Publishing.

RD Web Access

This certificate is used for the RD Web Access portal and RD Web Feed. If this certificate isn't trusted, users accessing the portal will be given a warning in their web browser. RemoteApp and Desktop Connections fails to connect to RD Web Feed if the certificate isn't trusted.

In an RDS deployment with only one RD Web Access server, the certificate should have the FQDN of the RD Web Access server. If you have configured RD Web Access for high availability, you should use the load-balanced name in the certificate.

RD Gateway

When clients access RDS resources from the Internet, the RD Gateway role service acts as an entry point to an organization's network, which encapsulates RDP traffic into HTTPS envelopes. By default, an RD Gateway server uses a self-signed SSL certificate. You should replace that certificate with a certificate from a trusted CA.

The certificate must use the common name that matches the FQDN that clients use to connect to the RD Gateway role service. For a highly available deployment of the RD Gateway role service, the load-balanced name should be used.

Requesting and configuring RDS certificates

In Server Manager for RDS, you can create self-signed certificates, but you can't create certificate requests. In a production environment, you typically use certificates issued by a public CA. To obtain a certificate from a public CA, you need to do the following:

1. Generate a certificate request with the correct name(s).

2. Provide the certificate request to the public CA.

3. Import the response from the public CA.

To generate a certificate request and import the response, you can use either of the following:

*   **IIS Manager**   You can use IIS Manager to create server or wildcard certificate requests. For a server certificate, enter the appropriate FQDN in the Common Name box. For a wildcard certificate, enter the appropriate wildcard name such as *.adatum.com in the Common Name box.

*   **Certificates snap-in**   You can use the Certificates snap-in in the Microsoft Management Console (MMC) to create server, wildcard, and SAN certificates. To ensure that you can define all of the necessary options, you can create a custom request.

After you have completed creating the certificate, you need to export it as a Personal Information Exchange – PKCS #12 (.pfx) file. This type of file includes the private key for the certificate. The .pfx file is imported when you configure certificates for RDS.

CHAPTER 9

COMMON MISTAKES CREATING CERTIFICATES

When you generate a certificate request, you need to configure a key size for the request. Many of the user interfaces default 1,024 bits, but public CAs now require the key size to be a minimum of 2,048 bits to increase security of the certificate. If you have created a certificate request with a key size that is less than 2,048 bits, just re-create the request with the correct key size.

Another common mistake is creating a certificate for which the private key can't be exported. You need to be able to export the private key to a .pfx file. When you are creating a custom request in the Certificates snap-in, this option is located on the Private Key tab in the properties of the certificate, as shown in Figure 9-12.

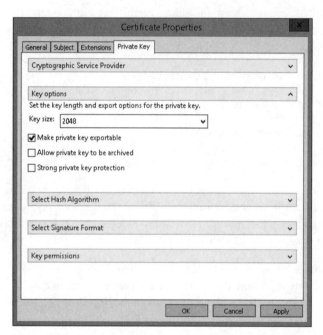

Figure 9-12 Custom certificate request, Private Key information

You configure certificates for an RDS deployment in the Deployment Properties on the Manage Certificates page, shown in Figure 9-13. For each type of certificate, you can choose Create New Certificate or Select Existing Certificate. If you choose Create New Certificate, a new self-signed certificate is created. For most deployments, you should choose Select Existing Certificate.

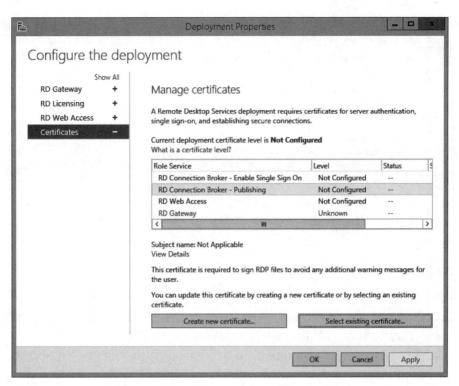

Figure 9-13 RDS Deployment Properties, Manage Certificates page

When you choose Select Existing Certificate, you are prompted for the location of the certificate, as shown in Figure 9-14. If you have a .pfx to import, select the Choose A Different Certificate option and enter the path to the .pfx file and the password for it.

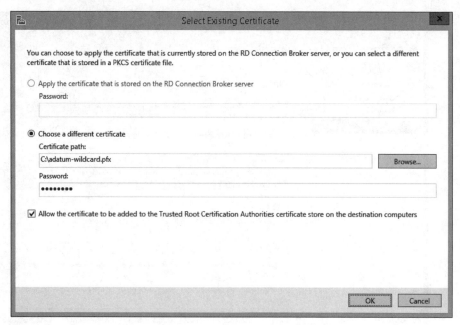

Figure 9-14 Select Existing Certificate dialog box

You must select the Allow The Certificate To Be Added To The Trusted Root Certification Authorities Certificate Store On The Destination Computers check box when adding a certificate. Selecting this option verifies that you understand the certificate will be copied to all servers performing that role. It doesn't mean that the certificate is configured as a trusted root certificate on the servers.

The Apply The Certificate That Is Stored On The RD Connection Broker Server option allows you to copy the certificate from the RD Connection Broker role service to other role services. This is appropriate when another role service such as the RD Web Access role is on the same server as the RD Connection Broker role service. This also is appropriate when you have a wildcard or SAN certificate that you have prepared for use on multiple RDS role services.

After importing and applying certificates, the Level and Status for the role services on the Manage Certificates page of the Deployment Properties will update. The Level is updated to Trusted and the Status is updated to OK.

Understanding single sign-on

SSO for RDS allows users to access RemoteApp programs and virtual desktops without authen-ticating a second time. Instead, the credentials from the local workstation are passed to the

RD Connection Broker role service. You typically use SSO when you deploy LOB applications or centralized applications and publish them as RemoteApp programs.

Before configuring SSO for an RDS deployment, you should be aware of the following requirements:

- The client computer and RDS deployment must be members of the same AD DS forest.

- If the server to which you are connecting can't authenticate via the Kerberos protocol or with an SSL certificate, SSO won't work.

- If the RD Session Host is configured to always prompt for credentials, SSO won't work.

The process for enabling SSO differs depending on how clients access RemoteApp programs and virtual desktops. If the client is using the RD Web Access portal, then you need to configure the RD Connection Broker – Single Sign On certificate. As long as clients trust that certificate, they aren't prompted for credentials after clicking an icon in the RD Web Access portal.

For clients that are using RemoteApp and Desktop Connections, you need to configure the Allow Delegating Default Credentials setting. This setting can be configured locally on each computer, but it typically is done by using Group Policy. The path for the setting is Computer Configuration\Policies\Administrative Templates\System\Credentials Delegation.

After you have enabled this setting, you need to add the RD Connection Broker role service FQDN as a server in the following format:

TERMSERV/*RDConnectionBrokerFQDN*

> **NOTE**
>
> It's possible to use wildcards when specifying the FQDN for the Allow Delegating Default Credentials setting. For example, you could enter TERMSERV/*.adatum.com. Be aware that this would allow credential delegation to all computers in the domain and may be a security risk.

CHAPTER 9

Planning and implementing pooled and personal virtual desktops

You can implement virtual machine (VM)–based desktops by using pooled and personal virtual desktops. The type of VM-based desktops you select is determined primarily by the needs of your users. For example, do your users need to install their own applications? The type of VM-based desktops also is influenced by how you want to maintain the virtual desktops.

An important part of planning pooled and personal virtual desktops is designing the configuration of virtual desktop templates that are used as the source for creating the VM-based virtual desktops. The virtual desktop templates are VMs that have been optimized for use as VM-based virtual desktops. You can perform optimizations to reduce the resources that each VM-based virtual desktop consumes.

To ensure that there is adequate performance for pooled and personal virtual desktops, you need to plan the implementation of Remote Desktop Virtualization Host (RD Virtualization Host) servers. This includes identifying the number of RD Virtualization Host servers and their hardware configuration, including storage for the VMs.

After planning is complete, you can deploy Remote Desktop Services (RDS) for pooled and personal virtual desktops. The deployment process is similar to the process used for session-based virtual desktops.

Understanding pooled and personal virtual desktops

Pooled and personal virtual desktops are based on VMs that run on a Hyper-V server. Unlike session-based virtual desktops, where users share resources on a single server, VM-based virtual desktops enable you to allocate specific resources to individual VMs. To ensure that you select and implement an appropriate solution, you need to understand the characteristics of pooled and personal virtual desktops. You also need to understand how to provide high availability for pooled and personal virtual desktops.

In a development or test environment, you often can meet your VM requirements by manually creating a few VMs and hosting them on a Hyper-V server or by using Client Hyper-V on a desktop computer. This type of solution isn't suitable for VM-based virtual desktops where you need to create many VMs to support users. You also need a method for connecting users to the appropriate VM.

When you implement VM-based virtual desktops, you implement many of the same server roles as when you implement session-based virtual desktops. The main difference is that, in VM-based virtual desktops, users are connected to a VM hosted on the RD Virtualization Host server instead of a session hosted on a Remote Desktop Session Host (RD Session Host) server. The resources of a VM are dedicated to the user of that VM, whereas the resources of an RD Session Host server are shared among multiple users.

Figure 10-1 illustrates the roles services used by the communication process for VM-based virtual desktops, as follows:

1. **Remote Desktop Web Access**   Clients connect to the Remote Desktop Web Access (RD Web Access) server first. The RD Web Access role service provides an .rdp file to the client that contains the configuration information necessary for the client to connect to the Remote Desktop Connection Broker (RD Connection Broker) role service.

2. **Remote Desktop Connection Broker**   Clients connect to the RD Connection Broker role service and are directed to an appropriate VM to which they have been granted access.

3. **Remote Desktop Virtualization Host**   Clients connect to VMs hosted on the RD Virtualization Host server. The RD Virtualization Host server has the Hyper-V server role installed.

If your organization provides external access to the VMs, you typically use the Remote Desktop Gateway (RD Gateway) role service to control access. The RD Gateway role service acts as a reverse proxy and allows all access to be tunneled in HTTPS packets that normally are allowed through firewalls from public locations such as hotels. It also authenticates access requests before allowing access to virtual desktops on the internal network.

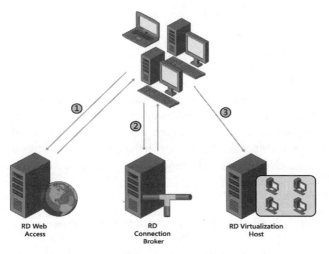

Figure 10-1 Communication process for a virtual desktop connection

Using pooled virtual desktops

Pooled virtual desktops are a type of VM-based virtual desktop where users connect to a pool of identically configured VMs. Each VM has identical resources and operating system configuration. If applications are installed in the VM, all pooled virtual desktops have those applications.

The VMs for pooled virtual desktops are not assigned to a specific user. Any user could be connected to any pooled virtual desktop that is available. The pooled virtual desktop for a specific user is selected by the RD Connection Broker role service during the connection process.

User state information is not retained when users log off from a pooled virtual desktop. When users log off from a pooled virtual desktop, the pooled virtual desktop reverts to the state in which it was before the user logged on. Any information stored on the pooled virtual desktop is removed.

The starting state for a pooled virtual desktop is defined from a virtual desktop template that you prepare and create. The virtual desktop template is a VM that you have installed and configured. The pooled virtual desktops have differential disks that use the virtual desktop template as a base. All changes to the hard disk of the pooled virtual desktop are stored in the differential disk. When the user logs off, the differential disk is removed.

CHAPTER 10

Using personal virtual desktops

Personal virtual desktops are a type of VM-based virtual desktop where users connect to a VM assigned to them. Unlike pooled virtual desktops, personal virtual desktops are not shared among multiple users. Each personal virtual desktop is dedicated to one user.

One of the main reasons to implement personal virtual desktops is to support user customization of the virtual desktop. A personal virtual desktop retains all changes when the user logs off. This allows personal virtual desktops to be customized with additional applications and user state information. If you want to provide users with the ability to install their own applications, you should give the users administrative permissions on their personal virtual desktop.

You can create personal virtual desktops in two ways:

- **Based on a virtual desktop template** When you create personal virtual desktops based on a virtual desktop template, all personal virtual desktops have an identical starting configuration. This method enables you to create many personal virtual desktops quickly for deployment, in much the same way as you would use imaging for operating system deployment on physical computers.

- **From an existing VM** When you create a personal virtual desktop from a specific VM, the VM is converted to a personal virtual desktop. This approach can be useful when you have existing VMs that you want to convert to personal virtual desktops.

Comparing virtual desktop options

Choosing the right type of virtual desktops for your users is essential because it ensures that you meet their needs in a cost-effective way. Table 10-1 compares the different types of virtual desktops in the areas of personalization, application compatibility, ease of management, and cost-effectiveness.

Table 10-1 Comparing types of virtual desktops

Characteristic	Session	Pooled	Personal
Personalization	Good	Good	Best
Application compatibility	Good	Best	Best
Ease of management	Best	Good	OK
Cost-effectiveness	Best	Good	OK

Personalization

The best option for personalization is personal virtual desktops. With personal virtual desktops, you can give users permissions to completely customize their personal virtual desktop, including applications. This option can be useful when users have unique application needs.

Pooled virtual desktops and session-based virtual desktops provide personalization options through other methods. You can implement user state virtualization to make user state persistent. To provide access to unique applications, you can use Microsoft Application Virtualization (App-V) or RemoteApp.

Application compatibility

Pooled and personal virtual desktops provide the best application compatibility. The majority of applications that can be installed on a desktop computer can be used on pooled and personal virtual desktops. The majority of applications can be installed for session-based desktops, but some end-user applications don't run properly on an RD Session Host because it uses a server operating system.

Ease of management

The ease of management for virtual desktop solutions depends on the amount of standardization. You can manage a few virtual desktop templates more easily than a large number of virtual desktop templates. Session-based virtual desktops have the best ease of management because you're updating applications and the operating system only on the RD Session Host server. Pooled virtual desktops also have good ease of management because you're updating only the desktop virtual template. Personal virtual desktops are managed by providing updates to each VM.

Cost-effectiveness

The cost to implement a virtual desktop solution is based on the resources required to support a specific number of users. Session-based virtual desktops are the most cost-effective because they have a much higher user density per server than VM-based virtual desktops. Pooled virtual desktops are more cost-effective than personal virtual desktops because they use much less storage. Pooled virtual desktops use less storage because they use a base image and differencing drive that is cleared when users log off. Personal virtual desktops can be customized, and the size of the disk for the personal virtual desktops grows over time as applications and updates are installed.

High availability for pooled virtual desktops

In a standard computing environment, each person has one desktop computer. An outage for that computer affects only the one user. When you implement virtual desktops, the infrastructure for virtual desktops provides an essential service for hundreds or thousands of users. If the virtual desktop infrastructure fails, the cost to your organization is very high due to the large number of users affected.

The process for providing highly available pooled virtual desktops is similar to the process for providing highly available session-based desktops. Each server role needs to be redundant, and there are multiple RD Virtualization Host servers. Table 10-2 shows how each server role is made highly available.

Table 10-2 High availability for server roles

Server Role	High Availability Method
RD Connection Broker	DNS round-robin and Microsoft SQL Server configured to store RD Connection Broker configuration
RD Web Access	Load balancing
RD Virtualization Host	Multiple RD Virtualization Hosts

When you configure high availability for pooled virtual desktops, individual VMs are not highly available, but the entire infrastructure is. When an RD Session Broker or RD Web Access fails, the failure doesn't affect users currently logged on to pooled virtual desktops. If the RD Virtualization Host server fails, all pooled virtual desktops currently running on that server fail, and users are disconnected.

When users reconnect, the RD Session Broker connects them to a pooled virtual desktop running on a different RD Virtualization Host server that is still functional. Any application data that wasn't saved before the failure is lost. All state information from the previous pooled virtual desktop is lost unless some type of user state virtualization has been implemented. Functionally, this is similar to the process when a user logs off from a pooled virtual desktop and then logs on again.

High availability for personal virtual desktops

Unlike pooled virtual desktops, which are interchangeable, personal virtual desktops are unique. You need to make individual VMs highly available for personal virtual desktops. To make VMs highly available, you need to configure RD Virtualization Host servers as nodes in a failover cluster. You also need to configure shared storage that is accessible to all nodes in the failover cluster.

Failover clustering is a feature in Windows Server 2012 R2 that provides high availability for services. You can use failover clustering to allow personal virtual desktops to be moved among RD Virtualization Host servers.

NOTE

Starting with Windows Server 2012, failover clustering is available in both the Standard and Datacenter editions of Windows Server. Earlier versions of Windows Server require the Enterprise or Datacenter editions to implement failover clustering.

If the movement of a personal virtual desktop to another node is unplanned due to the failure of an RD Virtualization Host server, the user is disconnected from the personal virtual desktop and must wait for the personal virtual desktop to be restarted on another node. If there was any unsaved work in progress at the time of the failure, that work is lost. This process is similar to what happens when a standard desktop computer loses power and is restarted.

If the movement of a personal virtual desktop between nodes in a failover cluster is planned, you can use Live Migration to move the personal virtual desktop. When you use Live Migration, the personal virtual desktop continues running while it's moved. A user is unaware that a Live Migration has been performed and continues working without interruption. You can use Live Migration to move VMs to other RD Virtualization Host servers before performing maintenance.

Live Migration uses the following process to move VMs without downtime:

1. **Live Migration setup**   During the initial setup of Live Migration, the source node connects to the destination node and transfers configuration information for the VM to the destination node. This enables the destination node to create a VM that is ready for content from the source node.

2. **Memory page transfer**   This stage copies the memory contents from the active VM on the source node to the destination node. During the copy process, any memory pages on the source VM that are modified are marked for later transfer.

3. **Modified memory page transfer**   Memory pages that were modified during the previous stage are transferred now. During this stage, memory in the source VM can't be modified. It's critical that there is high-speed network connectivity between the source and destination nodes to minimize outages. Once modified memory page transfer has started, you can't cancel the Live Migration.

4. **Storage movement**   After all memory contents for the VM are copied to the destination, the storage for the VM is transferred to the destination node. The virtual hard disks associated with the VM are connected on the destination node.

5. **VM startup**   At this point, the migrated VM on the destination node is started. Because the memory information was transferred while the VM was running, the VM state is the same now as before migration. The only difference is the node on which the VM is hosted.

6. **Network cleanup** The running VM now communicates on the network and forces the network switches to identify the new location of the VM. This allows network communication formerly being sent to the switch port of the source node to be directed to the new switch port to which the destination node is connected.

A personal virtual desktop is made available to all nodes in the failover cluster by placing it on storage that can be accessed by all nodes. This allows all nodes in the failover cluster to use the virtual disk and configuration files required to start the personal virtual desktop. Traditionally, shared storage for a failover cluster was as follows:

- Shared serial attached SCSI (SAS)

- Internet SCSI (iSCSI) storage area network (SAN)

- Fibre Channel SAN

In these traditional configurations, the shared storage normally is configured as a cluster shared volume (CSV). You can store multiple VMs on a single CSV because multiple nodes can access a CSV at the same time. Individual files are locked by a node when they are in use to ensure that files are not corrupted by two nodes accessing a file at the same time.

You also can use a file share as storage for Hyper-V VMs, which is less complex to implement than traditional shared storage. This is possible due to performance improvements in the Server Message Block (SMB) protocol version 3.0. SMB 3.0 was introduced in Windows Server 2012. You can make file shares highly available in Windows Server 2012 R2 by creating a Scale-Out File Server.

Inside OUT

Selecting shared storage for a failover cluster

Failover clustering can use several types of shared storage. With proper configuration, any of the shared storage options can meet your performance requirements. So, the correct type of shared storage is based on other factors such as the following:

- **How many RD Virtualization Host servers will be in the failover cluster?** Shared SAS has limited scalability because it requires each RD Virtualization Host server to be connected physically to the shared SAS bus. In most cases, this limits you to a maximum of four RD Virtualization Host servers.

- **What type of experience does your organization have with shared storage?** In general, Fibre Channel is the most complex type of shared storage to implement and is used primarily when your organization already is experienced in its use. Shared SAS, iSCSI, and Scale-Out File Server tend to be easier to configure.

> ● **Do you have dedicated staff for shared storage?**   If you don't have staff who are skilled in managing shared storage, you should consider using Scale-Out File Server. Scale-Out File Server is a failover cluster for file sharing. The back-end storage for that failover cluster is shared SAS, which often is simpler to deploy than SAN-based storage. All software configuration is done within Windows Server 2012 R2. This enables server administrators to manage the entire solution.

Networking

A failover cluster typically is configured with multiple networks. Each node in the failover cluster has access to all the networks. Table 10-3 lists common networks used when personal virtual desktops are made highly available by using a failover cluster.

Table 10-3 Common networks for a failover cluster

Network	Description
Management network	Used by administrators to connect to the failover cluster nodes to perform management actions
Virtual machine network	Used by clients to connect to the personal virtual desktops
Heartbeat network	Used by nodes to communicate with one another and identify when other nodes have failed
Storage network	Used by the cluster nodes to communicate with the shared storage

Planning and creating virtual desktop templates

A virtual desktop template is the base VM that is copied to create pooled and personal virtual desktops. At the most basic level, all you need is a VM with a desktop operating system that is configured to meet the needs of your users.

To create a virtual desktop template, perform the following steps:

1. Create a VM on a Hyper-V server.

2. Install the selected operating system in the VM.

3. Install selected applications in the VM.

4. Optimize application configuration for virtual desktops.

CHAPTER 10

5. Optimize operating system configuration for virtual desktops.

6. Run the System Preparation (Sysprep) tool to prepare the operating system.

After the virtual desktop template is configured, you can create a virtual desktop collection for the pooled or personal virtual desktops. The Create Collection Wizard requests the virtual desktop template and takes a copy of the VM you configured when the virtual desktops are created.

Selecting an operating system

The only Windows client operating systems that you can use with pooled and personal virtual desktops are the Enterprise editions of Windows 8.1, Windows 8, and Windows 7. Other Windows client operating systems are not supported.

The Enterprise editions of the supported operating systems provide features not available in the Pro or Professional editions. Table 10-4 shows the additional virtualization features supported by Windows 8.1 Enterprise, Windows 8 Enterprise, and Windows 7 Enterprise with RDP 8.0 installed. Note that the only difference is supported features for RemoteFX.

Table 10-4 Virtualization features

Feature	Description
RemoteApp	VM-based virtual desktops can be a host for applications that are provided to other computers by using RemoteApp. For example, if a user has a standard desktop computer with an operating system and applications installed, a pooled or personal virtual desktop using Windows 8.1 Enterprise can provide an installed application to the standard desktop by using RemoteApp. This can be useful when the application can't be installed on an RD Session Host or is required by only a few users.
RemoteFX Multi-Touch	Windows 8.1 Enterprise and Windows 8 Enterprise support the use of touch-enabled devices. This is important if you use touch-enabled devices such as tablets to access the personal and pooled virtual desktops. Windows 7 Enterprise doesn't support RemoteFX Multi-Touch.
RemoteFX USB Redirection	VM-based virtual desktops support redirection of USB devices from the local client to the pooled or personal virtual desktop. This allows various local USB devices such as printers, scanners, and audio devices to be used by the pooled or personal virtual desktop.

RemoteFX virtual graphics processing unit (vGPU)	The vGPU feature in VM-based virtual desktops enhances graphics processing in the VMs. For performance reasons, some applications require a graphics processing unit (GPU) to be present to run. The vGPU feature can provide the pooled and personal virtual desktops with a method to access a physical GPU in the RD Virtualization Host server.
User profile disk	You can use a user profile disk with VM-based virtual desktops to implement user state virtualization. This is useful for pooled virtual desktops where changes are not retained between sessions.

Windows 8.1 Enterprise, Windows 8 Enterprise, and Windows 7 Enterprise are available in 32-bit and 64-bit versions. Unless you have a specific reason for using a 32-bit operating system, you should use a 64-bit operating system. This ensures that you can support newer 64-bit applications as they become available.

The following are the main differences between 32-bit and 64-bit client operating systems:

- **Memory support**   A 32-bit operating system supports a maximum of 4 gigabytes (GB) of RAM. If you require more than 4 GB of RAM for application performance, you should use a 64-bit Windows client.

- **Resource utilization**   The memory usage for 32-bit and 64-bit operating systems is about the same. However, storage utilization for a 32-bit version of Windows 8.1 is approximately 6.5 GB, whereas storage utilization for the 64-bit version of Windows 8.1 is approximately 8.5 GB. When you're creating hundreds or thousands of pooled and personal virtual desktops, 2 GB per desktop can be significant. This can be mitigated if deduplication is enabled where the VMs are stored.

- **Application compatibility**   A 64-bit operating system can run 32-bit and 64-bit applications. If you currently are using or anticipate using 64-bit applications, you need to use a 64-bit Windows client. If you have older 16-bit applications, you must use a 32-bit operating system because 16-bit applications are not supported in 64-bit operating systems.

Activating the operating system

When you create a virtual desktop template with Windows 8.1, you need to consider how Windows 8.1 is activated. The operating system in the pooled or personal virtual desktops is activated after the pooled or personal virtual desktops are deployed. It isn't practical to enter product keys manually and perform activation after deploying pooled and personal virtual desktops. So, you must automate the activation process.

CHAPTER 10

Volume licensed versions of Windows 8.1 include a generic volume license key (GVLK). A GVLK instructs Windows 8.1 to look for an automated method of activation for volume licensing. For pooled and personal virtual desktops, you can use Active Directory–based activation or Key Management Service (KMS).

Inside OUT

Installing a generic volume license key (GVLK)

When you install Windows 8.1 from volume-licensed media, it automatically has a GVLK installed. If you accidentally make your virtual desktop template from retail media or you previously installed a Multiple Activation Key (MAK), you can install a GVLK manually in the virtual desktop template by performing the following steps:

1. Open a command prompt with administrative permissions.

2. Type slmgr /ipk *key*, where *key* is the GVLK for your operating system.

Microsoft provides a public list of GVLKs that you can use. You can access the list of GVLKs for Windows operating systems at *http://technet.microsoft.com/en-us/library/jj612867.aspx*.

Active Directory–based activation stores all of the necessary activation information for pooled and personal virtual desktops in Active Directory Domain Services (AD DS). When the unactivated pooled or personal virtual desktops join the domain, they read the activation object in AD DS and activate.

To configure Active Directory–based activation for an Active Directory forest, complete the following steps:

1. On a computer running Windows Server 2012 or Windows Server 2012 R2, install the Volume Activation Services server role.

2. Open Volume Activation Tools and select Active Directory–Based Activation in the Volume Activation Tools installation wizard.

3. Enter the KMS host key. This is the volume license key that you have purchased.

4. Activate the key. Typically this is done online, but it also can be done by phone.

5. Close the Volume Activation Tools installation wizard.

NOTE

Windows 8.1 and Windows 8 are the only Windows client operating systems capable of performing Active Directory–based activation. You also can activate Microsoft Office 2013 by using Active Directory–based activation.

Many organizations already have implemented KMS to support the activation of Microsoft Office 2010 or Windows 7. If you already have implemented KMS, you may prefer to continue using KMS rather than starting to use Active Directory–based activation for Windows 8.1 and Windows 8.

When you install KMS on a computer, a service is installed on that computer that can be used to activate software. Similar to Active Directory–based activation, you enter a KMS host key into KMS to make the licenses available for clients to activate. Client computers use DNS to identify the location of the KMS service. Most organizations use dynamic DNS, in which case, the KMS service creates a service resource record (SRV record) in DNS to advertise its location. If Dynamic DNS is not being used then you need to manually create the necessary SRV record. The KMS service listens on port 1688.

➤ **For more information about implementing KMS, see KMS Activation on the TechNet website at *https://technet.microsoft.com/en-us/library/ff793419.aspx*.**

Inside OUT

Comparing Active Directory–based activation and KMS

Active Directory–based activation automatically is highly available if you have multiple domain controllers. To make KMS highly available, you need to install two KMS servers. By default, clients will load balance between the two available KMS servers and, if one is unavailable, clients will use the other.

One critical consideration for KMS is the minimum activation threshold. KMS won't activate client computers until a minimum of 25 computers have contacted the KMS. This can be important for small virtual desktop deployments and pilot projects in which a small number of pooled and personal virtual desktops have been deployed. In contrast, Active Directory–based activation doesn't have minimum activation thresholds.

For both Active Directory–based activation and KMS activation, the client must be a domain member. In addition, clients must reactivate every 180 days. As long as clients are connected to the domain network, reactivation occurs automatically.

Table 10-5 Active Directory–based activation and KMS comparison

Characteristic	Active Directory–based authentication	KMS
Requires a KMS host key	Yes	Yes
Stores activation information in AD DS	Yes	No
Installs a service that clients use for activation	No	Yes
Automatically highly available	Yes	No
Has a minimum activation threshold	No	Yes
Clients must reactivate every 180 days	Yes	Yes

Updating applications and the operating system

When you plan the deployment of pooled and personal virtual desktops, you need to consider how applications will be installed and updated in the VMs. Pooled and personal virtual desktops have unique characteristics that require application installation and updates to be managed differently.

Updating pooled virtual desktops

Pooled virtual desktops have unique application installation and application update issues because they don't retain changes between logons. Application and operating system updates delivered by a solution such as Windows Server Update Services (WSUS) or System Center 2012 R2 Configuration Manager would be lost at each logoff. Consequently, those tools shouldn't be used. If applications include their own automatic update function, it should be disabled.

To deploy application and operating system updates to a pooled virtual desktop, you modify the pooled virtual desktop and update it. If you include many applications in the virtual desktop template for the pooled virtual desktops, you will need to update the pooled virtual desktops many times. Avoid this approach because it becomes a significant management burden. As an alternative, consider using App-V to deploy applications to pooled virtual desktops. App-V deploys applications quickly and can be customized for each user.

Updating personal virtual desktops

Application and operating system updates for personal virtual desktops are managed similarly to updates for standard desktop computers because they retain state the same way. Updates installed on a personal virtual desktop are retained between logons. This means that you can use standard application updating methods such as WSUS and Configuration Manager for personal virtual desktops. You also can use application deployment tools such as Configuration Manager to deploy applications to personal virtual desktops.

You are more likely to include applications in the virtual desktop template for personal virtual desktops than for pooled virtual desktops. This is because you can deploy updates to the applications without redeploying the personal virtual desktops. App-V is still a good choice for application deployment on personal virtual desktops, just as it is for standard desktop computers.

Eliminating the system partition

In a default installation of Windows 8.1, a 350-megabyte (MB) system partition is created. When Windows 8.1 starts, it begins loading from this system partition and then loads the remainder of the operating system from the boot partition (C drive). Having a separate system partition is required to implement BitLocker Drive Encryption.

BitLocker Drive Encryption is most commonly used to secure disk contents for mobile computers that are more likely than desktop computers to be lost or stolen. Because virtual desktops are stored in a data center, there seldom is a need to encrypt the disks. In addition, the best user experience for BitLocker Drive Encryption requires a Trusted Platform Module (TPM) to store encryption keys. Hyper-V has no method to provide a virtual TPM to virtual desktops.

A 350 MB system partition is mostly wasted disk space for VM-based virtual desktops. Depending on the volume of virtual desktops you implement, this can end up being a significant amount of disk space and should be eliminated.

The process to eliminate the system partition from the operating system installation varies depending on the deployment method:

- **Microsoft Deployment Toolkit 2013**   The Microsoft Deployment Toolkit (MDT) 2013 is a free tool provided by Microsoft to automate the installation of Windows operating systems. You can use it to automate the deployment of Windows 8.1 in a VM that you are using as the virtual desktop template. One of the configuration files MDT uses during operating system deployment is customsettings.ini. To prevent the operating system from creating a separate system partition, configure customsettings.ini to include DoNotCreateExtraPartition=Yes.

  ➤ For more information about MDT, see Microsoft Deployment Toolkit on the TechNet website at *https://technet.microsoft.com/en-US/windows/dn475741.aspx*.

- **Windows System Image Manager**   The Windows Assessment and Deployment Kit (Windows ADK) includes Windows System Image Manager (Windows SIM). You can use Windows SIM to create answer files for unattended installations of Windows operating systems. In the answer file, you can include instructions about how to configure disk partitions.

➤ For more information about Windows SIM and automated installation of Windows 8.1, see Windows Deployment Tools Technical Reference on the TechNet website at *https://technet.microsoft.com/en-us/library/hh825039.aspx.*

● **Manual installation**   When you perform a manual installation from Windows 8.1 installation media, you can configure the partitions during installation. You can do this by using diskpart at a command prompt or in the graphical interface. In both cases, you create a single large partition that uses the whole disk to prevent the Windows 8.1 installation from creating a system partition.

Inside OUT

Creating partitions during a manual installation

During a manual installation of Windows 8.1, you can open a command prompt by pressing Shift+F10 on the Windows Setup Screen that requests the language and keyboard settings. From this command prompt, you can use diskpart to create a single partition for installation manually by using the following commands:

```
Diskpart

Select disk 0

Create partition primary

Active

Exit
```

You can modify the disk partitions by using the graphical interface during a manual installation of Windows 8.1. The process isn't intuitive, but you can force the creation of a single large partition for installation by doing the following:

1.   On the Where Do You Want To Install Windows screen, click New and click Apply.

2.   Click OK to acknowledge the warning that Windows will create additional partitions, as shown in Figure 10-2.

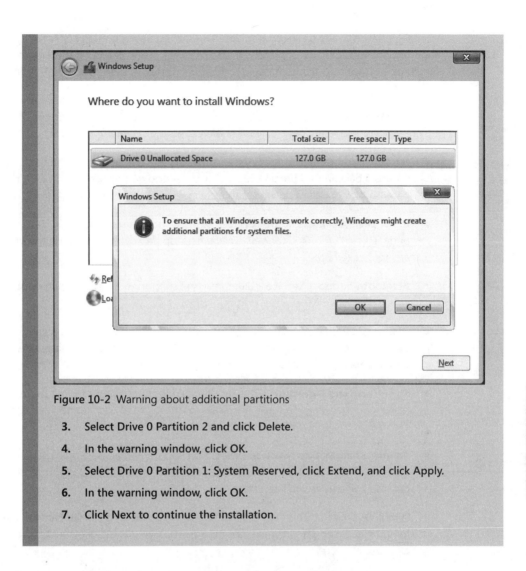

Figure 10-2 Warning about additional partitions

3.   Select Drive 0 Partition 2 and click Delete.

4.   In the warning window, click OK.

5.   Select Drive 0 Partition 1: System Reserved, click Extend, and click Apply.

6.   In the warning window, click OK.

7.   Click Next to continue the installation.

CHAPTER 10

Optimizing operating system configuration

It's important to optimize the configuration of virtual desktop templates to limit the resources used for each virtual desktop. When there are hundreds or thousands of virtual desktops, even minor optimizations can create significant resource savings on the RD Virtualization Host servers. For example, if an unnecessary service in Windows 8.1 uses 100 MB of memory on an RD Virtualization Host server with 50 virtual desktops, this equates to 5 GB of memory usage on the RD Virtualization Host server. Disabling that service in the virtual desktop template may allow you to run more VMs on the RD Virtualization Host server.

You can optimize virtual desktop templates by disabling any operating system or application functionality that increases resource load. When you start the optimization process, you should look for ways to reduce memory utilization, processor utilization, disk I/O, and storage utilization.

Many Windows 8.1 services aren't required in most virtual desktop deployments. The following are some of these services that you should consider disabling:

- **Background Intelligent Transfer Service (BITS)**   This service is used to download data as a background process. Most virtual desktop deployments don't require this because they have fast network connectivity.

- **Block-Level Backup Engine Services**   This service is used to back up data on the computer. This isn't required for most virtual desktop deployments because the VMs typically are not backed up.

- **Bluetooth Support Service**   Bluetooth isn't supported for pooled and personal virtual desktops.

- **Diagnostic Policy Service**   This service is used for problem detection and resolution, which isn't necessary for most virtual desktop deployments. If necessary, it can be enabled manually for troubleshooting.

- **Shell Hardware Detection**   This service provides notifications for hardware events that trigger AutoPlay. This isn't necessary for most virtual desktop deployments because events that trigger AutoPlay, such as inserting a DVD, typically are not performed.

- **Volume Shadow Copy Service (VSS)**   This service manages volume shadow copies for backup and restores points. This isn't necessary for most virtual desktop deployments because backups are not necessary.

- **Windows Search**   This service indexes local files, including cached Outlook mailboxes, for faster searching. You can disable this for virtual desktop deployments that don't store data locally.

NOTE

You can obtain a large list of services that you should consider disabling from the Windows 8 Virtual Desktop Infrastructure image client tuning guide at *http://aka.ms/VirtApps/ImageClientTuningGuide*

In addition to disabling unnecessary operating system services, you can adjust other settings in Windows 8.1 to enhance performance of pooled and personal virtual desktops. Consider the following:

- **Minimize event log sizes**   This is done to minimize storage utilization. You can increase the event log sizes when necessary for troubleshooting.

- **Disable unneeded scheduled tasks**   This is done to minimize overall resource utilization. For example, the disk defragmentation task that runs once per week isn't useful in a virtualized environment.

- **Minimize visual effects**   This is done to reduce utilization of the vGPU.

- **Disable features that increase storage utilization and activity**   You can disable several features to reduce storage utilization. Actions to take include the following:

  - **Disable the NTFS file system's last access time stamp**   This prevents files from being modified each time they are accessed.

  - **Disable System Restore**   This prevents system restore information from being saved on the disk. System restore information can be several GB.

  - **Disable hibernation**   This prevents hiberfil.sys from being created on the C drive, equal to the amount of memory in the computer.

Inside OUT

Optimizing Windows 8.1 with a script

If you're creating multiple virtual desktop templates to support various groups of users, invest your time in creating a script to perform the optimization process. The initial creation of the script takes some effort, but it will save you significant time on every virtual desktop template you create. Also, just as important as saving you time, a script ensures that the process is done properly every time.

To create an optimization script, you can start with a script provided by Jeff Stokes, a Premier Field Engineer with Microsoft. Use the script as a starting point for making your own script. Download the script at *http://blogs.technet.com/b/jeff_stokes/archive/2013/04/09/hot-off-the-presses-get-it-now-the-windows-8-vdi-optimization-script-courtesy-of-pfe.aspx.*

CHAPTER 10

Optimizing App-V

Just as it is beneficial to separate applications from physical desktop computers, it is beneficial to separate applications from virtual desktops. This enables you to update the applications independently of the pooled virtual desktops and to customize the applications to which individual users have access.

One of the best ways to deploy applications to pooled virtual desktops is by using App-V. You can customize App-V for use in virtualized environments. Consider the following App-V optimizations for virtualized environments:

- **Use a publishing server**   When you use a publishing server, applications are streamed to the pooled or personal virtual desktop with the most important files streamed first. As a result, the speed of deployment increases.

- **Disable pre-caching**   Pre-caching stores files for App-V applications locally on the pooled or personal virtual desktop before you start the application. This allows the application to start faster the first time it's used. If there are multiple App-V applications, the cache uses significant storage space for files that might never be required because the user didn't start the application before logging off from a pooled virtual desktop.

- **Enable shared content store mode**   When you enable shared content store mode, very little application data is stored on disk. Only feature block 0, which contains application metadata, is stored on a local disk. All other application files are streamed over the network and stored in memory as they are required. This minimizes storage utilization, but it also increases network utilization. So, you need to ensure that the network has sufficient capacity to support shared content store mode.

Optimizing antivirus software

When you implement pooled and personal virtual desktops, you need to consider the impact of antivirus software on system performance. Just like desktop computers, pooled and personal virtual desktops can become infected with malware that can steal personal information or control the infected system.

You should use antivirus software for pooled and personal virtual desktops. Even though logging off from a pooled virtual desktop reverts its state and removes malware, the malware is functional and can propagate while the pooled virtual desktop runs. Also, depending on the user state virtualization that you use, malware might be installed in the user state information and remain there even after logoff. Ideally, antivirus software prevents infection from occurring rather than just removing the malware afterward.

Antivirus software might adversely affect performance for pooled and personal virtual desktops. Using antivirus software increases storage I/O because each time a file is scanned, it uses the storage subsystem. On a desktop computer, this effect is minimal because only one computer is using the storage. For pooled and personal virtual desktops, hundreds or thousands of I/O per desktop adds up to a large amount of I/O.

Check with your antivirus software vendor to see if the vendor has any specific recommendations for implementing its product with pooled and personal virtual desktops. Here are some generic recommendations for configuring antivirus software for pooled and personal virtual desktops:

- **Disable scheduled scans on pooled virtual desktops**   Scheduled scans read the entire disk looking for malware, which causes a high amount of I/O. A scheduled scan isn't necessary on pooled virtual desktops for which logging off effectively cleans any malware that has been installed.

- **Randomize scheduled scans on personal virtual desktops**   If your organization runs scheduled scans on desktop computers, you also should run scheduled scans on personal virtual desktops. Because personal virtual desktops share the same storage infrastructure, you need to ensure that scheduled scans on personal virtual desktops are randomized and don't run at the same time. If scheduled scans run at the same time on all personal virtual desktops, there is a large burst of I/O on the storage infrastructure. If the scheduled scans are randomized, the load on the storage infrastructure is evened out.

- **Randomize virus signature updates**   Updating the virus definition updates for antivirus software causes a brief burst of I/O. Randomize the updates to minimize the impact on storage infrastructure.

- **Do not scan after virus signature updates**   Antivirus software offers the option to perform a scan of the entire system after updating virus signatures. The purpose of this scan is to identify recently installed malware that wasn't detected by the previous set of virus signatures. Note that this scan places a large load on the storage infrastructure, similar to running a scheduled scan.

- **Prevent scanning of the virtual desktop template files**   If possible in your antivirus software, exclude files from the VM template from being scanned. The files in the VM template are known to be malware-free from your original build. Preventing their scan reduces overall resource utilization.

Using Sysprep to prepare a virtual desktop template

Before you can create a virtual desktop collection that contains pooled or personal virtual desktops, you need to complete preparation of the virtual desktop template by using Sysprep. Sysprep is used to generalize the operating system and make it ready for deployment. This

CHAPTER 10

is similar to what you would do when preparing a system image for deployment to standard computers.

To prepare a virtual desktop template by using Sysprep, perform the following steps:

1. Use File Explorer to browse to C:\Windows\System32\Sysprep.

2. Double-click sysprep.exe to open the graphical interface, as shown in Figure 10-3.

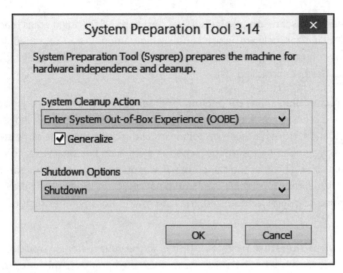

Figure 10-3   Using Sysprep

3. In the System Preparation Tool 3.14 window, in the System Cleanup Action box, select Enter System Out-of-Box Experience (OOBE).

4. Select the Generalize check box.

5. In the Shutdown Options box, select Shutdown.

6. Click OK.

Inside Out

Optimizing virtual desktop template deployment

Normally, when you generalize an operating system by using Sysprep, the information about detected hardware is removed from the operating system. When the operating system is deployed, the hardware is detected again. This is reasonable because Sysprep was designed to allow you to move Windows images to different hardware platforms. When you are deploying a virtual desktop template, the hardware does not change.

Starting with Windows 8, Sysprep includes VM mode for more efficient deployment of VMs. When you use VM mode, hardware information isn't removed from the operating system. So, when the operating system image is deployed, initial configuration is much faster because hardware information does not need to be detected and configured.

VM mode is a command-line option that only is available when Windows 8 or newer is running in a VM. The following example shows how to use VM mode:

```
Sysprep.exe /generalize /oobe /mode:VM /shutdown
```

Planning storage for pooled and personal virtual desktops

Storage performance is a critical consideration when planning personal and pooled virtual desktops. If you don't configure storage for RD Virtualization Host servers appropriately, users will experience slow performance on their pooled or personal virtual desktops. The appropriate storage option to select depends on whether you are implementing pooled or personal virtual desktops. If you are implementing highly available personal virtual desktops, then you must use shared storage. For pooled virtual desktops, shared storage isn't required.

Using local storage for pooled and personal virtual desktops

Many administrators assume that to provide storage for personal and pooled virtual desktops, you need to implement a SAN. However, if you are using pooled virtual desktops, local storage can be a cost-effective alternative to a SAN. Local storage might not be suitable for personal virtual desktops.

Local storage that is attached to an RD Virtualization Host server generally is much less expensive than the equivalent storage on a SAN. In part, this is because a SAN has many additional features that local storage does not provide. The main disadvantage to local storage is that it lacks scalability for highly available VMs.

CHAPTER 10

You can attach local storage to multiple RD Virtualization Host servers at the same time with a shared SAS bus, but the scalability is limited. Typically, a maximum of four RD Virtualization Host servers can attach to a shared SAS bus. This means that large deployments of personal virtual desktops can't use local storage, but pooled virtual desktops are well suited to local storage because pooled virtual desktops don't require shared storage for high availability.

The total number of disks that can be attached limits the total storage capacity of an RD Virtualization Host server that uses local storage. Depending on the physical server and the physical size of the drives, it's unlikely that you can physically insert more than 8 to 12 hard drives in a server. You can overcome this physical limitation by attaching an external storage array with additional hard drives. You can get external storage arrays with up to 50 hard drives. If necessary, you can add multiple external storage arrays for even greater storage capacity.

When you use locally attached storage, you typically implement redundancy in the disk subsystem. You can implement hardware-based or software-based redundancy. Hardware-based redundancy is implemented as a physical storage controller card in a server that allows Redundant Array of Independent Disks (RAID) to be implemented on a set of disks.

The following are commonly used RAID types:

- **RAID 1 (mirroring)**   When you implement RAID 1, two disks are mirrored copies of each other. This type of RAID is similar to a single drive in write performance, but it might have increased read performance because data can be read from both disks at the same time.

- **RAID 5 (disk striping with parity)**   When you implement RAID 5, data is spread across multiple disks in an array along with parity information. If a single disk in a RAID-5 array fails, then the missing information can be calculated from parity information. RAID 5 has excellent read performance but poor write performance. Performance is very poor when a disk in the array fails.

- **RAID 6 (disk striping with double parity)**   When you implement RAID 6, you get similar performance characteristics to RAID 5, but the array can survive the failure of two disks. When you use large disks, this is important to minimize the chance of an array failing during a rebuild after a disk failure.

- **RAID 10 (striping across mirror sets)**   When you implement RAID 10, data is striped across multiple mirror sets. This type of RAID offers high read and write performance. Multiple drive failures can occur without losing data if two drives in a mirror are not lost.

Hardware RAID controllers also include a cache to increase overall performance. However, using this cache can cause data consistency issues during power outages. To mitigate this, you can get a battery-backed cache or a cache that uses non-volatile memory. Both of these methods allow data that has not yet written to disk to remain in a cache until power restores. When power restores, cached data writes to a disk to make the data consistent.

The Windows Server 2012 R2 operating system includes Storage Spaces to provide data redundancy at a software level, rather than at a hardware level. Storage Spaces moves beyond simple RAID and virtualizes storage to provide increased flexibility in how storage allocates.

Storage Spaces provides the following redundancy options:

- **Two-way mirror storage space** A two-way mirror is similar to RAID 1 and has similar performance characteristics.

- **Three-way mirror storage space** A three-way mirror provides extra redundancy by having three copies of the data, and its performance is similar to a two-way mirror.

- **Parity storage space** A parity storage space with one copy of the parity information is similar to RAID 5 and is protected from single-disk failure. It also has performance characteristics that are similar to RAID 5. A parity storage space with two copies of the parity information is similar to RAID 6 and is protected from disk failures. It also has performance characteristics that are similar to RAID 6.

> ➤ For more information about Storage Spaces, see Storage Spaces – Designing for Performance on TechNet at *http://go.microsoft.com/fwlink/?LinkID=510053*.

Using a SAN for pooled and personal virtual desktops

Locally attached storage is a potential solution for pooled virtual desktops. However, for personal virtual desktops, you typically require shared storage to support high availability. One method for providing shared storage is a SAN. A SAN also can be used for pooled virtual desktops, but there is no advantage to doing so.

A SAN generally is more complex to implement and more expensive than local storage, but the additional cost does provide additional features. Some of the features that a SAN might provide include the following:

- **Snapshots** Some SANs allow you to take hardware-based snapshots for almost instantaneous backups of SAN data. This functionality is similar to VSS in the Windows operating system, but it is implemented within a SAN.

- **Offsite replication** If your SAN provides offsite replication, you can use this functionality for disaster recovery.

A SAN also provides more flexibility in storage allocation than local storage. A SAN has one large pool of storage that can be allocated to various servers. If required, reallocating storage from one server to another is relatively easy. For high availability, multiple servers can share the storage.

The two common types of SAN are Fibre Channel and iSCSI. Fibre Channel is a complete networking system that has specialized switches and Fibre Channel host bus adapter cards that must be in servers. In contrast, iSCSI uses standard Ethernet networking equipment to communicate between servers and storage. Table 10-6 summarizes the characteristics of iSCSI and Fibre Channel.

Table 10-6 Comparison of iSCSI and Fibre Channel

Characteristic	iSCSI	Fibre Channel
Cost	Lower	Higher
Complexity	Lower	Higher
Performance	Slightly lower	Slightly higher

Because iSCSI uses common networking hardware, it generally is less expensive to implement than Fibre Channel. Fibre Channel hardware is more expensive than Ethernet networking hardware. It also generally is easier to configure than Fibre Channel unless your organization already has Fibre Channel expertise.

Traditionally, Fibre Channel has been considered faster than iSCSI, but newer implementations of iSCSI offer similar speeds. Fibre Channel commonly is found at 8 gigabits per second (Gbps) and uses a protocol that is designed for storage networking with very low latency. In high-performance environments, the higher latency of iSCSI might result in lower performance. In many environments, however, the small amount of additional latency in iSCSI does not significantly affect performance. The performance of iSCSI has increased as faster Ethernet has become available. Ethernet up to 10 Gbps commonly is available, essentially matching the most common implementation of Fibre Channel.

Using scale-out file servers for pooled and personal virtual desktops

Scale-out file servers make application data highly available on file shares. In this context, the application data is data for an application server such as Microsoft SQL Server databases or .vhd files for Hyper-V VMs. These applications minimize the number of open connections to data on a file share. Scale-out file servers can't make data files such as Microsoft Word documents on a file share highly available.

You use the failover clustering feature in Windows Server 2012 R2 to make a file share highly available. Traditionally, a highly available file share only is available on one node of a failover cluster at a time. If a node fails, another node in the cluster presents the highly available file share. In most cases during the failover process, clients disconnect from a file and might need to restart their application. Any type of data can use these types of highly available file shares.

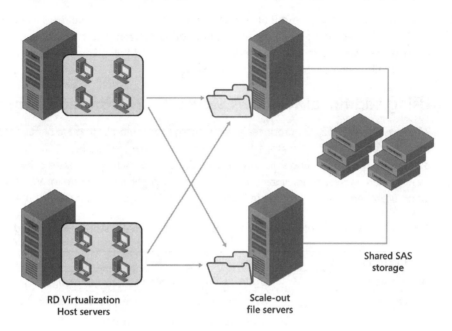

Shared SAS storage

RD Virtualization Host servers

Scale-out file servers

Figure 10-4 Scale-out file server architecture

Scale-out file servers are optimized for application data and allow all nodes in a failover cluster to actively provide access to a file share at the same time. All nodes accept and respond to client requests for data on scale-out file shares at the same time. Adding cluster nodes increases the bandwidth that is available for accessing data on scale-out file shares. Additionally, access to files isn't interrupted when a cluster node fails. The architecture of scale-out file servers is shown in Figure 10-4.

The shared storage for scale-out file servers is a shared SAS bus. Disks on a shared SAS bus are configured by using Storage Spaces. Storage Spaces provides redundancy. The disk space that Storage Spaces manages is configured as a cluster shared volume (CSV) on the cluster nodes. Scale-out file shares then are created on the CSV.

You can store VMs on a file share because of the efficiency of Server Message Block (SMB) 3.0, which Windows Server 2012 and newer use to provide access to file shares. For an administrator who manages Hyper-V Server 2012, it's easier to manage access to a file share than to manage access to SAN storage. To place a VM on a file share, you specify a universal naming convention (UNC) path rather than a local path when creating a VM. Connecting to a SAN is more complex because client software or hardware requires configuration.

When you implement scale-out file servers for VMs, you should isolate the network communication for access to scale-out file servers from other network traffic. This prevents regular network communication from interfering with access to VM files. Effectively, connectivity to a scale-out file server becomes a new type of SAN.

Using additional Windows Server 2012 R2 storage technologies

Windows Server 2012 R2 introduces several storage technologies that are beneficial for personal and pooled virtual desktops. Storage Spaces now has storage tiers that optimize data between spinning disks and solid-state drives (SSDs). CSV caching increases overall performance when a CSV is used. Finally, using the Data Deduplication feature for VM disks results in a significant reduction of storage utilization. Table 10-7 summarizes these technologies.

Table 10-7 Summary of additional Windows Server 2012 R2 storage technologies

Storage technology	Description
Storage tiers	Optimize data between SSDs and spinning disks
CSV cache	Uses server memory to increase read performance
Write-back cache	Uses SSD storage as a write cache
Data deduplication	Minimizes storage utilization

Storage tiers

SSDs offer much faster performance than spinning disks, but they are relatively expensive per gigabyte. Rather than putting all data on SSDs, it's more cost-effective to use two storage tiers with SSDs for frequently accessed data and spinning disks for less frequently accessed data. The difficult part of implementing storage tiers is identifying the data that should be located on each tier and providing access to it.

When you configure storage tiers in Storage Spaces, you don't need to identify the data manually that you will place on the faster and slower tiers. Storage Spaces automatically places the most-accessed data blocks on the faster tier and optimizes the configuration over time. When you configure a new virtual disk in Storage Spaces, you specify how much space a virtual disk allocates from the faster tier and how much space it allocates from the standard tier.

NOTE
Storage tiers do not support parity spaces.

You can pin commonly used files to the faster tier by using the Set-FileStorageTier cmdlet. Files also can be unpinned from the faster tier by using the Clear-FileStorageTier cmdlet. The example below demonstrates the *base.vhdx* file being pinned to the faster tier.

```
Set-FileStorageTier –FilePath C:\disks\base.vhdx –DesiredStorageTierFriendlyName
NameOfSSDTier
```

CSV cache

When personal virtual desktops have been clustered for high availability, you can use a CSV cache to increase data storage read performance on CSVs. The CSV cache is memory that you allocate in a server as a write-through cache. A write-through cache does not cache disk writes, only disk reads. This is important to preserve data consistency. If disk writes were cached and a power outage occurred on a server, then data on a disk might become corrupted because some data still was in memory cache and was not yet written to disk.

In Windows Server 2012, you need to enable the CSV cache. In Windows Server 2012 R2, the CSV cache is enabled already, but you need to specify the size of the CSV cache. Up to 80 percent of Windows Server 2012 R2 memory can be allocated for the CSV cache.

The following example demonstrates how to set the CSV cache at 10 GB by using the Windows PowerShell command-line interface.

```
(Get-Cluster).BlockCacheSize = 10240
```

Write-back cache

To help ensure data consistency for Storage Spaces, Windows Server 2012 R2 introduced the write-back cache. If you have implemented tiered storage with SSDs, a portion of the faster tier allocates as a write-back cache for each virtual disk. A write-back cache stores disk writes before they transfer to an appropriate physical disk. Because SSDs are non-volatile, a power outage does not affect cached data. Cached data still can write to the appropriate physical disk, thus preserving data integrity on physical disks.

The size of a write-back cache varies depending on how a virtual disk is created. A virtual disk that has not been allocated any space on the faster tier is given a 32 MB write-back cache. A virtual disk that uses the faster tier allocates 1 GB of the faster storage as the write-back cache.

You can specify the size of the write-back cache if you create a virtual disk by using Windows PowerShell. The example below creates a two-way mirror, 100 GB virtual disk with 20 GB on the faster tier and 2 GB allocated for the write-back cache.

The faster tier is stored in the $tier_ssd variable, and the standard tier is stored in the $tier_hdd variable. Use the Get-StorageTier cmdlet to put the appropriate tiers into these variables.

CHAPTER 10

```
New-VirtualDisk -StoragePoolFriendlyName "StoragePoolName" -FriendlyName "VirtualDis-
kFriendlyName" -StorageTiers @($tier_ssd,$tier_hdd) -StorageTierSizes @(20GB,100GB) -
ResiliencySettingName Mirror -WriteCacheSize 2GB
```

NOTE

You can't change the size of the write-back cache after virtual disk creation.

Data Deduplication

You can use the Data Deduplication feature in Windows Server 2012 R2 to reduce the amount of storage that personal and pooled virtual desktops require. The Data Deduplication feature was first included in Windows Server 2012, but it didn't support VM deduplication. Windows Server 2012 R2 allows you to deduplicate CSVs that store live VMs for virtual desktops. This can help you store more of your VM data on SSDs when using Scale-Out File Server and Storage Spaces.

The Data Deduplication feature works by identifying duplicate chunks of data on a disk that are between 32 kilobytes (KB) and 128 KB. When duplicates are found, only one copy of that data chunk is retained. When complete, the Data Deduplication feature moves all file data into a chunk store container. Files on disk are now stubs that reference appropriate chunks in a chunk store container. This change is completely transparent to users and applications.

For VM-based virtual desktops, the amount of storage savings is very large because a great deal of data is duplicated across VMs. For example, a deployment with 30 personal virtual desktops would use approximately 8 GB for just the operating system. After data deduplication, the 30 personal virtual desktops will consume a total of 8 GB for the operating systems instead of 240 GB.

To use the Data Deduplication feature for VM-based virtual desktops, you must enable it for use in virtual desktops by specifying the usage type as Hyper-V. Specifying the usage type as Hyper-V enables the optimization of open files and partial files. Optimization of open files is important because virtual hard disks that are used by personal and pooled virtual desktops are likely to be open most of the time. Optimization of partial files is important because it allows specific parts of virtual hard disks to be optimized when files within have not been changed for a specified period, which is three days by default.

The following example shows how to enable deduplication for virtual desktops by using Windows PowerShell. This command is run on the file server cluster hosting the CSV where the Data Deduplication feature has been enabled, not on the RD Virtualization Host servers that access the share over the network.

```
Enable-DedupVolume C:\ClusterStorage\Volume1 -UsageType HyperV
```

NOTE

Data deduplication increases CSV cache performance because multiple files can reference a single cached disk block.

Capacity planning for pooled and personal virtual desktops

Before you begin to build a solution for personal and pooled virtual desktops, you need to ensure that the infrastructure can support the required number of virtual desktops. You need to go through a capacity planning process to determine the correct infrastructure. This includes understanding the use of virtual desktops and the resources that are available. Similar to performance monitoring, the main considerations for capacity planning are storage, memory, networking, and processing. Each of these four areas can become a bottleneck and affect virtual desktop performance.

You must plan your infrastructure capacity to ensure that the system meets user expectations. There are multiple parts of the planning process, including identifying usage patterns for virtual desktops and verifying that your infrastructure meets performance requirements.

The first step in capacity planning is to understand what your users currently do. You can do performance monitoring for users to understand how much storage, memory, networking, and processing are used. Once you have measured performance characteristics for users, you can extrapolate that across the multiple virtual desktops that are hosted on an RD Virtualization Host server. For example, if you determine that a single user requires 2 GB of memory, then 50 virtual desktops will require 100 GB of memory on the RD Virtualization Host server.

The number of virtual desktops that you will host determines how many RD Virtualization Host servers you require. When you reach the capacity of a single RD Virtualization Host server, you need a second RD Virtualization Host server. When determining the number of RD Virtualization Host servers that you require, you should allocate enough unused capacity in the infrastructure to survive the failure of at least one RD Virtualization Host server. This ensures that performance for users isn't affected by the failure of an RD Virtualization Host server.

In addition to identifying usage patterns and planning your virtual desktop hardware based on those patterns, you should perform load testing on live systems to ensure that your resource utilization estimates are accurate. One common way to perform load testing is to run load simulations. You can use software that is capable of connecting to many virtual desktops and perform a predefined set of tasks. The tasks need to simulate the work that users actually will perform with software such as Microsoft Office. Ideally, you should be able to create customized tasks that also allow the use of your custom applications.

CHAPTER 10

NOTE

The most commonly used load simulation software for virtual desktops is Login VSI. Hardware vendors that provide preconfigured virtual desktop solutions that are rated for a specific number of users typically use Login VSI for their testing.

If you are flexible in your deployment plan, a pilot project might be useful to perform capacity testing. When you perform a pilot project, you design your infrastructure to be scalable and start with a small deployment. Based on this initial deployment, you can identify the actual performance characteristics that users generate rather than create estimates from simulations. You then can extrapolate performance data for the pilot project to a larger number of users and build an infrastructure that meets those performance requirements.

Capacity planning for storage

When you are planning capacity for storage, you need to consider the amount of data that needs to be stored and the storage throughput. The amount of data that needs to be stored depends on the number of virtual desktops and how much data besides the operating system is stored in the virtual disk files. Storage throughput is based on the type of activity that users perform.

You can calculate the total volume of data that needs to be stored on a disk by identifying the storage required for a single virtual desktop and multiplying it by the number of virtual desktops you intend to implement. Keep in mind that if you use data deduplication for a CSV that is storing VMs, you significantly reduce your storage volume.

As a broad generalization, pooled virtual desktops take 20 GB to 30 GB for a virtual desktop template and an additional 5 GB per pooled virtual desktop. Personal virtual desktops generally are larger and typically range from 40 GB to 60 GB. Personal virtual desktops also are more likely to grow over time as users install additional applications that are retained across sessions.

Storage system throughput is measured in I/O operations per second (IOPS). You can measure the IOPS that are required for each running virtual desktop to determine the IOPS that are required to support all of your virtual desktops. Ensure that you plan the IOPS capacity of your infrastructure to support the peak IOPS that are generated rather than the average IOPS. Otherwise, you will experience slow performance during peak utilization periods.

One of the peak times for IOPS is in the morning at initial sign-in. The process of starting virtual desktops and signing in generates significant IOPS. A general rule for acceptable performance is that users must be able to begin working on their virtual desktops within 30 seconds of connecting to them.

Inside Out

Increasing storage performance

One way to increase storage performance is by implementing faster disks. SSDs are much faster than spinning disks and have much higher IOPS. A single 15,000 RPM (revolutions per minute) SAS drive supports approximately 200 IOPS. The IOPS for a typical SSD is 100,000 or more. Placing virtual hard disks on SSDs makes a system much faster, but it has a significantly higher cost per GB. It might not be practical to put all of your storage on SSDs because of cost concerns. If you are using pooled virtual desktops, all of the VMs share the virtual desktop template to which differencing disks are linked. Placing the virtual desktop template for pooled virtual desktops on an SSD significantly speeds up all of the pooled virtual desktops.

Tiered storage in Storage Spaces is another option for increasing performance that is less costly than putting all VMs on SSDs. If you are using Storage Spaces on a local RD Virtualization Host server or scale-out file servers, then tiered storage significantly increases IOPS by automatically moving frequently accessed data blocks to SSD storage.

Finally, if VMs are stored on a CSV, implementing a CSV cache can increase read IOPS even if an SSD isn't present.

Capacity planning for memory

You need to identify the memory requirements for individual virtual desktops based on performance monitoring. As an estimate for initial planning, consider the memory usage for the following categories of users:

- **Small**   1.5 GB to 2 GB

- **Medium**   2 GB to 3 GB

- **Large**   2 GB to 4 GB

The amount of physical memory in a server limits the number of virtual desktops you can place on an RD Virtualization Host server. It's common for new servers to support 192 GB to 256 GB of memory. For medium workload virtual desktops, that means each RD Virtualization Host server can support approximately 100 to 125 virtual desktops.

You should use Dynamic Memory for personal and pooled virtual desktops. Specify 1 GB of memory to start and allow it to grow to an appropriate maximum. When you enable

CHAPTER 10

Dynamic Memory, it allocates to virtual desktops as it's needed. This minimizes the amount of memory that each virtual desktop actually uses.

If you use Dynamic Memory for virtual desktops, you can use the average memory utilization rather than the maximum memory utilization when you calculate the memory that virtual desktops require. This is because Dynamic Memory is allocated and reclaimed dynamically. The assumption is that peak memory utilization occurs for different users at different times and that the overall memory used at any given time does not vary significantly.

Capacity planning for networking

When you plan network capacity for personal and pooled virtual desktops, you first need to identify the types of network traffic that will be generated. You need to consider whether the different types of network traffic will be isolated or will travel on the same network. Some types of network traffic include the following:

- User communication with personal and pooled virtual desktops

- Personal and pooled virtual desktops that are accessing shared data on file and application servers

- RD Virtualization Host server communication with shared storage

When you allocate network capacity for each virtual desktop, you can use a network utilization average rather than peak utilization. The assumption is that network utilization is randomized and evens out overall, but you should consider that certain times of day might generate increased overall network utilization, such as sign-ins at the beginning of the workday.

Users communicate with personal and pooled virtual desktops by using Remote Desktop Protocol (RDP). RDP is an efficient protocol—on average, an RDP client generates about 500 kilobits per second (Kbps) of network traffic. For 100 VMs, an RD Virtualization Host server would require 50 megabits per second (Mbps). However, this can vary depending on the amount of user activity and the type of tasks users perform. Therefore, you should verify that your users meet this profile.

Activities that users perform on their virtual desktops also generate network traffic. Some actions that generate network traffic include the following:

- Accessing file shares

- Applications accessing databases and other data sources

- Applications accessing the Internet

- Printing

- Displaying audio and video files

NOTE

Printing can occur directly from a virtual desktop to a printer, or it can redirect over RDP to a printer that is attached to a user's local device. Both scenarios generate print traffic over a network, but with different network usage patterns.

You need to assess the level of network activity accurately to ensure that your RD Virtualization Host server has sufficient network capacity to support user connections and access to data from virtual desktops. In most cases, a virtual desktop has a single virtual network adapter, and both types of network communication share a network infrastructure.

If you use an iSCSI SAN or scale-out file servers for storage, then you also need to consider the impact of network communication with shared storage. Even though network communication with shared storage is IP-based, it always should be isolated on a separate network that is dedicated for storage. The storage network typically needs to be much faster than a network for user communication. In a very small virtual desktop implementation, the storage network must be at least 1 Gbps. For larger implementations, you should consider 10 Gbps Ethernet.

Inside OUT

Optimizing network utilization

You can do very little to minimize network communication for pooled and personal virtual desktops. You can adjust some options in the RDP client, but the effect is minimal without degrading the user experience. Segmenting network traffic allows you to better control the traffic and build the network to support the level of network communication that you require.

You can use network interface card (NIC) Teaming to increase the network capacity of RD Virtualization Host servers. You can use the NIC Teaming feature that is included in Windows Server 2012 R2, or you can use hardware-based NIC Teaming that is configured with specialized drivers from network adapter vendors. NIC Teaming allows you to combine multiple network ports into a single logical connection. Combining two network ports makes overall communication twice as fast. For example, in a large virtual desktop deployment, you could use NIC Teaming to combine two 10 Gbps connections for a total of 20 Gbps.

CHAPTER 10

Capacity planning for processing

You can calculate the processing capacity that is required for an RD Virtualization Host server by determining the processing capacity that is required for a single virtual desktop and multiplying that by the number of virtual desktops on a server.

Be aware that it is difficult, if not impossible, to determine the precise value of processing power used by a desktop computer. A reasonable estimate of processing power used on a desktop computer can be generated by identifying both the overall processing power of the desktop computer and the CPU utilization on that computer. Processing power for many specific computer and processor combinations can be obtained from the Standard Performance Evaluation Corporation website.

> ➤ **For more information about performance ratings for various computers and processors with their SPEC CPU2006 results, see SPEC CPU2006 Results on the Standard Performance Evaluation Corporation website at** *http://go.microsoft.com/fwlink/?LinkID=510054.*

When you calculate the processing capacity that is required for a single virtual desktop, you can use the average value rather than peak values. It's unlikely that all virtual desktops will experience peak processing utilization at the same time, but you should allow some room for bursts in processing requirements because usage won't always be at average levels. For example, sign-ins in the morning are likely to result in a burst of processing utilization by virtual desktops.

When you identify the hardware for your RD Virtualization Host servers, the characteristics of the processors are important. Different processors have different levels of processing capacity. Some processor characteristics that influence processing capacity include the following:

- **Processor cores**   Each processor core can work on a task independently of other processor cores. Generally, more cores results in more processing capacity. Server processors commonly are available with six or eight cores.

- **Processor clock speed**   Processors are available in various clock speeds. Generally, a faster clock speed results in more processing capacity.

- **Processor family**   Different processor families have different performance characteristics. This means that you can't just compare cores and clock speeds to identify total processing capacity accurately.

If you require a high level of processing capacity, consider using smaller RD Virtualization Host servers and scaling out by adding RD Virtualization Host servers. The cost difference between single-processor and dual-processor servers is minimal. The cost difference between dual-processor and quad-processor servers is significantly more. It generally is more cost-effective to use a dual-processor server and then add RD Virtualization Host servers if required. A single host with 24 cores has approximately the same processing power as two hosts with 24 cores.

Capacity planning example

To apply some capacity planning principles, let's look at a scenario. In this scenario, your organization is opening a remote office where computer support isn't readily available. To simplify management of this remote location, you have decided to implement virtual desktops. To support the widest possible variety of applications and licensing schemes, you have decided to implement pooled virtual desktops. There are 100 users at the remote site.

Your testing of a single pooled virtual desktop indicates the following:

- Network utilization of 400 Kbps

- Storage utilization of 10 GB

- Disk IOPS of 10

- Average RAM utilization of 1 GB

- Average central processing unit (CPU) utilization of 8 percent of one core

To provide high availability, you need at least two RD Virtualization Host servers. Because this is a production environment, the infrastructure should be highly available. It's possible to configure a single RD Virtualization Host server to support all of the necessary desktops. Each RD Virtualization Host server must have enough capacity to run 100 virtual desktops to support all users.

The following hardware configuration is required for the RD Virtualization Host servers:

- **Memory** To support 100 pooled virtual desktops at an average of 1 GB of memory each, an RD Virtualization Host server must have at least 100 GB of memory. A server is likely to have 128 GB or 192 GB of RAM. Given that RAM is relatively inexpensive, 192 GB of RAM offers more flexibility in case workloads change over time.

- **CPU** With each pooled virtual desktop requiring 8 percent of one core, 10 pooled virtual desktops require one core for 80 percent utilization. This is a good level of utilization because it allows some room for bursts of activity. To support 100 pooled virtual desktops at this level, 10 cores are required. Server CPUs commonly are available with six or eight cores. Although two processors with six cores each are sufficient, two processors with eight cores each offer additional flexibility in the future.

- **Storage** To support 100 pooled virtual desktops that use an average of 10 GB of disk space, the total space that is allocated to the 100 pooled virtual desktops must be at least 1 terabyte (TB). The IOPS that are required for 100 pooled virtual desktops is 1,000 IOPS. The storage subsystem must be configured to support this. If local storage is used, RAID 10 likely is the best option to provide this level of storage; you could use an eight-disk RAID 10 array of 300 GB, 15,000 RPM serial-attached SCSI drives. This would provide 1.2 TB of storage space and approximately 1,200 IOPS.

- **Network** To support 100 pooled virtual desktops that use 400 Kbps, you must have a total of 40 Mbps available for RDP communication with the pooled virtual desktops. You also must ensure that the wide area network (WAN) link to the remote location has this amount of bandwidth allocated for communication with the pooled virtual desktops.

Inside OUT

Planning for increased performance

Calculations based on testing a single desktop can be used only as a rough estimate for hardware purchases. You still need to confirm adequate performance on the physical hardware that is purchased and the final VM configuration.

As part of your planning process, you need to consider what you'll do if performance isn't adequate. Identifying this ahead of time ensures that you can implement an alternate plan instead of being stuck with poorly performing virtual desktops. You need to consider how you could improve all aspects of the solution. The following are some potential methods of improving performance:

- Adding an RD Virtualization Host server to add processing, memory, or networking capacity
- Adding memory or network adapters to RD Virtualization Host servers
- Adding SSDs for increased disk performance
- Changing RAID configuration for increased disk performance

Implementing pooled and personal virtual desktops

After you have planned a personal or pooled virtual desktop deployment, you can begin building an infrastructure to support the personal or pooled virtual desktops. First, you need to install RD Virtualization Host servers. After installing the RD Virtualization Host servers, you can create virtual desktop collections with personal or pooled virtual desktops. After deployment, you occasionally will need to update pooled virtual desktops to incorporate operating system and application updates. You also may want to deploy RemoteApp programs from VMs by using RemoteApp for Hyper-V.

Deploying RD Virtualization Host servers

Similar to RD Session Host server deployment, RD Virtualization Host server deployment is part of an integrated RDS deployment. To implement VM-based virtual desktops, you require at least one instance of the RD Virtualization Host server role that integrates with the RD Connection Broker and RD Web Access server roles. In a small test environment, these three roles can exist on the same server, but in a production environment, an RD Virtualization Host server is separate from the RD Connection Broker server and the RD Web Access server.

You can deploy an RD Virtualization Host server either when you initially deploy RDS or afterward by adding individual RD Virtualization Host servers. If you are adding an RD Virtualization Host server as part of an RDS deployment, you select the Microsoft Virtual Machine-Based Desktop Deployment scenario in the Add Roles And Features Wizard. If you already have deployed RDS, you can add an RD Virtualization Host server from the Overview of Remote Desktop Services in Server Manager.

When you deploy an RD Virtualization Host server, you don't need to add the Hyper-V server role before deployment. The Hyper-V server role is added as part of the deployment process. However, the deployment wizards work properly if Hyper-V already is installed.

You have the option to create a new virtual switch on an RD Virtualization Host server during installation. If you select this option, a new virtual switch is created for an external network on the RD Virtualization Host server. This ensures that an external network is configured on the RD Virtualization Host server. This isn't required if you already have configured an external network on the Hyper-V host. RD Virtualization Host server deployment fails if an external network isn't configured.

> ### NOTE
> **Remember that all servers in the RDS deployment must be added to Server Manager before you begin the installation process.**

To create a new VM-based RDS deployment, perform the following steps:

1. In Server Manager, click Manage and then click Add Roles And Features.

2. In the Add Roles And Features Wizard, on the Before You Begin page, click Next.

3. On the Select Installation Type page, click Remote Desktop Services Installation and click Next.

4. On the Select Deployment Type page, click Standard Deployment and click Next.

CHAPTER 10

5. On the Select Deployment Scenario page, shown in Figure 10-5, click Virtual Machine–Based Desktop Deployment and click Next.

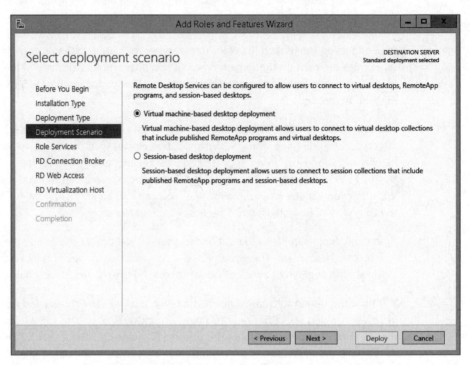

Figure 10-5 Add Roles And Features Wizard, Select Deployment Scenario page

6. On the Review Role Services page, click Next. This page provides a brief description of each role service, but there is nothing to configure. The currently logged-on account is being used to create the deployment and is displayed here as a reminder.

7. On the Specify RD Connection Broker Server page, in the Server Pool box, double-click the server on which you wish to install the RD Connection Broker role service and click Next.

NOTE

Do not install the RD Session Broker role service on a domain controller when you are implementing VM-based virtual desktops. The RD Session Broker server must create computer accounts for virtual desktops, and this process can fail when the RD Session Broker role service is installed on a domain controller.

8. On the Specify RD Web Access Server page, select the Install
The RD Web Access Role Service On The RD Connection Broker Server
check box and click Next. Alternatively, you can select another server on
which to install the RD Web Access role service.

9. On the Specify RD Virtualization Host Server page, shown in Figure 10-6, in the
Server Pool box, double-click the server on which you wish to install the
RD Virtualization Host role service.

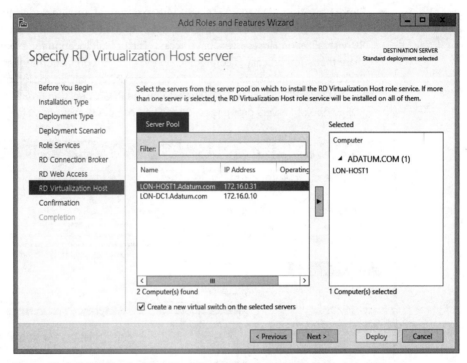

Figure 10-6 Add Roles And Features Wizard, Specify RD Virtualization Host Server page

10. If you have not already configured Hyper-V on the RD Virtualization Host server,
then select the Create A New Virtual Switch On The Selected Servers check box and
click Next.

11. On the Confirm Selections page, select the Restart The Destination Server Automatically
If Required check box and click Deploy.

12. On the Completion page, click Close.

After RDS deploys, most of the deployment settings are the same as those that are
used for session-based desktop deployments of RDS. Settings for RD Gateway,

Remote Desktop Licensing (RD Licensing), RD Web Access, and certificates are the same, but the following settings are specific to VM-based desktop deployments:

- **Active Directory settings**   In the Active Directory configuration settings, shown in Figure 10-7, you define an organizational unit (OU) where computer accounts for personal and pooled virtual desktops can be created. This setting configures the permissions to allow an RD Connection Broker server to create computer accounts when virtual desktops are configured. This is necessary before you create a virtual desktop collection.

- **Export location**   When you select a virtual desktop template during the creation of a collection, the virtual desktop template exports to a location to which all RD Virtualization Host servers have access. The default location for exports is a file share that automatically is configured on the first RD Connection Broker server in an RDS deployment. The file share is *Servername*\RDVirtualDesktopTemplate, and it's located at C:\RDVirtualDesktopTemplate on the RD Connection Broker server. The RDS Endpoint Servers group is assigned Full Control permissions to this share and folder.

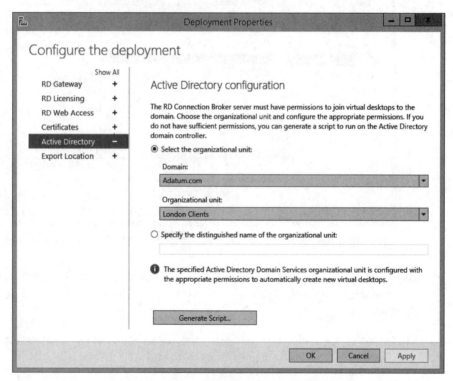

Figure 10-7 Deployment Properties, Active Directory Configuration page

To configure the Active Directory settings for an RDS deployment, perform the following steps:

1. In Server Manager, in the navigation pane, click Remote Desktop Services.

2. On the Remote Desktop Services > Overview page, next to Deployment Overview, click Tasks, and click Edit Deployment Properties.

3. In the Deployment Properties window, in the navigation pane, click Active Directory.

4. On the Active Directory Configuration page, click Select The Organizational Unit.

5. In the Domain box, select the domain where the computer accounts will be created.

6. In the Organizational Unit box, select the OU where the computer accounts will be created.

7. Click Apply to assign the permissions. Permissions are granted to the RD Session Broker server computer accounts.

Understanding user profile disks for VM-based virtual desktops

User profile disks for VM-based virtual desktops fulfill the same purpose as user profile disks for session-based virtual desktops. User profile disks for VM-based virtual desktops allow user state information to be retained across sessions, even when a user does not reconnect with the same VM.

You can use user profile disks as an alternative to roaming user profiles. A user profile disk stores the same information as a roaming user profile, but it does not require user state information to download from a file share at sign-in and upload at sign-out. Instead, a user profile disk is a virtual hard disk (VHD) that is stored on a file share. The virtual hard disk is attached to a VM when a user signs in and detached when the user signs out.

You define a network share as the location for user profile disks, and a separate user profile disk is generated for each user. Each VHD is named based on the security identifier (SID) of the user. You can back up user profile disks if your organization determines that user state information is important enough to retain for disaster recovery.

You can select which information is stored on a user profile disk. You can store an entire user profile or just selected folders on a user profile disk. For example, if you determine that you only want to retain application settings between sign-ins on pooled virtual desktops, then you can enable only roaming user profile data and user registry data. If you want to include more folders, you can manually specify individual folders to include. This can be useful if an application stores data in a specific location that isn't included in the predefined folders.

CHAPTER 10

When you configure user profile disks for a virtual desktop collection, you specify the maximum size for each user's VHD. The default value is 20 GB, but you can modify this to suit your environment. In the shared folder that you specify for user profile disks, the file *UVHD-Template.vhdx* is created. This file is a dynamically expanding VHD with the maximum size that you specify. When a user signs in for the first time, this file is copied to create a user profile disk for the user.

User profile disks offer similar functionality to roaming user profiles and Folder Redirection, but they are applicable only to virtual desktop collections. You can't implement user profile disks to support roaming among different environments, such as a desktop computer and a virtual desktop. However, they are an excellent method for retaining user state for pooled virtual desktops. User profile disks are not available for personal virtual desktops.

NOTE

User profile disks can't be shared among virtual desktop collections. If users require user state information to roam across different collections of pooled virtual desktops or to session-based desktop deployments, then you must implement an alternative method for synchronizing user state information.

Creating a virtual desktop collection

VM-based desktop deployments are managed through virtual desktop collections. When you create a virtual desktop collection, you select a virtual desktop template to create VMs for users. During the creation process for a virtual desktop collection, you need to select many options.

First, you need to specify whether you want a virtual desktop collection to be a pooled virtual desktop collection or a personal virtual desktop collection. The options for the remainder of the Create Collection Wizard vary slightly depending on which you select.

At this time, you also select whether to create and manage virtual desktops automatically. If you select this option, then virtual desktops are created from a VM template that you specify. In most cases, you will use this option because it simplifies virtual desktop deployments. If you don't select this option, then you select VMs to use in a collection from a list of existing VMs. The wizard won't create additional VMs.

Inside OUT

Automatic VM creation

When you automatically create and manage virtual desktops from a template, the template exports to a shared folder where all RD Virtualization Host servers can access it. RD Virtualization Host servers copy the template from the shared folder when creating VMs.

Because each VM is created from a virtual desktop template that has been prepared by using Sysprep, you need to provide information to automate the initial VM configuration process. To do this, you can provide a Sysprep answer file that you create, or you can provide settings in the Create Collection Wizard. If you choose to provide unattended installation settings, then the Create Collection Wizard prompts you for time zone information and the OU for computer objects.

You also need to provide a setting for the computer name in the wizard. You can define a prefix and suffix for the computer name. The default prefix is XXX-, where XXX is the first three letters of the virtual desktop collection name. The default suffix is 0, where 0 is the number of the VM that is being created. For example, a prefix of PER- and a suffix of 0 results in computers named PER-0, PER-1, and so on.

When you automatically create VMs, you need to specify how many VMs to create. You also have the option to specify how the VMs are allocated among RD Virtualization Host servers. By default, VMs are evenly distributed among RD Virtualization Host servers.

Finally, you need to specify the storage location for VMs. You can select to store VMs locally on an RD Virtualization Host, in a shared folder, or in a CSV. If you select to store VMs locally on an RD Virtualization Host server, the default location is %ProgramData%\Microsoft\Windows\RDVirtualizationHost. You need to ensure that the location that you specify has sufficient capacity and performance to support the virtual desktops that you create.

When you create a pooled virtual desktop collection, you don't manually assign users to specific virtual desktops. Instead, users automatically are assigned to an available pooled virtual desktop. You specify users and groups that have access to a pooled virtual desktop collection.

When you create a personal virtual desktop collection, you need to determine how users are assigned to their personal virtual desktop. The simplest method for assigning users to personal virtual desktops is to enable automatic user assignment. This option functions similarly to the assignment for pooled virtual desktops. You give users and groups access to a virtual desktop collection, and users are assigned permanently to the first personal virtual desktop to which they connect. This method works well when all personal virtual desktops start with the same configuration and users don't have specific needs.

You also can select to disable automatic user assignment. Without automatic user assignment, you need to assign each user manually to a personal virtual desktop. This is most useful when personal virtual desktop configuration is highly customized and you want to ensure that a user is assigned to the correct personal virtual desktop.

When you configure user assignment for personal virtual desktops, you also can select the option to add the user account to the local Administrators group on the virtual desktop. Select this option if you want users to have administrative rights on their personal virtual desktop to perform customization such as installing software.

To create a pooled virtual desktop collection, perform the following steps:

1. In Server Manager, in the navigation pane, click Remote Desktop Services.

2. In Server Manager, in Remote Desktop Services > Overview, click Create Virtual Desktop Collections.

3. In the Create Collection Wizard, on the Before You Begin page, read the requirements to complete the wizard and click Next.

4. On the Name The Collection Page, in the Name box, type the name of the collection and click Next. You also have the option to enter a description.

5. On the Specify The Collection Type page, shown in Figure 10-8, select Pooled Virtual Desktop Collection.

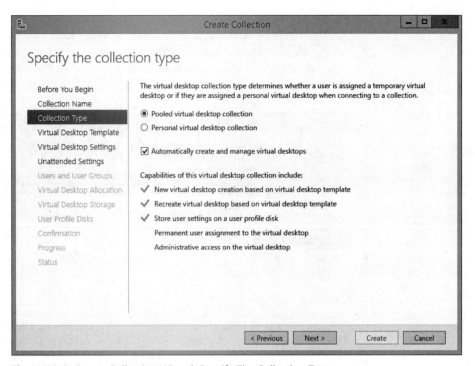

Figure 10-8 Create Collection Wizard, Specify The Collection Type page

NOTE

If you select the Personal Virtual Desktop Collection option, then the feature Store User Settings On A User Profile Disk isn't used. The features Permanent User Assignment To The Virtual Desktop and Administrative Access On The Virtual Desktop are enabled.

6. Select the Automatically Create And Manage Virtual Desktops check box and click Next.

7. On the Specify The Virtual Desktop Template page, click the VM you want to use for the virtual desktop template and click Next.

NOTE

Sometimes a VM that you have configured to be a virtual desktop template does not appear in the list of virtual desktop templates from which to select. This usually can be resolved by restarting the RD Session Host server with the virtual desktop template and running the Create Collection Wizard again.

CHAPTER 10

8. On the Specify The Virtual Desktop Settings page, shown in Figure 10-9, select the Provide Unattended Installation Settings option and click Next. When you select this option, the wizard asks you for the unattended installation settings. If you select Use An Existing Sysprep Answer File, then you can provide an INF file containing the necessary settings.

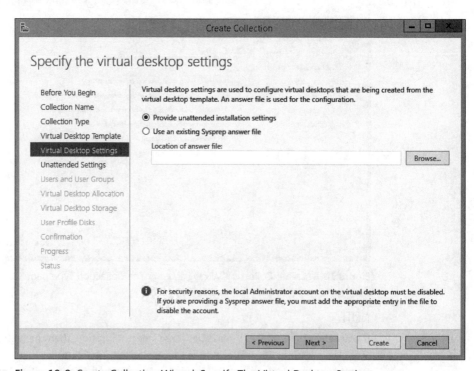

Figure 10-9 Create Collection Wizard, Specify The Virtual Desktop Settings page

9. On the Specify The Unattended Installation Settings page, shown in Figure 10-10, in the Time Zone box, select an appropriate time zone for the virtual desktops.

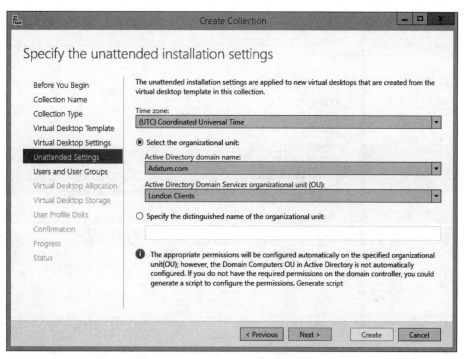

Figure 10-10 Create Collection Wizard, Specify The Unattended Installation Settings page

10. To select the OU where computer accounts for the virtual desktops will be created by using drop-down lists, click Select The Organizational Unit. In the Active Directory Domain Name box, select the appropriate domain. In the Active Directory Domain Services Organizational Unit (OU) box, select the appropriate OU and click Next.

11. On the Specify Users And User Groups page, shown in Figure 10-11, in the User Groups box, specify the users or groups that you want to have access to the desktop collection. Domain Users are listed by default.

CHAPTER 10

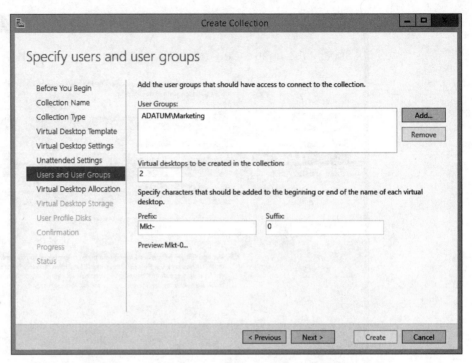

Figure 10-11 Create Collection Wizard, Specify Users And User Groups page

12. In the Virtual Desktops To Be Created In The Collection box, enter the number of virtual desktops that will be created in the collection. If there are multiple RD Virtualization Host servers, some of these virtual desktops can be allocated to each one. You can expand the number of virtual desktops later.

13. In the Prefix box, enter the text that you want the computer names of virtual desktops to start with. For example, if the Prefix value is Mkt-, then all computer names will start with Mkt-.

14. In the Suffix box, enter the starting number you want to include in the computer names of the virtual desktops and click Next. For example, if the Suffix value is 0, then the first VM created will be Mkt-0, and the next will be Mkt-1.

15. On the Specify Virtual Desktop Allocation page, shown in Figure 10-12, specify the number of virtual desktops to create on each RD Virtualization Host server in the RDS deployment and click Next. If there is only one RD Virtualization Host server, then all virtual desktops are created on that server.

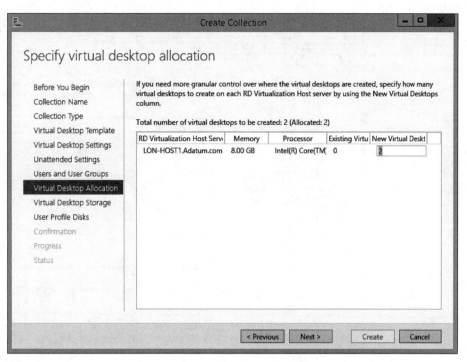

Figure 10-12 Create Collection Wizard, Specify Virtual Desktop Allocation page

16. On the Specify Virtual Desktop Storage page, shown in Figure 10-13, select the storage location for the virtual desktops.

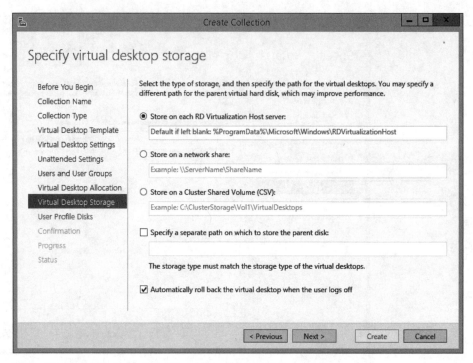

Figure 10-13 Create Collection Wizard, Specify Virtual Desktop Storage page

17. If you want to store the parent disk in a separate location from the differencing disks for each virtual desktop, then select the Specify A Separate Path On Which To Store the Parent Disk check box and type the path.

18. If you want the virtual desktops to reset to their starting state each time a new user connects, then select the Automatically Roll Back The Virtual Desktop When The User Logs Off check box and click Next. This option is enabled by default and is used in most deployments.

19. On the Specify User Profile Disks page, if you want to enable user profile disks, select the Enable User Profile Disks check box and specify the location for the user profile disks.

20. In the Maximum Size (In GB) box, type the maximum size to be used for each user profile disk and click Next.

21. On the Confirm Selections page, click Create.

22. Wait while the virtual desktop template is exported and the virtual desktops are created from the exported virtual desktop template. This activity is disk-intensive and can take an extended period of time. When this activity is complete, click Close.

The settings for a virtual desktop collection are similar to those for a session-based desktop collection. In addition to the settings that you can configure during creation, you can configure the following:

- Client settings for device redirection

- Detailed configuration for user profile disks

Inside OUT

Implementing save delay

The only setting that is unique to virtual desktop collections and is not available during creation is Enable Save Delay (In Minutes) on the General tab. When you enable save delay, you specify a number of minutes that a virtual desktop is unused before it's saved.

Saving a virtual desktop reduces resource utilization on an RD Virtualization Host server. When a virtual desktop is saved, it uses no memory, processing, or disk I/O on the server. If you have many virtual desktops that are seldom used, then you can enable save delay for the virtual desktop collection to limit resource utilization without a significant impact on users.

Connecting to a saved virtual desktop is slower than connecting to a virtual desktop that already is started. To mitigate this, at least two desktops in a pooled virtual desktop collection stay started.

Updating pooled virtual desktops

Personal virtual desktops retain their state between uses. Consequently, operating system and application updates can be handled in the same way that updates are handled for desktop computers. Pooled virtual desktops lose their state, so there is no point in applying updates each time a new user signs in. Instead, you need to have a defined update process for pooled virtual desktops.

To update pooled virtual desktops, you first update the virtual desktop template that you use to create pooled virtual desktops. To simplify virtual desktop template management, consider taking a snapshot of the VM before you run Sysprep. This saves the time of waiting for the specialization and OOBE phases to complete before you can make your updates. You also can use an automated deployment tool such as the MDT to ensure consistent configuration when building updated virtual desktop templates.

CHAPTER 10

After you have updated the virtual desktop template, you need to update the virtual desktops that are created from that template. To do this, you select the Recreate All Virtual Desktops task from the collection node in Server Manager. The Recreate All Virtual Desktops Wizard guides you through the process of updating pooled virtual desktops. The first step is selecting the updated virtual desktop template, as shown in Figure 10-14.

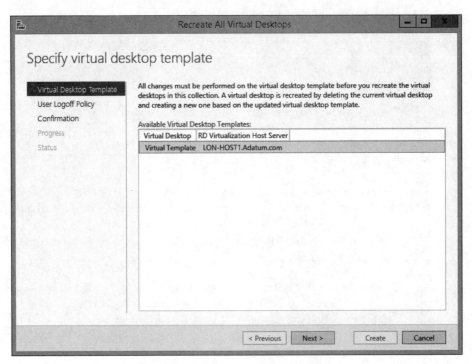

Figure 10-14 Recreate All Virtual Desktops Wizard, Specify Virtual Desktop Template page

On the Specify User Logoff Policy page, shown in Figure 10-15, you define when virtual desktops are recreated. In most cases, you want to update virtual desktops when users sign out from their virtual desktop. This prevents users from being disconnected from a virtual desktop while they are working. If you configure a start and end time for an update, any remaining virtual desktops will update at the end time if users have not signed out.

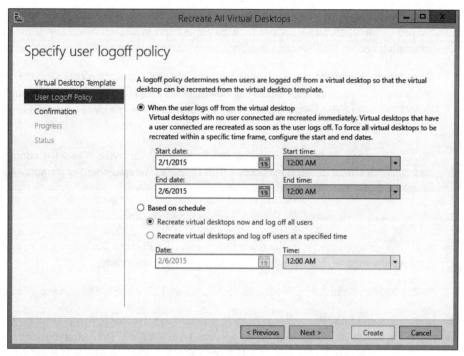

Figure 10-15 Recreate All Virtual Desktops Wizard, Specify User Logoff Policy page

When you perform a scheduled update, the update happens regardless of whether users are signed in. You can schedule an update to happen immediately or at a specific time. When a scheduled update is performed, any signed-in users are signed out before the updates are performed. You would schedule an update outside typical work hours.

When you complete the wizard, the virtual desktop template is exported to an RD Session Broker server and then imported on the RD Virtualization Host servers. This process is the same as when you create a new virtual desktop collection.

Implementing RemoteApp for Hyper-V

RemoteApp typically presents applications that are installed and run on an RD Session Host server to users. You also can implement RemoteApp for Hyper-V to allow personal and pooled virtual desktops to present applications to users. Unlike an RD Session Host server, a single virtual desktop allows only one user to connect at a time. Therefore, to support 10 simultaneous users, you need to have 10 virtual desktops available for RemoteApp.

CHAPTER 10

You should use this solution if you can't implement RemoteApp on an RD Session Host server to present an application. For example, an application might not run properly on a server operating system, or licensing might not allow installation on an RD Session Host server.

In some cases, you can use RemoteApp for Hyper-V for application compatibility when multiple versions of an application can't be installed locally. For example, you could maintain a few VMs with older versions of Internet Explorer to support older web-based applications that don't work properly in newer browsers.

RDS in Windows Server 2012 R2 integrates RemoteApp for Hyper-V into the configuration interface for virtual desktop collections. This simplifies a deployment of RemoteApp for Hyper-V in a virtual desktop deployment.

To configure RemoteApp for Hyper-V, perform the following steps:

1. In Server Manager, in the navigation pane, click Remote Desktop Services and click the name of the virtual desktop collection you want to update.

2. Next to RemoteApp Programs, click Tasks, and click Publish RemoteApp Programs.

3. In the Publish RemoteApp Programs Wizard, on the Select Virtual Desktop page, shown in Figure 10-16, select a virtual desktop and click Next. The virtual desktop that you select is used to generate a list of applications that are available in the collection.

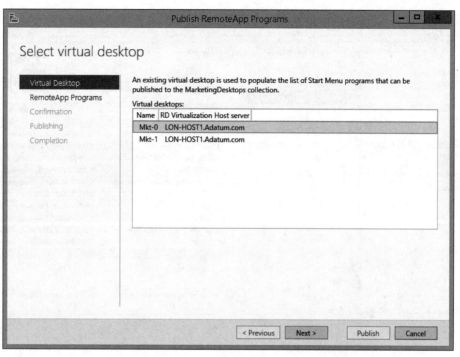

Figure 10-16 Publish RemoteApp Programs Wizard, Select Virtual Desktop page

4. On the Select RemoteApp Programs page, shown in Figure 10-17, select the applications installed on the virtual desktop that you want to be available as RemoteApp programs and click Next.

CHAPTER 10

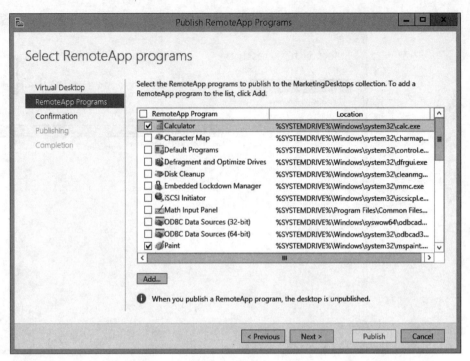

Figure 10-17 Publish RemoteApp Programs Wizard, Select RemoteApp Programs page

5.   On the Confirmation page, click Publish.

6.   Wait until the RemoteApp programs are published and click Close.

After you publish RemoteApp programs from a virtual desktop collection, the virtual desktops in that collection are no longer available to users. Only RemoteApp programs are available. If you remove all RemoteApp programs from the collection, then virtual desktops become available again.

Clients follow the same connection process for RemoteApp programs in a virtual desktop collection as they do when connecting to a virtual desktop. Users launch their connection from the RD Web App page and contact an RD Connection Broker server that directs them to an appropriate virtual desktop that presents the RemoteApp application.

Inside OUT

RemoteApp for Hyper-V with Windows XP

Although the RDS solution in Windows Server 2012 R2 only supports the Windows 7 Enterprise and Windows 8 Enterprise operating systems, you can create Windows XP Professional Service Pack 3 (SP3) and Windows Vista Enterprise Service Pack 1 (SP1) VMs and enable RemoteApp for Hyper-V on them. Windows XP Professional SP3 and Windows Vista Enterprise SP1 require an update to present RemoteApp for Hyper-V applications.

To configure RemoteApp for Hyper-V on Windows XP, perform the following steps:

1. On the VM that is running Windows XP, set the HKLM\Software\Microsoft \Windows NT\CurrentVersion\Terminal Server\TsAppAllowList\fDisabledAllowList registry key to a value of 1.

2. Create an RDP file with the appropriate settings for RemoteApp:

   ```
   remoteapplicationmode:i:1

   Alternate shell:s:rdpinit.exe

   RemoteApplicationName:s: friendly name

   RemoteApplicationProgram:s:path to the application

   DisableRemoteAppCapsCheck:i:1

   Prompt for Credentials on Client:i:1
   ```

➤ For more information about RemoteApp for Hyper-V, see RemoteApp for Hyper-V (VDI) Deployment on the Remote Desktop Services Blog at *http://go.microsoft.com/fwlink/?LinkID=510056*.

Implementing Remote Access for VDI

A recent trend in IT is users bringing their personal computing devices to the office. This is often called Bring Your Own Device (BYOD). It started when smartphones became popular and users asked IT departments for access to email from the smartphones. It has expanded, and now it is common for users to bring personal tablets and laptops into the office, too. IT departments have been supporting these devices, sometimes limitedly, ever since.

What started as users using their personal devices in the office has expanded to users using their personal devices outside the office. As a result, IT departments are being challenged to provide a seamless user experience no matter which device users are using. Users expect to have access to the same technologies from any device and from any network. They also want the experience to be consistent across multiple platforms. In this chapter, we will discuss providing remote access for Virtual Desktop Infrastructure (VDI), which helps bring users closer to seamless access from any device and any network.

Extending VDI outside the organization

Extending VDI outside your organization is a big endeavor that requires careful planning. One of the biggest factors in such a project is security. Any time you open your environment to the outside world, there are new avenues available for malicious individuals. As the administrator, it is important to understand the security ramifications of extending VDI externally. Later in this chapter, we will describe some of the available access control methods.

Why remote access is important for VDI

Whenever you deploy a technology solution that benefits users, there will be an immediate surge in requests for access to the solution from personal devices, both from users who travel and work in hotels and from users who work at home. Users today have high expectations, and they can boost productivity when access to their work is seamless. There are multiple reasons why remote access is important for VDI, including the following three:

- **Increasing demand for mobility** Users expect to be able to perform their job while at the office. But they also want to be able to perform their job at lunch, at home, on an airplane, and at a client site. They prefer that their location doesn't affect their productivity. Increasingly, users also have access to mobility-friendly computing devices—for example, a computing device at work, a computing device at home, a smartphone for a bag or pocket, and a tablet computer for anything in between.

- **Desktop on demand from anywhere**   Some users, especially those who often switch computing devices, find a desktop on demand a great way to work with a common computing environment. Whether they are at work or home and whether they are working from a tablet computer or any other computing device, they want to be able to access a desktop on demand. Such a desktop has all of their productivity applications and access to shared network drives.

- **RD Client for Android, iOS, and Windows Phone**   The RD Client for mobile devices brings new features to mobile devices. The RD Client can access computers at the office, VDI desktops, session-based desktops, and RemoteApp applications. Now, instead of just working with email on their mobile devices, users can connect to a virtual desktop and perform any of the tasks that they normally would on a desktop computer, but with a smaller screen.

Methods for securing remote access to VDI

Once you decide to offer remote access to your VDI, you need to begin evaluating the remote access methods to determine which one is the right choice for your environment. Each method has some pros and cons. The following three methods are the most common methods for securing remote access to a VDI:

- **Virtual Private Network (VPN)**   VPN technology has been around a long time. It is a stable technology that is well understood by IT administrators, and users are comfortable connecting by using a VPN. You don't have to deploy anything new or different, so using a VPN remote access method is a quick way to provide remote access. On the downside, the user experience isn't as good as with some other methods because users have to connect to the VPN before they can connect to the VDI, so an extra step is involved. In addition, in some environments, such as high-security environments, network restrictions prevent users from connecting to a VPN, which would prevent users from connecting to the VDI. This is true especially for sales professionals or others that travel to various company sites.

- **RD Gateway**   You can deploy Remote Desktop Gateway (RD Gateway) servers, which will accept connections from external users. The RD Gateway access method provides enhanced security because you have to authenticate and be authorized to use the RD Gateway and to use additional services such as virtual desktops. In comparison, many VPNs offer full network access once connected. The RD Gateway servers are easy to use because users generally only configure the gateway once. Thereafter, they can use the Remote Desktop Connection (RDC) client as though they were connected to the company network internally. The RD Gateway server works in tandem with the RD Web Access server to proxy communication from the Internet to the internal network. We look at the RD Gateway access method later in this chapter in a section titled "Controlling RD Gateway access."

- **Open the firewall, allowing communication from the Internet to the LAN**   A third option, which isn't recommended, is to open ports from the Internet to the resources on the company internal network. For example, you could open a port to allow external users to connect to the port that you use for your Remote Desktop Connection Broker (RDC Connection Broker) server. As a general rule, you should avoid opening ports from the Internet directly to the internal network. Instead, connections from the Internet should be authenticated—and, if possible, authorized—in the perimeter network first. That way, you can minimize the load on your internal resources and ensure that nobody who hasn't been authenticated and authorized already can get to the VDI environment. In the next section, we describe a network scenario that is a variation of this option.

Network configuration for RD Gateway

Sometimes, the best way to understand something is to see it displayed. This is true of the different RD Gateway network configurations available. Many configurations are available, and we will look at some popular options.

One of the simplest network configurations for RD Gateway is one that has the RD Gateway server placed onto the local area network (LAN) with a firewall separating the Internet from the LAN, as shown in Figure 11-1.

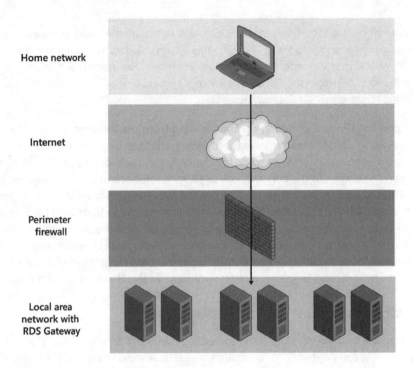

Home network

Internet

Perimeter
firewall

Local area
network with
RDS Gateway

Figure 11-1 RDS Gateway in LAN

Although having the Remote Desktop Services (RDS) Gateway server on the LAN provides simplicity, it also reduces the security of your environment. So it's a big tradeoff that usually isn't worth it. In this scenario, an unauthorized user is able to attempt authentication to your internal Active Directory Domain Services (AD DS) domain controllers from the Internet. This can lead to a denial of service attack, degraded performance, or service outages. In a worst-case scenario, it could lead to compromised credentials and data loss. In a high-security environment, it's a good practice to authenticate and authorize users prior to allowing them into your LAN.

A second network configuration is one in which the RDS Gateway server is placed into the perimeter network. It's separated from the LAN by an interior firewall, and it's separated from the Internet by a perimeter firewall, as shown in Figure 11-2.

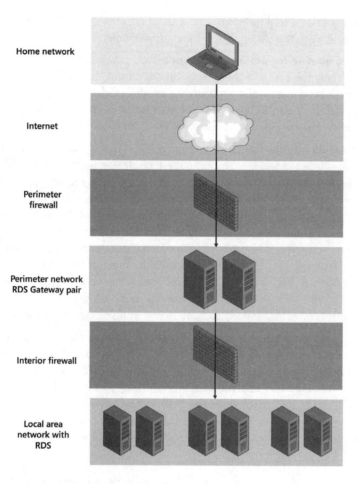

Figure 11-2 RDS Gateway in perimeter network

Moving the RDS Gateway server to the perimeter network enhances the security of your environment, especially compared to having Internet users come straight into the LAN. There are two variations of this model:

- **RDS Gateway in a workgroup**   In this variation, the RDS Gateway server(s) are in a workgroup. This model ensures that users are authenticated in the perimeter network before communicating with servers in the LAN. But, because the RDS Gateway servers are in a workgroup, the users have to authenticate twice: once to an RDS Gateway by using a local user account and a second time to RDS in the LAN, which relies on AD DS authentication.

- **RDS Gateway joined to a domain**   In this variation, the RDS server(s) are joined to an AD DS domain. With this variation, there are a few options:

    - **AD DS domain for perimeter network**   You can use an AD DS domain that serves only the perimeter network. With this option, there is a one-way forest trust so that the perimeter domain trusts the internal domain. This is a recommended approach if your RDS Gateway server must be in the perimeter network, because it doesn't have some of the downsides discussed in the next two options.

    - **Use AD DS internal domain**   You join the RDS Gateway server(s) to the internal AD DS domain. There is a big drawback, though: you need to open your firewall to support the domain membership. Most network and security teams aren't comfortable with the firewall changes required. In many organizations, there are security policies in place that do not allow the internal AD DS domain to be joined from a perimeter network. One way to make this option more palatable is to use IPsec, which can sign and encrypt communications, for all domain communication. This enhances security and reduces the number of firewall ports that have to be opened. But, some network teams oppose network tunnels that fall outside their control. Also, IPsec adds complexity to your deployment, which often leads to more administrative overhead and slower troubleshooting scenarios.

    - **Use a read-only domain controller (RODC)**   You can deploy a couple of RODCs for your internal AD DS domain to the perimeter network. This is an improvement over extending the internal domain with read-write DCs in the perimeter network. But, this still requires opening your firewall to support the RODCs. It also may violate any existing security policies that prohibit the internal AD DS domain from servicing perimeter networks. You can use IPsec for all domain communication, but you should weigh the added complexity of that to ascertain whether it makes sense for your environment.

Often, your design decision will be based on your defined perimeter network authentication strategy and whether you have a way to accept AD DS authentication in the perimeter network.

Another network configuration is one that deploys the RD Gateway server(s) to the internal LAN and uses reverse proxy services to handle communication from the Internet, as shown in Figure 11-3.

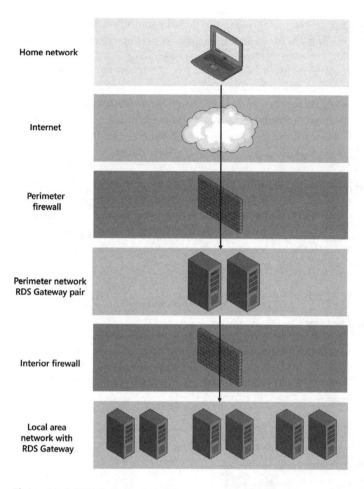

Figure 11-3 RDS Gateway in LAN

Of all of the options, this option is the most recommended. The benefits of this option are as follows:

- **SSL inspection**   A reverse proxy server, such as Microsoft Forefront Threat Management Gateway (TMG) 2010, can be configured to decrypt inbound communication, inspect it for security issues, re-encrypt it, and then send the acceptable communication on to the RDS Gateway server in the LAN. This provides enhanced security.

- **Domain joining not required**   A reverse proxy server does not have to be joined to a domain to authenticate domain-based traffic securely. Although firewall ports need to be opened from the proxy server to the domain controllers, they will be used only for authentication and not for regular domain membership communication.

- **Flexible for other services**   A reverse proxy server also can service Microsoft Exchange, Microsoft SharePoint, Internet Information Services (IIS) websites, and other services on your LAN. An RDS Gateway is a dedicated solution for RDS, which isn't as flexible because it can't be used for other services. For organizations that have several technologies that require communication from the Internet and into the LAN, a reverse proxy solution often is the best choice.

Configuration options for RD Gateway

There are a few key configuration items to review after deploying an RD Gateway server, such as Secure Sockets Layer (SSL) settings, transport settings, and logging. These options are housed within the RD Gateway Manager management console. To access the management console, perform the following steps:

1.   Open Server Manager and click the Tools menu.

2.   Locate and highlight Terminal Services from the list.

3.   Select Remote Desktop Gateway Manager.

You can access the configuration options that we will be discussing by right-clicking the server and clicking Properties, as shown in Figure 11-4.

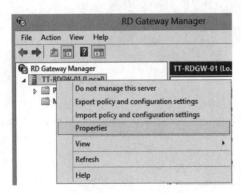

Figure 11-4 RD Gateway Manager management console

TCP and UDP ports

For each external user session, the RD Gateway server creates three connections: one HTTP connection and two UDP connections with the client. The HTTP connection maintains client communication with the target RDS server though TCP port 443 by default, while the UDP connections are used to support a rich multimedia experience. If you have multiple RD Gateway servers in a server farm, you can use hardware or software load-balancing solutions to distribute user sessions among all servers in the farm.

The port configurations are shown on the Transport Settings tab of the RD Gateway server properties, as shown in Figure 11-5.

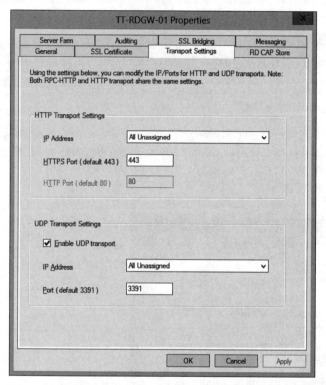

Figure 11-5 RD Gateway Properties window, Transport Settings tab

In addition to client communication, there is back-end communication. The ports being used vary depending on the network model you have. At a high level, you need to investigate the following communications so that you can configure your firewalls accordingly:

- **Authentication** Users have to be authenticated. If you are authenticating locally to the RDS Gateway server, then you don't need to do anything for the authentication communication because it doesn't leave the server. However, if the server is joined to a domain or a trusting domain, then there are many ports that must be configured.

- **Authorization** Users have to be authorized as valid users before proceeding. One example of this is communication between the RDS Gateway server and a central

Network Policy Server (NPS) server, which would require some ports being opened, depending on the location of each server.

- **Name resolution**   The RDS Gateway server needs to be able to resolve the fully quali-fied host names of other servers with which it will communicate, such as domain con-trollers and NPS servers. The RDS Gateway server, if it resides in the perimeter network, would not have direct access to the DNS servers. Thus, you need to allow the server to communicate over DNS ports to the DNS servers.

- **Public Key Infrastructure (PKI)**   You need to be able to communicate with an internal PKI or a third-party PKI to validate that the certificate being used hasn't been revoked.

For a complete list of the ports used in an RDS deployment, see the article at *http://aka.ms/VirtApps/rds2012ports*.

All communication to and from the RD Gateway is encrypted and therefore requires a valid SSL certificate to function correctly. The first time you open the RD Gateway SSL Certificate settings, a warning is displayed at the top of the tab, as shown in Figure 11-6, instructing you to import a valid SSL certificate.

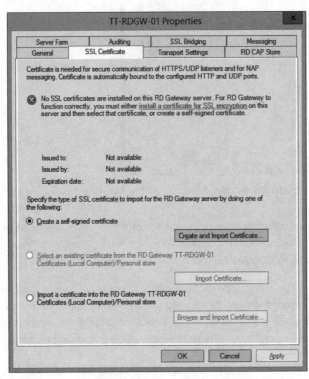

Figure 11-6 RD Gateway Properties window, SSL Certificate tab

From this property window, you are given the option to create and import a self-signed certificate. This should be used only for technical evaluation and testing purposes. In a production environment, you use a certificate provided by a trusted public certification authority (CA). You do not need an internal PKI if you can use another method to obtain an externally trusted certificate that meets the requirements for RD Gateway. However, if you have an existing PKI and your clients will all trust the PKI, you can use a certificate issued by the internal CA.

In the following example, we import a certificate from an internal PKI.

1. On the SSL Certificate property page, select the Select An Existing Certificate From The RD Gateway <server hostname> Certificates (Local Computer)/Personal Store option. Then click Import Certificate.

2. In the Import Certificate window, click the desired certificate in the list of available certificates and then click Import, as shown in Figure 11-7.

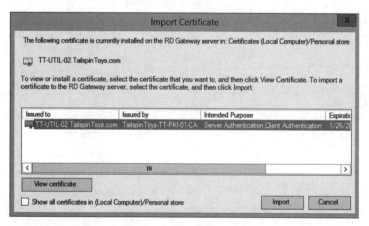

Figure 11-7 Import Certificate window

3. Click Apply after the certificate is imported. You will see the information on the SSL Certificate tab updated to reflect the import, as shown in Figure 11-8.

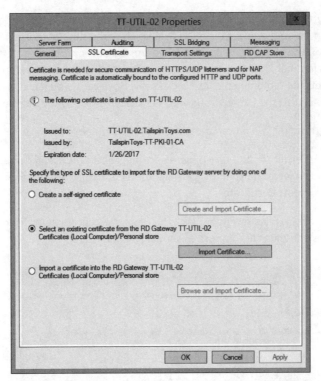

Figure 11-8 RD Gateway Properties window, SSL Certificate tab

Inside OUT

A deeper look at certificates for RD Gateway

Some key details often can create trouble for administrators when they try to import a certificate. First, the certificate must be installed, and it must be in the Local Computer /Personal key store. Otherwise, the import process won't see a valid certificate and you can't proceed with an import. This information occasionally is shown in the user interface. There also are some lesser-known requirements for certificates in RD Gateway, as follows:

- **FQDN name match**   The fully qualified domain name (FQDN) of the RD Gateway server, or the FQDN that users use to connect to it, must match the name in the Subject line of the certificate.

- **Server Authentication**   The certificate must be configured with Server Authentication as a part of the Enhanced Key Usage. It also can be configured for other uses, but Server Authentication must be one of them.

- **Private key**   The installed certificate must have a corresponding private key. If you exported the certificate from another server, make sure that you export it with the private key so that you can import it with the private key.

- **Computer certificate**   The two types of certificates that you can acquire are computer certificates and user certificates. User certificates typically are used for encryption or code signing. Computer certificates often are used for authentication. For the RD Gateway certificate, you must use a computer certificate.

SSL Bridging

Earlier in this chapter, in the section titled "Network configuration for RD Gateway," we discussed using reverse proxy services in the perimeter network to enhance security and simplify your environment. If you opt to go that route, you should configure SSL Bridging. The RD Gateway supports SSL Bridging. The options are available on the SSL Bridging tab of the RD Gateway Properties page, as shown in Figure 11-9. In this example, we enable SSL Bridging with the HTTPS–HTTPS bridging option.

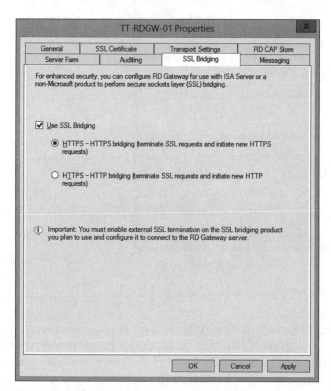

Figure 11-9 RD Gateway Properties window, SSL Bridging tab

Simultaneous connections

The RD Gateway server enables you to control the number of incoming connections. On the General tab, as shown in Figure 11-10, you can allow as many connections as the server hardware supports, you can allow only a certain number of connections, or you can disable any new connections. Not allowing any new connections allows you to remove a server from servicing new connections. Eventually, the server will not have any connections, and then you can perform maintenance. In such a case, you can disable new connections early in the day to prepare for maintenance work in the evening. This is sometimes referred to as drain stopping a server.

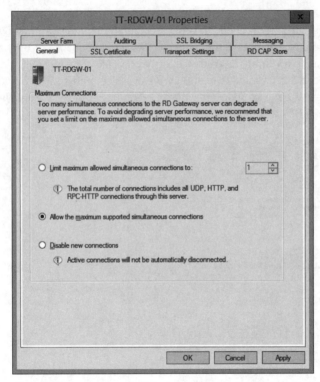

Figure 11-10 RD Gateway Properties window, General tab

Logging

Logging is another key component that should be reviewed in your environment. With RD Gateway Manager, you can specify the types of events that you want to monitor, such as unsuccessful or successful connection attempts to internal network resources through an RD Gateway server.

When the events occur, you can monitor the corresponding events by using Windows Event Viewer. RD Gateway server events are stored in Event Viewer under Application and Services Logs\Microsoft\Windows\Terminal Services-Gateway\.

The logging options are available on the Auditing tab of the RD Gateway properties page, as shown in Figure 11-11.

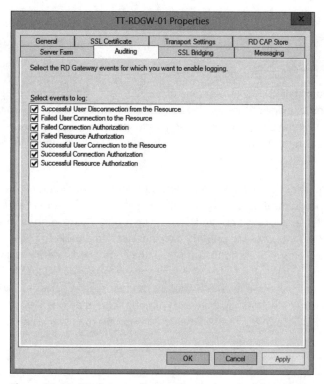

Figure 11-11 RD Gateway Properties window, Auditing tab

Remote access from mobile devices

Historically, users connected to RDS through their organization's network, from their desktop or laptop computers. Today, things have changed dramatically: users have multiple devices, including smartphones and tablets, with them at all times. At work, they still use laptop computers, but when they aren't at the organization's location, users want to connect to RDS from their mobile devices. If a device has an RDC client and network connectivity, users can run RemoteApp programs or access their virtual desktops from almost everywhere and from almost any device.

CHAPTER 11

RDC is built into Windows client and server operating systems. Additionally, it is freely available for other operating systems and platforms, including the following:

- Android

- iOS

- Mac

- Windows Phone

- Windows RT

You can download and install RDC from the same place you would obtain other programs for your device. Because mobile devices are touch-enabled, users can control RDC with touch. Most clients provide the same basic features as the Windows version, including access to remote desktop, support for RemoteApp programs, editable RD settings, and a configurable RD Gateway.

Depending on the mobile device, you also can connect to RemoteApp programs. RemoteApp enables you to make programs that are accessed remotely through RDS appear as if they are running on the end user's local computing device. The programs are referred to as RemoteApp programs. Instead of being presented to the user in the desktop of the Remote Desktop Session Host (RD Session Host) server, the RemoteApp programs are integrated with the client's desktop, which is why they appear to be running locally. The RemoteApp program runs in its own resizable window, can be dragged across multiple monitors, and has its own entry in the taskbar. If a user is running more than one RemoteApp program on the same RD Session Host server, the RemoteApp programs will share the same RDS session.

TROUBLESHOOTING

Some clients work, some don't

Now that the RD Gateway server supports so many different client operating systems and device types, there are additional complexities for troubleshooting scenarios. Sometimes, the best way to build up your troubleshooting skills is to spend some time troubleshooting. Unfortunately, that means that you need some real issues to troubleshoot! If you run into a situation in which some clients work and some clients don't, one thing to check immediately is the operating system and device type of the nonfunctional clients. If the nonfunctional clients are not Windows clients, check if your RD Gateway configuration is set to allow only connections from clients that support RD Gateway messaging. RD Gateway messaging is a feature that allows you to configure a logon message to clients as they log on. On the RD Gateway server, you can configure the server to allow only connections from clients that support RD Gateway messaging. Unbeknownst to many, some RD Gateway clients, such as Mac clients, Android clients, and iOS clients, don't support messaging and thus can't connect when it is required.

Controlling RD Gateway access

Now that you have a thorough understanding of the options for extending your VDI outside your organization, you need to learn about the available options for controlling who can access your VDI from the outside. In this section, we will look at some of the options, discuss the role of the Network Policy Server (NPS) server, and discuss when cloud-based, multi-factor authentication comes into play.

Overview of controlling RD Gateway access

After you install an RD Gateway server, users can establish a secure connection through the RD Gateway server to the internal RDS resources. The internal RDS resources include RD Session Host servers, RemoteApp programs, virtual desktops, and computers with enabled Remote Desktop features.

In most environments, you need to be able to control who can access internal RDS resources and which RDS resources can be accessed from the Internet. You can use Remote Desktop connection authorization policies (RD CAPs) and Remote Desktop resource authorization policies (RD RAPs) to achieve this goal when using RD Gateway. RD CAPs and RD RAPs are stored locally on the RD Gateway server by default. If you have multiple RD Gateway servers, you can configure them to use centralized RD CAPs, which are stored on an NPS server. If you want to provide an additional layer of security for users who connect to the internal RDS resources, you can integrate RD Gateway with Microsoft Azure Multi-Factor Authentication.

RD CAPs

The first tool that you can use to control who can access your RD Gateway servers is an RD CAP. An RD CAP allows you to control access to the RD Gateway server by offering the following configuration options:

- **Specify user groups** As part of creating an RD CAP, you must specify a minimum of one security group. It can be a local group or an AD DS group, depending on whether the RD Gateway server is joined to the domain. Only members of the specified groups can connect to the RD Gateway server.

- **Specify computer groups** Specifying computer groups is optional. It allows for further filtering of who can connect to your RD Gateway server. It is used mostly in high-security environments because it isn't very compatible in a network in which you aren't familiar with or aren't controlling the client computers, such as a network with users using personal computing devices.

- **Specify authentication type**   You can require password authentication only, require smart card authentication only, or allow either one.

- **Configure device redirection**   Device redirection is a feature that redirects hard drives, the Clipboard, printers, some ports, and some Plug and Play devices. This allows you to use them in an RDC session. In an RD CAP, you can enable all redirection or only allow a subset of redirection.

- **Configure timeout settings**   You can enable and configure time-out settings for idle connections or active sessions. This enables you to ensure that users don't stay connected indefinitely.

An RD CAP is dependent on an RD RAP. You need to have both to enable users to connect. An RD CAP is shown in Figure 11-12.

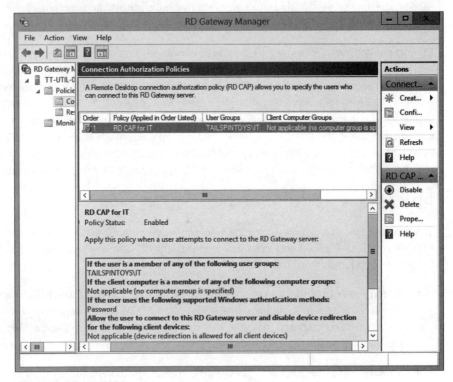

Figure 11-12 RD CAP

RD RAPs

An RD CAP specifies which groups can access an RD Gateway server, and an RD RAP specifies the resources to which they can connect. You can use the following configuration options in an RD RAP:

- **Specify groups**   You can limit the RD RAP to specific local or AD DS security groups by adding them to the RD RAP. In most cases, you should specify the same groups for corresponding RD CAPs and RD RAPs.

- **Specify resources**   You can grant users access by configuring one of the following three resource options:

    - **Specify an AD DS group**   You can specify a group that contains the computers to which you are allowing users to connect.

    - **Specify an RD Gateway–managed group**   You can specify an RD Gateway–managed group that contains computers or a remote desktop farm.

    - **Allow users to connect to any resource**   You also can allow users to connect to any resource, which effectively takes off the resource filter.

- **Specify the allowed ports**   You can specify that only port 3389 is allowed. Or, you can specify a custom list of ports. To remove port filters completely, you can allow any port. If you use the default port, then the default configuration of allowing 3389 is what you want because RDC sessions use 3389 by default.

An RD RAP is dependent on an RD CAP. You need to have both to enable users to connect. An RD RAP is shown in Figure 11-13.

CHAPTER 11

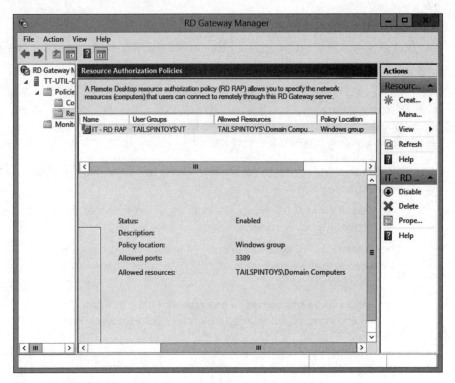

Figure 11-13 RD RAP

Central RD CAP store

Many organizations have multiple RD Gateway servers in an RDS deployment. This enables external users to connect to internal RDS resources even if a single RD Gateway server fails. However, because each RD Gateway server uses local RD CAPs by default, it can be challenging to configure all of your RD Gateway servers with the same configuration. In such environments, using a central store for RD CAPs is beneficial.

When you install RD Gateway, NPS installs on the same server. By default, RD Gateway uses that local NPS to store RD CAPs. You can configure the RD Gateway server to use centralized RD CAPs, in which case it will store them on the remote server that runs NPS. When you have multiple RD Gateway servers, they all can use the same NPS server. This provides all RD Gateway servers with the same set of RD CAPs.

To configure RD Gateway with a central RD CAP store, perform the following steps:

1. Install the NPS role service on a server that will be the central store. In NPS, you need to add all RD Gateway servers as Remote Authentication Dial-In User Service (RADIUS) clients by specifying their IP address and shared secret.

2. On each RD Gateway server, configure a central RD CAP. You must specify a central server that runs NPS and a shared secret, which must match the shared secret that was specified for the RD Gateway server.

3. Use the Network Policy Server console to create RD CAPs on a central server that runs NPS. You should be aware that when a central RD CAP store is used, you manage RD CAPs in the Network Policy Server console and not in RD Gateway Manager.

TROUBLESHOOTING

Switching to a centralized RD CAP store

Often, administrators opt to store RD CAPs locally in their initial configuration. Later, as the infrastructure grows, it is common to switch to a centralized model to store RD CAPs, especially as the number of RD Gateway servers grows. If you decide to switch to the central store, be aware that the local RD CAPs won't copy over to the central store. Instead, you need to create new RD CAPs on the central NPS server.

Integrating Microsoft Azure Multi-Factor Authentication

One of the primary concerns with opening your internal environment to your users on the Internet is security. Often, users connect to internal environments by using unsecured public wireless networks at coffee shops, in airports, and on airplanes. To add to the risk, users often use personal computing devices that don't have the typical corporate security software installed and maintained. Some organizations want to add security to their external connectivity. One way to do that is to add multi-factor authentication, which is available as a service in Microsoft Azure. By adding Azure Multi-Factor Authentication (Azure MFA), you will be able to secure your environment by requiring a user name and password or smart card plus an additional authentication from Azure, which uses a mobile app, a telephone call, or an SMS message. The diagram in Figure 11-14 shows the high-level flow of authentication when you integrate Azure MFA.

CHAPTER 11

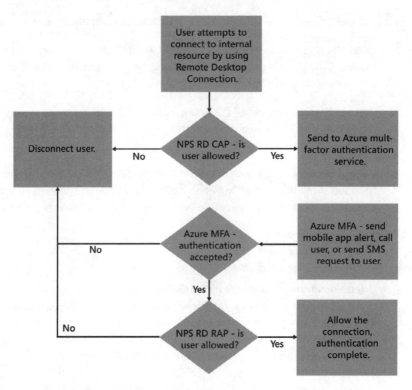

Figure 11-14 Azure MFA flowchart

Besides having a Remote Desktop environment up and running, you will need to meet the following prerequisites to establish multi-factor authentication:

- **Azure multi-factor cloud service**   You need to add the Azure MFA service to your Microsoft Azure subscription. To add Azure MFA to your subscription, perform the following steps:

1. Sign into the Microsoft Azure management portal.

2. In the lower-left corner, click New.

3. In the New menu, click App Services, click Active Directory, click Multi-Factor Auth Provider, and then click Quick Create.

4. In the Name text box, type a name for your Azure MFA.

5. In the Usage Model drop-down window, select the usage model. You can select Per Enabled User or Per Authentication. You generally should opt for the model that costs less for your environment. For example, if you are going to have a small number of users

but a large amount of authentication activity, you should opt for
Per Enabled User. In contrast, if you are going to have a very large number
of users who only will authenticate occasionally, you should consider the
Per Authentication model. In this model, you are charged for every
10 authentications, but you can have an unlimited number of users.

6. In the Subscription drop-down menu, select the subscription with which you want to
associate the Azure MFA. If you have a single subscription, you won't need to perform
this step. The charges will be handled by the subscription that you select.

7. In the Directory drop-down menu, select the Azure Active Directory instance that you
want to use with Azure MFA. Or, if you don't want to use one or don't have one, select
Do Not Link A Directory.

8. Click Create.

● **Multi-Factor Authentication Server**   You need to download the
Multi-Factor Authentication Server from the Microsoft Azure management
portal. It's a free download because Azure MFA charges you for users or
authentication activity, not for the server software.

After you have the Azure MFA added to your subscription, you should see it in the management portal, as shown in Figure 11-15.

active directory

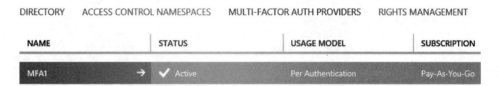

Figure 11-15   Azure MFA in management portal

You can have multiple Azure MFA providers in an Azure subscription. After you install the
Multi-Factor Authentication Server, you will be able to manage your multi-factor configuration
from a management console, which is shown in Figure 11-16.

CHAPTER 11

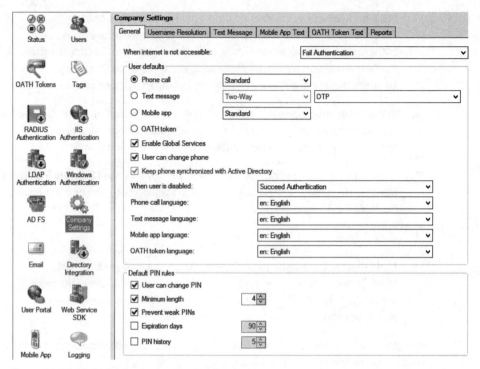

Figure 11-16 Multi-Factor Authentication Server

There is a detailed step-by-step write-up about integrating RD Gateway with Azure MFA by two RDS MVPs named Kristin L. Griffin and Freek Berson at *http://aka.ms/virtapps/ws2012r2RDgateway*.

Performance and Health Monitoring of Virtual Desktop Infrastructure

Virtual Desktop Infrastructure (VDI) performance and health monitoring is a critical part of managing VDI to meet user performance expectations and avoid outages. The Windows Server 2012 R2 operating system includes tools that you can use for troubleshooting performance issues. If you need active monitoring, you can use System Center 2012 R2 Operations Manager. There are unique performance counters that you should monitor for different parts of a VDI deployment. For example, you should monitor different performance counters on a Remote Desktop Session Host (RD Session Host) server than on a Remote Desktop Virtualization Host (RD Virtualization Host) server. In this chapter, you will learn how to monitor VDI performance and health.

Monitoring desktop and application virtualization

Windows Server 2012 R2 includes a number of tools that you can use to view performance information. Event Viewer and Server Manager help you monitor service health. Task Manager, Resource Monitor, and Performance Monitor provide detailed information about the resources that applications and services use, which you can use when troubleshooting. You also can download tools, such as Process Monitor, from Windows Sysinternals that provide even more detailed performance information.

Understanding monitoring for desktop and application virtualization

Most organizations don't actively monitor standard desktop computers because performance issues are rare and affect only one user. If a single computer, and consequently a single user, has a performance problem, that user calls the help desk for assistance. Computer issues for a single user generally don't result in significant costs for an organization.

The infrastructure for desktop and application virtualization supports many users. Consequently, a single performance problem or service outage for desktop or application virtualization infrastructure affects many users and might have a large impact on your organization's productivity. If you monitor your desktop and application virtualization infrastructure, you

CHAPTER 12

quickly can identify when performance issues or outages are occurring and resolve them. This minimizes performance issues and outages that affect user productivity.

Desktop and application virtualization infrastructure that you should monitor includes the following:

- **Microsoft Application Virtualization (App-V) servers**   You should monitor App-V publishing servers to ensure that they are available for application distribution. In addition, you should ensure that resources such as the network and disk aren't becoming bottlenecks in application distribution.

- **RD Session Host servers**   You should monitor RD Session Host servers to ensure that users can access Remote Desktop Services (RDS) session-based desktop deployments. You also can use monitoring to ensure that RD Session Host server performance is adequate. For example, you can monitor resource utilization on a server to ensure that there are no bottlenecks.

- **RD Virtualization Host servers**   You should monitor RD Virtualization Host servers to ensure that users can access personal and pooled virtual desktops. You should use monitoring to ensure that no resource bottlenecks affect the performance of personal and pooled virtual desktops.

- **Other RDS roles**   You also should monitor the availability and performance of other RDS server roles such as Remote Desktop Gateway (RD Gateway), Remote Desktop Connection Broker (RD Connection Broker), and Remote Desktop Licensing (RD Licensing). If any of these server roles is unavailable or suffering from performance issues, it can affect users.

Event monitoring for desktop and application virtualization

You can use event logs in Windows Server 2012 R2 to identify errors that affect application and desktop virtualization. You can use Server Manager in Windows Server 2012 R2 to view the health of server roles. In the Server Manager dashboard, you can see the health of server roles, including RDS. If you click on Events in the RDS area, a window opens that allows you to view Warning and Error events.

Event Viewer, shown in Figure 12-1, is the most commonly used tool for viewing event logs on a specific server. For basic event log monitoring, you can browse each event log individually. There also is an Administrative Events custom view that you can use to review Error and Warning events quickly. The Administrative Events custom view filters all of the event logs on a local computer and shows all Error and Warning events. You also can create your own custom views to simplify monitoring specific event logs or event sources.

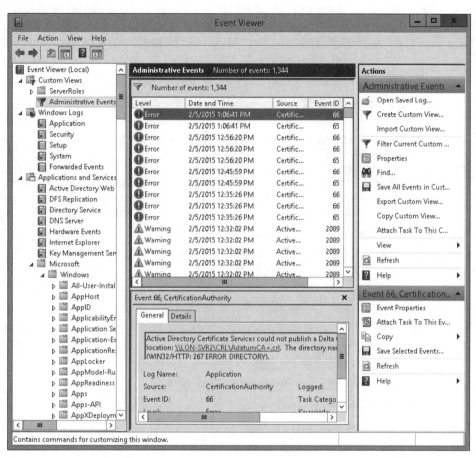

Figure 12-1 Event Viewer

Although it's most common to use Event Viewer to view event logs on a local computer, you can use Event Viewer from a desktop to view event logs on remote servers. In many cases, this is faster than using a Remote Desktop session to open Event Viewer on a remote computer.

To simplify monitoring event logs on multiple servers, you can configure event log subscriptions. You can use an event log subscription to gather specific events from multiple servers to an event log on a single central server. Then, instead of connecting to multiple servers, you can view and filter events in a single event log on a central server.

NOTE

Very few organizations use event log subscriptions. Organizations that need to perform event log monitoring across many servers typically use a different tool.

As part of monitoring, you should monitor the System and Application event logs on all servers. The System event log shows generic server-level events such as services starting and stopping and networking configuration. The Application event log has application-specific events from many services. You are more likely to find application-specific events that are useful for troubleshooting in the Application event log.

Windows Server 2012 R2 uses event logs for specific services and server roles. You should include the appropriate event logs for specific services in your infrastructure monitoring for application and desktop virtualization. Some of the service-specific event logs to monitor include the following:

- **App-V** The most useful troubleshooting information for App-V client connectivity is located in the Applications and Services Logs\Microsoft\AppV\Client\Admin event log, which is located on the App-V clients. Additional logs that you can use for troubleshooting are on the App-V Management Server:

  - Microsoft\App-V\Server-Management\Admin

  - Microsoft\App-V\Server-Publishing\Admin

  - Microsoft\App-V\Server-Publishing\Operational

- **RDS** There are several service-specific event logs for RDS. These event logs include logs for RD Licensing, RD Connection Broker, RD Virtualization Host, and other RDS server roles. The names of some event logs are as follows:

  - Remote-Desktop-Management-Service

  - RemoteApp and Desktop Connection Management

  - RemoteApp and Desktop Connections

  - RemoteDesktopServices-RdpCoreTS

  - RemoteDesktopServices-SessionServices

  - TerminalServices-SessionBroker

  - TerminalServices-TSV-VmHostAgent

- **Hyper-V** Several event logs that are specific to Hyper-V can be useful when monitoring Microsoft virtual machine (VM)–based desktop deployments of VDI. The Hyper-V event logs include the following:

  - Hyper-V-Hypervisor

  - Hyper-V-VMMS

  - Hyper-V-Worker

Performance monitoring tools for desktop and application virtualization

Windows Server 2012 R2 includes several tools that you can use to monitor server infrastructure performance for application and desktop virtualization. These tools provide information that can be useful when identifying performance issues. The main drawback of these tools is the lack of centralized monitoring. The tools included in Windows Server 2012 R2 primarily focus on monitoring a local server.

You are most likely to use Task Manager, shown in Figure 12-2, when you need to troubleshoot a performance issue quickly. In Task Manager, you can view which processes run on a server and identify the resources those processes use. When there is a performance issue, you can use this information to identify a process that uses a high level of resources, which might cause the performance issue.

Figure 12-2 Task Manager

You also can use Task Manager to identify quickly all of the users who are signed in to an RD Session Host server. You can identify the processes that each of these users started. You also can see a summary of the processing and memory resources that each user and each of the user's processes use. You can monitor additional resources on the Details tab by right-clicking the column headers and selecting additional columns.

CHAPTER 12

You can use Resource Monitor, shown in Figure 12-3, to view more detailed information than Task Manager provides about processor, memory, disk, and network utilization. For example, you can view disk utilization and identify whether disk I/O is a bottleneck. If disk I/O is a bottleneck, you can identify which processes and files are causing the large amount of disk activity that is slowing down the system. Like Task Manager, you can use Resource Monitor to troubleshoot performance problems when they occur.

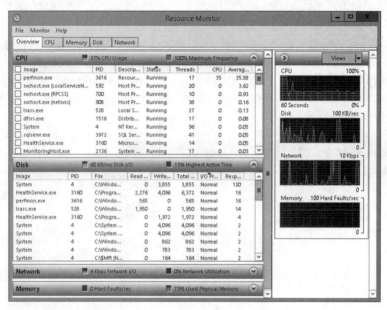

Figure 12-3 Resource Monitor

You can use Performance Monitor, shown in Figure 12-4, to record and view performance counter values in Windows Server 2012 R2. Many detailed performance counters that you can monitor are available. The performance counters that are available for monitoring vary depending on the server roles that are installed. Some applications also include performance counters as part of application installations. Some commonly used counters relate to central processing unit (CPU) utilization, memory utilization, disk I/O, and network utilization.

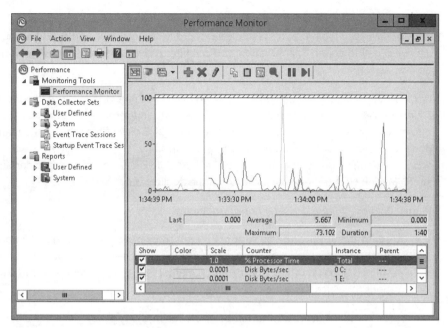

Figure 12-4 Performance Monitor

You can view current performance counter values to troubleshoot current issues. For intermittent issues, you can create data collector sets in Performance Monitor. When you create a data collector set, you can define which performance counters are recorded, when performance counter recordings start, the interval for sampling the performance counter, and when performance counter recordings end. After you have recorded data with a data collector set, you can view the data and try to correlate anomalies in the data with performance issues.

Using Process Monitor to identify application issues

Windows Sysinternals is a set of free tools that is available from Microsoft to perform low-level monitoring and troubleshooting of Windows clients and servers. Sysinternals tools are available to monitor and view process activity, disk activity, and security settings. One utility that is useful for identifying compatibility issues with RD Session Host servers is Process Monitor.

Process Monitor is a utility that monitors and logs the activity of processes on a computer system. The activity that you can monitor includes access to the following:

- Registry keys

- Files

- Network

After you capture application activity by using Process Monitor, you can filter it in a number of ways. You can use toolbar buttons to display registry, file, network, and thread activity. If you are investigating a specific application, you can filter activity to show actions that a specific process performs.

When an application isn't running properly, you can use Process Monitor to identify which action is failing. For example, you might use Process Monitor to identify that an older application modifies information in the HKEY_LOCAL_MACHINE hive of the registry. Standard users don't have permissions to modify registry keys in this hive. Only administrators typically have access to modify registry keys in HKEY_LOCAL_MACHINE. This means that standard users on an RD Session Host server are unable to run the application.

In this situation, there are several possible solutions:

- **Update the application to support standard user permissions**   Ideally, you can update an application to a more recent version that does not require users to access restricted portions of the registry. But in many cases, this problem occurs in older applications for which there are no replacements.

- **Give standard users additional permissions in the registry**   In some cases, you might be able to update permissions on the registry keys that an application accesses to allow standard users to modify the registry keys. This solution often works on traditional desktop computers, pooled virtual desktops, and personal desktops. However, on an RD Session Host server, you might be allowing multiple users to overwrite information at the same time, which might cause problems for the application.

- **Implement the application by using personal desktops**   On personal virtual desktops, you can give users local administrator permissions to resolve registry permissions issues. You also could use RemoteApp applications on personal desktops instead of providing access to entire personal virtual desktops.

- **Implement the application by using App-V**   App-V virtualizes an application's registry activity. This functionality isolates application activity from the local operating system and can allow the application to be used on an RD Session Host server.

➤ To download Process Monitor from the Windows Sysinternals, go to *https://technet.microsoft.com/en-us/sysinternals/bb896645*.

Using Operations Manager for monitoring

Most of the monitoring tools included with Windows Server 2012 R2 primarily are used to react when users notify you of performance issues. Operations Manager is part of System Center 2012 R2, and it can monitor servers actively. Active monitoring raises alerts so that you can address problems immediately. You also can monitor resource utilization trends to predict when upgrades are required before performance affects users.

Operations Manager is a monitoring solution for network infrastructure, servers, and applications. You can use it to gather essential monitoring information into a single central console that you can use to track anomalies, such as failed services, and to record their resolution. Actively monitoring your infrastructure minimizes downtime because you can identify potential problems before they affect users. When a problem does occur, you are notified quickly and are given information about the problem almost immediately.

The following are the main functions of Operations Manager:

- **Collecting data**   To support data collection from servers and clients, you need to install the Operations Manager agent. This agent monitors a local system and sends data back to a management server that stores the collected data in a database. The data to be collected is defined based on rules that you can create and modify.

- **Generating alerts**   In Operations Manager, you can define acceptable values for the data that the Operations Manager agent collects. Management servers send the rules to the agents. If monitored values fall outside defined parameters, the agent notifies the management server and an alert is generated. The alert appears in the Operations console, where administrators can view information about the alert and begin to resolve the issue.

- **Sending notifications**   Most likely, an administrator does not use the Operations console constantly to monitor whether alerts have been generated. Therefore, Operations Manager can send notifications to administrators to indicate when an alert is generated. You can implement rules to identify which administrators should be notified by specific systems in your organization. The notifications can be sent by email, SMS, or instant messaging.

Parts of an Operations Manager implementation

Operations Manager includes several parts that work together to provide monitoring, alerts, and notifications. You should understand each of the Operations Manager parts to understand its overall capabilities. In addition, understanding the communication process among parts aids you when troubleshooting is required. Figure 12-5 shows the communication process.

CHAPTER 12

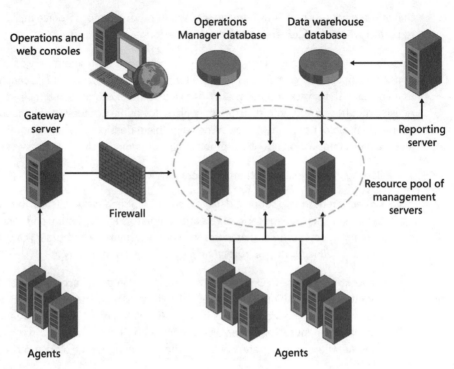

Figure 12-5 Operations Manager

Operations Manager has the following parts:

- **Agents**   In most cases, you install agents on computers that Operations Manager monitors. Agents can be installed on Windows-based, UNIX-based, and Linux-based systems. It's also possible to perform monitoring without an installed agent, but this isn't very efficient and has limited functionality. You typically use agentless monitoring on systems on which an agent can't be deployed, such as secure systems with restricted access.

- **Management servers**   Agents report status information to management servers. One management server is required, but for high availability or additional capacity, you can have multiple management servers in a single resource pool.

- **Operations Manager database**   Management servers store information collected by agents in an Operations Manager database. This database is used for short-term storage of information that relates to current status and alerts.

- **Data warehouse database**   Management servers also store information collected by agents in the data warehouse database. This database is used for long-term data storage and for reporting.

- **Reporting server**   The reporting server is a server that runs Microsoft SQL Server Reporting Services (SSRS). This server generates reports that typically are viewed by using the Operations console.

- **Operations console**   The Operations console is the primary interface for managing and working with Operations Manager. You can use the Operations console to view status, manage alerts, and view reports. The web console provides many of the same functions as the Operations console, but through a web-based interface.

- **Gateway server**   You can use a gateway server to support environments where Kerberos authentication isn't possible between agents and management servers. Agents report to a gateway server, which reports information to management servers. Authentication between a gateway server and management servers is performed by using certificates. It's also possible to configure agents to use certificate-based authentication, but when there are more than a few agents, it's easier to use a gateway server.

Inside OUT

Understanding the Operations console

After Operations Manager is installed, the Operations console, shown in Figure 12-6, is the most commonly used way to interact with the monitoring information. Functionality in the Operations console is divided into workspaces. The Operations console has several workspaces for configuring and managing Operations Manager. The workspaces are as follows:

- **Monitoring**   This workspace contains various views for monitoring systems. Views import as part of management packs, but you also can create your own customized views. The most common views show alerts and system state.

- **Authoring**   You use this workspace to configure customized monitoring of applications and servers.

- **Administration**   You use this workspace to configure various aspects of Operations Manager. The most common actions that you perform here are discovering computers for agent deployment and importing management packs.

- **My Workspace**   You can customize this workspace to contain the views that you use most often.

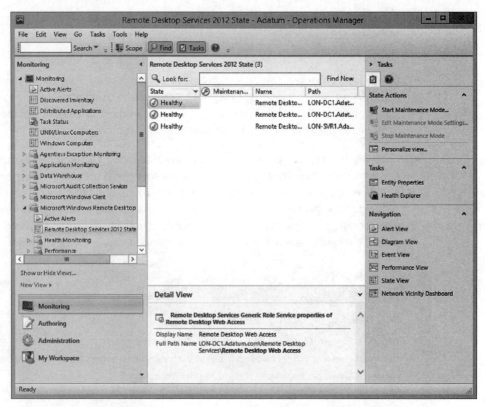

Figure 12-6 Operations console

Before you can monitor servers providing application and desktop virtualization, you need to install the Operations Manager agent. You can install the agent manually from the Operations Manager installation media, but it's more common to deploy it by using the Operations console. The process for selecting the computers for deployment is referred to as discovery.

To install the Operations Manager agent on a server, perform the following steps:

1. On the taskbar, click Operations Console.

2. In the Operations console, click the Administration workspace.

3. In the Administration workspace, on the Administration Overview page, shown in Figure 12-7, click Required: Configure Computers And Devices To Manage.

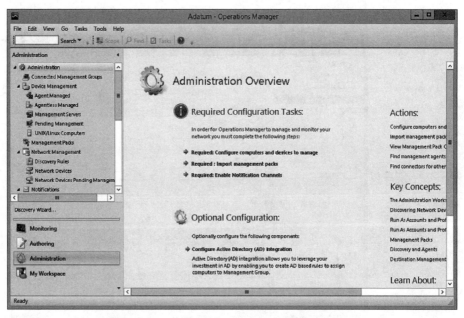

Figure 12-7 Operations console, Administration Overview page

4. In the Computer And Device Management Wizard, click Windows Computers and click Next. You also can select UNIX/Linux computers and network devices for monitoring.

5. On the Auto Or Advanced page, select Automatic Computer Discovery and click Next. This option queries Active Directory Domain Services (AD DS) for all computer objects. If you choose Advanced Discovery, you can limit the results to Servers Only or Clients Only or specify specific computer accounts.

6. On the Administrator Account page, select Use Selected Management Server Action Account and click Discover. This page defines an account that has administrator rights on the computers on which you are installing the agent. The Management Server Action Account defined in Operations Manager has local administrator permissions in most cases, but you can specify an alternate account if you prefer.

7. On the Select Objects To Manage page, shown in Figure 12-8, select the servers on which you want to install the agent and then click Next. In most cases, you want to use the default Management Mode of Agent.

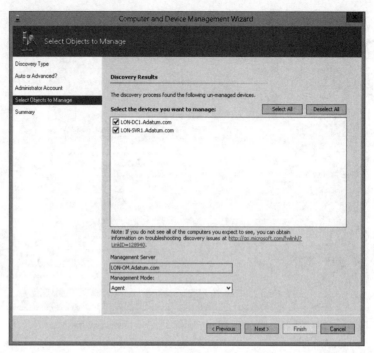

Figure 12-8 Computer And Device Management Wizard, Select Objects To Manage page

8. On the Summary page, shown in Figure 12-9, click Finish to begin deployment. On this page, you can change the installation directory and credentials used to run the agent service on managed computers, but this is done rarely.

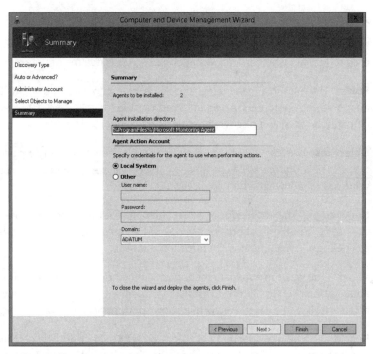

Figure 12-9 Computer And Device Management Wizard, Summary page

9. In the Agent Management Task Status window, click Close. You can close this window at any time. Agent installation completes as a background task.

NOTE

After installing the agent on a computer, it can take 10 to 15 minutes for the status to appear in the Operations console.

Understanding management packs and overrides

In Operations Manager, the rules for data collection and raising alerts are stored in management packs. At the simplest level, a management pack is a file that contains information about how to perform monitoring and how to display that monitoring information.

Although creating your own management packs is possible, downloading predefined management packs is more common. Many management packs are available that include rules that reflect a recommended starting point for monitoring systems. For example, management packs are readily available to monitor common applications such as Microsoft SQL Server and Microsoft Exchange Server, in addition to infrastructure such as Windows Server 2012 R2.

CHAPTER 12

Management packs can include the following parts:

- **Monitors**   A monitor identifies the status of a particular item. In general, monitors are used to identify whether an application or service is healthy or unhealthy.

- **Rules**   The rules in a management pack are instructions for the agents that are running on monitored computers. An agent is responsible for collecting data, generating alerts, gathering events, and discovering objects to monitor.

- **Object discoveries**   An object discovery defines how to identify a particular object that can be monitored. For example, an object discovery could define a registry key and value to identify whether an application is installed.

- **Knowledge**   The knowledge in a management pack is information that administrators can use for troubleshooting. For example, when an alert is generated, the knowledge can define a known method for resolving the issue.

- **Views**   The views in a management pack define how to display information about an application or service. In most cases, a management pack has separate views for state and alerts. In some cases, a view that shows performance data also is included.

- **Reports**   Some management packs include reports that provide detailed information about the monitored application or service. These reports are generated from long-term data that is stored in the data warehouse database. Reports generally are used to identify long-term trends rather than for short-term troubleshooting.

- **Tasks**   A task is a script or executable code that runs on a managed computer. Tasks can be triggered automatically in response to an alert or manually. You create tasks to perform common actions that might be required to resolve problems.

- **Run As profiles**   A Run As profile contains a set of credentials that are used to run tasks on monitored systems. Using Run As profiles allows Operations Manager users to run tasks even if they don't have permission to perform an action directly. For example, a task could use a Run As profile with local administrator permissions on a computer to restart a service. This is possible even if the user who triggers the task does not have permission to restart the service. The credentials from the Run As profile are used to restart the server when the task runs.

Inside OUT
Tuning management packs

Management packs contain thresholds for monitoring based on best practices, but not all of the thresholds in a management pack will be suitable for your environment. Adjusting the default thresholds and alerts in a management pack is called tuning a management pack. The goal of tuning a management pack is to eliminate irrelevant alerts that the default configuration settings generate.

During the tuning process, you should create overrides rather than edit a management pack that you downloaded. Overrides are stored in a separate management pack that you create for this purpose. If you store your overrides in separate management packs that you create, it's easier for you to back up and restore overrides. Also, many management packs that you can download are sealed and can't be modified.

In addition to the monitoring that downloadable management packs provide, you can create customized monitoring to meet your organization's needs. For example, you can create alerts that are triggered based on performance counters that fall outside a specific range. You also can create alerts based on particular events in an event log.

When an application, such as a web-based application that stores information in a database, is composed of multiple parts, you can configure distributed applications that monitor all of the parts. Then you can receive an alert that informs you which part of the application failed.

Management packs for monitoring application and desktop virtualization

Every environment that uses Operations Manager to monitor a Windows Server–based infrastructure should use management packs for monitoring. To do this, you download a management pack for each version of Windows Server that you are using, and then you import it into Operations Manager. After you have imported management packs for the Windows-based servers, you can tune them.

Management packs for Windows-based servers provide basic operating system monitoring that you can use to ensure the general health of a Windows-based server. For example, an alert will be generated when volumes on a server are low on free space.

CHAPTER 12

Management packs that are useful for monitoring desktop and application virtualization include the following:

- System Center Management Pack for Microsoft Application Virtualization Server 5.0

- Microsoft Remote Desktop Services 2012 Management Pack for System Center 2012

- System Center Management Pack for Windows Server 2012 R2 Hyper-V

The System Center Management Pack for Microsoft Application Virtualization Server 5.0 is used to monitor App-V 5.0 servers. It monitors the health of the management server, publishing service, and reporting service. Most monitoring occurs by monitoring events in event logs. When specific events are generated on an App-V 5.0 server, the agent reports an alert to the management server.

> ➤ **For more information about the System Center Management Pack for Microsoft Application Virtualization Server 5.0, go to the Microsoft Download Center at** *http://go.microsoft.com/fwlink/?LinkID=510068&clcid=0x409.*

The Microsoft Remote Desktop Services 2012 Management Pack for System Center 2012 provides monitoring for the RDS server role and all RDS role services. Even if RDS role services are installed on different servers, overall RDS health is monitored as a single unit.

The following information is monitored:

- **RD Session Host server performance**   For RD Session Host server performance, the management pack monitors active sessions, inactive sessions, and total processor time per session. You are alerted when the number of active sessions reaches the performance limit of the server, when there are too many inactive sessions, and when sessions consume more than 80 percent of the processing capacity for 15 minutes or more.

- **RD Session Host server monitoring**   For RD Session Host server monitoring, the management pack verifies that the RDS service is running. It also verifies connectivity to required role services such as the RD Licensing server and RD Connection Broker.

- **RD Licensing server monitoring**   For RD Licensing server monitoring, the management pack verifies that the RD Licensing role service is running. The management pack also verifies that client access licenses (CALs) are available.

- **RD Gateway server monitoring**   For RD Gateway server monitoring, the management pack verifies that the RD Gateway role service is running. It also verifies connectivity to RD Session Host servers and monitors the number of current connections.

- **RD Connection Broker server monitoring**   For RD Connection Broker server monitoring, the management pack verifies that the RD Connection Broker role service is running. It also monitors connectivity to Remote Desktop Web Access (RD Web Access).

- **RD Web Access server monitoring**   For RD Web Access server monitoring, the management pack verifies that the RD Web Access role service is running. It also monitors connectivity to the RD Connection Broker server.

- **RD Virtualization Host server monitoring**   For RD Virtualization Host server monitoring, the management pack verifies that the RD Virtualization Host agent service is running. It also monitors RD Virtualization Host server performance.

➤ **For more information about the Microsoft Remote Desktop Services 2012 Management Pack for System Center 2012, go to the Microsoft Download Center at** *http://go.microsoft.com/fwlink/?LinkID=510070&clcid=0x409.*

The System Center Management Pack for Windows Server 2012 R2 Hyper-V monitors the things on a Hyper-V host that are specific to Hyper-V. On an RD Virtualization Host server, you might have sufficient information about the RD Virtualization Host server from the RDS management pack, but this management pack provides more information that is specific to Hyper-V.

The following are some of the things that the Hyper-V management pack monitors:

- Hyper-V services, to ensure that they are running

- Free disk space on VMs

- Microsoft RemoteFX configuration

➤ **For more information about the System Center Management Pack for Windows Server 2012 R2 Hyper-V, go to the Microsoft Download Center at** *http://go.microsoft.com/fwlink/?LinkID=510071&clcid=0x409.*

Installing management packs

Management packs that you download from Microsoft are distributed as an MSI file that performs an installation process. The installation process for management packs extracts the management files to a folder in C:\Program Files (x86)\System Center Management Packs. After the files are extracted, they need to be imported by using the Operations console.

To import a management pack, perform the following steps:

1. In the Operations console, in the Monitoring workspace, on the Monitoring Overview page, shown in Figure 12-10, click Required: Import Management Packs.

CHAPTER 12

Figure 12-10 Operations console, Monitoring Overview page

2. In the Import Management Packs window, click Add and click Add From Disk.

3. In the Online Catalog Connection window, click Yes. Some management packs are dependent on other management packs. Using this option automatically downloads any management pack dependencies.

4. In the Select Management Packs To Import window, browse to the location of the .mp files for the management packs you want to import, select the files, and click Open.

5. In the Import Management Packs window, shown in Figure 12-11, click Install.

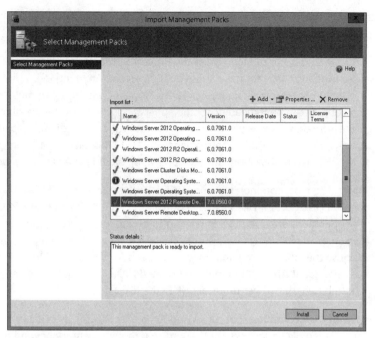

Figure 12-11 Import Management Packs window

6.   When the import is complete, click Close.

Monitoring desktop virtualization infrastructure

When you monitor desktop virtualization infrastructure, you need to consider that multiple users share the infrastructure at the same time. The actions of one user can affect performance of other users. Monitoring is particularly difficult for VM-based desktop deployments because the performance counters within a VM aren't an accurate indicator of the overall performance of an RD Virtualization Host server. You also need to be aware of specific counters that you should monitor for RD Virtualization Host servers and RD Session Host servers.

Understanding resource bottlenecks

Monitoring any computer's performance generally means identifying and reducing perfor-mance bottlenecks on a computer that runs the Windows 8 or Windows Server 2012 R2 oper-ating system. The most common performance bottlenecks occur with four main resources: CPU utilization, memory utilization, disk I/O, and network utilization. If any of these four resources are consumed fully, a bottleneck occurs.

You can use counters in Performance Monitor to identify when resources are fully utilized. Each resource has unique counters that you can use:

- **CPU**   A CPU is utilized fully when the Processor Information\%Processor Time counter in Performance Monitor has a value of 100 percent. Anything less indicates that the processor has additional unused capacity. However, with modern multicore processors, this counter can be misleading. Some applications aren't written to allow the use of all processor cores. As a result, when such an application uses the full capacity of a single processor core, application performance peaks. In this case, a four-core processor could show 25 percent utilization, but the application would have reached a bottleneck.

- **Disk**   The most common measure of disk performance is Physical Disk\Current Disk Queue Length. This counter describes how many disk operations are queued and waiting to be processed. If this counter registers a value greater than two for a sustained period, it's considered a performance concern because the disk isn't keeping up with requests for disk activity. In cases in which you use Redundant Array of Independent Disks (RAID), you should evaluate disk queue length based on two per physical disk in the RAID array.

- **Memory**   A computer that runs Windows Server 2012 R2 is capable of using disk space for a paging file to support applications that require memory beyond the physical memory in the computer. When the paging file is used as virtual memory, it creates a high level of disk utilization. As a best practice, you should ensure that computers have sufficient memory to limit use of the paging file. The Memory\Pages/sec counter indicates information that reads and writes to the paging file. A sustained high level of pages in the counter typically indicates a shortage of physical memory. You also can monitor the Memory\Available MBytes counter to identify available physical memory.

- **Network**   On a modern computer network that uses switches, network utilization can reach approximately 80 percent before performance concerns appear. You can use the Network Interface\Bytes Total/sec counter for a specific network interface to monitor throughput of a network virtual adapter. You can compare this to link speed to identify overall network utilization.

Considerations for monitoring desktop virtualization

When you monitor a single computer, you are monitoring a single operating system and a single user or application. This direct relationship among computers, operating systems, and users makes it easy to identify the source of performance issues. When you monitor VDI implementations, there is no direct relationship among computers, operating systems, and users.

A VDI implementation that uses virtual desktops that are hosted on an RD Virtualization Host server has multiple operating systems that are hosted on a single physical computer. Monitoring performance is more complex because monitoring each virtual desktop computer's performance characteristics does not provide you with a complete performance picture. For example, when you monitor CPU utilization on a virtual desktop, high CPU utilization does not indicate that the physical processor on the RD Virtualization Host server also has high utilization. When you monitor virtual desktops, you need to monitor the RD Virtualization Host server in addition to the virtual desktops.

Monitoring a session-based desktop deployment of VDI that uses RD Session Host servers to provide virtual desktops is more complex than monitoring desktop computers. When you monitor an RD Session Host server, you need to consider the relationships among all of the users who access the RD Session Host server. Because all users share resources on an RD Session Host server, you need to consider whether an application that is used by one user is affecting the performance of another user.

In general, because an RD Virtualization Host server or RD Session Host server has multiple users, you need to consider the resource utilization of all users on that host. When you design the RD Virtualization Host server or RD Session Host server, you need to ensure that there is sufficient capacity in the following:

- CPU

- Memory

- Disk I/O and free space

- Network

Monitoring RD Session Host server performance

Because an RD Session Host server is accessed by multiple users at the same time, there are unique requirements for monitoring performance. Unlike RD Virtualization Host servers, the resources that individual users consume aren't isolated. On an RD Virtualization Host server, you can control the resources assigned to a VM and thereby limit the resources consumed by a user of that VM. On an RD Session Host server, all users have access to a single pool of resources.

RD Session Host servers are more prone to spikes in processor utilization that most servers. Spikes in processor utilization typically are driven by a few highly active threads. Each thread can fully consume the processing capacity on a single processor core. On single-user systems with fewer applications running, spikes occur less frequently. An RD Session Host server's best performance occurs when there are many processor cores. This way, when a thread monopolizes a processor core, the remaining processor cores can service other threads. When you monitor processor utilization, you need to be aware of utilization on individual processor cores, not just overall utilization.

An RD Session Host server requires much less memory than an RD Virtualization Host server because an RD Session Host server avoids loading the same content into memory multiple times. For example, an application loads into memory once, and then each user has dedicated memory for the application while it's working.

The total memory required for an RD Session Host server is the memory that is required for the operating system and for each user session. The amount of memory that each session requires varies depending on the work that each user performs. The only way to optimize the amount of physical memory is to measure system performance under load.

To optimize memory in an RD Session Host server, you should monitor the Memory\Available MBytes and Process\Working Set counters. The point at which both of these counters reach a steady state is the optimal point for memory configuration. Past this point, performance degradation can occur.

Each user connected to an RD Session Host server generates additional disk I/O. In addition to disk activity that user applications generate, disk activity is generated by reading and writing to user profiles. In general, you should place user profiles on a separate physical disk to increase disk performance.

The RD Session Host server role might have higher page file utilization than other server roles due to the high number of processes running. To accommodate this, you can place the page file on a separate physical disk.

High rates of disk activity can indicate that an RD Session Host server does not have sufficient physical memory. You can verify this by monitoring the Memory\Pages/sec counter. If this counter is a consistently high value, the RD Session Host server requires additional memory.

The network activity that users generate is composed of the Remote Desktop Protocol (RDP) communication between clients and the RD Session Host server and network activity generated by the applications that users are running. For example, an application might query a database on another server. Network activity is specific to each implementation because it depends on the applications that are being used.

Optimizing RD Session Host server performance

When Windows Server 2012 R2 is configured as an RD Session Host server to support hosting applications, a common concern is resource contention among multiple users of the RD Session Host server. Resource contention happens when a single user runs applications that use a high percentage of resources, such as processor, network, disk I/O, and memory. To control resource utilization, you can use Fair Share.

A Windows Server 2012 R2 RD Session Host server includes Dynamic Network Fair Share, Dynamic Disk Fair Share, and Dynamic CPU Fair Share. These features control the allocation of network bandwidth, disk I/O, and processor capacity, respectively. Each Fair Share feature distributes resources across user sessions to prevent one user's resource utilization from affecting the performance of other users. For example, if one user runs an application on an RD Session Host server that attempts to use 100 percent of the CPU capacity, Dynamic CPU Fair Share ensures that other users still can access processing capacity by limiting the first user's CPU utilization.

Fair Share is enabled by default for the CPU, disks, and the network. You can use Group Policy to disable CPU Fair Share by enabling the Turn Off Fair Share CPU Scheduling policy setting in Computer Configuration\Policies\Administrative Templates\Windows Components\Remote Desktop Services\Remote Desktop Session Host\Connections. You can't disable Dynamic Network Fair Share and Dynamic Disk Fair Share by using Group Policy. Table 12-1 shows the registry keys that you can use to disable Fair Share.

Table 12-1 Registry keys to disable Fair Share

Description	Registry key
Dynamic CPU Fair Share	HKEY_LOCAL_MACHINE\SYSTEM\CurrentControlSet \Control\Session Manager\Quota System \EnableCpuQuota
Dynamic Disk Fair Share	HKEY_LOCAL_MACHINE\SYSTEM\CurrentControlSet \Services\TSFairShare\Disk\EnableFairShare
Dynamic Network Fair Share	HKEY_LOCAL_MACHINE\SYSTEM\CurrentControlSet \Services\TSFairShare\NetFS\EnableFairShare

Inside OUT

Windows System Resource Manager

If you are searching for information about controlling resource utilization on RD Session Host servers, you likely will find documentation for Windows System Resource Manager (WSRM). WSRM was an alternative mechanism to control per-user resource utilization in older versions of Windows Server. WSRM was deprecated in Windows Server 2012 and has been removed from Windows Server 2012 R2. Fair Share is used instead of WSRM.

CHAPTER 12

Use the following guidelines to increase RD Session Host server performance:

- **Eliminate unnecessary per-user processes**   Identify and remove unnecessary processes that run at user sign-in. These applications might be found in the Run key in the registry or as scheduled tasks. Because many users sign in to a single RD Session Host server, eliminating unnecessary user processes can affect performance significantly.

- **Remove unnecessary desktop notification icons**   Some notification icons consume significant resources when refreshing. If a desktop notification icon is required, it might be possible to reduce the refresh frequency to reduce resource utilization.

- **Reduce application synchronization frequency**   If there are applications that synchronize data, reduce the synchronization frequency as much as you can without affecting application functionality. For many applications, you should disable synchronization to the virtual desktop. For example, if you are using Microsoft Outlook 2013 on a virtual desktop, you should not use cached mode.

- **Disable device redirection to reduce network utilization**   Device redirection such as redirected printers and other local resources can consume significant network resources, but the primary concern is whether the functionality is required.

Inside OUT

Identifying startup processes

Many applications install additional helper applications that perform tasks such as displaying in the notification area of the taskbar. When you want to prevent these applications from starting automatically, it can be difficult to identify how they are starting. In older versions of Windows, System Configuration had some functionality for identifying and disabling startup programs. In Windows 8 and Windows 8.1, the ability to modify startup programs has been moved to Task Manager.

Windows Server 2012 and Windows Server 2012 R2 don't include the ability to modify startup programs in either System Configuration or Task Manager. Instead, you should use the Sysinternals Autoruns program. Autoruns provides a comprehensive list of all software that loads automatically in Windows, and you can remove any item.

➤ For more information about Autoruns, see
http://go.microsoft.com/fwlink/?LinkID=510072.

Index

About the authors

BYRON WRIGHT is a partner in a consulting firm, where he designs and implements solutions using Windows Server, Exchange Server, and Office 365. Byron is also a sessional instructor for the Asper School of Business at the University of Manitoba, teaching management information systems and networking. Byron has designed, authored, and coauthored a number of books on Windows Server, Windows clients, and Exchange Server, including Microsoft Official Curriculum courses and the Windows Server 2008 Active Directory Resource Kit. To recognize Byron's commitment to sharing knowledge with the technical community, he has been given the Microsoft MVP Award for Exchange Server.

BRIAN SVIDERGOL specializes in Microsoft infrastructure and cloud-based solutions built around Windows, Active Directory, Microsoft Exchange, Microsoft System Center, virtualization, and the Microsoft Desktop Optimization Pack (MDOP). He holds a bunch of Microsoft and industry certifications, including the Microsoft Certified Solutions Expert (MCSE), Server Infrastructure. Brian authored the *Active Directory Cookbook* 4th Edition and the Exam Ref 70-695 Deploying Windows Devices and Enterprise Apps book. He served as an MCT Ambassador at TechEd North America 2013 and at Microsoft Ignite 2015. He also delivered Exam Prep sessions at TechEd and Ignite. He works as a subject matter expert (SME) on many Microsoft Official Curriculum courses and Microsoft certification exams. He has authored a variety of training content, blog posts, practice test questions, college exams, and has been a technical reviewer for over 25 books.

From technical overviews to drilldowns on special topics, get *free* ebooks from Microsoft Press at:

www.microsoftvirtualacademy.com/ebooks

Download your free ebooks in PDF, EPUB, and/or Mobi for Kindle formats.

Look for other great resources at Microsoft Virtual Academy, where you can learn new skills and help advance your career with free Microsoft training delivered by experts.

Now that you've read the book...

Tell us what you think!

Was it useful?
Did it teach you what you wanted to learn?
Was there room for improvement?

Let us know at http://aka.ms/tellpress

Your feedback goes directly to the staff at Microsoft Press,
and we read every one of your responses. Thanks in advance!